Exceptional
A Guide for Understanding

Stuart E. Schwartz
University of Florida

McGraw-Hill, Inc.
College Custom Series

*New York   St. Louis   San Francisco   Auckland   Bogotá
Caracas   Hamburg   Lisbon   London   Madrid   Mexico   Milan   Montreal
New Delhi   Paris   San Juan   São Paulo   Singapore   Sydney   Tokyo   Toronto*

EXCEPTIONAL PEOPLE *A GUIDE FOR UNDERSTANDING*

Copyright © 1991 by McGraw-Hill, Inc. All rights reserved. Printed in the United States of America. Except as permitted under the United States Copyright Act of 1976, no part of this publication may be reproduced or distributed in any form or by any means, or stored in a data base retrieval system, without prior written permission of the publisher.

    4 5 6 7 8 9 0 MALMAL 9 5 4

ISBN   07-055962-7

Editor: Judy T. Ice

Cover Design: Dale Novak, Full House Creative Group
Cover Photograph: Courtesy of Kurt Lischke

Printer/Binder: Malloy Lithographing

 This book is printed on recycled, acid-free paper containing a minimum of 50% recycled de-inked fiber.

Dedication

This book is dedicated to those persons--

> with disabilities who have suffered due to the ignorance of others--

> with disabilities who have demonstrated to the world that they are just as good, and many times far ahead, of everyone else--

> who are not disabled, but who treat those individuals with fairness and respect.

Acknowledgements

It is almost impossible to give proper thanks to all of the individuals who have assisted with this large project. This is my attempt.

Thanks to the chapter authors for their great contributions and very positive attitudes. It was a pleasure working with each of you. What a great group of pros!

Thanks to each of the individuals who contributed Personal Perspectives. These "slices of life" are meaningful and valuable.

Thanks to Dr. Paul Sindelar, the Chairperson of Special Education at the University of Florida, for being supportive during these times when I was extremely busy with this project.

Thanks to Dr. Catherine Morsink for the challenge which assisted me in developing the course, Exceptional People.

Thanks to Dr. Harry Hurst and to Dr. Bob Algozzine; both friends and colleagues who motivated me to undertake this project. You are the best.

Thanks to the many persons who served as staff members for the Exceptional People course during the past years. Each of you has made significant contributions.

Thanks to my students. Your positive attitudes and motivation for learning are truly inspirational.

Thanks to Judy Ice, the McGraw-Hill Editor who coordinated this project. It has been a pleasure working with you.

Thanks to J. D. Ice, the McGraw-Hill Sales Representative who initiated this project. Your assistance was excellent.

Thanks to David Lustgarten, Richard Goos, and Darren Salinger for their research and editorial assistance. What a great job you guys did!

Thanks to Kurt Lischka for developing the Study Guide and for contributing photographs. As usual you did an excellent job.

Thanks to Leila Cantara for taking the entire manuscript and putting it in final, finished form. Thanks friend!

Thanks to Dr. Gary Clark, my doctoral advisor at the University of Kansas. You continue to inspire me.

And, finally, thanks to you, the student who is using this book. You are on your way to respecting everyone in your life who is different.

SES

Preface

As a child I vaguely remember visiting my aunt, who was mentally retarded, in a large institution in Pennsylvania. We played and I knew that she enjoyed my family's visits and I realized that she liked playing with me. It was many years later, while working as a camp counselor in Bear Mountain State Park in New York with underprivileged inner-city youth, that I was again given an opportunity to interact with exceptional individuals. The camp director, while making assignments for the third two-week period, asked for volunteers to supervise programming for and to live with disabled campers. I volunteered because, unlike most of the other counselors, I knew I would be comfortable thanks to my experiences with my aunt.

As a result of these valuable experiences, I decided to make working with exceptional people my career. I was a house parent for adolescents who had behavior problems, a teacher of emotionally disturbed and mentally retarded high school students, and a supervisor of a work experience program for adolescents who had a variety of disabilities. Finally I joined the faculty at the University of Florida after completing my doctoral studies at the University of Kansas. For years I taught classes of college students who were studying to become teachers of exceptional children.

It was over lunch one day that I expressed a bit of frustration to my Department Chairperson, Dr. Catherine Morsink. I told her that it seemed to me that by only training future special education teachers, we, as a special education faculty, were not doing all we could to assist disabled individuals in reaching their potentials. I suggested that we begin an introductory class about exceptional persons for undergraduate students who were not planning on entering education. The course would be designed to teach persons from every possible university major about exceptional people and would assist these college students in improving their attitudes toward and their "comfort level" with disabled people. Dr. Morsink could have said no. However, she sent me on my way with a new mission and challenge.

That was in 1984 and the first class had 76 students who had been recruited from among students who were desperately seeking another elective in long registration lines. Today, at the University of Florida, more than 2,000 college students from every possible major enroll annually (without any recruitment activities) in that same course, EEX 3010, Exceptional People. These students, upon graduation, enter leadership positions in their home states and communities and through business, political, and social opportunities have the ability to have a positive influence on society's attitudes toward and interactions with exceptional persons. Former students have repeatedly expressed how their experiences in EEX 3010 have benefitted them and disabled persons.

Most books written by special educators stress the education of disabled students. Recognizing the need for a book that could be used by students who are not education majors, I began to plan the development of this book a few years ago. Other demanding obligations kept me from serious work until strong words of encouragement came from two very close colleagues. Dr. Harry Hurst, Director of the Association for Retarded Citizens in Indian River County, Florida, and Dr. Bob Algozzine, Professor of Special Education at the University of North Carolina, Charlotte. Each twisted an arm and encouraged me to get started so that a book for non-education majors would be available.

This project has given me the opportunity to work with many fine professionals in special education who were willing to contribute their expertise. The chapter authors are all persons who are recognized as content experts. These individuals have many years and types of experiences with exceptional persons and it is apparent that, due to the contributions of these people, the book is a valuable learning tool.

This book, although specifically designed for the college student who is not entering a profession dealing with exceptional individuals, is certainly appropriate for non-education, education, and special education majors. Persons who are entering professions in related fields, such as physical therapy, psychology, and vocational rehabilitation, should also benefit from using this book.

Before beginning with your reading I suggest that you review the entire book so that you know what components exist and which ones will assist you with your studying. Note that the chapters in Section II have similar organization so that you can use the same note taking and outlining format for those chapters. Appendix A provides you with a descriptive listing of organizations and agencies which either provide services for exceptional people or are actually comprised of persons with different types of exceptionality. Appendix B presents you with an opportunity to learn selected sign language words and fingerspelling.

Following the appendices is the Student Study Guide which has been designed to assist you as you study the material. Find all of the terms and concepts which are identified in the study guide in the corresponding chapters. Complete the exercises to insure that you are familiar with the terms and concepts which are regarded as important content. Then attempt, without turning back to the chapter, to answer the true/false, multiple choice, and essay style questions. If you do this task seriously you should be better prepared for a similar test on the content which may be given by your instructor. You can check your answers to the questions by using the key which is provided at the end of the study guide.

In Chapters 1 and 18 you will find a series of "Personal Perspectives." These are manuscripts which were submitted by exceptional persons, members of their families, or their friends. The ones which are included were selected from among many papers and their purpose is to give you a more thorough insight into the lives of persons who are exceptional. The willingness of these authors to share "a slice of life" should be applauded and beneficial to you as you discover what exceptionality is.

No matter what your major educational pursuit is, I trust that this book will enable you to learn about and improve your attitude toward people who are different. The more you learn about exceptional individuals the more you will realize that they are more like you than different. The more you learn about what is correct social behavior the more you will feel comfortable interacting with disabled people. And the more you know and experience about people who are different the more prepared you will be to be a friend, neighbor, or parent of an exceptional person.

It is my sincere hope that you find this text to be valuable and enjoyable to read. I invite your comments and suggestions. Please write to me at G-315 Norman Hall, University of Florida, Gainesville, FL 32611, or call me at (904) 392-0701.

S. E. Schwartz

About the Authors

Editor

Stuart E. Schwartz, Ed.D., Professor of Special Education
University of Florida

Dr. Schwartz. a former teacher of children and adolescents with various disabilities, has been a professor at the University of Florida since 1974. He is the author of numerous instructional materials, journal articles, monographs, and book chapters, and he regularly teaches "Exceptional People," a course about disabled persons for non-education undergraduates. Dr. Schwartz's professional interests include attitudes about and vocational preparation of disabled people.

Chapter Authors

Miriam Adderholdt-Elliott, Ph.D., Clinical Assistant Professor
University of North Carolina-Charlotte

Dr. Adderholdt-Elliott teaches master's level courses in gifted education and is a member of numerous professional groups. She has authored two books, two book chapters, and 20 journal articles regarding gifted education.

Sherwood J. Best, M.A., Lecturer and Supervisor in Teacher Education
The University of California at Riverside and
California State University, Los Angeles

Ms. Best teaches courses and supervises student teachers in special education. Before she began her university career, she taught children with physical and health impairments. She has co-authored chapters on physical and health impairments and psychosocial aspects of disabilities.

Glenn H. Buck, M.Ed., Doctoral Candidate
University of Florida

Mr. Buck has a Bachelors Degree in Music Education from Nazareth College and a Master's Degree in Special Education from George Peabody College of Vanderbilt University. He has extensive experience as a preschool, elementary, and junior high special education teacher.

Carl T. Cameron, Ph.D., Associate Professor
George Mason University
  Dr. Cameron is an Associate Professor at George Mason University. He is a senior member of the management team at the Center for Human Disabilities and is responsible for the development of supported employment demonstration projects, technology applications, and is the producer of a wide variety of video productions related to special education.

Kay Alicyn Ferrell, Ph.D., Associate Professor
Teachers College, Columbia University
  Dr. Ferrell coordinates the Program in Education of Blind and Visually Impaired Learners at Teachers College, Columbia University. Dr. Ferrell has directed numerous research projects and has authored many journal articles in the area of visual impairment.

Timothy J. Landrum, Ph.D., Research Associate
Commonwealth Institute for Child and Family Studies
  Dr. Landrum received his B.S. from the University of Virginia and his M.Ed. from the College of William and Mary. He has taught children and adolescents who are emotionally disturbed in public school and residential settings. Dr. Landrum has authored numerous journal articles on the topic of emotional disturbance and behavior management.

Julia M. Lee, Ph.D., Associate Professor of Special Education
Valdosta State College
  Dr. Lee has been teaching at Valdosta State College for five years. She received her Ph.D. in special education with an emphasis in education of students who are physically impaired and/or multiply handicapped. Her teaching interests have focused on services for people with severe handicaps.

Elliott Lessen, Ph.D., Professor of Special Education
Northern Illinois University
  Dr. Lessen has served as Chair, Faculty of Special Education, and has taught undergraduate and graduate courses in the area of learning disabilities. He teaches a course for non-education majors, "Exceptional Persons in Society," and serves as the special education coordinator for the Genoa-Kingston School District. Dr. Lessen has authored numerous journal articles and has consulted widely.

Kurt R. Lischka, B.S., Visual and Editorial Consultant
Supplemental Creations
Mr. Lischka is a professional photographer and writer, specializing in photographic illustration and technical writing. His education includes basic and advanced studies in technical communications, science, and mathematics.

James K. McAfee, Ph.D., Associate Professor/Coordinator of Special Education
The Pennsylvania State University/Great Valley Graduate Center
Dr. McAfee has been a teacher of children and adults with emotional disorders and mental retardation. He has also been a principal of a special school and has authored numerous articles on mental retardation and special education law.

Jeanne B. Repetto, Ph.D., Visiting Assistant Professor
University of Florida
Dr. Repetto is currently director of two transition projects and she offers coursework in the areas of transition, vocational special needs education, and leadership skills for special educators. Her research interests are focused on the provision of technical assistance, transition, and equal access issues.

Deborah C. Simmons, Ph.D., Research Assistant Professor
George Peabody College of Vanderbilt University
Dr. Simmons received her Ph.D. from Purdue University and has been a speech and language pathologist and special education practicum supervisor for local and state education agencies. Her current research and teaching interests focus on means of enhancing the quality and quantity of mainstream instruction for students with academic learning problems.

Deborah Bott Slaton, Ph.D., Assistant Professor
University of Kentucky
Dr. Slaton's professional experience includes teaching special classes for children and adolescents with learning disabilities and tutoring college-aged students with learning problems. She currently coordinates the Learning and Behavior Disorders Programs at the University of Kentucky where she is involved with teacher education and applied research.

Maureen A. Smith, M.A., Instructor
State University of New York at Geneseo
    Prior to working at Geneseo, Ms. Smith taught hearing impaired and multiply handicapped children and youth. She has written numerous articles and book chapters and has co-authored four books in the area of hearing impairment.

Beth Tulbert, M.Ed., Doctoral Candidate
University of Florida
    Ms. Tulbert has 17 years teaching experience working with mentally retarded, learning disabled, emotionally disturbed, and multiply handicapped students. Her interests include training college-level learning disabled students, multicultural issues, learning strategies, and effective teaching practices.

Donna L. Wandry, M.Ed., Doctoral Candidate
University of Florida
    Ms. Wandry received her B.S. in Special Education from the University of Wisconsin and her M.Ed. in Special Education from the University of Utah. Ms. Wandry's study and research interests include transition services for secondary students and adults with mild to moderate disabilities, educational leadership, policy development, and interagency collaboration.

Carole Zingari, M.Ed., Doctoral Candidate
Purdue University
    Mrs. Zingari has worked as a speech-language pathologist for adult clients. She has also designed individualized communication programs, as well as trained care staff in implementing these programs. She is a co-author of several journal articles and has made many presentations concerning communication and special education.

Contents

SECTION I   **INTRODUCTION**

1   Exceptional people.. 1
           Stuart E. Schwartz

2   On being different.. 29
           Elliott Lessen

3   A family perspective.. 53
           Deborah Bott Slaton

SECTION II   **TYPES OF EXCEPTIONALITIES**

4   People who are hearing impaired... 77
           Maureen Smith

5   Visually disabled persons.. 105
           Kay Ferrell

6   People with health impairments... 129
           Sherwood Best

7   Physically disabled individuals... 153
           Julia Lee

8   Persons who are mentally retarded... 179
           James McAfee

9   Learning disabled individuals... 205
           Deborah Simmons

10   Emotionally disturbed persons... 231
           Tim Landrum

11	Individuals with communication difficulties.................................	253
	Carole Zingari	
12	Gifted and talented individuals..	283
	Miriam Adderholdt-Elliott and Donna Wandry	

SECTION III   SERVICES FOR EXCEPTIONAL PERSONS

13	Special education..	307
	Beth Tulbert	
14	Related services and support professionals.................................	337
	Glenn Buck	
15	Community and consumer groups..	363
	Donna Wandry	

SECTION IV   TRENDS AND THE FUTURE

16	Laws and legislation..	391
	Carl Cameron	
17	The exceptional adult...	415
	Jeanne Repetto	
18	The future..	439
	Stuart E. Schwartz	

APPENDICES

A	List of agencies...	467
B	Sign language..	475

STUDENT STUDY GUIDE... 485
                Kurt Lischka

CHAPTER 1

EXCEPTIONAL PEOPLE

Stuart E. Schwartz

Introduction

Have you ever stared at someone who was disfigured due to an injury or disability? Do you ever wonder if you should avoid words such as "see" or "beautiful" with blind persons? Have you ever felt uncomfortable when interacting with someone who is different from you? Do you ever wonder what causes deafness or mental retardation? These questions and reactions are very common among those individuals who do not have knowledge about persons who are exceptional. This book will help you understand what an exceptionality is and what the causes of the various exceptionalities are. More important than the acquisition of knowledge, however, is the ability to interact comfortably with individuals who are different. That should also be an outcome for you as you read this book and complete the activities which are suggested.

Before beginning your reading, take a look through the book so that you know what to anticipate. In the first section emphasis is given to the understanding of exceptionalities in general. Two authors who have extensive experiences with and who teach classes about exceptional individuals provide insightful discussions for your consideration. The effects of being exceptional on the person himself or herself and upon that person's family is thoroughly explored. You will be introduced to the concept of exceptionality, learn a variety of terms, and review myths and misconceptions about exceptional people. Attention is given to your comfort level in this first section as well so that you can explore and reduce any fears which you may have.

The second section of the book includes a thorough overview of the different types or categories of exceptionality. Professionals with nationally recognized expertise in the specific areas of exceptionality have developed each chapter in Section II so that you will be introduced to the latest research and intervention options. You will also benefit from suggested guidelines in each of the chapters for comfortable and appropriate social, family, and professional interactions with exceptional persons.

Section III is an overview of services which are available for exceptional individuals. Three individuals, who have done extensive research in dealing with the needs of exceptional individuals, have contributed to this portion of the text. The role and responsibility of the schools is described and specific therapies, from a variety of professional disciplines and which are commonly utilized, are presented. In addition, you will find a presentation which overviews the various community agencies and consumer organizations which can be helpful for obtaining further information and support services. Appendix A is an extension of this section as it provides a comprehensive listing of various groups and organizations which offer services for exceptional persons or are actually designed for the membership of exceptional individuals and/or their families.

The final part of the book, which includes contributions from experts in the areas of legal issues and adult adjustment, contains three critical topics; a review of laws and legislation which affect the lives of exceptional individuals, a discussion of employment and adult options for exceptional people, and a presentation of future options and directions for you and this special group of people.

At the end of each chapter you will find additional valuable material. Suggested readings about exceptional individuals are listed and should be readily available in your library. Your opportunity to interact with the material is also provided at the end of the chapters through individual activities, group projects, and reaction papers. These interactive materials, prepared by David Lustgarten, Richard Goos, and Darren Salinger, will give you the opportunity to further explore the chapter's topic and to reflect upon what you have learned. You are urged to complete all of the suggested activities and reaction papers.

Immediately following Section IV are the appendices. As mentioned previously, Appendix A is a listing of groups and organizations which provide services for exceptional persons or which are comprised of persons who are exceptional. The complete address and phone number for each agency is provided so that you can easily contact the organization and obtain information about their current programs and services. Appendix B contains fingerspelling and selected words for you to learn in sign language.

The final portion of the book is a study guide which should prove to be useful as you review the material in the text and should also assist you when preparing for any tests which your instructor may give. You are urged to complete all of the exercises in the study guide so that you can determine if you have grasped the main ideas and retained what is considered to be the most important information which was provided by the chapters' authors. A key to the study guide is provided at the end of the section so that you can check your work.

You should be ready to begin your exciting study of exceptional persons. Keep an open mind, be prepared to modify any existing attitudes and expectations, and be ready to learn about persons who are, in almost every respect, very similar to you.

Exceptional People

Persons who are exceptional are individuals who significantly differ, in one or more ways, from those who are considered to be average. This definition could, of course, refer to every person depending upon the group to which that person is currently being compared. Usually adults, heterosexuals, and English speakers are not considered to be exceptional or different. However, an adult who is walking down the street with a group of children would be exceptional, a straight person who attends a meeting of a gay organization would be exceptional, and a person who speaks English in a group of Italian speaking people would be considered exceptional. You, no matter how "average" you may be, would be considered different or exceptional in a group or society where you are not part of the majority.

The expectations that a certain population has upon members of its group for specific behaviors or group standards also affect whether the individual is considered to be exceptional. A group of teens which expects its friends to dress in a specific style might consider the person who dresses differently to be exceptional. Parents who have high academic achievement expectations might believe that their child, who gets C's and D's, is exceptional while that same child could be thought to be average or a good achiever by parents who emphasize physical or athletic ability instead of academic development.

Therefore, it would be appropriate to consider every possible difference from the norm, every possible norm, and every level of expectation as you study the concept of exceptionality. That, however, would not be practical. Since it is expected that you will be interacting with exceptional persons in school, your home, while employed, and within your family, the most common types of exceptionalities are presented in this book. The categories selected should enable you to have a thorough understanding of these areas of exceptionality and should assist you in being a better friend, neighbor, family member, or employer of these people and of others who may, from time to time or from group to group, be considered different.

You may now, or in the future, be a person who is characterized as exceptional. This book should assist you, as well, in having a better understanding of yourself as an exceptional person in our complex society.

Labels

A person who wears the label "exceptional" may be above or below average in a variety of ways. For instance, the person who wins a national chess tournament, who runs faster than most, or who is selected to play first chair violin in a major orchestra may be labeled as gifted or talented. Another person who struggles to learn to read, who is unable to follow complex directions, or who requires assistance with many common tasks may be thought of as a mentally retarded or developmentally delayed individual. Both persons are exceptional even though it is clear that their differences from the norm are in opposite directions.

The use of labels to identify exceptional individuals may be viewed as both positive and negative. Certain school and community programs are funded based upon the number of individuals who have been labeled as eligible for programming (Hardman et al., 1990). Additionally, it is important for certain labels to be used so that professionals, family members, and exceptional persons can all communicate. Labels may be somewhat negative as many common labels applied to exceptional individuals appear to have a negative connotation. When labels are negative, some people may have reduced expectations of exceptional persons and poor attitudes toward them all due to labels which may be misleading and which may simply be furthering the myths which often surround disabled people.

We are all a product of our environment and have been influenced by the thinking and attitudes of others. Now, however, is a great opportunity for you to re-examine your own attitudes about persons who are different. If you determine that your attitudes need some major overhaul or minor fine tuning, now is the time to make the necessary adjustments.

Disability or Handicap?

Those persons whose labels suggest that they are below the norm in some respects are often thought of as disabled or handicapped. The concept of disability suggests that the person has a permanent impairment, such as blindness or a missing limb (Schwartz & Sindelar, 1990). On the other hand, the handicap is the problem which is created as a result of the disability and it should be the goal of all persons involved to assist the individual in reducing the handicap. Methods to reduce a handicap, such as the learning of sign language for communications between deaf and hearing individuals and the use of behavior management techniques for reducing behavior outbursts in emotionally disturbed persons will be provided in Chapters 4-12.

It would be beneficial if the letters "dis" could be removed from the word "disability." Then, perhaps, people would be able to focus on what exceptional persons can do, on their skills, and positive attributes. As you learn more about exceptional people you will easily recognize that these people are every bit as able as those who are not exceptional. They simply need to find ways to overcome their handicaps caused by their disabilities. And, non-exceptional people need to forget about the labels and focus on the person.

Disabilities may be quite apparent or they may be hidden. An individual who uses a wheelchair or a person who is missing a limb is considered to have a visible disability. Likewise, a person who has epilepsy or who is deaf has a hidden disability. When a person with epilepsy has a seizure or when a deaf person begins to use sign language, others will note the exceptionality. Some persons who have disabilities which are hidden will make efforts to hide their differences while others will freely point them out to their friends and acquaintances so that they are not surprised at a later time. Recognize that persons who are exceptional, but with a hidden disability, are different from those who have visible differences.

It is important to point out that the label which a person wears may cause that individual to behave or perform in a certain way. Other persons may have different expectations of the exceptional person depending upon their understanding of the label. Further, the labeled person may feel differently about himself or herself due to the wearing of a label. The next section should assist you in developing a greater awareness of the effects of labeling upon an individual.

A friendly visit

Imagine your excitement when you learned recently of winning a free balloon ride. Just think, a full afternoon of floating quietly among the clouds while observing native animals in the lush countryside. You arrive, greet your pilot, and begin loading your belongings into the balloon's basket. How exciting it all looks to you. There are people holding the basket, your guide is giving her staff some last minute instructions, and the burner is giving off a warm glow while keeping the balloon inflated.

As you stoop down to stow the last of your belongings, however, you stumble and grab hold of an overhead rope to avoid falling. This rope causes the burner to blast into a high position. Amid much yelling from the guide and her startled staff you lift off alone. Grabbing the rope in hopes of shutting down the burner it comes off in your hands, the burner continues its furious blast, and you drift higher and higher. A feeling of dizziness overcomes you as you slump to the floor of the hot air balloon basket.

Minutes later (or is it hours?), you pick yourself up off the floor and realize that you are still drifting with the burner chugging at full blast. But where are you? How far have you gone? How will you get home? As you near a mountainous area, the burner sputters due to a depleted fuel supply and you brace yourself for a crash landing. Fortunately, you drift down softly into a rather swampy area near the top of the mountain.

Who are these people coming toward you? They are so different looking! At least eight feet tall, they are all wearing green masks and white gowns. Their language is one which you have never heard and they are screaming and laughing at you. Some of them, especially the children, seem to be afraid to come near you.

As you sit there crouched and filled with fear, you quickly realize that you are in a place where people like you have rarely been seen before. You look different from these people. You speak and behave differently. And you are greeted with apparent fear by some and disgust by others.

Why, these strange people don't want you in their midst! You realize that they are afraid of you when the adults pull their children away from you and they keep their weapons and shields in front of them. Some of the strange folks are throwing things at you and others seem to be mocking you and laughing at you. If only they knew that in reality you are a decent, pleasant person who only drifted into their midst by accident and that you would not do anything to harm them. But they have you labeled--you are different. One of the stones thrown by a strange child suddenly hits you in the head and you begin your second state of unconsciousness for the day.

What is this? A bell ringing? Are those strangers trying to awaken you? To harm you? Reach out and defend yourself! Grab something to throw! You have it in your hand and that's what is ringing. What is it? You know--now you know--it is your alarm clock awakening you from this terrible nightmare!

How did it feel to take a simple balloon trip and find yourself wearing the label of "different" among those people in the mountain? Realize that because of your label these people feared you, ridiculed you, and couldn't (or wouldn't) communicate with you. What they didn't know was that, in spite of being different from them, you really are a wonderful, skilled, and kind person. Unfortunately, they could not see beyond the label. They had negative expectations just because you were different.

Attitudes

Consider your attitude toward persons who are different. When you see someone who is using a wheelchair or someone who has an artificial arm or leg, how do you react? How do you feel? What about someone who stutters badly or someone who uses gestures and sign language for communications? Or a person who is walking down the street with a guide dog? Are you uncomfortable? Do you try to avoid the person? The attitude that others display toward persons who are exceptional is critical.

It appears that an attitude is learned early in life while children interact with others and observe human interactions displayed by family members and friends. The child who hears his or her parents make negative remarks about persons who are exceptional, or who observes his or her playmates ridicule and tease other children who have disabilities, will probably be greatly influenced by these experiences. The normal or typical child who grows up in an environment where individual differences are noted and treated with respect will more likely not have negative expectations, feelings of discomfort, and negative attitudes.

Can you improve the attitudes of children and adults toward exceptional individuals? You certainly can by being a good model and following these guidelines.

Always display your respect and comfort. It is important for you to set a good example. If you interact with exceptional individuals in a respectful manner and if it appears that you are comfortable in your interactions with those persons, your friends, family members, fellow employees, and your children will follow your lead.

Remember that others will copy your behaviors; especially if they know that you have read this book and taken a course about exceptional individuals!

Tell children about differences. Encourage children to ask questions as their curiosity is quite normal. If children are given correct information in a matter of fact manner, they will perceive that being different is not mysterious or something to fear. People tend to fear that which is unknown so it is critically important to teach children about disabled individuals so that all possible fears about exceptional people are eliminated.

Allow children to ask disabled persons about their disability. If a child asks another child or adult who is disabled about his or her disability don't scold and yank the child away! Situations which encourage interactions between children and disabled people are wonderful learning opportunities for the non-disabled child and, in most cases, a positive experience for the exceptional individual. Most disabled persons recognize that it is natural for children to be curious. This is an excellent opportunity for the disabled person to assist a child toward developing a positive attitude and the ability to comfortably interact with persons who are different.

Stop someone who is ridiculing or joking about exceptional persons. If someone begins to ridicule or joke about an exceptional individual, challenge that person to stop. If you sit there and laugh along with the crowd, you are just as guilty as the joke teller. By participating you are giving others the impression that you condone such negative behavior. It really takes guts to stop a friend or co-worker but, if done in a serious and positive manner, others should respect you for your position. Comments such as, "Excuse me, but the joke you are telling is making me uncomfortable," or, "If you don't mind I'd appreciate your saving any jokes about disabled people for a time when I'm not around," usually will work. Another way to handle the situation would be to tell the group you are leaving because of the types of jokes which are being told. Then walk away.

Expect normal behaviors and achievement from exceptional persons. Remember that expectation may greatly influence actual outcomes. If you expect that a retarded person can never learn to ride a bus or subway and if you are an influential person to that individual, you are setting a major roadblock in the way of that person's learning to use public transportation. If you think that your good friend, who is deaf and uses sign language, will be unable to get the job he or she is applying for, you will be hampering the employment success of that person. The expectations of influential people, such as parents, teachers, and friends, have a strong influence on the disabled person's confidence level and motivation to achieve. The potential of disabled people is usually only limited by opportunities to learn and the inappropriately low expectations of significant others.

Be yourself around those who are exceptional. If you are normally crabby, be crabby. Putting on an act around disabled people will be recognized as patronizing or demeaning behavior. It is not necessary for you to sprint ahead and open a door for someone in a wheelchair unless you usually do that for everyone. If you are walking through a shopping mall and your normal behavior repertoire includes saying hello to everyone then, by all means, say hello to that blind person who is walking by. If you usually ignore persons whom you don't know, and you don't know that blind person, then ignore him or her as well. Exceptional persons want to be treated like everyone else and they can tell when you are acting. Therefore, be yourself and don't change your behaviors around disabled people.

Use your common, everyday vocabulary. The vocabulary you commonly use should be fine with exceptional persons. With blind people it is appropriate to say, "It's nice to see you," or, "Isn't it a beautiful day?" It is also acceptable to say to a friend of yours who uses a wheelchair, "Let's take a walk to the park." Exceptional individuals use common, everyday language all the time so don't feel the least bit awkward using your everyday vocabulary. If you stop to think about the "right" words to use, you will come across as uncomfortable and the substitute words you select will probably be wrong.

Suggest activities in which you are interested. Exceptional individuals often enjoy the same hobbies as you do. If you like tennis, ask your friend who has epilepsy to play. If you are going to a car race invite your friend who is mentally retarded to accompany you. If you want to go to an art museum don't hesitate to invite your blind friend along. Disabled persons should not be excluded from activities just because you think those activities would not be appropriate for them. Ask your disabled friends to participate. They are fully capable of selecting the activities which they will enjoy and which fit their interests.

Look at but never stare at someone who is different. It is fine to look, note any differences in your mind, and then go on with your interaction with an exceptional person in a normal fashion. Staring at someone who is disabled, however, is rude and makes that person feel uncomfortable. Some disabled persons will stare right back or will bluntly ask you why you are staring. It is very appropriate, however, to look at the disabled person with whom you are interacting in a normal fashion. Avoiding eye contact, or looking away, is just as rude as staring.

Talk to the disabled person and not to his or her companion. When interacting with a disabled person who is with a family member or companion, be sure to address the disabled person rather than the family member or companion. A disabled person can usually answer questions or respond appropriately in conversation without assistance. Likewise, if you are with a friend who is disabled, don't respond for the friend. When put in that situation, such as a waiter or waitress asking you what your disabled companion would like to eat, don't respond for your friend. Politely suggest to the waiter or waitress that he or she ask your friend. Although that situation may be a bit uncomfortable it will be a good learning experience for that insensitive restaurant employee.

The guidelines suggested above should assist you in your efforts to improve your interactions with exceptional people and they should serve as excellent examples for children and other adults who observe your behaviors. By interacting correctly and comfortably you will greatly aid those persons who are uncomfortable or afraid due to ignorance, myths, and misconceptions.

Language

The terms you use to describe or identify persons who are different should be positive, current, and correct. You probably can think of many inappropriate terms which have been used to identify disabled people. Examples of such terms, which are considered to be insulting and degrading and which should be avoided include idiot, Mongoloid, cripple, deaf & dumb, and spastic. Also some disabled persons dislike such terms as physically challenged, handicapable, and mentally different (The Research and Training Center on Independent Living, 1990).

If you are in doubt about a specific word it is probably best to go right to an expert; a friend of yours who has a disability. Feel free to ask what is correct and obtain your friend's viewpoint. Or, discuss this issue with your peers and try to reach a consensus regarding what is correct and appropriate. You will probably develop a list of terms which are not negative or demeaning such as people who are disabled, mentally retarded person, and person with epilepsy. The best guideline is to always remember that the person comes first and the label simply identifies a specific characteristic about that person. Don't use the adjective in noun form; whenever possible use the label to modify the person. For instance, don't say, "The deaf are hard-working people." Try, "People who are deaf (or deaf persons) are hard-working individuals."

Personal Perspectives

To assist your development of positive attitudes about and understanding of exceptional individuals, this section includes essays which were submitted from across the United States by exceptional people, their friends, and their family members. The essays are true "slices of life" or real-life experiences, whether positive or negative, from the individuals who submitted them. The Personal Perspectives are presented in their original form, with only minor editing, so that each author's true meaning and intended messages were not altered. Additional Personal Perspective papers will be presented in the final chapter.

While reading each of the stories try to picture the people and their lives. As much as possible, put yourself "in their shoes" so that you can continue to explore the concept of exceptional.

"I had no idea . . ."
Suzy Adams

While I attended high school, I participated as a member of the school swim team. We competed against many other schools in meets. One day, while swimming against another high school, I was made aware of something quite interesting. There was a girl who swam the 500 yard freestyle for the other team. What was different about her was not only that she swam the longest individual event in the meet, but that she was completely blind.

Although she generally finished last in her event, she never stopped trying to achieve her personal best. While she swam, something interesting came over all those who watched. People from not only both teams, but others on the pool deck, would not only watch, but cheer her on the entire way. This was not just because she was blind, but because she was a special individual trying to achieve a special task for herself. You could tell this made her feel not only more confident, but more accepted. Until I was told she was blind, I had no idea that she was.

"Shattered Dreams"
L. O. Crosby

  When your dreams shatter, there is no sound, just the slow motion vision of icebergs sliding off of a glacier, making huge soundless waves and looking so calm--unless you happen to be swimming under the iceberg.
  That's what it was like the day we learned that our beautiful two year old had a hearing problem. It was hard to wrap our minds around the word "deaf" immediately, but in recent months, we had become increasingly aware that Dorothy Jane didn't seem to hear. The moment of knowing, really <u>knowing</u>, that our lives had taken an unexpected turn came in the audiometry booth, when DJ sat in my lap happily playing with a colorful puzzle, but showed no response to the sounds coming over the speakers--louder and louder and **LOUDER**. This wasn't happening to us, these things always happen to other people, this was <u>not</u> happening! **God, are you really sure you've picked the right family? Can we talk?**
  It was to be ten more days before we were able to get the definitive test, a measurement of her brain-wave response to sounds. When the nurse stopped chatting happily and became all business, we knew things weren't going well. A few minutes later the doctor gave us the devastating news--there was no response detected at any volume or frequency. We had a deaf child, cause unknown.
  Somehow we drove home, and began the process of grieving. Mother's Day weekend was spent asking how could this be true, searching for strength, blaming ourselves for not knowing sooner, imagining what the future would bring, crying over our shattered dreams, and mourning for our poor little girl who couldn't possibly have a happy or normal life now.
  I'm glad to say that time was to prove us wrong on some counts. Also, we were fortunate enough to trust in the power of prayer, and we had previously learned something about grieving. So when feelings of denial, shock, anger, and more denial washed over us, we tried to accept them as early stages of the healing process. Our knowledge didn't make the experience any less intense or wounding, but with time we were able to move through the initial emotional firestorm toward acceptance and a pragmatic plan for the future.
  Immediately after getting the diagnosis, the days weren't so bad, but for several nights I found myself making lists at 2:00 AM of what DJ would <u>not</u> be able to do. Unwelcome thoughts of music, dancing, movies, piloting an airplane, singing, talking after lights out, etc., etc., formed themselves into endless lists night after sleepless night. Positive thinking didn't even help as I tried to focus on the myriad of opportunities that were still open to her. It was only when I began to list things that

*I probably will be unable or unwilling to do in the rest of my lifetime (fly on the space shuttle, run a sub 3:00 marathon, learn to draw and paint) and **these things weren't on DJ's list,** that the whole issue evaporated in a flash!*

Sometimes I awake and have to remember, "Oh yes, Dorothy will be deaf again today." It's not something you eventually recover from, like the chicken pox. When I dream, Dorothy still talks and speaks. But life continues--DJ is interested in getting on with it even when we are not. You can attempt to cling to your own sense of tragedy, but not when the central character isn't playing her part.

We're so glad that we had time to know DJ first, before getting the diagnosis. We were fortunate to come to know and love her as a beautiful, bright, inquisitive child with a sunny personality. If we had received the news sooner, we probably would not have appreciated these qualities as fully. It's comforting to realize that they didn't switch children on us when we went to the audiologist.

Besides, nature doesn't give us what we can't handle. In a surprisingly short time, the emphasis returned to the same issues that all parents face, but without the luxury of making the necessary decisions unconsciously. Since our child was the first deaf person we had known, for better or worse, we had no role models or peer support. How could we best nurture this bright, inquisitive intelligence that seemed so apparent? I feared that one of my shattered dreams would be the hope that DJ could soar in the realms of learning. It seems to take so much work, so much pushing, for deaf people to excel in this arena. And at what cost to a balanced, rounded personality? Clearly, this was more of an issue for me than for DJ, but it hurt so much to let go of some of my dreams and fantasies for her so soon! It felt like a part of me, the parent, had been ripped away.

The educational issue also brought up the ramifications of our making cultural choices for our child. But isn't that just what we do in deciding on an inner city magnet school vs. private prep school? On the other hand, sometimes these choices seemed more analogous to deciding to raise a child as a Christian vs. Moslem, or having them grow up in South Africa vs. Sweden. Boy, does Dorothy's condition ever bring a lot of parenting issues into sharper focus! Conscious parenting becomes inescapable--and that's probably good.

Questions, questions, questions. . . . But then I sit on the floor with Dorothy Jane and she signs "cat" for the first time and I smile/cry/laugh. We are explorers together in an unknown land. The maps are nonexistent, contradictory, or confusing. What adventures await us? What secrets will be revealed? Will there be treasure? Magic? Will she push back the borders of the known world? How far will we journey together? Now those are the real questions, and the answer sleeps in my arms . . . dreaming silent dreams.

"No One Asks to be Born Disabled"
Susan B. Blocker

I was born on April 21, 1962 in Jamaica Queens, New York. In the early sixties a drug known as Thalidomide was prescribed by physicians to women who were pregnant in hopes of alleviating some of their discomfort. During my mother's pregnancy she was taking Thalidomide, as a result I was born prematurely and physically disabled.

Because of Thalidomide many babies were born physically disabled. We were known as Thalidomide babies. I was born two months prematurely and without arms; I joined a very large family of thirteen sisters and brothers.

Because of my parents' personal hardships they were unable to raise me. When I was fourteen months old I was placed into New York City's Foster/Adoption care system. I spent the next thirteen years of my life being shuffled in and out of foster homes, group homes, and hospitals.

I started running away when I was eight years old. I was physically and emotionally abused by my foster mother for six years. I was permanently removed from the home at age fifteen. By this time I had lost all my self-worth. I was a very scared and angry disabled teenager. I trusted no one, yet I needed to be loved and accepted.

At age sixteen, I was placed in my fourth foster home. It was very hard for me to adjust to a "normal" family life, because I had been shuffled around so much. I put my foster parents through hell, but they stuck by me, because they truly believed in me.

I am now an independent twenty-eight year old woman. I graduated from Francis Lewis High School in June of 1980 and I completed a year of college. For the past seven years I have lived, independently on my own in my apartment, in St. Albans, Queens.

I manage daily living by the use of my feet. I do everything from cleaning house to driving a car. I started working at age sixteen and I've been employed ever since. I've been employed for the past three years with a local telecommunication company.

I am also in the process of starting my own home-based computer company. Life has been hard on me, but I've managed to overcome my obstacles through my stubbornness and my will to survive.

As for my biological parents/family; well, I was reunited with them two days after my eighteenth birthday. For the past twenty-eight years of my life my mother has been blaming herself for the way I was born. At this present day I live less than five minutes away from her and she still cannot bare to look at me.

If there is only one point that I can make out of this story, it is that "I don't at all blame my parents for my disability." On the other hand, my parents, as well as the mainstream population, must realize that no one asks to be born disabled.

"A Trip to the Bottom"
Gregory J. Ruediger

As we walked 117 feet down into a state geological site, his eyes said what his voice could not. He was terrified of an everyday event! With sweat dripping from his brow, he hung onto the railings with all his might. Each step was a new adventure into the unknown. As he looked at me (his teacher), his eyes appeared to say; what is this teacher trying to prove; what did I do to deserve this; am I going to fall?

His fears lessened with each step. He was able to hear the trickle of the stream under him, the leaves brushing against each other, and see the beauty of the surrounding vegetation. As his teacher, I was smiling inside for I knew he was growing from the experience, not only in his mobility skills but as a person. As we came up the slippery steps sweaty and dirty, we both had big smiles on our faces. Other people thought we were crazy, but we both had gained from our "trip to the bottom."

Even though this young man is profoundly mentally retarded, he can experience the many beauties of nature and life. Society has to overlook individual deficits and allow people the opportunity to explore the environment and use their many abilities!

"The Time-Test"
Marguerite Koenig

When I was about one year old, I was playing with our kitchen french doors, and I accidently cut my finger off. As I look back on the past twenty years of my life, I have come to realize that that phrase flows freely from my lips without hesitation. It doesn't take naturally curious children very long to notice and ask why one of their peers is different. My most vivid memories of kindergarten are those of myself surrounded by kids, explaining my missing finger.

I never thought of myself as exceptional; I don't think that I ever wanted to admit it to myself. I never considered myself special, impaired, or different. That was for people with severe handicaps--not me! I am a girl, and girls are supposed to be beautiful--not some freak with part of a finger missing. (Not to mention the fact that it happened to be the pinkie finger next to my left ring finger.) For many of my preteen hours I wallowed in self-pity. I had dedicated myself to concealing my "exceptionality" if it was the last thing I did. I became insecure and a nervous wreck when it came to involvement with the opposite sex. God forbid the occasion should ever arise if I had to hold something, wave to someone, or demonstrate in front of a class. Consequently, I based my relationships on a "time-test." The longer it took a boyfriend to notice my "exceptionality" the less interested in him I became.

But something happened to me towards the end of high school; I began to develop a new attitude of self-respect. I let my nails grow long and painted them in bright shades of color. I didn't mind outstretching my hands when a girlfriend asked to admire my long nails. I not only faced the challenge of taking the required course of Typing I (which I had put off until the very end of my senior year), but I also won the Typing I award for that school year. I also stopped putting guys through my "time-test," embarrassed by how unfair I was being to them. For I came to realize that they weren't responsible for my finger. No one was. It was just how things happened; and it was just a part of my life that I needed to accept. Everyone has a special cross to bear, and in this essence, mine is no exception.

"What is Normal?"
Miriam Kimmelman

When I was in the fifth grade my arm took on a life of its own. It moved constantly, jerking up and down, calling attention to me, ruining my handwriting. I just wanted the arm jerking to stop because it hurt to have everyone, teacher and classmates, laughing at my sudden inability to write more than "chicken scratches."

I learned to type and the arm jerking stopped. It was replaced by subtle and progressive difficulty controlling my legs. In less than a year I could not walk normally. At home I crawled on the floor. In public I could only move backwards, holding on tightly to another person or to the walls. People were always looking at me, I thought, and I often cried because I was so self-conscious.

My mother took me to many doctors. There finally was some consensus. I had dystonia, a progressive neurological disorder that no one ever heard of. One doctor after another said it was hopeless. I wanted everything to go away magically and to become "normal," so that I could blend into a group without people looking at me.

Three years had gone by and I was referred to a specialist who told me that he thought he might be able to help me with some experimental brain surgery. He explained that he would freeze the spot in my brain that seemed to be causing the problem. It was a chance and I took it, without guarantees.

The surgery, actually there were two separated by three months, helped me a great deal. I could walk upright, with a minimal limp. I finished high school and college. I still had some nightmares that everything would come back and I would be a helpless spectacle again.

I had a relapse of some symptoms and one additional surgery, which was not quite as successful as the first two had been. But I finished graduate school and got a job as a rehabilitation counselor in a psychiatric hospital. Now I have been working for 18 years and don't think that much about my walking.

Sometimes I just forget how I look, until I catch a glance in a store window and realize that I seem to be tilted. Dystonia is just as much a part of me as my white-gray hair. However, every now and then I am stopped with comments like "Gee, isn't it early in the day for you to be drinking?" and I remember that dystonia isn't "normal." But what is?

"Walk On"
Liz Petruzzi

Our son, Joseph Richard Petruzzi, was diagnosed at birth with a rare, genetic disorder called Rubinstein-Taybi Syndrome. The following passage describes some of the things we went through after his official diagnosis. Rubinstein-Taybi involves developmental delay and possible mental retardation. There are other associated symptoms that go along with this syndrome. Joey is presently enrolled in an early intervention center and is doing very well. He is very close to his age developmentally and socially. Joey is one of the lucky ones.

When we found out Joey had RTS, we felt numb, devastated, and nauseous all at the same time. My husband, Mark, refused to believe it, but I knew in my heart of hearts that it was true. How could this have happened to our beautiful, sweet little baby? I couldn't understand how this could have happened to us. The early days are so blurred for me. It was a very confusing and hard time for us. I felt so cheated; cheated by the hospital for missing out on the first few days which should have been the happiest days of my life. Cheated because I had done everything I could to make sure I had a healthy baby and this happened. I was in complete shock. I over-reacted to everything and everyone and became highly overprotective of my infant son.

Soon, the chromosome test came back normal (RTS is not chromosomal) and I allowed well-meaning friends and relatives to lull me into a comfortable state of denial. "There's nothing wrong with this baby that time won't fix" and, "You can't compare babies, they all develop at different rates" were some of the rationales. Deep down I knew Joey was different.

I allowed myself to be convinced until Joey was five months old and still was not strong enough to lift his head. Enough was enough--something had to be done. Over my husband's objections and with mixed emotions, I called my pediatrician who readily agreed. She had tried to discuss this with me several times, I just wasn't ready. The doctor recommended Easter Seals Early Intervention Center where Joey would receive physical and occupational therapy twice a week and get the extra stimulation she felt he needed.

This opened up all the old fears and anxieties. I wished with all my heart that this wasn't happening, but I knew the problem wouldn't go away. For my son's sake, I had to pull myself together and get my head out of the sand. If nothing else, to give him every opportunity to overcome his disability.

I was so afraid for him and his future. I couldn't help but remember how the mainstreamed disabled children were treated when I was in school. This was not what I wanted for my son. We had to learn to take one day at a time, to rejoice with his successes and to leave the future alone.

I know now that the whole ordeal was a process we had to go through. No one can tell you how to deal with all of it; it's almost like a grieving process. There are lots of times, even now, that I have to force myself to work through, but the worst is behind us, and we are stronger because of it. I don't regret having Joey for one second; he is the light of my life--he brings so much joy to us he is worth anything I or my husband have had to go through.

"On Becoming Invisible"
Beverly Maszdzen

In December of 1978, at the age of 22, I suffered a massive stroke. Diagnosed as left hemiplegic, with unintelligible speech, I was presented with a fairly dismal prognosis--that I would never walk again. Of course, I was not presented with the prognosis, as no one spoke directly to me; rather I gathered my information from overheard conversations, or those directed at my family.

I tried to ask questions, unaware that my speech was not intelligible. My family reacted as though they understood me, but I slowly realized that their answers were always an affirmative or negative nod, or word. I tested the waters--began to ask concrete questions, like "Is it cold out?" (it was December). I began to get very incongruous answers, and thus discovered I could not be understood! Why did no one tell me? And did they think I would never catch on? Perhaps they were worried at my reaction. The doctors, those who did speak directly to me, always shouted their words, using language I would expect in a nursery school. I realized, finally, that they thought I was cognitively unable to understand them. I was extremely fortunate in that my speech recovered spontaneously within three weeks. Suddenly these professionals talked to me, as though my ability to speak implied my ability to understand.

Regaining movement on my left side was not as fortuitous. Following 2-3 times a day occupational and physical therapy, I was beginning to show improvement. The staff at the hospital and my family were wonderful! Any improvement, no matter how minor was received with overwhelming excitement. I improved sufficiently to be moved to a rehabilitation center. Thus I continued therapy 2-3 times a day, until the point at which I could be released to my parents' home.

The shock of so suddenly being disabled was one thing, but the "armor" of the disability was quite another. I was embarrassed at the splint, the sling, and the cane. The concept of going unnoticed was out of the question. Little did I realize how this armor would shield me from the buffets of the world, however. On my first excursions out of doors for a brief walk, I would often find I could not get across a street fast enough, becoming caught in the middle of the road against the light. Folks would smile, sympathetically, and allow me extra time. I continued to set my sights on eliminating the need for the unattractive adapted equipment I carried. I was so proud the day I could take a walk sans cane, splint, and sling. I finally felt "invisible," as though I blended in. I was a bit slower, and more unsteady, however, without the help. Again, I found myself stranded in the middle of the street, no matter how fast I seemed to go. Suddenly, no one smiled and waved me on. I was beset with an onslaught of curses and one finger salutes. I had worked so hard to get better, and suddenly found myself much worse. I recall I retrieved that armor the next few times out, because I just couldn't deal with this angry rejection. Being invisibly disabled was so much harder than being starkly visible!

Summary

You have had an opportunity, in this first chapter, to begin an exploration of exceptional people. Correct terms, the effects of labels, the importance of positive attitudes, and guidelines for comfortable and correct interactions have all been offered. Personal perspectives written by persons who are exceptional and by their friends and family members were also included. But, this is just the beginning. In the next two chapters you will have the opportunity to become more aware of individual differences and how those differences affect the exceptional individuals themselves and their families and friends. Enjoy learning about people who are exceptional!

References

Hardman, M. L., Drew, C. J., Egan, M. W., & Wolf, B. (1990). *Human exceptionality: Society, school, and family.* Boston: Allyn and Bacon.

Research and Training Center on Independent Living. (1990). *Guidelines for reporting and writing about people with disabilities.* (Available from Bureau of Child Research, University of Kansas, Lawrence, KS 66045.)

Schwartz, S., & Sindelar, P. (1990). Introducing today's exceptional children. In E. L. Meyen (Ed.), *Exceptional children in today's schools.* Denver: Love.

Suggested Readings

Buscaglia, L. F., & Williams, E. H. (1979). *Human advocacy and PL 94-142: The educator's roles.* New Jersey: Charles B. Slack.

De Felice, R. J. (1986). A crippled child grows up. *Newsweek, 108*(18), 13.

Dickman, I., & Gordon, S. (1985). *One miracle at a time.* New York: Simon and Schuster.

Donaldson, J. (1980). Changing attitudes towards handicapped persons: A review and analysis of research. *Exceptional Children, 46*(7), 504-512.

Gourse, L. (1989). The amazing Anderton's. *McCall's, 116*, 92-96.

O'Hara, J. (1987). A hero comes home. *Macleans, 100,* 34-40.

Turnbull, H. R., & Turnbull, A. P. (1985). *Parents speak out.* Columbus, OH: Merrill.

EXCEPTIONAL PEOPLE

Exploration

An Exploration Section is provided at the end of each chapter. The Exploration activities should assist you as you consider the meaning and implications of the content of the chapter.

Individual Activities

1. You are an exceptional person! How, you ask? Well, there are things you do much better than others, and there are some things you don't do as well. List 8 things that make you an exceptional person. Circle those which are extremely higher or lower than what you consider normal.

   _____   _____
   _____   _____
   _____   _____
   _____   _____

2. Now is the time to get all the negative terms you can think of for describing disabled people out of your system. You've probably heard many. List 20 of those terms. Then decide to never use them again!

   _____ _____ _____ _____
   _____ _____ _____ _____
   _____ _____ _____ _____
   _____ _____ _____ _____
   _____ _____ _____ _____

Group Activities

1. Get into a group of 4 or 5 people; persons whom you don't know well. Have each person write down a list of 5 adjectives which are guesses about the skills and weaknesses of each person in the group. Now discuss what everyone in the group wrote. Were the people in the group right or wrong about you? Did you find out something about yourself you didn't already know? How correct were you about others? Welcome to the world of labels!

    Reactions:

    _____

    _____

    _____

2. Stay in your group of 4-5 people. Review the guidelines presented in the chapter for interacting with exceptional people. Now, as a group, discuss and rank these guidelines from most to least important.

    Reactions:

    _____

    _____

    _____

Reaction Paper 1.1

Imagine yourself as the person in the runaway balloon story. You will now have to become accustomed to living in a world where everything is suited for people who are at least eight feet tall. How are you going to climb a flight of stairs, when each stair comes up to your waist? What would be easier to deal with, the stairs or the stares? Why?

_____

Continue on back if needed.

24

Notes

28

CHAPTER 2

ON BEING DIFFERENT

Elliott Lessen

Introduction

Each of us is different. These differences are evident as we compare ourselves to those around us and these differences are evident even within ourselves as we contrast our abilities from our weaknesses. We tend to pride ourselves on being unique and some of us are, perhaps, more unique than others. Exceptional persons are unique, a statement that on the surface seems so simplistic. Yet, as unique as we are from each other, we all share so much.

As human beings, we have many different experiences and believe many different things. However, there are commonalities that bind us together as such. Human beings have, among their capabilities, those of higher-order thinking, communicating, and responding emotionally. Although as part of the animal kingdom, albeit the highest phylum, we also have instinctual responses, our thought processes, and empathic sense of compassion which are among those things that set us apart from all other phyla.

We have all said at one time or another that, "it takes all kinds." If this statement is a truism, we are inferring acceptance of difference. To do any less, would be neither human nor humane. Included in these "kinds" are those persons who are exceptional and thus the focus of this chapter.

In this chapter, you will meet several exceptional people at different points in the life-span. For each person, you will be given a glimpse of what she or he encounters as a person who is exceptional. And for each person who does not fall under the rubric of exceptional, you will follow this person's relationship with someone who is exceptional.

What is it like to be exceptional? Perhaps only one who is exceptional can answer this question, but the collective experience of those who are can be presented as you begin to learn about yourself in relation to them.

Dan and Franco

Dan is 7 years old, has blond hair and blue eyes. His sense of humor and warmth attract his peers and teachers to him. He can read and do his math. He's the class leader. His inquisitiveness gets him into everything. While pretending to pay attention, he is actually looking at the new gym shoes he's wearing to school today.

Franco is 7 years old, has brown hair and brown eyes. He doesn't say much, but when he does, all his friends listen. He and Dan do things together in and out of school as friends. Dan's new gym shoes have caught his attention and he looks at them while pretending to pay attention. Franco, however, can't pull it off. The teacher has asked him a question to which he doesn't respond. She has already given him several warnings about his needing to pay attention to her. Franco is deaf.

Franco is indeed lucky to have such a good relationship with Dan. For without having a highly respected peer as his friend, his existence in this 2nd grade class might indeed be very lonely. Franco has an interpreter who is with him all day. She is with him for everything except for her own lunch. She goes with him on the playground so that he can communicate better with the other students and to help maximize his social interactions.

Dan has learned some sign language and that has encouraged others to do so as well. Some of the older students have tried making fun of Franco but Dan and the other second graders have been very protective of Franco. Now, even some of the older students want to learn some signs. Chances are, Franco will grow up and be able to feel comfortable in the deaf community as well as in general society.

Only a very few years ago, Franco would have been educated in a segregated classroom or in a segregated school for deaf students. The obvious reasons for the segregation would have been to protect him from being ostracized by others and to provide him with a "more appropriate" education. However, underlying those conscience pacifiers, there are other reasons; fear, ignorance, myths, and just basic discrimination.

Reactions toward persons with handicaps

"Handicaps are . . . made as well as born" (Buscaglia, 1983, p. 10). Disabilities can be either congenital, with the onset present or in some latent form at birth, or adventitious, with the onset at some point after birth. Regardless, however, the restrictions placed on persons with disabilities are more a function of the attitudes of society than it is a function of the disability itself (Buscaglia, 1983). Thus, although a handicapping condition may limit an individual's ability to participate in some aspect(s) of life, we, society-at-large, are the major stumbling block.

Gordon (1974) indicated that handicaps are created by society. That is to say, the perception we have about a handicap allows us to believe as we might have learned and to act the way we have been taught to act; and that is that persons with disabilities tend to be viewed as inferior to those without disabilities. However, it is less the limits or differences of the handicapping condition itself than the stereotypes we believe or the manner in which we treat people with handicaps which "...reflect the assumption that people with disabilities have neither interest nor ability to interact with the larger society" (Gordon, 1974, p. 1). Implicit in Gordon's assertion is our history of institutionalizing and segregating persons with disabilities from the mainstream of society, whether as children or as adults.

We still have these fears, ignorance, myths, and discrimination. We still have these stereotypes that form the basis for segregation. So why is it that Franco is integrated educationally and socially instead of being segregated? The answer is PL 94-142, The Education for All Handicapped Children Act of 1975. Because of this federal law, most students with handicaps are educated for all or at least part of the school day with their non-handicapped peers. As a result, students lose more of the negative feelings they have long had about persons with disabilities. Students like Franco are more able, therefore, to have friends like Dan.

Franco is rather lucky. His handicap is not visible on first appearance and most people are fascinated by sign language. But, what if Franco had cerebral palsy and walked "funny" and had slurred speech? What if Franco were blind? What if Franco were facially disfigured?

Views of persons with handicaps

Beyond your initial responses toward persons with handicaps is the way you view these individuals and what they do. Ysseldyke and Algozzine (1990) indicated that a disability we can see, such as a blind person using a cane for mobility or a person in a wheelchair, is more acceptable to us. Those disabilities we cannot see or which are difficult to understand evoke less compassionate responses in us. It is more difficult to understand why persons with an emotional disturbance cannot just control their behaviors than it is to understand why persons who use wheelchairs may need more time to get someplace on campus. Thus, the "visible" nature of an impairment contributes to our view of the persons, to the way we respond to their handicaps, and to the empathy we might accord them.

When you think of Beethoven, what do you think of first; that he was a musician/composer or that he was deaf? When you think of Franklin D. Roosevelt, what do you think of first: that he was a President of the United States or that he had polio? When you think of Jim Abbott, what do you think of first: that he is a major league pitcher or that he has one arm? Why do these people conjure up positive images for us when people in our everyday lives may not?

Scott and Lenny

Scott is 37 years old, married, and the father of three young children. Scott is a successful real estate agent who finds time for his family as well as his leisure-time passions; he is on two softball teams and in two weekly foursomes for golf. His buddy Lenny is a couple of years older than Scott. Lenny is also married and has two children. He has climbed the "ladder of success" and is now a corporation vice-president. He and Scott have played golf and softball together for almost 20 years. About two years ago, Lenny was diagnosed as having multiple sclerosis (MS).

Scott's and Lenny's relationship has not changed even though Lenny now uses a cane to walk and occasionally has to use a wheelchair. On a recent two-family vacation to Disney World, Lenny had to spend almost the entire time in the wheelchair. He and his wife have started looking for a new home; one that is all on one floor, has enough room at the entrance in the front and from the garage for a ramp, and has relatively wide doorways and hallways for the wheelchair. They know that they'll also need an architect to redesign the kitchen and one bathroom to make those rooms wheelchair accessible.

Lenny's relationships at work have not changed too much, although at the beginning several co-workers shied away from him. People, however, are getting used to his needing a bit more time to get places and the fact that he tires more easily. Do you think they initially thought they were going to get MS from being near or perhaps touching Lenny? Socially, Scott is still his close friend, but as Lenny has become progressively more incapacitated, some others have begun to include him and his wife less often.

Lenny's friendship with Scott and his family has been long-lasting and has endured the impact of this situation. Why have others chosen to stay away? Could it be that they really didn't choose not to call or include Lenny, but it just "sort of happened?" Although the reactions toward Lenny may not be conscious ones, they are indeed ones of which his friends are aware. So why have they begun to exclude him? Is it fear? "People in wheelchairs scare me. I don't know how to act." Is it ignorance? "I've never been around someone with MS and I don't know what to do." Is it because of myths about MS? "I heard you can catch MS by touching someone who has it?" Or is it a form of discrimination? "He's different now and we can't do things like we always used to." Actually, it is probably some of each of these reasons.

Unlike Franco, Lenny's handicap is visible. Most people will tend to stay away from him or stare at him, especially as his condition deteriorates. The sight of him as he becomes more debilitated will evoke responses similar to those shown to Christy Brown in the movie "My Left Foot." Some will pity him, some will be repulsed by him, and some will be afraid to go near him for fear of some uncontrolled physical movement. But ultimately there will be some level of compassion accorded him because of all that he is enduring.

Relationships with persons with handicaps

Have you ever thought about how you interact with people and why you interact the way you do? Interpersonal relationships, difficult at times for all of us, present a different set of circumstances for persons with disabilities. All of us interact with others, i.e., family, friends, co-workers, and strangers. When we feel good about ourselves, these interactions have a greater chance of being positive. But what about the times when we feel less than good about ourselves? Have you ever had a bad haircut that made you want to avoid everyone until it grew out? Have you ever tried to avoid having people see you because of that zit that blossomed on your nose overnight? Although these were somewhat inconsequential in the long-term of life, you felt conspicuous.

Persons with disabilities are conspicuous each and every day of their lives. There is always something that sets them apart from the mainstream. These differences, no matter how small, can have a cumulative effect that may make these individuals want to avoid others. Just as you did not want to have people stare or point a finger at you for your haircut, people with disabilities do not want people to stare or point a finger at them because of their difference.

Developing "typical" relationships with others can become a matter of adjustment that takes time. Relationships, for many persons with disabilities, can be experiences that connote rejection and isolation (Ysseldyke & Algozzine, 1990), and these experiences can come to be their expectations about all relationships. If being in public has been painful for a person with a disability, isolation from public places may become this person's manner of coping. Thus, how we interact with one another has a great likelihood of bringing about the same response from the other person. Increasing our awareness of differences in people and accepting these differences can have a positive impact on the lives of others and upon our own lives as well.

In our everyday lives, we (society-at-large) are much more likely to turn away, to cross to the other side of the street, to avoid completely, to stare while a person with a handicap is trying to do something, and maybe even to laugh. These are very typical responses, however, and ones we need to consider. Why do they occur? What precipitates our actions and reactions toward these persons we see every day who are handicapped?

Because we don't know about a particular handicap, because we don't know how to interact with a person with a handicap, because we are thrust into an interpersonal situation which is different from the usual, we may be afraid of persons with handicaps (Bowe, 1978). Are we born with this fear? Is the fear instinctual? The answer is no! Then how do we get this fear? We get it just like any other fear; we learn it through watching and listening to others around us, particularly our parents and other family members.

Intolerance or tolerance?

Actually, we start out very ignorant about handicaps and assume that many of the myths to which we have been exposed are true! But then we learn that some of them are not true. People with epilepsy are not mentally retarded; they're not insane; they're not . . .; they're not . . .; they can hold jobs; they can drive cars; they can . . .; they can . . . The problem arises when we realize that what we've been told is actually not true and yet we choose to ignore this new information.

You have so many pieces of information through which you must sort in order to arrive at what your adult views, values, and beliefs are going to be. Take for example any religious, gender, or racial myth you held to be true as a young child. Once you were made aware that your belief or myth was incorrect, you had two options. You could have elected to continue to believe as you always had and thus, to ignore that which disputed your belief; or you could have changed your belief by incorporating what you had heard, seen, or experienced.

For those of you who change your beliefs, humanity is forever grateful. For those of you who do not change, human progress is stalled by prejudice. Ignorance can be viewed with a positive connotation at one time in your lives. For example, having a stereotype about someone who is racially or religiously different is understandable in three-year-olds who don't know any better and who are only mimicking what they hear from their parents. Ignorance changes rapidly to prejudice when you refuse to see a side to an issue that is different from what you might have thought. When three-year-olds become teenagers or young adults, the racial or religious stereotypes they may have held as toddlers should have been replaced by facts.

A long-held societal myth is that women are poorer at mathematics than men. Many societal reasons have sustained this myth over the years, but now, with the number of women in executive positions, finding careers in accounting, etc., this myth or belief has been disputed. Therefore, for those of you who want to continue believing this type of nonsense, your thoughts and actions are marked by prejudice and prejudicial behaviors. For those of you who realize the myth of this particular belief and change your thinking and attitudes about it, or at least try to change, ignorance has given way to tolerance and understanding; tolerance for differences and understanding of these differences as they affect your daily lives.

The time when we start allowing our ignorance, based on myth and stereotypes, to give way to broader dimensions of thinking is perhaps the moment of truth in our thinking. For at this time we truly have to look at who we are and in what we believe about the value of humanity. It is at this time that our unfounded fears, or our ignorance, can either be discarded or ignored. Those of you who have discarded at least some of your fears of persons who are different are further ahead of those of us whose ignorance has changed to prejudice. When we know that some of what we had learned is not true and start changing how we behave toward or interact with all persons, including persons with handicaps, the irrational fears we once had start to dissipate. The change toward acceptance is a long and difficult process. We need to get over our irrational fears and replace them with thoughts and actions that are based on reason and facts.

Nancy and Laura

Laura and Nancy have known each other since they started kindergarten and have been college roommates for the past three years. Although their majors are different, they joined the same sorority and have many of the same friends. Recently, Laura contracted AIDS as the result of a blood transfusion. Nancy's first reaction upon learning that Laura is HIV-positive, was to be supportive, but as she went through the first several days, she found herself using the other bathroom, putting all dishes through the dishwasher, avoiding even brushing up against Laura, or sitting on her bed while they were talking, and so on. Nancy even found that she didn't want to wash Laura's clothes with hers or wear Laura's clothes. As the saying goes, her actions spoke louder than her words; she was showing Laura behavior that was different from what she was saying. Could you blame Nancy? Would your reactions have been any different?

Luckily for Laura, Nancy began to see what she was doing to herself and to Laura and stopped all the "fussiness," as she called it. She read everything she could about AIDS and decided that by behaving as if nothing were different, she would not only be supporting Laura emotionally, but also modeling for others how they should behave toward and interact with Laura.

But Laura's future isn't exactly rosy. Her T-cell count is very high although she has thus far not suffered any real symptoms of the disease. When that will happen is pure conjecture at this point. However, Laura knows that her college degree may never be put to use. Will her "secret" follow her everywhere she goes? Can she keep her disease a secret? Will everyone who finds out shun her? Will rooms clear out when she walks in? Laura spends her days trying to be positive and outgoing; but her private moments and nights are filled with anxiety and nightmares.

What if you were Laura? What if you were Laura's friend? Each question begs a different response. Being a person with a handicap is something out of the realm of reality for almost everyone reading this chapter. Oh, some of you wear glasses and maybe a few have experienced a learning problem. But for the most part, you are all relatively healthy. It won't be until you are about 40 that "things start to fall apart." (Doesn't that sound like something familiar your parents have said?) But the truth of the matter is that until you are senior citizens, most of you will not experience anything that is permanently debilitating.

Being the friend or relative of a person with a handicap is somewhat different. You can only imagine what it is like for your friend. You can only imagine what physical and/or emotional pain your friend is experiencing. In Nancy's case, she was afraid, she was ignorant, she only knew myths about AIDS, and she initially discriminated against her friend Laura. Nancy's ignorance and the myths she had changed. She lost her fear of Laura and of Laura's AIDS. She stopped discriminating against Laura. In fact, although she didn't become a crusader, she did speak out on campus about AIDS and the mistreatment of persons with AIDS, especially among her college-age peers. Are you capable of doing the same?

Lou and Rob

Lou and Rob are brothers, with Lou being two years older. They are in high school. Lou has just started his senior year and Rob has started "ninth" grade. Lou, who skipped a grade is academically gifted and is in several accelerated classes. Rob, on the other hand, is mildly retarded. He idolizes his older brother and can't wait to be in the same school with him. He is in all special education classes except for things like physical education, music, home economics, and lunch. He has a girlfriend and wants to go to all the school dances.

Until this year, Lou and Rob have not attended the same school since their elementary years when Rob's being "a bit behind" wasn't quite as noticeable. Lou has troubles of his own. He has been perceived as a "know-it-all," a "nerd," and just plain different. But he worked very hard to overcome these stereotypes that others had of him and since coming to the high school, has been on the football team. Now all of that is about to change. He is afraid that new differences will become associated with him as Rob's brother.

Rob has been in a self-contained special education class and now, upon entering high school, he will be mainstreamed into some low-level regular classes. His slowness will be more evident, his lower social skills will be more evident, and his devotion to his older brother will become a burden to Lou. Luckily, however, for both Lou and Rob, their parents took Lou to see a counselor with whom he talked about his fears and his concerns. Lou sees Rob's being in high school with him something that could strengthen their sibling relationship. Lou also realizes that he is going to have to educate his friends about all the strengths that Rob has.

Just as Franco, Lenny, and Laura had to learn or relearn ways to cope with their peers, Lou and Rob also will have to go through that process. Rob may never fully realize what others are saying about him behind his back or even to his face. Lou, however, will understand all the subtle and not-so-subtle comments that are made. Lou's own experience may help him to help his brother.

How to refer to persons with handicaps

Why do we say things about persons who are different? Why are we cruel at times? Why do we laugh? We do so because of fear, ignorance, and myths about the unknown. We have all made fun of someone who is handicapped, either in a passing comment or in a joke. We have all laughed at someone who has done something different or bizarre. We have all been cruel, perhaps without even knowing it!

Have you ever called a friend who constantly made mistakes in athletics a "spaz?" Have you ever made fun of the kids who rode the little yellow school bus? Have you ever called someone who wore glasses "four-eyes?" Have you ever called a friend who didn't catch on quickly to something in school a "retard," or "moron," or "idiot," or "imbecile?" Yes, you probably have; but of course that was out of ignorance! These quirks of our language need to disappear if we, both individually and as a society, are going to be more accepting of individual differences. For it is only with consciousness of what we actually say and do that we can truly change how we accept differences in others.

Have you ever laughed at someone who has slipped on a wet floor or on ice and fallen down? Have you ever laughed about your friend's cast and signed it? People laugh at moments such as these and make light of a broken leg or arm by signing a cast for several reasons. Among these reasons are that it is important for our own spirit to make light of the event. We laugh as if to say, "Whew, it isn't me." We sign a friend's cast to make light of his or her predicament and to signify its temporary nature. If something is temporary, it is much easier to accommodate. If we know it will go away, it is easier to accept.

The next time you walk down the street and see someone who is limping or walking "funny" coming toward you, check your reaction as that person gets nearer. Our natural response is to brush off any emotion if the limp is caused by something temporary. But if the limp is caused by something permanent, such as cerebral palsy or a prosthetic leg, our emotions run the gamut from pity for the person to relief for ourselves.

As with Franco, Lenny's handicap will be such that people will look at him and "see" his handicap. However, Laura, Lou, and Rob are exceptional in ways that are not readily evident, although the ravages of Laura's AIDS will eventually worsen and people will stare at her. For Lou and Rob, our responses to them will vary but will be less compassionate than our responses to the others. Why? Because the differences between ourselves and either Lou or Rob are difficult to "see." When Lou wasn't on the football team, he was categorized as a "geek." He wore glasses, and "set the curve" in every class. His peers treated him as being different and thus, treated him less compassionately. In Rob's case, it is difficult for us to understand how someone in "ninth" grade can't add basic sums, or can't recite the names of the 50 states, or can't respond in a socially appropriate way in different situations. Therefore, Rob is treated differently and less compassionately by those who do not understand his retardation.

Views of persons with handicaps

Your perceptions of others are based on how different they are from you and what you consider to be normal. But as society treats people who are disabled differently it is necessary to realize that they too are people and have feelings and emotions. The sense of who persons with disabilities are falls into several different types (Barnes, Berrigan, & Biklen, 1978). The types represent the stereotypes to which you assign exceptional people and thus govern how you act and react toward them; and it is society and your parents who have raised you to view persons with disabilities in the following ways.

Few, but some, persons with disabilities are seen positively, and thus almost held in a place of honor. We have already mentioned people like Beethoven and

Roosevelt. How about adding Ray Charles and Terry Fox to the list? And even in fictional situations, how about the Incredible Hulk and Corky in "Life Goes On?" They are different from most persons, but different in very dissimilar ways.

Another way we see persons with handicaps is as people to be pitied. We have seen or read about circus freak shows, or seen handicapped children on telethons, or seen blind people begging on street corners. There is a tendency to allow these people to make us feel guilty.

Sometimes we view persons with handicaps as berserk, or frenzied, or even sinister. How about Captain Hook? or Frankenstein? or one of James Bond's nemesis, Jaws? Perhaps, because their handicaps make them look so different and even grotesque, our fear of them is intensified. Of course, think of the roles they play. Are they ever the heroes?

Many exceptionalities, however, have been portrayed over the years by characters that are ridiculous or inept caricatures. Don't the Three Stooges represent a view often held of persons who are mildly retarded--sort of bumbling through life? Or consider the pity engendered by Mickey Rooney as "Bill." What about Tattoo on Fantasy Island; why doesn't Ricardo Montalban call _him_ Boss? Chester from "Gunsmoke" always seemed to be the "town charity" week after week. And although we are all aware of Einstein, don't we first think of him as sort of a frumpy person? And Dr. Strangelove or Dr. Jekyll or Dr. No, why are these gifted men portrayed as such weirdos?

Finally, and encompassing the way in which most persons who are handicapped are portrayed, is that they are children incapable of taking care of themselves. Even adults with handicaps are portrayed as childlike rather than as adults. This depiction of persons with handicaps as children seems to allow able-bodied individuals to perpetuate a sense of inferiority for anyone who is not "whole." Our stereotype of someone who is handicapped is that that person can't do things or can't think independently. Thus, non-disabled persons have placed themselves in a position of superiority.

Have you ever watched a telethon for a particular disease or handicap? Have you seen adults with handicaps or children and adolescents with handicaps on the telethon? Jason, a college student, appeared on a telethon just several months before he died at age 20 from complications from muscular dystrophy (MD). He did so to help raise money for MD research. However, he said he was treated like an incompetent child. He was patronized. Why? Fear, ignorance, myths, discrimination, and even the misconception that persons with handicaps are inferior to those who are not handicapped!

ON BEING DIFFERENT

Perceptions about and attitudes toward persons who are exceptional are subjective and arbitrary. They typically represent unconscious judgments we make when we act and react toward persons who are different from what we consider to be normal. These judgments place persons with handicaps into a category of humanity that is mutually exclusive from ourselves. Can our behaviors and beliefs be changed? Simply answered, yes. But how?

Changing our interactions with persons with handicaps

The next time you see someone who is blind, for example, address the person directly and don't shout; chances are the individual isn't deaf, too. When you interact with someone who may have a learning problem, or may be retarded, or may even have an emotional problem, realize that the inability to function in a way that you think is normal is not of this person's own choosing. Have compassion, not pity, for someone with cerebral palsy.

Try spending an hour at home blindfolded. Go through your morning routine, watch TV, try to make something to eat. What is it like being blind? Put in ear plugs and then try watching TV or talking to friends. What is it like being hearing impaired? Borrow a wheelchair and try to get around your house or apartment or dorm. Try going different places on campus or using the restrooms on campus from a wheelchair. What is it like being in a wheelchair?

Tape your dominant hand into a fist with masking tape and try going through a day; getting dressed for class, cooking, and taking notes. What is it like having a physical impairment? Try sensing what it is like to have a learning disability by sitting in on a class of advanced calculus or physics. You should understand the majority of words used, but when you listen to the lecture, it will probably make little sense to you. What is it like having a learning disability?

After you try one or more of the ways mentioned that simulate being handicapped, ask yourself: how did it feel having your daily life inconvenienced, even for a short period of time? How did you feel having people laugh at you? How did you feel having people stare at you? How did it feel not understanding when someone spoke to you?

Just as persons from different ethnic or racial backgrounds cannot escape identification with their backgrounds, persons who are exceptional cannot escape from their handicaps. So the next time you meet an exceptional person, remember that "it takes all kinds!" Have a little tolerance for differences and show that person the same dignity that you would want for yourself!

References

Barnes, E., Berrigan, C., & Biklen, D. (1978). *What's the difference? Teaching positive attitudes toward people with disabilities.* Syracuse, NY: Human Policy Press.

Bowe, F. (1978). *Handicapped America: Barriers to disabled people.* New York: Harper & Row.

Buscaglia, L. (1983). *The disabled and their parents: A counseling challenge* (rev. ed). New York: Holt, Rinehart, and Winston.

Gordon, S. (1974). *Sexual rights for the people who happen to be handicapped.* Syracuse, NY: Syracuse University.

Ysseldyke, J. E., & Algozzine, B. (1990). *Introduction to special education* (2nd ed.). Boston: Houghton Mifflin.

Suggested Readings

Blatt, B. (1966). *Christmas in purgatory: A photographic essay on mental retardation.* Boston: Allyn and Bacon.

Brown, C. (1955). *My left foot.* New York: Simon & Schuster.

Keller, H. (1911). *The story of my life.* Garden City, NY: Doubleday.

Rivera, G. (1972). *Willowbrook: A report on how it is and why it doesn't have to be that way.* New York: Random House.

ON BEING DIFFERENT

Exploration

Individual Activities

1. What makes a person different? Clothing? Skin color? Religion? Attitude? This is a difficult question which you must answer every day. Think of three persons whom you believe are different. Then list five characteristics of each of those persons.

   Person 1   Person 2   Person 3

   _____   _____   _____

   _____   _____   _____

   _____   _____   _____

   _____   _____   _____

   _____   _____   _____

   Do you think that any of the characteristics you listed above are important enough so that the persons should be considered to be different? If so, identify which characteristics and your reason.

   Characteristic   Reason

   _____   _____

                               _____

   _____   _____

                               _____

   _____   _____

                               _____

   _____   _____

                               _____

2. Have you ever been walking along and noticed a person with a visible disability? The significant question is, did you stare at the person? How do you think staring affects individuals who are disabled? This is your opportunity to explore what it is like to have someone stare at you. Make a sign on cardboard which is 5 inches by 8 inches (minimum) which says, "I AM DIFFERENT." Wear this sign from the moment you leave your home in the morning until you return home at night. Keep a record of your experience in the provided spaces by listing the reactions you received from others.

   Reactions of others:

   a. _____

   b. _____

   c. _____

   d. _____

   e. _____

   f. _____

ON BEING DIFFERENT

Group Activities

1. In class, break up into groups of five people. Assume that you are a world famous acting troupe that has been given the assignment to write and act out a short skit portraying what it is like to be different. Take 15 to 20 minutes to write and rehearse your skit. After everyone is ready get up and perform your creation. There are no bounds as to how you are to get your point across except to keep it to within 5 minutes. Good luck and break a leg!

   Reactions:

   _____

   _____

   _____

2. This is an opportunity to further explore the issue of labeling. Select one specific item of clothing (green socks, white shirt, black pants, white sneakers, etc.) and have everyone in your class who is wearing the item stand. Now indicate that those individuals, who have the label of wearing the type clothing you have identified, are lazy, incompetent, impolite, and smelly. Explore how the persons who are standing feel due to their negative labels which are simply due to the clothing they are wearing.

   Reactions:

   _____

   _____

   _____

Notes

Reaction Paper 2.1

When you wore your "I AM DIFFERENT" sign, what were the reactions of other people? How would you feel if this sign were permanently attached? Relate your feelings to those a person with a visible exceptionality, such as someone in a wheelchair or someone missing a limb, would feel.

Continue on back if needed.

Reaction Paper 2.2

You are a successful business person who is in need of some additional help. It turns out that one of your two best applicants has a noticeable disability. If all qualifications were equal and both could do the job equally well, how would you decide who gets the position? Take time with this question and be honest!

Continue on back if needed.

50

Notes

CHAPTER 3

FAMILIES' PERSPECTIVES ON EXCEPTIONALITY

Deborah Bott Slaton

Introduction

Every person with a disability is a member of a family. If you are part of a family coping with disability, or you know such a family, you likely have insights into the complexities of families' perspectives on exceptionality. Just as every family is a unique mix of personalities, values, cultural heritages, expectations, and communication styles, so the family with a member who is disabled is unique in the way the family unit and individual members respond to the disability. It may appear that families with a loved one who is exceptional face many issues distinct from those faced by "normal" families. In fact, families of people with disabilities deal with issues that face every family--communication, safety, independence, financial security--but these issues are in a different context because one or more members of the family have a handicap. Despite the similarities they have with other families, families with a member who has special needs are undeniably influenced by the handicap. The purpose of this chapter is to briefly describe how a disability changes the context of family life and to give examples of how some families have learned to meet the challenge of exceptionality.

Learning of the Disability

When family members retell their experiences of first learning about their relative's disability, they often recall vivid details about that moment. It is common to hear or read of awkwardness on the part of professionals (often physicians) who must tell anxious family members that their relative has some sort of impairment. Some individuals are thankful that they were treated with respect and given clear, accurate information about the disability. Other individuals remain angry about the behavior of professionals during these very sensitive moments. It is common to hear of professionals who withheld information, delivered the news and left without answering questions, or immediately gave advice about sending the family member with a disability to an institution of some sort.

Family members may learn of a relative's handicap at any time. Many parents learn of birth defects during pregnancy or soon after the child is born, but some handicaps do not manifest themselves immediately. It may not be until an infant misses some developmental milestones such as tracking objects with the eyes or lifting the head, that parents and pediatricians suspect some skills or functions are not developing normally. Sometimes parents endure weeks and months of nagging worry about their child before a clear diagnosis is available. In the cases of mild mental retardation, learning disabilities, and mild hearing losses, the handicap may not be detected until the child reaches school age and is confronted with academic learning tasks at which he or she fails to perform as well as peers.

Some disabilities have slow onsets during childhood or later in life. Progressive diseases such as muscular dystrophy cause the individual to lose functions and skills that were previously intact. Some family members react to progressive loss of function with careful planning; other individuals react with an extreme dread of the future (Coombs, 1984).

Disabilities may also result from serious injury or illness later in life. Automobile accidents, strokes, and diabetes may result in permanent disabilities for individuals who were previously healthy and able. Families may receive news of a relative's disability at any point in time. Parents may learn of an infant's physical disability in the hospital delivery room; children may learn of a grandparent's stroke after overhearing their parents' telephone conversations; a husband may learn of his wife's paralysis from physicians working in a hospital emergency room. Whenever or however news of a handicap is delivered, it is always a difficult, emotional moment.

Families have specific needs during this vulnerable time (Turnbull & Turnbull, 1986). The first need is for complete, straightforward information about their relative's condition. Any attempt to filter or withhold information, although probably prompted by a desire to be kind, may actually impede the family's ability to accept the situation. Children are often adversely affected by adults' incomplete or inaccurate descriptions of the disability. If children do not have clear descriptions they can understand, they often will create fantasy explanations that may be more scary than the actual situation (Powell & Ogle, 1985).

A second need of some family members is to have the information repeated at different times and in different ways. The strong emotional response people have to learning of a handicap may prevent them from comprehending all the information the first time around. Family members may need a phone number they may call for more information, and the thoughtful professional will recognize the need for follow-up contacts with the family to answer questions and offer support. A final need experienced by many people at this time is for the opportunity to express feelings and emotional reactions to learning of the disability.

Reacting to the Disability

Much has been written about emotional stages through which people progress as they work to cope with the disability of a family member, but this concept is highly controversial (Blacher, 1984). First, if individuals in a particular family do progress through common stages of reaction, nothing is to say that those reactions will happen at the same time. This can lead to misunderstandings and miscommunication among members of the family (Coombs, 1984). Others suggest that stages oversimplify what are actually more intricate dynamics within the family. Featherstone (1980) provided additional insight into the issue by stating, "Certainly these stage models tell a part of the story: people do change; many follow rather similar paths; for the most part, life improves. I think, however, that most stage theories oversimplify a complex and diverse process" (p. 10).

Given the concerns regarding stages of emotional reaction or adjustment, there is one emotion that is widely reported as an initial reaction to the news of a disability, and that emotion is grief. Many family members in this situation speak of a sense of loss similar to that of death. In the case of an infant, the healthy child that parents dreamed of is in a sense "dead." In his or her place is an infant with an uncertain future and limitations that probably were not considered as the parents anticipated the birth of their child. In the instance of a loss later in life, the affected individual and his or her family may grieve for a lost ability, talent, or future. Many people view the grieving process as important for later healthy adjustment, and although it is a common initial reaction, some people report an enduring sense of grief over any loss caused by the disability.

The emotional reactions people experience toward disabilities are not unique emotions. Most parents, grandparents, brothers, and sisters, experience fear, anger, guilt, and loneliness. Again, it is the disability itself that gives a different context to these emotions. For example, it is normal for parents to experience some level of fear for their child's safety and future, but parents of a child with hemophilia probably experience a more intense and constant fear for their child's safety. Apparent severity of the disability to an outside observer doesn't predict an individual's or family's reaction. More important is ". . . the degree to which it threatens our goals and security" (Coombs, 1984, p. 17). Coombs offered the example of a concert pianist who loses a finger. To many other people, this may not cause drastic changes in lifestyle; it may not actually result in a handicap. But to a musician such an injury may mean loss of career, income, and status. Age, vocational goals, and familial expectations all influence any sense of loss resulting from a disability.

Featherstone (1980) described the four most prominent emotional reactions to a family member's disability as fear, anger, loneliness, and guilt or self-doubt. Fears include not only fears for the individual's health, safety, and happiness but also fears related to how the disability will impact the lives of non-handicapped family members. Featherstone described these "fears for self" as anticipated loss of personal freedoms, threats to financial security, and the fear of failure at caring for or loving the family member. Often, family members report that their most intense fears happened soon after learning of the handicap. Fear can be somewhat mitigated by experience, knowledge, and the passage of time.

Anger is another prominent emotional reaction to disability. Indeed, there is much for family members to be angry about when a loved one experiences a disability. Many people are intensely angry at the disability itself. As one parent stated, ". . . life has ripped us off" (Featherstone, 1980, p. 33). The reactions of people inside and outside the family can also prompt anger--at ignorant reactions, at insensitive professionals, or at cruel acts of teasing or ridicule. Finally, some family members experience anger at the exceptional individual; this is an especially conflicting type of anger because it can seem inappropriate to be angry at a person with a disability.

Many family members also experience a strong sensation of loneliness. The loneliness can be self-imposed as when the family isolates itself due to embarrassment or overprotectiveness. For example, families that include a member with a history of behavioral problems may avoid social situations that could prompt a much-feared tantrum or outburst. Isolation can also result from the logistics of caring for a member who needs extensive physical assistance. Families, caring for a member who is severely handicapped, may find it difficult to organize outings, and environmental barriers in recreational facilities or friends' homes may make going to a party or a picnic a complex ordeal. Siblings of individuals with handicaps may be cut off from their peers if they are called upon for extensive child care responsibility for the brother or sister with a handicap. Finally, segregated services for persons with disabilities may also serve to isolate their families. Parents of children attending a special school for children with handicaps usually do not attend PTA meetings with their neighbors. Sometimes the isolation from others is subtle, but the loneliness that results is very real.

Guilt and the accompanying self-doubt are also prominent emotional reactions to a family member's handicap. All family members may at some time feel guilty for being healthy and able when their loved one is not. For many years, professionals in medicine and education pointed to parents as the cause of many of children's disabilities. Parents were told that their child's autism resulted from inadequate parental affection during early years, that mental retardation was only due to heredity, and that emotional disturbance was rooted in the parents' behavior. While some handicaps do result from genetic conditions (i.e., Down Syndrome) or parental behavior (i.e., ingestion of alcohol during pregnancy), in many cases the precise cause of a disability is unclear (Turnbull & Turnbull, 1986). Parents are especially vulnerable to feelings of guilt about their child's disability. All family members involved in caring for the relative with a disability may experience self-doubt about their ability to do enough of the right kind of thing to help their loved one.

Every individual has a unique collection of knowledge, attitudes, and experiences that influence that person's behavior. Religious background is but one example of how an individual's history influences his or her view of disability; one may view a handicap as punishment, a test of his or her own worth, fate, or an event predetermined by God. Regardless of philosophical viewpoint, disabilities are often stressful for people, and an individual's approach to dealing with stress is a key factor in how he or she will cope with disability.

The first step to dealing with stress is to recognize it; there is nothing shameful about the admission that a loved one's disability results in stress for other members of the family. A disability can cause many difficult changes in the lives of everyone in the family; areas in which these changes occur may include health, finances, work, living conditions, recreation, social contacts, and the daily routines of eating and sleeping. Many people find that stressful situations are somewhat relieved if those things that can be changed or controlled are separated from those that cannot. After this distinction is made, individuals are free to work to change those things under their control, and develop acceptance of the things they cannot change.

Learning About the Disability

If family members are to learn to cope with a relative's disability and assist that individual in their growth and development, it is imperative that they learn all that they can about the disability and available services. As Turnbull, Turnbull, Bronicki, Summers, and Roeder-Gordon (1989) stated when describing families' need for information about disabilities, "Knowledge is power" (p. 306). Sources of information include the following: books and periodicals in public, university, and personal libraries; parent and professional organizations; U.S. Department of Education parent information and training centers (see Turnbull & Turnbull, 1986, for a comprehensive list of addresses); professionals including special educators, physicians, therapists, or counselors; and state planning councils for developmental disabilities (see Turnbull et al., 1989).

Families searching for printed information will soon distinguish two broad categories of information about disabilities: (a) technical information written by professionals for professionals, and (b) information written for families and other interested non-professionals. Although the information aimed at families may certainly be more pertinent and jargon-free than the professional literature, family members should not shy away from the professional literature if they seek answers to technical, in-depth questions. When looking for information in a library card catalog or index, the following descriptors will lead to information about families and disabilities: Handicapped children--Care; Handicapped children--Family relationships; Handicapped--Family relationships. Many libraries also list materials under descriptors for specific handicaps, and these may include: physically handicapped, mentally handicapped (or mental retardation), deafness, blindness, learning disabled, autism, and so forth.

The following periodicals address the needs of families with a member who has special needs:

-*ERIC Clearinghouse on Handicapped and Gifted Children Information Bulletin.* 1920 Association Drive, Reston, VA 22091.

This free, quarterly bulletin describes new books and other literature on the topic of exceptionality. It also contains brief articles describing trends and developments pertinent to people with disabilities. To receive copies of the bulletin, write the above address and ask to be placed on the mailing list.

-The Exceptional Parent. 605 Commonwealth Avenue, Boston, MA 02215. This magazine, directed at parents of children with disabilities, is published eight times each year.

-Accent on Living. Cheever Publishing, Gillum Road and High Drive, P. O. Box 7000, Bloomington, IL 61701. Aimed at adults with disabilities, some pieces in this periodical may also assist children with disabilities to understand how disabilities do not automatically prevent success as an adult.

A realistic view

One goal of learning about a family member's handicap is to develop a realistic view of disabilities and abilities. Sometimes lack of information can cause a family to underestimate the exceptional person's abilities and thus not allow that individual to fully develop to his or her potential. Family members also need information about resources that can assist them and the disabled person in the family. For example, for some physical disabilities, it may be possible that a specially designed computer or a trained animal can enhance the disabled person's ability to be independent in self-care, eating, or leisure tasks.

Another purpose in seeking information is to alleviate some of the fear, anger, loneliness, and guilt the family may be experiencing. Many books have been written by relatives of people with disabilities, and vicariously sharing these individuals' experiences may prove helpful. Parents and siblings have written especially eloquent and revealing descriptions of life with a son or daughter, brother or sister with a handicap. Examples of books within this category are listed in the "Suggested Readings" section at the end of this chapter. These books offer emotional comfort and practical advice to other exceptional families.

Meeting the Needs of a Family Member with a Disability

If the individual with a disability has extensive needs for care and attention, the impact on all members of the family can be considerable. Some family members report that they cope with the need for long-term care by taking each day, one at a time. In de Vinck's (1988) moving book about his severely handicapped brother who died at the age of 32, he described the following conversation with his father:

> *I asked my father, "How did you care for Oliver for thirty-two years?"*
> *"It was not thirty-two years," he said. "I just asked myself, 'Can I feed Oliver today?' and the answer was always, 'Yes I can.'"*
> *We lived with Oliver moment by moment. (p. 13)*

Long-term planning

The challenges presented by a disability on a day-to-day basis, are the same challenges which compel family members to engage in long-term planning for the member who experiences a disability. Long-term planning should consider the entire life span. Future planning is difficult but important for such key issues as financial security, life in the community, where to live, what kind of job to prepare for, how to spend money, and many other issues. Turnbull et al. (1989) provided very detailed information about future planning for children, young adults, and adults with disabilities. Their text emphasizes that parents need to make informed, purposeful decisions about the legal status of the son or daughter with disabilities; these decisions include mental competence (degrees of), consent, and guardianship. The text provides a series of worksheets and exercises families may use to aid decision-making. Turnbull et al. also suggested the following general approach to long-term planning and problem-solving: (a) define the problem or need; (b) brainstorm a range of possible solutions; (c) evaluate the alternatives and choose one; (d) communicate this decision to others; (e) take the action necessary to implement the alternative; (f) finally, evaluate the outcomes of the action.

Empowerment

When families undertake future planning, it is important to involve the person with a disability in decision-making to the maximum extent possible. Many families and professionals are now implementing the idea of empowerment. Empowerment means that whenever possible, persons with disabilities are accorded the same level of control over their lives that non-handicapped people expect. Empowerment may involve confrontations with service providers who are accustomed to making decisions for people with handicaps rather than with them. Empowerment can also mean less dramatic behavior such as family members avoiding speaking for the exceptional individual when he or she is present and a stranger asks a question. Being over-assistive or over-protective toward a relative with disabilities inhibits that individual's growth and optimal self-sufficiency.

Community integration

Long term planning involves many considerations, one of which is the degree of community integration the family finds desirable. Although the trend in services for people with disabilities is to promote mainstreaming, not every community is moving in that direction at the same speed. While services for school-aged children are covered by a federal law that states children should be served in the "least restrictive environment," integration for adults with disabilities is under no such legal imperative. Families who prefer a mainstream job placement to a sheltered workshop may need to engage in some creative problem-solving and persuasion to create such opportunities for their relative with a disability. Recently, President Bush signed federal legislation designed to prohibit discrimination of persons with handicaps in the workplace, and this may prove helpful to families with a preference for integration. (For more information on federal legislation, please see Chapter 16.)

Related to the issue of mainstreaming, families with members who are moderately or severely handicapped often face a decision regarding where the individual with a disability should live. The decision to place a child or adult member in institutionalized care is often reached only after much anguish. But the decision to care for the family member at home can also be difficult. Jones (1985) provided a great deal of detailed, yet practical and easy-to-understand information about home care for children who are disabled or chronically ill. Home care may require more professional support for a family than does sending a family member to an institution such as a special school or a nursing home. Families who live in rural or remote areas often find this decision especially difficult, as expert care and services may not be locally available. Families who are helping a relative recuperate from surgery, illness, or injury may find it helpful to use strategies that allow the exceptional individual and other family members to detect progress. Coombs (1984) suggested setting reachable short-term goals, recording surgeries and milestones in recovery on a calendar, and taking photographs at milestones to document improvement.

Financial planning

Future planning for both the short- and long-term requires consideration of finances. In some instances, a family member's disability may not result in a need for additional financial resources. In the case of a learning disability, the free public education to which the individual is entitled may be sufficient service, and that individual may go on to be a self-sufficient adult. But in the case of an individual with a health impairment or severe disability, additional funds may be necessary to adequately provide for the family member through adulthood. Turnbull et al. (1989) suggested the following guidelines for financial planning: (a) inventory the family's assets, (b) involve other family members and professionals in planning, (c) consider the whole family when planning, not just the individual with a disability, and (d) consider the role of taxes, especially estate taxes, within the plan. Financial resources available to individuals with a disability include benefits from private health, accident, liability, or disability insurance, and benefits from government programs such as Social Security, Medicare, Medicaid, food stamps, and federally supported housing programs. One outcome of long-term financial planning for some families may be a trust fund designed to provide for the individual with a disability after the death of parents or guardians.

Meeting the Needs of Other Members of the Family

A disability has the potential to affect all interrelationships within a family. Sometimes the effects are positive, as when a family rallies to meet this special challenge in ways that they would not have otherwise. The potential is also there for the handicap to induce unique stresses to all the relationships found within a family including those between husband and wife, parents and children, and brothers and sisters. Step-families that include an exceptional individual may be especially vulnerable to stress during the process of combining two previously separate family units. Turnbull and Turnbull (1986) described interrelationships within families using a systems approach. They stressed that understanding families requires considering a complex and extensive number of factors including the resources of the family (financial and otherwise), the family's interactions, the functions served by the family, and the family life cycle. While grandparents, cousins, aunts, uncles, and in-laws may be affected by a relative with a disability, the following sections highlight the special concerns of parents and siblings.

Parents

Parents of children with disabilities experience special concerns, problems, and needs. Featherstone (1980) discussed the stress that an exceptional child can bring to a marriage. She stated that this stress can derive from the powerful emotions associated with the disability, the perceived parental failure that may be implied by the handicap, and the reorganization of the family that a child's disability may impose. In addition, not all parents of children with disabilities have a partner who participates in the child's care. Parents have found a variety of solutions to stressful situations. For some, professional counseling provides the supportive atmosphere in which they may express emotions, resolve conflict, and learn improved communication skills. For others, the solution lies in seeking support groups of other parents of handicapped children.

Many parents find that respite care is an important part of coping with a child's disability. Respite care means that other people outside the family unit may supplement or replace care by family members. Sometimes these people are volunteers, other times they are professionals. This type of arrangement may be necessary for other members of the family to hold a job or complete an education. It is not a sign of weakness for parents to arrange for others to help with the care of a son or daughter with a disability.

Siblings

Relationships among siblings are often intense and complex for non-handicapped brothers and sisters, and the addition of a disability to the interactions can make these relationships all the more complicated. Children who are siblings of an exceptional person experience the same range of emotions described earlier, but often children are ill-equipped for dealing with such new and complicated feelings. Adult brothers and sisters of individuals with disabilities have their own unique set of concerns that include their own ability to have healthy children, the care of the exceptional sibling after the parents' deaths, and insuring that the sibling has a high quality of life (Powell & Ogle, 1985).

Often, in an effort to protect children, adults give sisters and brothers incomplete and vague information about their sibling's handicap. A great deal of the fear and confusion experienced by siblings of persons with disabilities is due to incomplete or inaccurate description of the handicap itself. Meyer, Vadasy, and Fewell (1985) provided a very informative book directed at siblings of children with disabilities, that includes clear, factual descriptions of disabilities and helpful strategies for dealing with their own emotions and the actions of others. For example, the following is a strategy Meyer et al. suggest to children for dealing with teasing and rejection of their exceptional sibling by their peers: (a) don't join in the teasing, (b) state that joking about a handicap isn't fair, and (c) state something positive about the sibling with a disability.

Many siblings develop a strong sense of responsibility toward their brother or sister with a disability, and adults sometimes report that the sibling is often more mature than his or her peers. Some siblings experience loneliness as a result of feeling that others do not know or understand about this prominent part of his or her life. Powell and Ogle (1985) related a poignant story about two men who grew up together in a small Southern town during the 1940's. Even though they were close friends as boys, neither visited the other's home. It wasn't until they were both adults that they discovered they each had a sibling with a disability, and that they were afraid what their friend would say or do if he were invited into the home. Had the boys shared their secrets, they would have felt less alone. By not trusting the other person to understand or accept, they cut each other off from a potential source of support.

Communication

The two boys just described may have reacted differently if their families had promoted open and honest communication about the family member with a disability. Somehow those two boys had the idea that a sister with Down Syndrome and a brother with cerebral palsy were an embarrassment that others were likely not to understand. Certainly, we do not know what type of communication took place in the homes of the two boys, and societal prejudices in the 1940s probably did not make their behavior that unusual. But present day writers also describe incidents of children being reluctant to have others know that they have a sibling with a handicap (Featherstone, 1980; Meyer et al., 1985). Children who see models of clear communication and acceptance of the disability are more likely to imitate that behavior than those who do not.

The topic of the disability is an important one about which family members must communicate. If the disability is treated as a taboo, all family members are cut off from an important source of support--each other. Many people find that "I" messages" are an important communication tool. Here is the formula for such a message: "I" + how you feel + what makes you feel that way. "I" messages can prevent anyone feeling put down, and they can help point to solutions for family members' concerns.

Advocating Change

Historically, the role of family members, especially parents, as advocates for persons with disabilities has been extremely important. Much of the early litigation and legislation leading to legal mandates for special services and protections for persons with disabilities resulted directly from actions taken by family members. As Kirk (1984) stated, "If I were to give credit to one group in this country for the advancements that have been made in the education of exceptional children, I would place the parent organizations and parent movement in the forefront as the leading force" (p. 41).

There are many examples of family members being influential advocates. Litigation and legislation are major examples, but in most every sphere of family and community life, there are examples of family members advocating on behalf of their relatives. Special Olympics and the Challenger Division of Little League Baseball are examples of recreational opportunities resulting from families acting as advocates for exceptional individuals. Advocacy may involve large, public gestures such as demonstrations or testimony to government panels, but it may also involve smaller, more private acts that enhance the quality of life of an exceptional individual. Families have accomplished a great deal of progress in the way that people with disabilities are treated by society, but there is still much to be angry about and much work to be done. Family members often have the insight, compassion, and motivation necessary for successful advocacy.

Summary

When a family becomes involved with a family member's disability, either at the birth of a child or later in life, all members of the family are affected. The disability itself can cause intense reactions and often prompts people to learn new skills. Communication, daily care, financial planning, and advocacy are but a few of the skills that people must learn in response to a family member with special needs. Each family is different in how it manages the challenges and learns to become an exceptional family.

References

Blacher, J. (1984). Sequential stages of adjustment to the birth of a child with handicaps: Fact or artifact? *Mental Retardation, 22,* 55-68.

Coombs, J. (1984). *Living with the disabled: You can help.* New York: Sterling.

de Vinck, C. (1988). *The power of the powerless.* New York: Doubleday.

Featherstone, H. (1980). *A difference in the family: Life with a disabled child.* New York: Basic Books.

Jones, M. L. (1985). *Home care for the chronically ill or disabled child: A manual and sourcebook for parents and professionals.* New York: Harper & Row.

Kirk, S. A. (1984). Introspection and prophecy. In B. Blatt & R.J. Morris (Eds.), *Perspectives in special education: Personal orientations.* Glenview, IL: Scott, Foresman.

Meyer, D. J., Vadasy, P. F., & Fewell, R. R. (1985). *Living with a brother or sister with special needs.* Seattle, WA: University of Washington Press.

Powell, T. H., & Ogle, P. A. (1985). *Brothers and sisters--A special part of exceptional families.* Baltimore: Brookes.

Turnbull, A. P., & Turnbull, H. R. (1986). *Families, professionals, and exceptionality: A special partnership.* Columbus, OH: Merrill.

Turnbull, H. R., Turnbull, A. P., Bronicki, G. J., Summers, J. A., & Roeder-Gordon, C. (1989). *Disability and the family: A guide to decisions for adulthood.* Baltimore, MD: Brookes.

Suggested Readings

Buck, P. (1930). *The child who never grew.* New York: John Day.

de Vinck, C. (1988). *The power of the powerless.* New York: Doubleday.

Dougan, T., Isbell, L., & Vyas, P. (1983). *We have been there: A guidebook for families of people with mental retardation.* Nashville: Abingdon Press.

Featherstone, H. (1980). *A difference in the family: Life with a disabled child.* New York: Basic Books.

Greenfeld, J. (1972). *A child called Noah.* New York: Holt, Rinehart, & Winston.

Greenfeld, J. (1978). *A place for Noah.* New York: Holt, Rinehart, & Winston.

Jablow, M. M. (1982). *Cara: Growing with a retarded child.* Philadelphia: Temple University Press.

Turnbull, A. P., & Turnbull, H. R. (1985). *Parents speak out: Then and now.* Columbus, OH: Merrill.

Exploration

Individual Activities

1. You are the parent of two young children, Johnny and Suzy. Johnny is physically disabled. Your children are intelligent and inquisitive and Suzy asks, "Why can't Johnny come out and play with me?" Johnny wants to know why he is different from everyone else. Why can't he go out and play? How would you handle these questions? Write down two answers you would give to each child.

   Suzy

   1._____

   _____

   2._____

   _____

   Johnny

   1._____

   _____

   2._____

   _____

2. Take a moment and think about what it takes to raise a child. This is a question that many of us have answered; bathing, discipline, feeding, teaching. Have you ever thought what extra considerations you would have to make to raise a disabled child? List five extra concerns or considerations that you would need to do to raise an exceptional child.

1. _____
2. _____
3. _____
4. _____
5. _____

Group Activities

1. In class divide yourselves into groups of 4 or 5 students. This is your new family! Choose a mom and dad and brothers and sisters. You have a terrific family and your sister Julie is not with you at this time. She is at a special school for mentally retarded individuals as she is severely retarded. Discuss your opinions of the effects Julie has on your family. In addition, talk about what needs to be done for Julie's normal daily functioning.

    Reactions:

    _____
    _____
    _____

2. Have a panel assembled for an in-class discussion with parents of exceptional children. Try and get five different sets or individual parents with children possessing varying types of disabilities. Have them give a description of their child, what they do special for the child because of the exceptionality, and their personal feelings towards their situation. Before class write down three questions you would like to ask the panel.

    Reactions:

    _____
    _____
    _____

Reaction Paper 3.1

You and your spouse are expecting. Congratulations! Two months before the birth you find out that your child will be seriously disabled. What are your reactions? What type of mental preparations will you need to make?

Continue on back if needed.

Reaction Paper 3.2

In a family with an exceptional child, whom do you think is affected the most--the parents, the siblings, or the child? Discuss effects on each member if you like.

Continue on back if needed.

74

Notes

CHAPTER 4

PEOPLE WHO ARE HEARING IMPAIRED

Maureen Smith

Introduction

Information gathered through the five senses enables you to function effectively, enjoyably, and safely in the world around you. Vision is essential for reading, allows you to appreciate a beautiful painting, and facilitates unencumbered movement through the physical environment. Taste and smell increase the appeal of food required to sustain life while allowing you to detect substances which may be hazardous to your health. Through touch, you can detect textural differences and minimize or avoid contact with objects that may be physically harmful such as scalding water. Finally, hearing allows you to participate in conversations and enjoy music while alerting you to sirens, car horns, fire alarms, and other warning signals.

Of the five senses, hearing is perhaps the most flexible. Taste, touch, and to a lesser extent, smell require close proximity to perform their functions. Although vision and hearing provide information regarding distant events, only through hearing are you aware of events occurring in dark settings, around corners, or in other rooms. In addition to keeping you in touch with the environment, hearing is the sense primarily responsible for the development of language and speech. These skills facilitate social interactions, the development of academic skills, and, ultimately, the transmission of cultural values (Lowenbraun & Thompson, 1986).

A variety of circumstances can affect your ability to hear. Perhaps, as a child, you had ear infections that reduced your hearing acuity. You have probably attended a loud concert or a fireworks display and experienced some difficulty with your hearing afterwards. These experiences give you a vague idea of what it is like to have a hearing impairment; however, your ability to empathize is limited by the relatively mild and temporary nature of your experiences. Individuals who are hearing impaired are challenged on a daily basis to communicate effectively and to ensure their safety either by making maximum use of the hearing they do have or using techniques that do not rely on hearing.

Definitions Related to Hearing Impairment

A variety of terms have been used to describe people who are hearing impaired. These terms and definitions are listed below. You should note that one term, "deaf and dumb", does not appear in this table. In the past, this phrase was used frequently to describe individuals with hearing impairments; however, it is considered by individuals who are hearing impaired as an extremely outdated, erroneous, and offensive label. Historically, dumb referred to people who could not speak. In fact, most people with hearing impairments do have some speech skills.

Terms related to hearing impairment:

Deaf - A hearing loss that is so severe that, even with amplification, an individual will not be able to use audition to develop speech and language skills.
Hard of hearing - A hearing loss that disables a person but does not prohibit the development of speech and language skills, with or without amplification.
Hearing impaired - A generic term that refers to all individuals who have a hearing impairment regardless of its severity.
Prelingual hearing impairment - A hearing impairment that occurs either at birth or before speech and language skills have been acquired.

- Postlingual hearing impairment - A hearing impairment that occurs after speech and language skills have been acquired. Another term for this is an adventitious loss.
- Conductive loss - A hearing impairment that is located in the outer or middle ear. With proper amplification, sounds will be heard without distortion.
- Sensorineural loss - A hearing impairment that is located in the inner ear, typically resulting from damage to the cochlea or auditory nerve. Even with amplification, sensitivity to sounds is reduced and/or distorted.

Prevalence

According to Moores (1987), approximately 15,000,000 people in the United States have a hearing impairment. Of these people, 2,000,000 are deaf. Ten percent of this latter group is prelingually deaf; another 10% became deaf between the ages of 3 and 19 years. According to the U.S. Department of Education (1989), there are 56,937 students with hearing impairments between the ages of six and twenty-one.

Causation

Your ability to hear is the result of a complex sequence of events. Sound waves are collected by the outer ear and channeled through the auditory canal. The tympanic membrane, or eardrum, conducts sound waves through three tiny bones in the middle ear. The third bone is connected to the inner ear which houses the cochlea and the semicircular canals. At this point, sound waves are transformed into neural impulses that travel along the eighth nerve to the brain, which adds meaning.

Factors present before, during, or after birth can disrupt the hearing process along any of three sites: the outer ear, the middle ear, or the inner ear. Despite the number of known causes, it is interesting to note that the cause of 25% of all hearing losses remains unknown (Morgan, 1987).

Prenatal factors

Prenatal factors affect the development of the hearing mechanism prior to birth. One factor is heredity, which accounts for anywhere from 11% (Trybus, 1985) to 33% of all hearing losses (Morgan, 1987). Other congenital factors are not related to heredity. In the mid-1960s, hearing impaired children were born to many women who contracted rubella (German measles) during the first three months of pregnancy. Fortunately, a vaccine routinely given to all preschool children has reduced the number of cases of hearing impairment attributed to this factor. More recently, cytomegalovirus (CMV), a herpes virus that can be passed through the placenta, has been linked to hearing impairments. There is currently no vaccine for this infection. Other congenital factors include Rh-factor incompatibility and toxoplasmosis, an infection caused by germs in raw meat.

Perinatal factors

A child can be hearing impaired as a result of conditions present during the birth process. Examples include prolonged labor, prematurity, anoxia (a lack of oxygen to the brain during birth), apnea (the failure to breathe during or immediately after birth), or a birth trauma that requires the use of obstetric equipment. CMV also poses a risk if it is being shed in cervical secretions during the birth process.

Postnatal factors

A number of conditions can result in a hearing impairment any time after birth. The most common cause of a loss at this time is infection, such as measles, mumps, scarlet fever, and meningitis. Fortunately, medical science has made great strides in reducing the incidence and impact of these diseases. Unfortunately, CMV continues to pose a threat if it is transmitted to the baby in breast milk. Other postnatal conditions contributing to a hearing loss include a high fever, head trauma, drugs, and repeated exposure to noise such as jet engines, sirens, jackhammers, and loud music.

In fact, noise-induced hearing loss is currently the leading cause of a sensorineural impairment. Finally, otitis media, an inflammation of the middle ear, is another factor that can either result in a temporary loss in normally hearing individuals or increase the loss experienced by a child with a hearing impairment.

Characteristics

Throughout the years, a number of rather unflattering labels have been used to describe individuals who are hearing impaired. Lane (1988) compiled a list that includes phrases and terms such as "cannot think clearly," "naive," "easily frustrated," "explosive," "paranoid," "impulsive," and "rigid." There are few empirical studies verifying the appropriateness of these labels. Generally, people who are hearing impaired experience the same feelings and behave in the same manner as you do when you are confronted with joy, sorrow, a challenge, or a disappointment. That is not to say that a hearing impairment has little or no influence on daily functioning; however, other factors must be considered including the degree of loss, intelligence, educational experiences, and family support.

Auditory Characteristics

Your hearing is measured by recording your sensitivity to sounds that vary by their intensity (loudness) and frequency (pitch). Intensity is reported in decibels (db) and pitch or frequency is reported in hertz (Hz). The chart in Table 4.1 lists some common sounds and the decibel and hertz levels associated with each.

A hearing loss is reported in decibels and is generally categorized as mild, moderate, moderately severe, severe, or profound. The chart in Table 4.2 shows the range of decibel loss associated with each category of hearing impairment. A person with a mild loss may experience difficulty with faint or distant speech. A moderate loss makes speech beyond five feet difficult to understand. This individual may benefit from amplification and speech therapy. A person with a moderately severe loss needs to have conversation loud if it is to be understood. In addition, speech will probably be noticeably impaired; thus, the need for speech therapy increases. A person with a severe loss is unlikely to hear a loud voice if it is more than 1 or 2 feet away although he or she may be able to distinguish between different environmental sounds. Finally, a person with a profound loss may be able to hear only very loud environmental sounds.

Table 4.1
Decibel Levels of Common Sounds

Stimulus	dB Level	Hz Level
Threshold of hearing	0 dB	0 Hz
Speech	20-50 dB	250-4000 Hz
An air conditioner	60 dB	125 Hz
A crying baby	60 dB	750 Hz
A barking dog	80 dB	500 Hz
A piano	80 dB	1,000 Hz
A lawn mower	100 dB	250 Hz
A helicopter	100 dB	4,000 Hz
Threshold of pain	140 dB	---

Table 4.2
Levels of Hearing Impairment

Level of Loss	dB level
Mild	27-40
Moderate	41-55
Moderately Severe	56-70
Severe	71-90
Profound	91 +

Language and Speech

Because of the importance of normal hearing to the development of language and speech, it is not surprising that many people who are hearing impaired have difficulty mastering language and speech. This may not be the case for all hearing impaired people. A postlingual loss may leave language and speech unaffected, particularly if the individual receives therapy to maintain skills. Although rare, an individual with a more severe prelingual impairment may have normal language and speech if the loss was identified early and amplification and intervention were provided.

Impaired hearing makes it extremely difficult to learn the rules of the English language. Therefore, hearing impaired people may have smaller vocabularies, less well developed syntax skills, and difficulty using morphological endings such as "-ing", "-ed", and "-s". In addition, words with multiple meanings, such as "run", and figurative expression, such as "The cat is out of the bag," may pose challenges.

Ling (1976), in a comprehensive review of the literature, identified some of the major speech problems experienced by individuals with more severely impaired hearing. These problems included limited pitch, slower rates of speech, and difficulties with the production of vowels and consonants. All of these problems have a detrimental effect on intelligibility.

Intelligence

The cognitive functioning of individuals who are hearing impaired, particularly those with more severe prelingual losses, has been discussed at length. Investigators have suggested that lower scores on intelligence tests do not reflect inherent cognitive deficits; rather, they indicate difficulties with the language used to administer the tests. Recent research has used intelligence tests that involve nonverbal directions and do not require oral responses. Results indicate that individuals with hearing impairments have a distribution of intelligence scores that is comparable to that displayed by the hearing population.

Academic Development

Formal instruction in academic areas relies heavily on the child's ability to use language. A solid foundation in oral language is the basis for the development of reading which, in turn, increases success in content areas such as science and social studies. Despite the difficulties encountered with English, approximately 10% of students with hearing impairments achieve levels of academic competence comparable to those of their hearing peers. Most high school seniors with more severe hearing impairments typically achieve scores of third and sixth grade respectively on standardized tests of reading and mathematics. These achievement levels are expected to rise as educational interventions improve.

Social and Emotional Development

Individuals with hearing impairments follow the same sequence in their social and emotional development as their non-disabled peers and, as mentioned earlier, are capable of experiencing a full range of emotions. However, some subtle differences in the nature of early experiences may have an impact on subsequent development. Impaired hearing may restrict access to social cues that hearing people take for granted. Thus, hearing impaired individuals may appear socially inept or clumsy.

There may also be differences in the ways parents interact with their hearing impaired children. Out of concern for safety, some parents may limit their child's exposure to activities that you took for granted such as unescorted trips to shopping areas or holding a summer job. Without the benefit of experience afforded during such informal experiences, some hearing impaired learners may appear naive.

Intervention

Several intervention techniques are available to meet the needs of individuals of all ages who are hearing impaired. Initially, parents, in consultation with professionals, select a technique or a combination of techniques that increases the child's development of language and speech. Later, the mature individual who is hearing impaired selects the technique or combination of techniques that produces the greatest amount of personal satisfaction and allows him or her to function effectively and enjoyably in the community.

Prevention

Obviously, the need for intervention upon the diagnosis of a hearing impairment would be completely eliminated if hearing impairments could be prevented in the first place. This goal is extremely difficult to accomplish given the current status of medical technology. This is not to undermine the many advances that have been made in minimizing or eliminating the threat of some causes of hearing impairment before, during, or after birth. Widespread use of vaccinations and better prenatal and postnatal care have reduced the number of children with hearing impairments.

Identification

If another member of the family is or was hearing impaired or if there have been birth complications, then it is likely that the hearing status of a newborn will be closely monitored. Parents of a child who appeared normal at birth may become concerned when they notice the child does not respond to sounds or has stopped babbling. They may discuss their concerns with their pediatrician who may make a referral to a specialist. Unfortunately, many parents of hearing impaired children report being told by their doctor that their anxieties stemmed from overactive imaginations. Continued persistence resulted in the appropriate referral; however, valuable time that could have been devoted to diagnosis and intervention was lost.

A number of behavioral and medical indicators suggest that an older child or an adult may have a hearing impairment. These indicators are listed in Table 4.3. Individuals who display these behaviors are candidates for referral. Regardless of the age of the person, it is important that a hearing loss be detected early. Subsequent intervention can alleviate some of the effects of a hearing impairment.

The definitive tool used to diagnose and measure a hearing impairment is an audiological examination. It is conducted by an audiologist in a sound proof booth and consists of the presentation of pure tone sounds and speech at varying decibel and hertz levels. Results are plotted on a special graph which is called an audiogram.

Table 4.3
Behavioral and Medical Symptoms That May Indicate a Hearing Loss

Behavioral	Medical
Inattentiveness	Frequent earaches
Poor speech	Fluid running from the ears
Inability to follow directions	Frequent sore throats
Difficulty working in large groups	Frequent colds
Depending on others for instructions	Recurring tonsillitis
Turning/cocking head	Complaints of head noise
Disruptive behavior	
Withdrawn behavior	
Limited interest in oral activities	
Turns up volume so high that others complain	
Frequent requests for directions or conversation to be repeated	

Intervention for the Preschool Child

Once the extent and type of hearing loss have been determined, parents and professionals should develop an intervention program. Frequently, the parents of a very young child with a hearing impairment are the focus of early efforts. They may receive counseling to help them deal with their feelings and understand the ramifications of a hearing impairment for their child. In addition, they may receive instruction on the use of amplification and how to communicate effectively with their child, thus enhancing the child's development of language and speech. Such instruction can be provided in a speech and hearing clinic, a nursery school, or perhaps even a public school or by a parent/infant specialist who visits the home on a regular basis.

Intervention for the School-age Child

Public Law 94-142 requires that all children with a disability receive a free appropriate public education in the least restrictive environment. It is this latter concept that has become an issue in the education of students who are hearing impaired. Many students with hearing impairments have been placed in classrooms with hearing students; however, for students with severe or profound losses, close proximity to normally hearing students with whom they cannot communicate may be restrictive indeed.

Depending on the severity of the impairment, the school-age child is typically assigned to any one of a variety of educational options. Some children with mild to moderate losses can function effectively in the regular classroom alongside their hearing peers. They may receive some assistance such as speech and language therapy or occasional instruction from an itinerant or resource teacher. In addition, the regular educator may receive the services of a consultant teacher who provides tips for minor instructional modifications, better communication, and effective use of the child's amplification system. It is possible that students with more severe hearing impairments could also function effectively in the regular classroom, particularly when services such as interpreting and notetaking are provided. It is more likely, however, that these students require placement in self-contained classrooms for hearing impaired students located in a public school, a day program, or a residential facility. Programs located in public schools allow for more mainstreaming opportunities while day or state-supported residential programs offer a greater quantity of specialized instruction and related services.

Communication Philosophies

Philosophies governing communication with and among hearing impaired people vary. The "best" philosophy has been the subject of countless debates in professional forums for over one hundred years with no clear winner emerging. The issue is not likely to be settled soon. Parents should find out as much as they can about each philosophy and its suitability given the unique characteristics and needs of their child. All philosophies have as their goal the development of speech and language so that the hearing impaired individual can acquire the academic, social, and vocational skills necessary for successful functioning in all aspects of daily living.

The Oral Philosophy. Proponents of the oral philosophy believe the best way to communicate with people with hearing impairments is through auditory methods. They advocate the use of speech, speechreading, and residual hearing with and among people with hearing impairments. It is believed that sole reliance on these techniques facilitates greater mastery of English, the language of the community in which most hearing impaired people must live.

The Total Communication Philosophy. Proponents of the total communication philosophy advocate the development of any and all methods of communication to facilitate interaction with and among people who are hearing impaired. They advocate the use of sign language, fingerspelling, speech, speechreading, amplification, reading, writing, gestures, pantomime, and drawing in isolation or in combination. Teachers using the total communication philosophy usually use speech, sign language, and fingerspelling simultaneously when communicating with hearing impaired learners. Typically, they require their students to wear amplification and use speech and sign language in return. The exact format of communication can be altered for different circumstances or as the individual matures and expresses specific preferences.

Sign Language

There are many varieties of sign language. American Sign Language is the native language used by deaf people in the deaf community. It is also known as Ameslan or ASL and is used by approximately one-half million deaf Americans and Canadians.

Another form of sign language is Sign English, which is the use of ASL signs in English word order. Articles, plurals, and verb endings are usually omitted. It is this form of sign language that is used most frequently in interactions between hearing and hearing impaired people. During the conversation, the hearing person generally speaks and signs simultaneously. The hearing impaired person may or may not vocalize while signing.

"Manual English" is a term that refers to forms of sign language in which English is exactly replicated. Manual English systems include Signing Exact English, Seeing Essential English, and Linguistics of Visual English. Authors of these systems incorporated many ASL signs and developed markers to indicate prefixes and suffixes. In addition, many signs from these systems are initialized; that is, the basic ASL sign has been modified by changing the handshape to a fingerspelled letter.

Another form of sign language is fingerspelling where each letter of the alphabet is represented by a distinct position of the hand. At one time, some hearing impaired people used fingerspelling as their sole form of sign language. Every word in the conversation was spelled out, requiring a high degree of concentration from all participants. Currently, fingerspelling is used in combination with other forms of sign language to represent words for which there are no formal signs.

Cued Speech. Although proponents of both the oral and total communication philosophies advocate the use of speechreading by hearing impaired individuals, it must be noted that many English sounds are either not visible on the lips or are easily confused with other sounds. Cued speech was developed in the mid-1960s at Gallaudet University by Dr. Orin Cornett to help hearing impaired people differentiate between various English sounds. It consists of four hand positions and eight configurations that only carry meaning when used simultaneously with speech. Cued speech has not been used widely in the United States.

Technological Interventions

People with hearing impairments have benefitted greatly from the explosion in technology. Several different devices have increased the accessibility of hearing impaired people to information and services that most hearing people take for granted.

Amplification. Perhaps the form of technology most frequently associated with hearing impaired people is amplification. Hearing aids are used to enhance the quality and quantity of speech and language heard and used by hearing impaired people. Improvements in technology have increased the power of hearing aids while reducing their size; however, it is important to remember that, unlike the effect that eye glasses have on most users, wearing a hearing aid does not restore hearing to normal.

Cochlear implants. A cochlear implant is a device that is surgically implanted in the ear. It converts sounds from the environment into electrical signals that are transmitted to coils implanted in the cochlea, thereby stimulating electrical impulses to the auditory nerve. Cochlear implants are still in the early stages of development and have been used almost exclusively with postlingually deafened adults.

Telecommunication devices. A telecommunication device for deaf persons (TDD) closely resembles a small typewriter. When hooked up to a phone, it allows a hearing impaired person to carry on a conversation. Many agencies, such as libraries, shopping services, and those providing emergency services, have TDD numbers that allow hearing impaired people to contact them directly. Some cities have a relay service whose employees transmit messages or act as intermediaries between a hearing impaired person using a TDD and a hearing person using the telephone.

Computer aids. There are a variety of computer programs available to assist hearing impaired people in their educational development. Software packages can reinforce and provide guided practice in academic instruction, language development, and speech production.

Captioned films. Over thirty years ago, the federal government funded Captioned Films for the Deaf to provide written narration on films and then loan them to agencies serving hearing impaired learners. In addition, this organization provides equipment that can be used by hearing impaired people, promotes the development of educational media, and trains personnel interested in educational technology.

Closed captioning. Closed captioned television has greatly increased leisure opportunities for hearing impaired people. Previously, people with hearing impairments either had to try to speechread dialogue or depend on family and friends to interpret. Now, dialogue from a television program is put into subtitles which are then converted into an electronic code. This code can be converted back into subtitles by a decoding device attached to the user's television set.

Signaling devices. Some people with hearing impairments may be unable to hear the ringing of a phone, doorbell, or alarm clock. Hearing impaired people who are parents may not realize their child is crying. There are devices which keep hearing impaired people in touch with the environment. Lights can be made to flicker each time the doorbell chimes or the phone rings. A special light can be set to flash when a child cries. A clock that sets off a blinking light or a vibrotactile device placed under a pillow or mattress can ensure a hearing impaired person awakens on time. Finally, some hearing impaired people are making use of "hearing dogs" who alert them when specific sounds occur.

Expectations

Most people with hearing impairments live within a hearing society and make adjustments to the world. However, their hearing impairment does increase the challenges everyone faces in daily living.

Postsecondary Opportunities

As is true for hearing people, most hearing impaired people need some postsecondary education to prepare them for employment. Hearing impaired people are enrolled in a number of community colleges and universities throughout the United States, although the number of available programs is limited. Most of these programs are primarily geared toward the hearing student but offer supportive services, such as interpreters, notetakers, and tutors, to assist the hearing impaired learner who is seeking advanced training. Other programs have been established solely to meet the needs of the hearing impaired learner working towards a degree. Such programs include the National Institute for the Deaf (NTID) in Rochester, New York and Gallaudet University in Washington, D.C.

Employment

Martin (1988) reported that one half of the hearing impaired population is available to the work force; unfortunately, only 50% of this group enjoy steady employment. Hearing impaired people make approximately 78% of the salary earned by hearing people.

Phillippe and Auvenshine (1985) stated that people with hearing impairments are more likely to be unemployed or underemployed than their hearing peers. Several factors contribute to these problems, including inadequate education, employer attitude and stereotype, and ineffective career counseling.

Marriage and Family

Deaf adults, particularly those with more severe prelingual impairments, tend to marry other deaf adults. While deaf parents are more likely to have deaf children, the majority of the children born to deaf parents have normal hearing.

The Deaf Community

It is not surprising that many individuals who are hearing impaired feel most comfortable around other people who are hearing impaired. Thus, the Deaf Community has developed and includes religious, social, and cultural organizations at local, state, national, and international levels (Moores, 1987). American Sign Language serves as the primary vehicle for communication. In addition, the National Association for the Deaf (NAD) was founded in 1880 and serves as an advocacy agency for people with hearing impairments. The NAD sponsors cultural activities, lobbies for legislation that will benefit hearing impaired citizens, and publishes books and magazines for and about hearing impaired people.

Interactions

Because it is at times a rather unobtrusive disability, you may not have realized that another person is hearing impaired until you saw a hearing aid or the individual began to speak or sign. If you ever took a sign language class, then you may feel less intimidated about the prospect of conversing with a hearing impaired person. Even if you have no signing experience, you still can interact successfully and enjoyably with a person who is hearing impaired. The following tips will be helpful.

PEOPLE WHO ARE HEARING IMPAIRED

The hearing impaired individual will be able to understand you better if he or she can see your face clearly.

Make sure you speak in moderate tones. Raising your voice will not help; in fact, it may distort your facial expressions, detracting from your comments and making you more difficult to understand.

If the hearing impaired person does not understand what you have said, then you should rephrase, rather than repeat your comments.

Do not stand where the light source falls over your shoulder and into the face of the hearing impaired individual.

Don't exaggerate your speech. You may also be exaggerating your facial expressions which is unnatural and distracting.

Avoid distractions such as excessive gestures, makeup, or jewelry.

Don't chew gum.

If you are in a group, one person should speak at a time to allow the hearing impaired person to follow the conversation better.

Perhaps you are making a presentation and know in advance that a member of your audience is hearing impaired. You can do several things to enhance communication.

The individual may be accompanied by an interpreter. Allow them to decide where the interpreter will be positioned. While you may feel somewhat intimidated, you should go on with your presentation. Communication is always improved by a knowledgeable speaker with an engaging presentation style.

Present an outline of your major points.

Use an overhead projector to avoid turning away from your audience.

Stay in the hearing impaired person's field of vision and avoid moving around.

The hearing impaired individual may have someone taking notes. Share your presentation notes with him or her.

When responding to a question asked through the interpreter, speak directly to the hearing impaired person using "You."

If you need to darken the overhead lights, make sure there is a small lamp or spotlight available to illuminate the interpreter.

Be prepared to define unusual vocabulary words.

If you are reading to the group, slow down so that the interpreter can better follow your presentation.

These tips should make you feel more comfortable when interacting with a person who is hearing impaired. In addition, you may wish to enroll in a course to learn more about sign language. Such courses are frequently available through adult education centers and community colleges. The administrative offices of your local public school district or of a nearby residential school for deaf students may also have information about sign language classes. Instructors of most sign language classes typically include information related to deafness that will be beneficial to you. Fingerspelling is included in Appendix B along with an opportunity for you to learn selected signs.

Summary

Your sense of hearing is key to your development as an individual and your ability to assume your place in society. Obviously, those with impaired hearing are no less human; however, their disability certainly poses a challenge in the attainment of their dreams and goals.

This chapter presented information about a hearing impairment and how it can influence every aspect of daily living. It has also described ways in which affected individuals can circumvent many of the barriers imposed by their disability to achieve their ambitions.

It is extremely likely that you have met or will meet a hearing impaired person. Armed with the information in this chapter and perhaps skilled in fingerspelling and some very basic signs, you will find your interactions more comfortable, enjoyable, and rewarding.

References

Lane, H. (1988). Is there a psychology of deaf? *Exceptional Children, 55,* 9-19.

Ling, D. (1976). *Speech and the hearing impaired child: Theory and practice.* Washington, DC: Alexander Graham Bell Association.

Lowenbraun, S., & Thompson, M. D. (1986). Hearing impairments. In N. G. Haring & L. McCormick (Eds.), *Exceptional children and youth* (4th ed.) (pp. 357-395). Columbus: OH: Merrill.

Martin, D. S. (1988). Directions for post-secondary education of hearing impaired persons. *Journal of the American Deafness and Rehabilitation Association, 22*(2), 37-40.

Morgan, A. B. (1987). Causes and treatment. In F. N. Martin (Ed.), *Hearing disorders in children* (pp. 5-48). Austin, TX: Pro-Ed.

Moores, D. F. (1987). *Educating the deaf* (3rd. ed.). Boston: Houghton-Mifflin.

Phillippe, T., & Auvenshine D. (1985). Career development among deaf persons. *Journal of Rehabilitation of the Deaf, 19*(1-2), 9-15.

Trybus, R. J. (1985). *Today's hearing impaired children and youth: A demographic profile.* Washington, DC: Gallaudet Research Institute.

U.S. Department of Education. (1989). *Eleventh annual report to Congress on the implementation of the Education of the Handicapped Act.* Washington, DC: United States Department of Education.

Suggested Readings

Bender, R. (1970). *The conquest of deafness.* Cleveland: Case Western Reserve.

Bruce, R. (1973). *Bell: Alexander Graham Bell and the conquest of solitude.* Boston: Little, Brown.

Bunde, L. (1979). *Deaf parents--hearing children.* Washington, DC: Registry of Interpreters for the Deaf.

Costello, E. (1983). *Signing: How to speak with your hands.* NY: Bantam Books.

Evans, L. (1982). *Total communication: Structure and strategy.* Washington, DC: Gallaudet University Press.

Gallaudet Research Institute. (1985). Some answers to frequently asked questions about hearing impaired young people. *Perspectives for Teachers of the Hearing Impaired, 3*(5), 9-10.

Jacobs, L. M. (1980). *A deaf adult speaks out.* Washington, DC: Gallaudet University Press.

Oberkotter, M. (1990). *The possible dream: Mainstream experiences of hearing impaired students.* Washington, DC: Alexander Graham Bell Association.

Ross, M. (1990). *Hearing impaired children in the mainstream.* Monkton, MD: York Press.

PEOPLE WHO ARE HEARING IMPAIRED

Exploration

Individual Activities

1. This activity may seem challenging at first, but don't worry, you should be able to handle it with some serious effort. Ready? . . . okay . . . Sit down on your couch or a comfortable chair and watch television. OK, maybe this will not be the hardest activity ever. Of course, there is a twist; you are going to watch television for one hour with the sound off. Pick any program you like except a sporting event.

    So, how did you do with this activity? Were you able to follow the show? If so, list the things that were most helpful. If not, list those items that made you lose track of what was going on.

Helpful	Problems

2. Get together with a friend and just talk for 10 minutes. Talk? Well, let's say, converse, using only sign language and gestures. You can have a conversation about anything you like but try to keep it interesting.

    How was it? Were you able to get your message across to your friend? What was the hardest part of maintaining your conversation?

    _____

    _____

    _____

Group Activities

1. In class or on your own, get into a group of 5 or 6 people. Your group will have the pleasure of being fashion designers. Using only sign language gestures, designate one person to be the model and create an original outfit for that person. You will each need to bring newspapers, magic markers, tape, and a stapler. It can be a costume, something stylish, or even something silly. Remember, no talking as you complete this group activity. Sign language and gestures only!

    Reactions:

    _____
    _____
    _____

2. Make a list of 10 items; movies, books, famous people--whatever you like.

1. _____	6. _____
2. _____	7. _____
3. _____	8. _____
4. _____	9. _____
5. _____	10. _____

    With a group of three or more people play charades with the list above. No, you can't just fingerspell the item. You can only use gestures and movements to help your group guess the thing you are describing.

    Reactions:

    _____
    _____
    _____

Reaction Paper 4.1

Do you think sign language should become part of one's normal learning topics, or should it be left to only those in contact with deaf persons? How would you feel if you were required to learn sign language fluently? When do you think the best time to learn it would be?

Continue on back if needed.

Reaction Paper 4.2

Do you think a deaf person is as qualified a worker as someone with normal hearing? State and support your position.

_____

Continue on back if needed.

Notes

CHAPTER 5

PEOPLE WITH VISUAL DISABILITIES

Kay Alicyn Ferrell

Introduction

People with visual disabilities are those who have some sort of impairment of the visual system. There are many terms used to refer to this type of exceptionality (see Table 5.1), but all basically indicate some difficulty in the process of seeing -- either in the physiological structure of the eye, or in how the brain interprets visual information. Many of the terms are misleading, as they encompass a range of functioning levels, from individuals who are totally blind to individuals who exhibit only reduced visual acuity.

Distance visual acuity (the measure familiar to most people as what results when you go to the eye specialist and read letters on a chart) is frequently used as a standard to identify persons with visual disabilities. Legal blindness, for example, a term used in federal and state legislation to establish a cutoff point for determining eligibility for various services, is defined as central visual acuity of 20/200 or less in the better eye with corrective lenses, or a visual field defect of 20 degrees or less in the better eye. Central visual acuity of 20/200 means that the legally blind individual must be as close as 20 feet in order to see what the individual with normal vision sees at 200 feet. A normal visual field (the visual space in front of you as you gaze straight ahead) is generally measured on a horizontal arc of 160 to 180 degrees. Obviously, legal blindness, either reduced acuity or reduced visual field, is a severe restriction.

Table 5.1
Taxonomy of Visual Disability[1]

Terms describing the disability	Terms describing the intervention
Blind	Functional vision
Functionally blind	Sight conservation
Legal blindness	Sight-saving
Legally blind	Utilization of low vision
Low vision	Vision rehabilitation
Partially blind	Vision training
Partially sighted	Vision stimulation
Reduced vision	Vision habilitation
Residual vision	Visual efficiency
Semi-sighted	
Visual disability	
Visual impairment	
Visually handicapped	
Visually limited	
Weak eyes	

[1]Many of these terms were first delineated in Corn, A. L., & Erin, J. N. (1986). How to speak visionese. *Journal of Visual Impairment & Blindness*, 80, 636-637.

But terminology can obscure function. Although blindness conjures up images of total darkness in the minds of the general public, people who are *totally* blind actually comprise a very small number of the people considered to have visual disabilities. Visual functioning, how the individual uses the vision that he or she has, is usually described along a continuum of visual abilities, ranging from normal or near-normal vision to total blindness (Tuttle, 1984). Many individuals who are "legally blind" at a distance are able to read regular size print at near point. Barraga (1983) estimated that as much as 75% of the legally blind population may actually be able to use vision as the primary means of getting information. And even this continuum is not static; regardless of visual diagnosis or measured visual acuity, visual functioning varies depending on the environmental conditions and the task being performed. Someone with albinism, for example, may read regular-sized print without spectacles or low vision aids when indoors. But that same person, when walking outside on a bright, sunny day, may be totally blind.

Visual disabilities and visual functioning are not always apparent. You may be surprised to learn that the man next to you has a severe visual impairment and can only see one letter of newsprint at a time, because he gives no outward appearance of visual disability--until you meet him at a coffee shop at night and notice his cane. At other times, you might wonder why your neighbor reads and writes braille, when she can see well enough to compliment you on the color you are wearing. In both situations, the demands, visual diagnoses, and environmental conditions are different; the lack of predictability is what is common to both.

The issues are even further complicated when eligibility for special education services are considered. The Education of the Handicapped Act (PL 94-142) uses the term "visually handicapped," and defines it as "a visual impairment which, even with correction, adversely affects a child's educational performance" (20 U.S.C. 1401(b)(1). Many states have adopted the same definition, but others utilize a cut-off point of 20/70 for including children in special education services (Kirchner, 1989), while some specialists have suggested that 20/50 would be more appropriate (Hatfield, 1975). Neither cut-off point seems very severe, unless you consider that vision is our primary learning modality and that even a small disturbance in how visual information is received may affect all future learning.

Prevalence

Estimates of the prevalence of visual disability are difficult to obtain with any certainty. There are numerous databases which collect information about visual disability, ranging from the U.S. Department of Education, Office of Special Education Programs (OSEP), which counts children receiving special education services, to the American Printing House for the Blind (APH), which maintains a registry of legally blind students who receive federal quota funds, to the National Center for Health Statistics (NCHS), which collects information on all ages. But no two agencies collect the same information in the same manner. Even OSEP is dependent on the statistics collected by state education agencies, and each state defines visual disability differently.

Suffice it to say that blindness and visual impairment is a low prevalence disability. The best estimate is that it affects about one-tenth of one percent of the school-age population of the United States (Kirchner, Stephen, & Chandu, 1988). Estimates of the prevalence of visual disability in the general population range from 2% (National Society to Prevent Blindness, 1980) to 18%, for the population over the age of 18 years (Kirchner, Stephen, & Chandu, 1988).

The fastest growing population of individuals with visual disability is elderly persons. The greying of America is not a new phenomenon. What has been overlooked, however, is that with advancing age comes deteriorating vision. Rosenbloom (1989) estimated that 25% of the over-65 population is visually impaired; a more conservative estimate is placed at 7.8% (Nelson, 1988). Lowman and Kirchner (1988) stated that as the population of elderly visually impaired Americans continues to grow larger, it will also become older and more predominantly female. Advances in medicine are at least partially responsible for extending the life expectancy of Americans, but medicine has simply not been able to halt the aging process and its effects on the sensory systems.

Medical technology has also been able to sustain the life of extremely premature, low birthweight babies. Fifteen years ago, babies born only six months after conception, or weighing less than two pounds, were not given much chance of survival. Today, it is not unusual for them to survive, albeit after a stormy course of treatment and prolonged residence in hospital neonatal intensive care units. But this, too, has had its effect on the population of persons with visual disabilities; evidence is accumulating that suggests that retinopathy of prematurity, a visual diagnosis closely associated with low birthweight, is quickly becoming the leading cause of blindness in young children (Ferrell, Deitz, Trief, Bonner, Cruz, Ford, & Stratton, 1990).

Causes

Visual disability may be either congenital (present at birth) or adventitious (occurring sometime after birth). As you might expect, most causes of visual impairment in children are congenital, and are either hereditary (such as cataracts or albinism) or due to some mishap before birth (microphthalmos, small eye) or during birth (cortical visual impairment, perhaps due to lack of oxygen). Retinopathy of prematurity, because it occurs so early in life, is also considered to be congenital.

In adults, most visual impairment is caused by injury to the eye or brain, although some eye conditions (such as retinitis pigmentosa) are hereditary conditions that do not become manifest until adolescence or adulthood. Other visual impairments may be the sequelae of other medical conditions (such as diabetes). As cataract and laser surgery have become commonplace, cataracts and diabetic retinopathy have given way to macular degeneration (a gradual loss of central visual acuity) as the leading cause of blindness among elderly adults. But generally even after surgery, the functional vision of elderly adults is not comparable to the vision they had in youth.

Visual impairment is frequently seen in conjunction with other disabilities -- usually associated with some form of neurological involvement, such as cerebral palsy, hydrocephaly, or hearing impairment in children (Ferrell et al., 1990), and hearing and orthopedic impairments in adults (Kirchner & Peterson, 1988b). Estimates of the proportion of persons with visual disabilities who also have additional handicapping conditions range from 48-66% (Erin, Daugherty, Dignan, & Pearson, 1990; Ferrell, 1987; Kirchner & Peterson, 1988b). This proportion is expected to be greater in persons over 65 years of age, since the aging process usually affects all body parts and not just the eyes. With children under 5 years of age, however, diagnoses of multiple impairment should be suspect, unless there is a physiological basis for the diagnosis. The reason for this caution is that infants with visual impairment frequently exhibit developmental delays early in life which are alleviated by the time the child enters school. These delays seem to be directly related to the limitations visual impairment imposes on the opportunities for learning and development. Suggesting that a child is multiply handicapped or mentally retarded before he or she has had a chance to learn what needs to be learned can become a self-fulfilling prophecy.

Characteristics

People with visual disabilities are people, first. Blindness and visual impairment affects *how* information is obtained; it does not necessarily affect *what* information is obtained. Neither does visual impairment alone provide any clues about an individual's school achievement, employment future, or success and happiness in life. There is as much heterogeneity within the population of people with visual disabilities as there is within the population of people without disabilities. Even two people with the same eye condition are unlikely to have the same visual acuity, or to be able to utilize their residual vision to the same degree. This heterogeneity, combined with the small prevalence of visual disability, make generalizations extremely difficult.

Lowenfeld (1973) suggested that visual disabilities impose three limitations on the individual; (a) the range and variety of experiences available, (b) the ability to move about, and (c) the control of the environment and the self in relation to it. Vision is the most predominant sense humans possess and the one sense that integrates all the others (Barraga, 1983). Think about how you use your vision every day: you hear a noise, and you look in its direction to determine what caused it; you read; you write; you choose clothes to wear based on their color and/or pattern; you recognize a friend walking across campus. Each one of these activities uses your vision, without any deliberate intent on your part.

What, then, happens if your vision is limited or missing altogether? Noises become clues that you have to think about, interpret, and then decide where they came from, perhaps never actually verifying their source. Reading is limited to what is available in an accessible medium (braille, large print, regular print with low vision devices, tape recordings). Handwriting may be difficult to read back, so you rely on computers with speech access or screen enhancements, electronic braille machines, or a slate and stylus. You organize your clothing by style and color, so that you can find it easily. But you don't necessarily recognize your friend, or even know that your friend is in the vicinity, unless your friend speaks to you first.

Obviously, Lowenfeld's limitations have implications for almost every area of life; personal and home management, travel, reading and writing, employment, and recreation (Tuttle, 1984). But limitations are not insurmountable. If visual impairment is congenital, it is a matter of learning about the environment in a different way than sighted children do. If visual impairment occurs adventitiously, it is a matter of adapting to a different way of doing things. Two principles may help you to understand how people with visual disabilities assimilate information:

Learning is not incidental. Much of the learning that occurs in childhood happens without a deliberate effort to make it happen. You cannot assume that people with visual disabilities know and understand something simply because it happened in their presence. For example, when you walk into a bank, you scan the room and see the tellers, the ATMs, the bank officers' desks, and a guard. Normally, you would interact with all these elements in the normal course of your business (except perhaps the guard). How would a person who is blind even know that a guard was there -- unless he or she had been told previously? Information cannot be left to chance.

Learning proceeds from parts to whole. For most people, reasoning proceeds deductively, moving from the large picture to the small details. People with visual disabilities, however, must use an inductive approach, taking all the parts and somehow putting them into a whole. A classic example of this is the cartoon which appeared in *The New Yorker* magazine a few years ago, where several adults, with dark glasses and canes, were circled around an elephant, touching an ear or the trunk or a leg, and verbally describing what an elephant was like. Each character had a different concept of what an elephant was, based on his experience of what an elephant felt like. And that experience was limited by what he could feel at any one point in time. Instead of a visual gestalt, people with visual disabilities have to put all the pieces together without knowing beforehand what the puzzle is supposed to look like.

People with visual disabilities differ among themselves about the implications and limitations of blindness. Some have referred to it as an extreme handicap, while others believe that blindness is only a nuisance or inconvenience. People with unimpaired vision, however, consistently view blindness as something of a disaster, often comparing it to death (Carroll, 1961). It is this attitude which probably does more to impose limitations than the visual disability itself. As a prominent leader in the field of blindness stated,

> I think it is clear that the disaster concept is widespread alike in popular culture and in the learned culture of the professionals. Moreover, I would submit that the concept itself is the *real* disaster -- the only disaster that we as blind people have to live with -- and that when we can overcome this monstrous misconception, we shall ring down the curtain forever on the fictional drama entitled "The Tragedy of Blindness." (Jernigan, 1971, p. 7)

Intervention

Visual disabilities will probably always exist. While medical research has certainly prevented some eye conditions from developing and even diminished the effects of others, it is unlikely that injuries to the eye and heredity will ever be eradicated entirely.

Lowenfeld (1981) described visual disability as "a loss or serious impairment of vision that demands adjustment in order to reduce its handicapping effects. Education and rehabilitation are the most important means of adjustment. Their success, however, is basically dependent upon the strengths of each individual" (p. 229). The goals of education and rehabilitation are simple and straight-forward for people of all ages who have visual disabilities; (a) teach the utilization of all the senses to obtain information, (b) promote adjustment, and (c) increase self-confidence. It is through knowing how to use the senses to do both everyday and extraordinary things, that adjustment and self-confidence flow. These goals also affect family members; as people with visual disabilities become more and more competent, family members begin to recognize the disability for its real (rather than imagined) effects and, hopefully, look at the things that can be accomplished, rather than those that cannot (Lowenfeld, 1981).

People with visual disabilities utilize various types of adapted equipment to assist them in school, work, and everyday living. Some of these are not exotic at all; for example, black felt tip pens to produce darker print, bookstands to bring reading material closer to the eyes and reduce fatigue, and adjustable lamps to increase the amount of and direct the position of artificial lighting. A list of the various aids commonly used by people with visual disabilities is given in Table 5.2. The increased availability of sophisticated technological aids, such as computers with speech output, braille printers, braille-to-print terminals, and enhanced computer screen images (in print color and size tailored to the individual's needs), has revolutionized the access of people with visual disabilities to both educational and employment opportunities. It is now possible to convert almost any printed material to braille, and the restrictions once imposed by the time needed to transcribe material into braille and the voluminous space it consumed after transcription are now largely a thing of the past.

Expectations

As Jernigan (1971) indicated, people with visual disabilities are handicapped more by people's attitudes and prejudices than they are by the disability itself. Most people with regular vision usually become aware of how much they depend on the visual sense when discussing visual impairments. In surveys asking people what disease they fear most, blindness rates at the top, along with cancer and AIDS. Unfortunately, this personal fear is often projected onto the person with visual disabilities; you don't know how you could do anything if you were blind, so of course you cannot understand how the blind couple next door can possibly take care of themselves. And there is no way, in your mind, that they can raise and support a family.

Table 5.2
Special (and not so special) Devices Utilized by
People with Visual Disabilities

Nonoptical devices
Bookstands
Felt tip pens
Acetate sheets
Adjustable lamps (with rheostats)
Large-type books
Bold-line paper
Page markers and reading windows
Sun visors
Friends
Classmates

Tactual devices
Braillewriter
Slate and stylus
Raised line drawing board
Cubarithm slate
Abacus
Raised line paper
Templates and writing guides
Needle threaders
Sensory Quill
Tactile graphics kit
Tactual maps or globes
Thermoform duplicator

Auditory devices
Cassette tape recorders
Variable speed attachments
Speech compressors

Optical devices
Bifocals
Field expanders
Spectacles
Contact lenses
Tinted lenses
Magnifiers
Telescopes
Bioptic lens systems

Travel devices
Cane
Laser cane
Pathsounder
Binaural sensory aids
Mowat Sensor
Dog guides

Reading devices
Optical scanners
Kurzweil Readers
Optacons
Closed circuit televisions
Stereotoner
Paperless braille
Viewscan

Computers
Speech programs
Screen enhancements
Braille printers
Braille translation programs

Historically, people with visual disabilities have been viewed as burdens to the community, subject to separation and death; as wards of the state, who needed care, solicitude, and guardianship; and more recently as equal, contributing members of society. It is significant that this change in treatment has occurred in large part because of the accomplishments of people with visual disabilities themselves (Lowenfeld, 1981). Beginning in the 18th century, people with visual disabilities have distinguished themselves as mathematicians, engineers, naturalists, musicians, and physicians. The American Foundation for the Blind maintains a Job Index which demonstrates that people with visual disabilities are presently involved in an extremely wide variety of occupations. These accomplishments have changed and challenged our expectations.

There is evidence that children with visual disabilities, despite the very real hurdles they face, "can attain levels of social and cognitive development comparable to those of sighted children" (Hollins, 1989, p. 167). Although many children do not compare favorably with the academic performance of typical children, just as many, if not more, do. Since it has not yet been determined why some children with visual disabilities do well and others do not, most specialists agree that children raised in a supportive family environment, who are given every opportunity to learn, to assume responsibility, and to take risks, and who receive appropriate education services from qualified special teachers, have a high probability of success both in school and later in life (Lowenfeld, 1981; Tuttle, 1984).

Employment

Although people with visual disabilities are succeeding in the academic world, this progress has not always been evident in the employment sector. People with visual disabilities are still subject to discrimination and under-employment. Kirchner and Peterson (1988a) reported that less than 1/3 of working-age visually disabled persons were in the labor force (i.e., able and looking for work), compared to almost 3/4 of the total US population; 80% of these were actually employed. The numbers are worse for women with visual disabilities, who apparently have not yet benefitted from the women's movement; only 20% of visually disabled women were in the labor force in 1976-77.

While people with visual disabilities are found in almost every job category, it appears that they are under-represented in the white collar (high prestige, high income) occupations, and over-represented in the blue collar jobs (Kirchner &

Peterson, 1988a). The new technology has started to impact on this distribution, however, as it has made employment in a wider variety of occupations possible. The American Foundation for the Blind's National Technology Center maintains a Careers and Technology Information Bank (CTIB), which contains information from over 1,100 individuals with visual disabilities about the adaptive equipment they utilize in a variety of jobs. A review of the database shows that almost all occupational categories are represented and that even within the same occupation, a range of adaptive equipment can be utilized.

For many people with visual disabilities, there are disincentives to work. Supplemental Security Income (SSI), a federal guaranteed income program, is structured in such a way that it is more costly to work than to drop out of the labor force. In 1986, 83,097 Americans received federal SSI payments and/or federally administered state supplementation, at an average SSI monthly amount of $235.38 (Kirchner, Stephen & Chandu, 1988). This does not seem like much, but compared to a low paying job that under-utilizes your talents and provides low self-esteem, SSI is probably at least equally attractive.

Interactions

Again, remember that people with visual disabilities are people, first. Your interactions with them are undoubtedly going to be influenced by your past experiences and your own feelings about disability in general and blindness in particular. Try to keep these points in mind:

Don't be afraid. Visual disability is not contagious. Neither is it frightening or intimidating to the person experiencing it.

Speak first. Remember that you have the advantage in a social situation, because you can see the other person, sometimes from a great distance, before the person with a visual disability even knows you are in the vicinity (unless, of course, you make a lot of noise or wear particularly strong perfume).

Identify yourself. People who are visually impaired are able to recognize familiar voices, but may not recognize yours until they know you better. Let them know who you are before they have to ask ("Hi, I'm Justin. It's good to see you again.")

Use the person's name. You have the advantage of making eye contact with most people during conversation, so it is easy to know who is being addressed. But the person with visual impairment does not know you're talking to him, unless you give a clue: "George, did you know . . . ."

Use natural language. It's okay to use visual terms such as "look" and "see," because they are part of everyday language. People with visual disabilities use them themselves.

Use a normal volume of voice. Remember, it is not hearing that is diminished, so you don't need to speak louder to a person who is visually impaired (although, by some strange phenomenon, many people think that they do).

Use a normal tone of voice. An overly solicitous or condescending tone can be easily discerned and can betray all your good efforts.

Be precise, particularly when describing something. People with visual disabilities cannot see what you are pointing at, and phrases like "over there" need some sort of reference point. Say, "The trash can is across the room, next to the door you came in."

Give directions that refer to the individual's experience, and/or relate directions to body parts. The statement, "next to the door you came in," allows people who are blind to retrace their steps mentally and form a mental representation of that to which you are referring. You can also give directions in relation to the body: "The bookshelf is on your left, about shoulder level."

Allow time. It sometimes takes longer to do simple tasks and activities when you can't rely on vision to guide you. You may be going crazy waiting for your roommate to iron a shirt so the two of you can go out, and you may be tempted to do it yourself. Don't. Give him or her the time to do it independently (and plan ahead next time). Your offer to take over may suggest that you don't think your roommate is capable of doing it alone.

Give tactual clues. People with visual disabilities rely on their other senses to provide information. Most will automatically establish a tactual orientation, but others may need help or may not feel free to tactually explore objects. Sometimes, you can provide those tactual clues: "Gene, let me take your hand and show you the parts of this engine."

Don't leave a person in open space. When guiding people with visual disabilities, do not walk away and leave them in open space. Try to "ground" them to an object in the environment, so that they have some orientation to the physical space around them. "Laurel, I left my backpack in the classroom. If you'll stay here next to the drinking fountain, I'll be right back."

Don't keep embarrassments to yourself. Remember that the public's impressions of people with disabilities is often based on surface characteristics. If you spill food on your shirt, or if your makeup is smeared, you can usually tell by people's expressions that something is wrong. In both cases, you pick up on nonverbal messages from others and can do something about it. It is okay to tell people with visual disabilities about faux pas that would be embarrassing if they found out about them later: "Excuse me, but did you know that you are unzipped?"

Don't assume that help is needed. Ask if help is needed, and if it is, follow the lead of the person who is blind. Blind people themselves will tell you how much help is needed and how they prefer to receive it.

Don't assume disability. You never know how much a person sees, or how much a person doesn't see. And you certainly know nothing about a person's impairment, disability, or handicap simply because you notice a white cane and dark glasses. Give the individual with visual disability the benefit of the doubt.

Expect competence. Blindness is not debilitating, nor is it visual impairment itself that limits what a person can or cannot do. In the absence of evidence to the contrary, assume that the individual who is visually impaired can succeed.

Summary

A striking characteristic about a study of people with visual disabilities is that it is impossible to make generalizations. As a whole, they demonstrate a range of visual loss, interests, experiences, academic achievement, job performance, and abilities and inabilities. Their visual impairment tells you nothing about what they are like as a person, what they might be like as a friend, or what quality of work they can do. Which, when you think about it, isn't that much different from everybody else.

References

Barraga, N. (1983). *Visual handicaps and learning: A developmental approach* (2nd ed.). Austin, TX: Exceptional Resources.

Carroll, T. J. (1961). *Blindness, what it is, what it does, and how to live with it.* Boston: Little, Brown & Co.

Corn, A. L., & Erin, J. N. (1986). How to speak visionese. *Journal of Visual Impairment & Blindness, 80,* 636-637.

Erin, J., Daugherty, W., Dignan, K., & Pearson, N. (1990). Teachers of visually handicapped students with multiple disabilities: Perceptions of adequacy. *Journal of Visual Impairment & Blindness, 84,* 16-20.

Ferrell, K. A. (1987). State of the art of infant and preschool services in 1986. *Yearbook of the Association for Education and Rehabilitation of the Blind and Visually Impaired, 1986.* Alexandria, VA: Association for Education and Rehabilitation of the Blind and Visually Impaired.

Ferrell, K. A., Deitz, S., Trief, E., Bonner, M. A., Cruz, D., Ford, E., & Stratton, J. (1990). The visually impaired infants research consortium (VIIRC): First year results. *Journal of Visual Impairment & Blindness, 84,* 404.

Hatfield, E. M. (1975). Why are they blind? *Sight Saving Review, 45,* 3-22.

Hollins, M. (1989). *Understanding blindness, an integrative approach.* Hillsdale, NJ: Lawrence Erlbaum Associates.

Jernigan, K. (1971). *The first thirty years: A history of the National Federation of the Blind.* Des Moines, IA: National Federation of the Blind.

Kirchner, C. (1989). National estimates of prevalence and demographics of children with visual impairments. In M. C. Wang, M. C. Reynolds, & H. J. Walberg, *Handbook of special education: Research and practice. Volume 3, Low incidence conditions* (pp. 135-153). Oxford: Pergamon Press.

Kirchner, C., & Peterson, R. (1988a). Employment: Selected characteristics. In C. Kirchner (Ed.), *Data on blindness and visual impairment in the U.S.* (2nd ed.) (pp. 170-177). New York: American Foundation for the Blind.

Kirchner, C., & Peterson, R. (1988b). Multiple impairments among noninstitutionalized blind and visually impaired persons. In C. Kirchner (Ed.), *Data on blindness and visual impairment in the U.S.* (2nd ed.) (pp. 101-109). New York: American Foundation for the Blind.

Kirchner, C., Stephen, G., & Chandu, F. (1988). Statistics on blindness and visual impairment. In *Yearbook of the Association for Education and Rehabilitation of the Blind and Visually Impaired* (vol. 5, 1987) (pp. 113-139). Alexandria, VA: Association for Education and Rehabilitation of the Blind and Visually Impaired.

Lowenfeld, B. (1981). *Berthold Lowenfeld on blindness and blind people: Selected papers*. New York: American Foundation for the Blind.

Lowenfeld, B. (Ed.). (1973). *The visually handicapped children in school*. New York: John Day.

Lowman, C., & Kirchner, C. (1988). Elderly blind and visually impaired persons: Projected numbers in the year 2000. In C. Kirchner (Ed.), *Data on blindness and visual impairment in the U.S.* (2nd ed.) (pp. 45-52). New York: American Foundation for the Blind.

National Society to Prevent Blindness. (1980). *Vision problems in the U.S.*. New York: National Society to Prevent Blindness.

Nelson, K. A. (1988). Visual impairment among elderly Americans: Statistics in transition. In C. Kirchner (Ed.), *Data on blindness and visual impairment in the U.S.* (2d ed.)(pp. 53-61). New York: American Foundation for the Blind.

Rosenbloom, A. A. (1989). Senior education and rehabilitation personnel: An untapped resource. *Journal of Visual Impairment & Blindness, 83,* 143-144.

Tuttle, D. W. (1984). *Self-esteem and adjusting with blindness.* Springfield, IL: Charles C. Thomas.

Suggested Readings

Attmore, M. (1990). *Career perspectives: Interviews with blind and visually impaired professionals.* New York: American Foundation for the Blind.

Corn, A., & Martinez, I. (1982). *If you have a visually handicapped child in your classroom: Suggestions for teachers.* New York: American Foundation for the Blind.

Koestler, F. A. (1976). *The unseen minority: A social history of blindness in America.* New York: David McKay.

Landau, B., & Gleitman, L. R. (1985). *Language and experience.* Cambridge, MA: Harvard University Press.

Lash, J. P. (1980). *Helen and teacher.* New York: Delacorte Press.

Lowenfeld, B. (1981). *Berthold Lowenfeld on blindness and blind people: Selected papers.* New York: American Foundation for the Blind.

Scholl, G. T. (Ed.). (1986). *Foundations of education for blind and visually handicapped children and youth: Theory and practice.* New York: American Foundation for the Blind.

Warren, D. H. (1984). *Blindness and early childhood development* (2nd ed.). New York: American Foundation for the Blind.

PEOPLE WITH VISUAL DISABILITIES

Exploration

Individual Activities

1. Wake up in the morning and blindfold yourself. Get out of bed and begin your day. Go to the bathroom and take a shower, brush your teeth, and do anything else you would normally do. After you've finished, still blindfolded of course, get dressed for your day.

   List three things you did that were difficult, frustrating, or even frightening for you.

   _____
   _____
   _____

   List three things you were able to do which surprised you.

   _____
   _____
   _____

2. You're hungry, and it's time for you to prepare a meal. Blindfold yourself before you assemble the ingredients and begin cooking. (For safety reasons have a friend observe and help only when needed.) After eating your culinary delight, clean up your dishes.

   Now think about what you just did. Give 4 or 5 examples of what this experience taught you.

   _____
   _____
   _____
   _____
   _____

Group Activities

1. Seated in your class, have everyone blindfold themselves. Now, take off a shoe and pass it two people to your right. After this, pass the shoe you have in your hand at the moment directly to a person behind you. Now pass it three people to your left. OK, time to return the shoe you have to its rightful owner, still blindfolded, of course. Try this same activity with another item (such as keys) but this time concentrate on the movement of the item you own. Are you able to locate your keys more easily than your shoe?

    Reactions:

    _____
    _____
    _____

2. Have your class take a "blind walk." Pair off in groups of two and take turns leading one another. Think of this activity as a type of obstacle course of life for blind people. Notice your surroundings through the use of your other senses. If you are the guide, notice the looks, stares, and behaviors of the people around you.

    Reactions:

    _____
    _____
    _____

Reaction Paper 5.1

Imagine yourself as a blind person. What parts of your normal daily routines would be changed from easy procedures to challenging tasks. Describe your new feelings and emotions concerning these alterations.

Continue on back if needed.

124

Reaction Paper 5.2

Discuss the differences you perceive between being blind from birth or acquiring blindness later in life. If you had to choose one, which would it be, and why?

Continue on back if needed.

Notes

CHAPTER 6

PEOPLE WITH HEALTH IMPAIRMENTS

Sherwood J. Best

Introduction

Persons with health impairments are extremely diverse in terms of types of exceptionality, educational and learning needs, and adjustment and employment outcome. When an attempt is made to arrive at an inclusive definition of health impairments, the diversity of conditions described by this label becomes apparent. The Education for All Handicapped Children Act, PL 94-142 (1975), has identified the categories of orthopedic and health impairments within the broader rubric of physical disability. Health impairments are defined in this law as conditions affecting school performance that result in "limited strength, vitality, or alertness due to chronic or acute health problems such as heart condition, tuberculosis, rheumatic fever, nephritis, asthma, sickle cell anemia, hemophilia, epilepsy, lead poisoning, leukemia, or diabetes" (*Federal Register*, 1977, p. 42478). These impairments can occur as the result of congenital (birth) conditions, occur adventitiously, or result from disease. While the federal definition notes that health impairments may be acute (time limited), those that are chronic (long lasting) are considered to be treatable but not curable. Since the management of many chronic health impairments is often taken over by the parent or the patient, such conditions can result in commitment to treatments that are complex, sometimes painful, and expensive (Johnson, 1985). In addition, if the impairment is a result of a disease that changes in severity and care level, changing intervention may be needed across the individual's life span. Drotar (1981) noted that "physical treatments have been developed with little consideration given to the psychological and social support necessary to enhance the quality as well as the length of the child's life" (p. 213). Health impairments therefore present a serious challenge to service care providers and the general community.

The Office of Special Education and Rehabilitation Services estimated that 52,638 children with health impairments between the ages of three and 21 received special education services in 1986-1987 (OSERS, 1988). Although this number is low in terms of the population of children in special education, chronic illness in the general population has been described as the nation's foremost health problem (Travis, 1976). It has been estimated that chronically ill children comprise approximately 50% of pediatric practice (Johnson, 1985). Because health impairments can occur in combination with other disabilities, exact prevalence figures are difficult to determine.

Several factors have contributed to changes in both the prevalence and clinical diversity of persons with health impairments. Some conditions have been either largely eradicated or made more amenable to treatment as a result of improved medical technology. While medical advancements have not yet altered the final outcome of conditions still considered terminal, persons with these conditions are surviving into adulthood in larger numbers. The presence of AIDS (Acquired Immune Deficiency Syndrome) as a new disease has added to the number of persons with health impairments, as well as having an impact on persons with health impairments who receive blood and blood products (Anderson, Bale, Blackman, & Murph, 1986). Thus, the category of health impairments is one that is not simple to define or describe.

Characteristics

Numerous social, psychological, and environmental factors affect the psychosocial development of persons with disabilities (including health impairments). Time of disability onset may have a profound effect on reaction to the disability. The person with a congenital condition may not have had experiences common to others, resulting in a feeling of difference. The person with an acquired health impairment may feel a loss of sense of the former self. In addition, many of the health impairments are "invisible"; they are not readily apparent to the casual observer. While this may allow the person with a health impairment to behave as if the condition does not exist, a sudden onset of symptoms may be misunderstood or even constitute a life threatening condition if prompt medical attention is not sought. Likewise, people who do not understand adaptive behavior patterns of a person who is health impaired may not be as accepting as when the impairment is clearly visible (Wright, 1983). Therefore, the psychosocial implications of health impairments need to be considered in any discussion of acceptance and adjustment.

The following discussion will focus on only a few health impairments. While many other important conditions (such as cancer, kidney disease, cardiac conditions, hemophilia, and sickle cell disease) exist, the following health impairments have been chosen because they are often the subject of some misunderstanding to the general public.

Diabetes

The human body supplies itself with energy by turning carbohydrates, fats, and proteins into glucose. The pancreas secretes a hormone called insulin which transports the glucose into the cells to be converted into energy to fuel the body. When we eat, glucose in the blood rises, and more insulin is produced. Extra glucose is stored as fat, which can be used when there is not enough glucose in the blood. Diabetes is a disorder of metabolism in which the pancreas does not produce enough insulin to meet bodily requirements. The cells feel a shortage of glucose, even if there is plenty in the blood. Fat is broken down to provide more glucose, and the person loses weight. If insulin is not placed into the bloodstream, the person will eventually die (Christiansen & Hintz, 1982).

In the adult with diabetes (called Type II diabetes), insufficient insulin is produced. Oral medication must be taken to "boost" the effect of naturally occurring insulin, or the person can inject additional insulin. A diet low in sugar and consistent exercise contributes to better health in the diabetic adult. Diabetes in adults is associated with obesity and sometimes pregnancy. In pregnancy-associated diabetes, the condition will disappear after the birth, although these women are more likely to develop permanent diabetes at a later time.

In contrast to the adult who develops diabetes, the child with diabetes produces no insulin (Type I diabetes). This child must inject insulin to survive. The use of insulin is therefore a life-long process for the juvenile-onset diabetic.

Diabetes has important side effects. If there is too little insulin, the person will experience fatigue, excessive hunger, thirst and frequent urination, and eventually diabetic coma. If there is too much insulin or the person engages in strenuous exercise and burns more glucose than usual, nausea, palpitations, irritability, disorientation, convulsions, coma, and death may ensue. The condition of too little insulin is called hyperglycemia or ketoacidosis, while too much insulin results in hypoglycemia or insulin reaction.

The person with diabetes looks normal. However, the child with diabetes may be smaller than normal if his/her body does not get enough glucose. The child must maintain a diet that is well-balanced and of consistent amounts. Exercise should be moderate. Furthermore, the blood or urine must be tested up to several times a day for glucose levels. One of the problems associated with diabetes is premature aging of the blood vessels. The adult with diabetes is therefore at risk for hemorrhage leading to blindness, poor circulation, and heart, liver, and kidney disease. These may be more life threatening than the actual diabetic condition.

Cystic Fibrosis

Cystic fibrosis is the most common hereditary disease of childhood and the most common cause of death in children due to a genetic disorder. Both parents must "carry" and "give" the gene for cystic fibrosis to the child for this disease to occur. Caucasians are most often affected, since about one in 20 carry the defective gene. Blacks and Asians are affected to a much lesser degree (Mangos, 1983).

In cystic fibrosis the secreting glands of the body are affected, particularly those that produce sweat, saliva, pancreatic juice, and mucus. The child might be diagnosed at birth or after several months. Parents might be the first to notice that their baby does not gain weight even though he/she eats voraciously. In addition, the sweat contains an unusual amount of salt. Both these conditions reflect abnormality of the secreting glands.

Cystic fibrosis is a progressive disease that ends in death from respiratory or other organ failure by the late teens or early twenties. While this is certainly a poor prognosis, it is much improved over previous expectations of death by the first or second year of life. Improved medical treatment to clear the lungs of mucus and prevent pneumonia, plus vitamin and enzyme supplements to aid digestion, allows a longer life with normal learning potential. The focus in treating the child with cystic fibrosis is on maintaining good health for as long as possible during the life span.

Children with cystic fibrosis have typical learning needs and can attend their neighborhood schools. However, they will increasingly require medical attention as the disease progresses. In addition, a lengthy home regimen of inhalation therapy and pulmonary percussion to loosen and remove the sticky mucus in the lungs becomes more frequent.

This situation may necessitate that one parent not seek employment outside the home and care for the child's needs. The often overwhelming tasks involved in maintaining the child's health compromises parental time spent with other siblings. A balance must be struck regarding provision of quality time with all family members.

Asthma

As the most common pulmonary disease of childhood, asthma accounts for one-fourth of school absences due to chronic illness (Travis, 1976). While it seems that some people have a predisposition toward developing asthma, an episode is triggered after exposure to an ingestant (allergic food), an inhalant (dust, pollen), or an injectable (insect bite). Exercise can also precipitate an attack. Strong emotion can initiate an attack, although it is often difficult to tell if the emotion actually triggered the attack, or vice versa. Sometimes only a small amount of the offending substance will trigger an attack, which consists of inflammation and blockage of the bronchial tubes, increased production of mucus in the lungs, and wheezing as the air passes in and out of the lungs.

Asthma was once believed to be the result of insufficient antibodies to the offending substance. Recent research indicates that the attack is actually a hyper-response from a body that has excessive antibodies. Reactions in the lungs result in asthma while hay fever, allergic conjunctivitis, and eczema or hives are reflective of extreme reaction in the nose, eyes, and skin, respectively. Some persons experience eczema and allergic episodes as infants, followed by asthma somewhat later in childhood. This type usually has a strong family history of asthma and is more difficult to control. Others experience asthma preceded by hay fever, which is a more controllable type (Harvey, 1982).

Not every person who wheezes has asthma. Babies have small bronchial tubes, and can wheeze when they have an ordinary cold. Wheezing may also result if there is a foreign object in the lungs, in persons with respiratory diseases such as cystic fibrosis, or when there are structural defects of the bronchial tubes.

Some people believe that chronic infections in the tonsils are related to asthma, but infection in another part of the body (such as the throat) will not cause an asthma attack in the lungs. Nor is it true that asthma leads to emphysema, in which the air sacs in the lungs become less elastic. Changes in the air sacs due to emphysema are permanent; in asthma they are not. Longer and more severe asthma attacks can have fatal consequences; every year more than 4,000 people in the United States die of asthma (Travis, 1976).

Epilepsy

Epilepsy is one of the oldest known disorders, mentioned in the writing of Hippocrates. The terms convulsions and seizures are used to describe a sudden alteration of brain function that begins and ends spontaneously and changes the individual's awareness of his/her surrounding environment. A person with recurrent seizures or convulsions is said to have epilepsy. About two million persons in the United States experience convulsive disorders, making it one of the most common neurological disorders (Nealis, 1983).

Epilepsy is not a specific disease, but is symptomatic of underlying brain abnormality (which might be disease-related). It can result from lack of oxygen during birth, head injury, tumors, parasitic infection, or stroke. Seizures are classified on the basis of whether the seizure involves the whole body (generalized) or only part (partial), and whether the individual remains conscious (Hermann, Desai, & Whitman, 1988).

When most people think of epilepsy, they visualize a generalized convulsion called a grand mal (tonic/clonic) seizure. This condition may begin with a premonition or aura that a seizure is beginning, followed by loss of consciousness, uncontrolled movements of the limbs, trunk, and head, and disorientation and sleepiness after the seizure ceases. In other types of seizures the individual may look like he/she is inattentive or engaging in somewhat purposeful but bizarre behavior. It is important to realize that the person is in no pain, and the seizure will generally stop without intervention. In some types of epilepsy hospitalization is required to contain seizures.

About 60% of children "grow out" of their seizures. This is less likely in the case in those children who develop seizures early in life or whose seizures are not well controlled by medication or who require high levels of medication to gain control.

Epilepsy can seriously interfere with life activities. The person may appear to be "daydreaming" when a petit mal seizure is in progress. Medication can result in drowsiness and impair the ability to complete work. If the person is fearful of having a seizure in public, social isolation may result. There is, however, no direct connection between epilepsy and mental retardation and the person with this condition is generally within the normal range of intelligence.

AIDS

The most recently identified of the health impairments discussed in this chapter, AIDS (Acquired Immune Deficiency Syndrome), was so labeled by the Centers for Disease Control in 1982. AIDS is viral in origin, and acts to attack and weaken the body's immune system. As a result, many "opportunistic infections" invade the body, causing discomfort and further disability. These opportunistic infections are frequently the actual cause of death, as is a rare form of cancer called Kaposi's sarcoma.

Many misconceptions exist as to the mode of transmission of the AIDS virus. AIDS cannot be transmitted through casual contact such as hugging, kissing, hand holding, spitting, or through insect bites. It cannot be contracted through donating blood. Transmission is possible through blood-to-blood contact that occurs in some sexual practices, through intravenous drug use, or from transfusion. Babies can acquire AIDS before or during the birth process by their infected mothers (U.S. Department of Health and Human Services, 1987).

Prior to actual AIDS symptoms, the infected person may experience other symptoms that contribute to a condition known as ARC (AIDS Related Complex). These include nightsweats, diarrhea, weight loss, and fatigue. It is possible for a person to be asymptomatic for an extended period of time prior to either ARC or AIDS symptoms, and still be capable of infecting others. While tests exist that will detect the presence of antibodies in the blood, infection is possible after viral exposure and before such tests yield a positive outcome. Therefore, the number of persons currently showing symptoms of AIDS is expected to grow as those who are currently asymptomatic progress to full expression of the AIDS virus.

Because there is no known cure for AIDS, measures to protect the health of the infected individual and those around him/her are important. Isolation is an extreme and unnecessary measure. Simple and effective measures such as proper handwashing, using a solution of bleach and water to clean areas soiled with urine, feces, or blood, and wearing disposable gloves constitute appropriate health measures. Best, Bigge, and Sirvis (1990) noted that because "these precautions constitute good hygiene for anyone who requires physical care, their universal adoption allows protection for care providers and preserves the privacy of the person with AIDS" (p. 297).

As with many other health impairments, persons infected with the AIDS virus will have periods of time when they feel good and can actively pursue a normal life style. However, because their systems are immunosuppressed, simple infections such as chicken pox or even colds may constitute a threat to life. In this respect AIDS shares with other conditions (such as cancer in the individual undergoing chemotherapy) low resistance to infection. While many fear the AIDS virus, the health of the person with this virus is more fragile than those around the individual.

Intervention

Treatment of health impairments will depend on the specific condition in question. Of course prevention is the most desirable choice, and some health impairments are wholly preventable. Adults who watch their weight and eat a balanced diet can sometimes avoid a diabetic condition. Counseling can assist a couple who carry the gene for cystic fibrosis to determine if adoption is an option for them. Avoidance of precipitating substances may prevent an asthma attack. Simple solutions such as use of mattress covers, synthetic fibers, or finding another home for the family pet may remove the need for more complex allergy injections or use of medication. Taking appropriate medications may control seizures. Abstaining from or taking specific precautions during various sexual practices or intravenous drug abuse will provide protection from AIDS for adults and for the children of mothers who engage in such activities.

If prevention is not possible, intervention to ameliorate the effects of a condition is the next choice. These interventions, whether medical/therapeutic, educational, or technological, have implications throughout the life span of the individual with a health impairment.

Children have a natural need to explore their environment. The physical status of a child with a health impairment might prevent him/her from touching, crawling, running, or engaging in other tactile experiences that are the cornerstone of early learning and environmental mastery. Separation, pain, boredom, and frustration engendered by hospitalization are not typically experienced by most children. The adolescent who is struggling with issues of body consciousness and independence may feel particularly self-conscious or rebel against medical treatment. If the condition compromises the ability to have children (as can be the case with diabetes, cancer, kidney, or heart disease), further estrangement from peers is possible. Extra care must be taken to provide a wide variety of experiences, with physical assistance and counseling if necessary. The delicate health of a person does not preclude involvement in normal family, school, or community involvement.

What are the goals of therapy and school for children with health impairments? Both occupational and physical therapists may be involved in the provision of therapy services. Traditionally, occupational therapists are concerned with fine motor development, activities of daily living, and sensorimotor integration. Physical therapists are involved with gross motor development in terms of gait (movement) training and assisting in use of adaptive devices such as wheelchairs, crutches, and other aids. You will find a more thorough discussion of these two therapies in Chapter 14. The person with a health impairment may require the services of both therapists, which, for school-age children, can be provided at school. Goals of therapy include increased mobility, self-care and independence, maintenance of equipment, and motor development. Younger children may be more "therapy intensive" then older individuals whose conditions have stabilized. However, with the advent of an acquired or later onset impairment, therapy may be an important consideration for the older individual.

For students with health impairments, school placement decisions should be made on an educational need with attention to what medical/therapy support is needed. Traditional placement for students with health impairments was based on a medical model, with classes located in hospital and residential convalescent facilities. Current educational policy and legislation supports education in the least restrictive environment. However, this must not be interpreted to mean that students with health impairments must all be educated in regular classrooms. While peer interaction, normalized school routines, and academic preparation are critical to any educational placement, least restrictive/most appropriate educational placement must address change in the health condition as that impacts functional ability. All decisions regarding educational placement must involve the parents as well as school personnel.

Advances in technology have helped persons with health impairments engage in relatively typical lifestyles. Many adaptations exist that allow persons with reduced coordination, strength, and vitality to use computers that can be equipped with switch access, synthesized voice, and special printers (Blackstone, 1986). Sophisticated environmental control systems are available that enable persons to operate their televisions, computers, and other business and household equipment independently. However, many "low tech" solutions to "high tech" problems can be utilized. For example, an electric typewriter or name stamp can be used by the person whose movement ability is compromised. Technological interventions should be tailored to the needs of the individual, yet be adaptable to his/her changing needs.

Finally, the older adult who has a health impairment must not be overlooked. Schienle and Eiler (1984) estimated that approximately 41 percent of the population of older individuals are limited by a chronic disabling condition. Of these, many can expect to live in some kind of institution (such as a hospital or nursing home). Whether such placement is permanent will depend on family and/or financial support. When health care is not enough to prevent the onset of a health impairment, intervention that is least disruptive to independent functioning is the most desirable for physical and mental health. Community-based programs such as senior centers or mutual assistance among neighbors are a creative alternative to institutionalization.

Expectations

As noted earlier, health impairments are frequently not noticeable to the general public unless an acute episode occurs. During periods of good health there may be no disease symptoms, which has both positive and negative aspects. The ability to engage in pursuits of everyday life should be encouraged, but not forgetting that a period of time without symptoms does not mean "cure." For those whose conditions require constant monitoring, this may prove especially frustrating. The teenager with diabetes, who has previously adhered faithfully to the testing and insulin regimen, may falter under pressure from the peer group and the desire to "be like others." Heightened awareness of the body at this time may pose a burden for those who must eat special foods at certain times, make frequent trips to the bathroom, or experience the results of bodily change as a result of treatment or medication (as in chemotherapy for cancer).

In all aspects of life, the focus should be on what the individual can do. Strauss (1975) provided guidelines that can be utilized by teachers, administrators, and parents to meet the needs of a child with a health impairment. These guidelines include knowledge of particular health impairments and related emergency procedures, management of the health regimen in a way that is unobtrusive and dignified, flexible scheduling to maximize productivity, understanding that symptom changes may trigger negative behaviors, awareness that the trajectory of an illness necessitates changes in goals and activities without overprotection, and assistance to the individuals whose condition results in loss of energy and corresponding declining social interaction.

While developed for providing an appropriate school experience for the child with a health impairment, such guidelines are applicable to the adult with a health impairment in the workplace. While work is an important transition to independence, issues of health insurance and employer concern about productivity, absenteeism, and employee appearance, constitute work disincentives. It is most important to remember that the presence of a health impairment should not preclude the individual from full participation to the extent of his/her abilities. Even when the prognosis is terminal, it is inappropriate to treat any person as dying or beyond the need of social interaction and participation in work.

Interactions

For the most part, persons with health impairments do not appear different and can engage in most typical life activities. However, people react to health impairments in a number of ways. Since many health impairments are often not cured but instead are approached from a perspective of symptom management, it is appropriate to talk about coping with these ongoing conditions. Coping involves the behaviors and thoughts that we use to confront life stress. It must be evaluated in terms of the resources that are available from the family, friends, co-workers, neighbors, and community associations, the personality characteristics of the individual in question, and the choice of behaviors to confront stress. When initially presented with a diagnosis, the person and his/her family may actively involve themselves in treatment or seek additional advice in the form of second opinions in an attempt to change the situation. The behavior of "doctor shopping," once thought to be an unhealthy response of denial, is now believed to be an appropriate and active behavior that allows the individual and family to take positive action. In the face of repeated diagnoses, most persons then begin whatever treatment regimen is advised.

Other coping strategies involve comparing oneself positively against the conditions of other persons with a similar condition, magnifying the importance of positive aspects of the situation ("It has brought us closer together"), and/or selectively ignoring that which is negative. These responses help give meaning to the situation.

Finally, acceptance, denial, or attribution of the condition to a higher authority may occur when the condition is recognized as chronic. These strategies may be used at different times and under different circumstances. It is important for the family member, friend, or co-worker to remember that coping is an active response and may be quite appropriate for the time. Under those circumstances, comments to "snap out of it," "get in touch with reality," or "go on with your life" can be counterproductive.

Wright (1983) noted that rehabilitation in persons with chronic illnesses was enhanced when certain goals were attained. These goals include enlarging the scope of values, subordinating the physique, containing the effects of disability, reordering priorities, valuing one's assets, sharing the load, and encouraging enablement. In a family whose cultural beliefs emphasize youth, physical strength, and traditional work roles, the person with a health impairment may be perceived as more helpless, shameful, and in need of protection (Rustad, 1984). The capacity for family change and acceptance of more flexible goals will enhance adjustment. Many self-help and advocacy groups related to specific impairments (See Appendix A) provide support and education to the individual, family, and interested community members.

If the condition has a terminal prognosis, there is the danger of overprotection, to the point that parents and friends of persons with such conditions avoid discussion of the disease outcome. While it is inappropriate to make the terminal aspect of any disease the focus of the individual's life, knowledge of various strategies and coping mechanisms can help in overall adjustment.

Very young children are developmentally unable to conceptualize death in adult terms. Their fears revolve around separation. For the child who requires frequent hospitalizations and medical treatments, the presence of a significant caregiver is important. The relaxation of visiting hours and "rooming in" reflects the response of hospitals to this need. The older child needs to gain a measure of control of his/her condition through active involvement in regimen compliance and/or acquaintance with facts of the condition.

Organizations exist that offer summer camps and similar programs in which affected children can meet with others, gain a measure of independence in a supervised setting, and receive instruction in self-care. The fact that a child with a terminal condition gets to know others with a similar prognosis argues against concealment, offering instead an opportunity to share information about treatment and strategies for successful living. Adults may express a need to "get their affairs in order," to the point of planning memorial services if the condition is terminal. This is not a morbid act but an attempt to gain a measure of control and protect other family members from these difficult chores.

Although reaction to people with health impairments is individualized, comfortable interaction is an important goal. Certainly it is permissible to use phrases like "Let's walk over here" to someone whose ability to ambulate is compromised. Such phrases are an accepted part of the language, and someone who consciously tries to avoid them will create more discomfort. It is certainly appropriate to offer to lend physical aid such as assisting a person to cross a street or to climb a flight of stairs, but many people do not do so out of fear of embarrassing themselves or the person with a health impairment. A good solution is to ask if assistance is needed in any situation in which you would typically lend aid to someone who is able-bodied. If someone can climb stairs unaided but is unsteady, follow the person up, and precede the individual down to block a possible fall. If more help is needed, ask the person how best to physically assist.

Finally, language is an important tool for influencing thoughts and actions. When making reference to someone with a health impairment, phrases like "He's my epileptic friend" define the person first in disability terms. This chapter has used the phrases "persons with health impairments," and "individuals who have health impairments." While these phrases may be more awkward than "health impaired people," it places the emphasis where it belongs--on the person and not the disability.

Summary

While the population of persons with health impairments is vast in terms of clinical diversity, it is also growing in terms of impact upon society. Many children with health impairments who might earlier have not survived are now living with their families and entering adulthood. New breakthroughs in medical technology extend life but necessitate lengthy and sometimes costly home treatment. The trend toward integration in the schools and community places responsibility for support not only on the family but the greater society. While health impairments pose a serious challenge, improvements in medical and rehabilitation technology, coupled with legislation that supports community accessibility and least restrictive/most appropriate educational placement, have a positive impact on potential for better health, independence, and improved quality of life.

References

Anderson, R. D., Bale, J. F., Blackman, J. A., & Murph, J. R. (1986). *Infections in children: A sourcebook for health care providers.* Rockville, MD: Aspen.

Best, S. J., Bigge, J. L., & Sirvis, B. (1990). Physical and health impairments. In N. G. Haring & L. McCormick (Eds.), *Exceptional children and youth: An introduction to special education* (pp. 284-324). Columbus OH: Charles E. Merrill.

Blackstone, S. W. (Ed.) (1986). *Augmentative communication: An introduction.* Rockville, MD: American Speech-Language-Hearing Association.

Christiansen, R. O., & Hintz, R. L. (1982). Juvenile diabetes mellitus. In E. E. Bleck & D. A. Nagel (Eds.), *Physically handicapped children: A medical atlas for teachers* (2nd ed.) (pp. 269-277). New York: Grune & Stratton.

Drotar, D. (1981). Psychological perspectives in chronic childhood illness. *Journal of Pediatric Psychology, 6*(3), 211-228.

Federal Register. (1977). *42*(163), p. 42478.

Harvey, B. (1982). Asthma. In E. E. Bleck & D. A. Nagel (Eds.), *Physically handicapped children: A medical atlas for teachers* (2nd ed.) (pp. 31-42). New York: Grune & Stratton.

Hermann, B. P., Desai, B. T., & Whitman, S. (1988). Epilepsy. In V. B. Van Hasselt, P. S. Strain, & M. Hersen (Eds.), *Handbook of developmental and physical disabilities* (pp. 247-270). New York: Pergamon Press.

Johnson, S. B. (1985). The family and the child with chronic illness. In D. C. Turk & R. D. Kerns (Eds.), *Health, illness, and families: A life-span perspective.* New York: John Wiley.

Mangos, J. A. (1983). Cystic fibrosis. In J. Umbreit (Ed.), *Physical disabilities and health impairments: An introduction* (pp. 206-213). Columbus, OH: Charles E. Merrill.

Nealis, J. G. T. (1983). Epilepsy. In J. Umbreit (Ed.), *Physical disabilities and health impairments: An introduction* (pp. 74-85). Columbus, OH: Charles E. Merrill.

Rustad, L. C. (1984). Family adjustment to chronic illness and disability in mid-life. In M. G. Eisenberg, L. C. Sutkin, & M. A. Jansen (Eds.), *Chronic illness and disability through the life span: Effects on self and family* (pp. 222-242). New York: Springer.

Schienle, D. R., & Eiler, J. M. (1984). Clinical intervention with older adults. In M. G. Eisenberg, L. C. Sutkin, & M. A. Jansen (Eds.), *Chronic illness and disability through the life span: Effects on self and family* (pp. 245-268). New York: Springer.

Strauss, A. L. (1975). *Chronic illness and the quality of life.* St. Louis, MO: Mosby.

Travis, G. (1976). *Chronic illness in children.* Stanford, CA: Stanford University Press.

U.S. Department of Labor/Department of Health and Human Services. (1987). *Joint advisory notice: Protection against occupational exposure to hepatitis B virus (HBV) and human immunodefiency virus (HIV).* Rockville, MD: Centers for Disease Control.

Wright, B. A. (1983). *Physical disability: A psychosocial approach.* New York: Harper & Row.

Suggested Readings

Best, G. A. (1978). *Individuals with physical disabilities: An introduction for educators.* St. Louis, MO: Mosby.

Bigge, J. L. (1990). *Teaching individuals with physical and multiple disabilities.* Columbus, OH: Charles E. Merrill.

Costello, A. (1988). The psychosocial impact of genetic disease. *Focus on Exceptional Children, 20*(7), 2-8.

Fithian, J. (Ed.). (1984). *Understanding the child with a chronic illness in the classroom.* Phoenix: Orynx Press.

Goldfarb, L. A., Brotherson, M. J., Summers, J. A., & Turnbull, A. P. (1986). *Meeting the challenge of disability of chronic illness: A family guide.* Baltimore, MD: Paul H. Brookes.

Hobbs, N., & Perrin, J. M. (Eds.). (1985). *Issues in the care of children with chronic illness: A sourcebook of problems, services, and policies.* San Francisco: Jossey-Bass.

Hobbs, N., Perrin, J. M., & Ireys, H. T. (1985). *Chronically ill children and their families.* San Francisco: Jossey-Bass.

Mattsson, A. (1972). Long term illness in childhood. *Pediatrics, 50,* 803-805.

Moos, R. H. (Ed.). (1984). *Coping with physical illness.* New York: Plenum.

Spinetta, J. J., Swarner, J. A., & Sheposh, J. P. (1981). Effective parental coping following the death of a child from cancer. *Journal of Pediatric Psychology, 6*(3), 251-263.

Stein, R. E. K., & Jessup, D. J. (1984). Relationships between health status and psychological adjustment among children with chronic conditions. *Pediatrics, 73,* 169-174.

Turk, D. C., & Kerns, R. D. (Eds.). (1985). *Health, illness, and families: A lifespan perspective.* New York: Wiley.

Wells, R. D., & Schwebel, A. I. (1986). Chronically ill children and their mothers: Predictors of resilience and vulnerability to hospitalization and surgical stress. *Journal of Developmental and Behavioral Pediatrics, 8*(2), 83-89.

PEOPLE WITH HEALTH IMPAIRMENTS

Exploration

Individual Activities

1. How would it feel not to eat your favorite foods, play sports, or have to take medication or shots on a daily basis? These are considerations that people with health impairments may go through every day. List 10 thoughts that are going through your mind while you think of this.

    1. _____ 6. _____
    2. _____ 7. _____
    3. _____ 8. _____
    4. _____ 9. _____
    5. _____ 10. _____

2. When you think of diabetes, asthma, and epilepsy there are several personal problems that go along with these conditions. Describe a few problems associated with each condition. Suggest strategies to overcome these problems.

    Diabetes_____
    _____
    _____

    Asthma_____
    _____
    _____

    Epilepsy_____
    _____
    _____

Group Activities

1. How would you feel if a member of your family had a severe health impairment? With four or five other students discuss ways you would deal with the situation.

   Reactions:

   _____

   _____

   _____

2. Arrange a class visit to a nursing home which specializes in caring for patients with severe health impairments. While there, be sure to notice the level of care that is required for some patients. Try to focus on the attitudes of both staff members and patients.

   Reactions:

   _____

   _____

   _____

Reaction Paper 6.1

Assume that you just read a Letter to the Editor of your local newspaper which suggested that persons with AIDS should not be allowed to shop in your community's food stores. Write your own Letter to the Editor as a response.

Continue on back if needed.

Reaction Paper 6.2

Maintaining a good quality of life is important for persons who have a permanent health impairment and for members of that individual's family. Suggest what can be done toward maintaining a good quality of life.

Continue on back if needed.

Notes

CHAPTER 7

PHYSICALLY DISABLED INDIVIDUALS

Julia Lee

Introduction

People with physical disabilities are very heterogeneous. Physical disabilities include cerebral palsy, limb deficiencies, multiple sclerosis, muscular dystrophy, spina bifida, spinal cord injuries, and many other impairments. Obviously, individuals with such different disabilities will vary greatly.

Frequently, physical disabilities are subdivided into two categories: health impairments and orthopedic impairments. Health impairments were discussed in Chapter 6; this chapter will focus on physical disabilities which are orthopedic in nature. In general, the primary characteristics of individuals with physical handicaps involve a difficulty of movement and/or absence of or lack of use of particular parts of the body. Additionally, most physical handicaps are quite visible to observers. In other words, you would be more likely to notice visible differences of people with physical disabilities than you would be when observing individuals with other disabilities (e.g., learning disabilities, hearing impairments). Another commonality of physical disabilities is that all are medically diagnosed and require some type of medical intervention.

Although these are three major features of individuals with physical handicaps, there are many different characteristics as well as etiologies of specific disabilities. Definitions of some frequently encountered physical disabilities will follow.

Determining the prevalence of individuals is difficult due to the nature of the impairments and classification systems. One classification system may include health impaired individuals as physically disabled, another may not. Prevalence figures are derived primarily from medical, vocational, and educational data. Some people with physical disabilities require no services, or require services at one time and not another. Prevalence data of each frequently encountered physical disability are included within the discussion of definitions and causes.

Cerebral Palsy

Cerebral palsy is a disorder of posture (ability to stay still) and movement (ability to move) caused by damage to the brain. A coordination of posture and movement is necessary in order for fluid mobility to occur. Cerebral palsy refers to a group of movement difficulties, rather than a single disorder. There are six major types of cerebral palsy: spasticity, athetosis, ataxia, rigidity, tremor, and mixed. Each of these types of cerebral palsy will result in different movement patterns in the person. The brain damage may occur before, during, or after birth, usually in infancy (Fraser & Hensinger, 1983). There are many causes of brain damage which result in cerebral palsy. Infections (maternal, fetal, or child), lack of oxygen, and accidents are a few things which can result in cerebral palsy. Estimated prevalence figures range from 1 to 6 per 1,000 live births (Mysak, 1986).

Limb Deficiencies

Limb deficiencies, or loss of one or more limbs, may be present at birth (congenital) or may occur later in life (acquired). Congenital limb deficiencies occur for several reasons; the causes of many of which are currently not known. During approximately the first month of embryonic development, arm and leg buds appear and later develop into arms and hands, legs and feet. Some interference occurs which stops the development in children born with congenital limb deficiencies.

Acquired limb deficiencies result most frequently from accidents and required surgical procedures for the management of health conditions (e.g., cancer). Acquired limb deficiencies occur more frequently in adults than in children. Prevalence data of limb deficiencies have been reported to range from 1.7 to 8.6 per 1,000 people (Hardman, Drew, Egan, & Wolf, 1990).

Multiple Sclerosis

Multiple sclerosis is a progressive disease of the central nervous system (brain, brain stem, and spinal cord) which results in muscle weakness, spasticity, and balance difficulties. Speech and hearing disorders may also occur (Fraser & Hensinger, 1983; LaPointe, 1986). Multiple sclerosis most frequently occurs in adults, and remissions (periodic absences of the disease) are common. The cause of multiple sclerosis is unknown, however it is currently believed that genetic factors may be involved. Prevalence estimates of multiple sclerosis range from 1 in 2,000 to 1 in 10,000 (Berkow, 1982).

Muscular Dystrophy

Muscular dystrophy is a group of inherited conditions which results in progressive muscular wasting. The four major types of muscular dystrophy are Duchenne, facioscapulohumeral, limb-girdle, and myotonic muscular dystrophy (Bauer & Shea, 1989). The dystrophies differ in age at onset, muscle groups involved, prognoses, severity, and male/female incidence. A prevalence figure of individuals with muscular dystrophy has been reported to be 0.14 per 1,000 people (Hardman et al., 1990).

Spina Bifida

Spina bifida is a congenital disorder caused by a failure of the spinal cord to develop appropriately prenatally. There are two major types of spina bifida; spina bifida occulta and spina bifida cystica. Spina bifida occulta is a malformation of the spinal cord which does not typically result in any physical handicap. In fact, most people who have spina bifida occulta do not know about it unless they have an x-ray. The more severe type of spina bifida is spina bifida cystica, of which there are two forms. Meningocele occurs when an infant is born with a sac on his/her back containing spinal fluid. Myelomeningocele occurs when an infant is born with a covered (by skin or tissue) or uncovered sac containing spinal fluid and nerve tissue. Paralysis or partial paralysis of certain body parts occurs in the person with myelomeningocele, and often additional disabilities are present.

The cause of spina bifida cystica is unknown, although there are several theories. The spinal cord is developed very early in the pregnancy (by the end of the first month) and genetic and environmental factors may combine as a cause. A prevalence figure of spina bifida has been reported to be 3 of every 1,000 live births (Bauer & Shea, 1989).

Spinal Cord Injuries

Spinal cord injuries occur whenever the spinal cord is traumatized or partially or totally severed. Spinal cord injuries are primarily caused by accidents such as diving, car accidents, and sports injuries, although some may be caused by disease. Frequently the person with a spinal cord injury will evidence partial or total paralysis of part of the body.

Spinal cord injuries are most common in males, and most frequently occur during the late teens and twenties (DeJong, 1984; LaPointe, 1986). A prevalence figure of 3 for every 100,000 individuals has been reported (Hardman et al., 1990).

Characteristics

As mentioned, due to the nature of the many physical disabilities, individuals vary greatly. Many of you know some people with physical disabilities. A common mistake some persons make is to assume that all individuals with physical disabilities are alike and share the same characteristics. Obviously, this is incorrect. Major characteristics of people with specific disabilities will be discussed under the same subheadings presented in the previous section.

Cerebral Palsy

People with cerebral palsy will display many different movement characteristics. Individuals with spastic cerebral palsy will exhibit very stiff movements and high muscle tone. The person with athetosis will move in involuntary, jerky motions. Ataxia is displayed by a lack of coordination and balance. Rare forms of cerebral palsy are tremor (rhythmic involuntary movements) and rigidity (constant muscle stiffness).

Individuals with cerebral palsy may have involvement in the entire body or in selected parts. A person may have hemiplegia, or an involvement of one-half of the body (one side). Entire body involvement is known as quadriplegia, while paraplegia refers to involvement of the legs or lower half of the body. People with cerebral palsy are not paralyzed; their brain is unable to send correct movement messages to muscles by nerves.

People with cerebral palsy often have other disabilities in addition to their physical impairment. Approximately half of the population with cerebral palsy test as mentally retarded (Mysak, 1986). This may be attributed to several variables. Testing may be difficult for some people due to reduced ability to respond. Additionally, one of the major ways individuals learn is through experiences and many people with cerebral palsy have had fewer opportunities for experiences due to their physical involvement. Many people with cerebral palsy exhibit speech and language disorders (Mysak, 1986). They may demonstrate speech which is very difficult to understand, or they may be unable to speak. Visual and hearing disorders may also be present. Some people with cerebral palsy of "normal" intelligence exhibit difficulties in learning which are similar to those exhibited by learning disabled populations.

When discussing interaction skills, speech and language difficulties probably interfere most significantly. Some individuals with cerebral palsy are unable to speak and must communicate using alternative methods. Others may be difficult to understand due to the unintelligibility of their speech.

Cerebral palsy may be mild, moderate, or severe. The severity label is not based upon the location of body involvement, but most typically is based on considerations of a combination of degree of mobility and independence in performing activities of daily living. Individuals with mild cerebral palsy are generally able to ambulate without assistance and/or are independent in personal daily living skills.

People with moderate cerebral palsy are able to ambulate with assistance and require some assistance in performing daily living skills. Individuals with severe cerebral palsy are unable to ambulate and require a great deal of assistance in daily living activities.

Limb Deficiencies

People with limb deficiencies, in general, learn like all other individuals. Their behavior may be very similar to other non-handicapped persons, with the primary exception of compensatory actions. A person with no arms, for example may eat, write, brush his/her hair with his/her feet. Use of the feet may be preferred by the individual to use of an artificial arm (prosthesis). Interaction skills of the person may differ from those skills of a non-handicapped persons; however, this is frequently due to inappropriate behaviors of unknowing persons. A person with a limb deficiency may feel uncomfortable around large numbers of novel persons, for example, because of stares received (Cassie, 1984).

People with limb deficiencies may be missing all or part of one to all four extremities (arms and legs). Determining severity of the condition depends not only on the number of extremities involved, but also on other variables such as which extremities are involved and the person's ability to compensate for the missing limbs. Many people born with limb deficiencies teach themselves, practically from birth, compensatory actions. Such individuals, even if missing three or four extremities, would be viewed as less severely disabled than a person who could not compensate for two missing limbs and was unable to perform some activities of daily living.

Multiple Sclerosis

Because the first symptoms of multiple sclerosis most frequently appear in late adolescence or early adulthood (DeJong, 1984; LaPointe, 1986), prior to this time, there are no overt differences between these individuals and non-handicapped persons. Some early symptoms of multiple sclerosis include paralysis or muscle weakness of an extremity, and visual difficulties such as dimness of vision or double vision (Berkow, 1982; Cassie, 1984).

As the effects of multiple sclerosis progress, individuals will typically experience frequent remissions and relapses for many years. Intervals between remission and reoccurrence become shorter and eventually permanent disability occurs. There is not a limited life span for most people with multiple sclerosis, but individuals who have an onset of the disease during middle age may face an earlier death (Berkow, 1982).

Multiple sclerosis can result in apathy, inattention, and a lack of judgement (Berkow, 1982), all of which can interfere with learning and interactions with others. Depression, euphoria, and large mood changes can also occur (Berkow, 1982). The person with speech and/or hearing involvement may be difficult to understand or may have difficulty in understanding others (LaPointe, 1986).

Most often, the mildest disabilities are present during remissions and during initial occurrences of the disorder. The disability becomes more severe throughout subsequent relapses in the years following initial diagnosis (LaPointe, 1986).

Muscular Dystrophy

Duchenne, the most common and most severe type of muscular dystrophy, occurs primarily in males as 90% of the time it is a sex-linked disorder. This means that most cases of Duchenne involve a carrier mother who passes the abnormal x chromosome to her son. It is most commonly diagnosed during the preschool years and follows a progressive course. Initial symptoms include awkward movements, toe-walking, and pseudohypertrophy (false enlargement) of the calf muscles. These muscles appear to be getting larger, but actually muscle tissue is turning to fatty tissue which increases the mass. Atrophy, or a wasting away, of the tissue later occurs. Most individuals with Duchenne muscular dystrophy are in wheelchairs by the teen years with death most typically resulting by the late twenties or early thirties.

Facioscapulohumeral, limb-girdle, and myotonic muscular dystrophies are most commonly diagnosed during adolescence or adulthood (Bauer & Shea, 1989). Facioscapulohumeral muscular dystrophy affects the muscles in the face, shoulder and upper arms. Limb-girdle muscular dystrophy is present in the shoulder or pelvic girdle and affects the arms and/or legs. Myotonic muscular dystrophy is usually evidenced by weakness in the face, hands, or feet. These types are less severe than Duchenne.

Individuals with Duchenne muscular dystrophy often test intellectually lower than would be expected. Additionally, as the body becomes weaker, endurance becomes a problem in learning. Emotional issues frequently surface as the individual gains in understanding of the nature of the disorder.

Spina Bifida

The individual with myelomeningocele, a form of spina bifida cystica, generally is paralyzed and lacks sensation at the point of the sac and below. There are often accompanying disabilities present such as hydrocephalus (an increase in fluid produced in the brain) and bowel and bladder incontinence. These persons frequently have IQ scores at the mildly mentally retarded to low average level (Hardman, et. al., 1990). Learning difficulties are most often present in people with accompanying hydrocephalus.

An individual with meningocele, a milder form of spina bifida would experience much less severe physical disabilities. Frequently, a weakening of the lower extremities or feet is the only physical involvement. Individuals with meningocele are also less likely to experience additional disabilities.

Spinal Cord Injuries

The physical effects of a spinal cord injury depend on two major factors; the amount of damage to the spinal cord and the location of the damage. If the spinal cord is completely severed, complete paralysis occurs to a portion of the body. Usually there is a partial severing or damage due to swelling and bleeding of the spinal cord following trauma. This results in partial paralysis and a loss of sensation (feeling). The location of the damage/injury is important because in general it is assumed that the parts of the body below that point are affected. This may include those systems responsible for respiration, bowel and bladder control, and ambulation.

The person with a spinal cord injury learns like all others. He/she may need an alternative way of demonstrating ability and knowledge, but the process of learning remains intact. Functions previously possessed and which were lost may influence interactions with others. For example, a person may be unable to feed him/herself and may, therefore, choose not to eat in public places so that observers won't view the assistance being given for feeding.

Intervention

There are many medical techniques used today to both detect physical disabilities early and to prevent them from occurring. Early detection allows for preventive treatment or for intervention to reduce the effects of the disability.

Cerebral Palsy

Early detection of conditions which can lead to cerebral palsy for prevention is critical. Diagnosis of infections such as meningitis, which may result in cerebral palsy, can be more easily treated if detected early. Fetal monitoring during pregnancy provides the obstetrician with information regarding fetal distress which is a common indication of lack of oxygen.

Early intervention of children with cerebral palsy provides them with adapted opportunities for experiences which contribute to learning. Early intervention programs are provided by hospitals, public schools, and organizations such as United Cerebral Palsy. Early intervention assists in preventing other problems from occurring due to inappropriate muscle tone. For example, shortening of muscles can be a problem which may occur if intervention is not provided (Peterson, 1987).

Physical and occupational therapy are frequently needed services for the person with cerebral palsy. Goals include the prevention of secondary problems as well as increasing the person's functional movement abilities (Peterson, 1987). Gross and fine motor skills are addressed to develop and/or improve ambulation and daily living skills. Orthotics, supportive and assistive devices such as braces and splints, are frequently used by people with cerebral palsy. Orthotics allow individuals with cerebral palsy better use of body parts and facilitate greater independence.

Many people with cerebral palsy need speech-language therapy to improve their communication skills (Mysak, 1986). Goals of speech-language therapy may include enhancing articulation, improving voice, and learning how to use augmentative communication devices. Special education services may be necessary to teach the person alternative methods of responding and specific academic skills. For the person with cerebral palsy who has additional disabilities, more intensive special education services will most likely be required.

Limb Deficiencies

Congenital limb deficiencies may appear on an ultrasound for early detection. There is no preventive technique for congenital limb deficiencies. Medical advances occurring in cancer management have led to some prevention of limb deficiencies due to surgical removal (e.g., a cancerous bone removed and replaced with a rod-like material in lieu of removing the limb. Obviously, early detection of the malignancy is the key, as this becomes more difficult to do if it has metastasized or spread.

Many people with limb deficiencies use prostheses (artificial limbs). These have, over the years, become more functional and more cosmetic. Prostheses now look more like the missing limb in color, shape, and size. Upper extremity prostheses allow a person to grasp and release objects more functionally. Some very young children with congenital limb deficiencies are not fitted with prostheses until they are older and can manipulate them with greater ease (Peterson, 1987). Physical and occupational therapy are typically required to teach the person with a limb deficiency how to walk with or use prostheses. Special education may also be necessary, in combination with occupational therapy, to teach alternative ways of performing activities of daily living. Counseling may be needed, especially for a person with an acquired limb deficiency, to adapt to the loss and the changes in his/her abilities.

Multiple Sclerosis

Early identification of multiple sclerosis is important so that medical treatment can begin. Early identification is difficult in many cases, because symptoms can be caused by other disorders (Berkow, 1982, Cassie, 1984). Drugs such as prednisone are prescribed as treatment; however, there is currently no cure (Berkow, 1982). Physical and occupational therapy is often provided to assist the person in maintaining use of muscles for movement. Speech and hearing services may be necessary for the person with multiple sclerosis who has involvement in these areas (LaPointe, 1986). Counseling and support/information services from the National Multiple Sclerosis organization may be beneficial.

Muscular Dystrophy

There is currently no method of prevention of muscular dystrophy. Early identification of Duchenne muscular dystrophy is important in order to begin the physical and occupational therapy so critical to preservation of function. Goals of these therapies include maintenance and improvement of movement abilities, especially ambulation. When ambulation becomes impossible, therapy involves positioning (placing the person in the best body position for muscle tension and posture) and selecting appropriate wheelchairs and orthotic devices. Medical management involves treatment of respiratory infections which frequently occur due to heart and lung involvement and medical maintenance services. At this time, there is no medical cure for Duchenne muscular dystrophy, but research supported by the Muscular Dystrophy Association of America is constantly occurring. Special education services may be required for reasons including absences, fatigue which impacts on learning, and access to a curriculum which includes content other than academics. Counseling may be necessary for the person to deal with his/her limited lifespan.

Spina Bifida

Myelomeningocele occurs early in a pregnancy and can be detected prenatally. Early detection is very important for medical treatment, especially if hydrocephalus is present. Shunts (tubes placed in cavities in the brain which drain the excess fluid) have been inserted via fetal surgery and are usually one of the first treatments if done after birth so that the negative effects can be lessened. Medical treatment of the sac occurs very soon after birth. Most children born with spina bifida have part of the spine that is exposed. Without intervention, infections can rapidly occur (e.g., meningitis).

Once the immediate medical interventions have occurred, focus typically is placed on educational and therapy needs. Early intervention is important to allow this child, like the child with cerebral palsy, access to experiences (Peterson, 1987). Alternative forms of mobility and use of those forms will also be emphasized during early intervention programs.

The person with myelomeningocele will most likely require physical and occupational therapy. These services will focus on developing mobility skills and abilities to perform daily living skills. The use of orthotics is common for individuals with myelomeningocele. Special education may be necessary, especially for the person who has accompanying hydrocephalus, to provide a comprehensive curriculum for these students. Medical services are often necessary for managing orthopedic difficulties and bowel/bladder control. Most children with myelomeningocele are cognitively able to catheterize themselves (drain urine from the bladder using a small catheter at specific times during the day) during the elementary school years. The person with accompanying hydrocephalus will need medical services to monitor the effectiveness of the shunt and replace the shunt if necessary.

Spinal Cord Injuries

Prevention of spinal cord injuries requires prevention of accidents. Care should be taken when diving, sports safety rules should be followed, and automobiles driven safely. Obviously, there are some injuries which are not preventable. Immediate diagnosis and treatment are critical after a spinal cord injury. Immobilization of the person is imperative to prevent movement and further damage. Surgical procedures are usually delayed until treatments are provided to decrease the swelling and bleeding of the spinal cord. Trauma to the spinal cord must be stabilized before physical and occupational therapy can be provided.

Physical and occupational therapy are frequently required to teach the individual how to use remaining muscles and residual muscles for function. Positioning, mobility, use of orthotics, and self-care skills are frequently the focus of physical and occupational therapy. Special education services may be required in the form of adapted physical education or to provide instruction in use of alternative modes of responding in regular classes. Counseling may be necessary to assist the person with his/her loss of function. As with myelomeningocele, medical services may be necessary due to orthopedic difficulties, lack of bowel/bladder control, and even body temperature regulation.

Individuals with all of the above disabilities will frequently require intervention in the use of adapted devices. Specialists from all areas work together to provide this instruction. The goals of all services need to be coordinated with family and individual input so that integration will occur.

Technology

Technological advances have had a major impact on the lives of many people with physical disabilities. Technology allows people, with very limited movement, the ability to control many materials in their environment. Switches can be connected to lights, televisions, computers, and many other things. Current technology has provided information so that these switches can be activated by any part of the body over which the person has control. Eyebrow switches, sound-control switches, and pneumatic (sip and puff) switches are a few examples of how technology has changed the life of the person with physical disabilities.

Electronic augmentative communication devices have been improved significantly in recent years. Technology has advanced so that systems with voice outputs sound more like voices than like computers as they did in the past. Devices are more portable and also are more frequently interfaced with computers to provide greater use.

Expectations

Motoric abilities of individuals with physical handicaps range from awkward movements to total paralysis. Medical research has provided a great deal of information about reasonable expectations for many of the disabilities. Some are quite predictable (spinal cord injury) while others are very unpredictable (multiple sclerosis).

Cognitive abilities in most individuals with physical disabilities are similar to those of non-handicapped persons. Persons may have difficulty in expressing or demonstrating knowledge, but learn using many of the same strategies as do their nonhandicapped peers. Cognitive abilities of persons with physical disabilities range from a gifted (Whitmore & Maker, 1985) to a mentally retarded level. Academic achievement also ranges from high achievement to below average achievement. A difficulty in school and in the community occurs when individuals view the physical involvement as more important than the mental abilities (Whitmore & Maker, 1985). Physically disabled students capable of average achievement should receive most of their education in a regular class with modifications made for the physical differences (Cassie, 1984; Whitmore & Maker, 1985).

In adulthood, non-handicapped persons make choices and decisions regarding lifestyle, career paths, marriage/family issues, and sexuality. It is important for people with physical disabilities to also make these choices and decisions. Vocational rehabilitation services may be necessary to provide assistance for individuals in receiving job training or retraining, college educations, and placement services (Cassie, 1984; Whitmore & Maker, 1985). The presence of a physical disability does not preclude the completion of postsecondary education programs, and many people with these disabilities complete college, graduate school, vocational training programs and other advanced training.

Adult independent living is frequently an issue for people with physical disabilities. Some live alone, with friends, or spouses with no assistance. Other individuals may need little assistance (e.g., driver) from others. There will be some people who require a great deal of assistance from others due to physical limitations (e.g., person with high spinal cord injury who cannot feed self and has a catheter). Services may be necessary to allow the more dependent person access to greater independent living.

During adolescence and adulthood, social and sexual issues typically are present. The person with a physical disability may have a distorted body image and may have difficulty positioning for sexual activities. However, most physiological sexual responses remain intact, even for individuals with spinal cord injuries (Griffith, 1984). Additionally, sexual feelings do not change as the result of a physical disability (Griffith, 1984).

Interactions

In many ways, interactions with people with physical disabilities will be the same as interactions with all other people. It is important to remember that the person with physical disabilities is a person first. This is not to suggest that the physical disability is not a part of the person, instead it is an attempt to encourage a view of physical disabilities as a part, and not the whole. This view as a person also encourages thoughts of individuality. All people are not the same. Therefore, some of the rules of etiquette which are suggested may not be accepted by all people with physical disabilities.

Interacting with a person with physical disabilities is most successful when you allow yourself to look beyond the disability. In other words, begin your interaction

PHYSICALLY DISABLED INDIVIDUALS

as you would with any other person. Staring, or "looking a person up and down," is obviously inappropriate. This really does not give you any information and is disliked intensely by most people with physical disabilities. If you have questions, ask. Ask your questions to the person with physical disabilities (unless a young child, perhaps), and not to others who are with the person. Although some individuals may not be comfortable when this occurs, you can generally tell if this is so. If so, say, "Thank you," and stop. This is also true when you are with children. Children tend to be very inquisitive and may ask, "What's wrong with that lady/man/?" Instead of silencing the child, have the child ask the person (appropriately, of course). This leads to education and can open the door to understanding.

The content of your questions and comments should also be appropriate. Do not assume total disability unless you have some evidence that this is fact. A young woman who has cerebral palsy and is in a motorized wheelchair was once approached by a stranger in a mall. The man came up to her and said, "You know, you should go over to the vocational school and make something of yourself." She is a professor of speech-language pathology at a college. Obviously, this comment was based on a lack of knowledge. Don't make that same mistake yourself.

Individuals with physical handicaps do not require assistance in performing all motor acts. Ask the person about the assistance needed or desired. Do not automatically open doors, push wheelchairs, or lift people. For example, it may be easier to maneuver a motorized wheelchair around a curve by pressing against a door with feet. Opening the door in this instance actually hinders the person instead of helping. When providing assistance it is best to ask the person, "How may I help you?" You will then know the most appropriate method of providing assistance and the type of assistance desired or needed.

You may have to adapt your interaction based upon the communication abilities of the person. Some individuals with cerebral palsy use augmentative communication devices. These devices may be difficult to understand or may be time consuming. Display patience and try not to finish the person's statement.

Do not talk about the person with physical disabilities to others as if the person is unable to hear or respond. Some people assume individuals in wheelchairs are deaf or unable to understand what is said around them. Do not assume that a person with a physical disability is unable to perform all motor tasks. Many people with physical disabilities can dance, skate, swim, and do other forms of rather rigorous activities. Base judgements on facts and knowledge, not stereotypes.

Many people with physical disabilities will tell you if your interactions and/or comments are inappropriate. They may tell you this using verbal or nonverbal messages. Listen to them.

Summary

As you can see, there are many different types of physical disabilities. Each of these disabilities results in a variety of characteristics. At this time, more than any other, society has demonstrated a commitment to prevention of these disabilities and the provision of interventions for people with physical disabilities. Technology has enabled severely physically disabled persons to exert control over their environment and allowed them to become more independent.

Individuals with physical disabilities can, and do, make significant contributions to this society. Most people with physical disabilities would like greater understanding from others and are willing to educate others about their physical differences. In order for this to occur, however, you have to display a desire to learn. You have demonstrated this by reading this text. Next you need to interact directly with physically disabled people. You can learn a great deal from them.

References

Bauer, A. M., & Shea, T. M. (1989). *Teaching exceptional students in your classroom.* Boston: Allyn & Bacon.

Berkow, R. (Ed.). (1982). *The Merck manual of diagnosis and therapy.* Rahway, NJ: Merck Sharp and Dohme Research Laboratory.

Cassie, D. (1984). *So who's perfect: People with physical differences tell their own stories.* Scottdale, PA: Herald Press.

DeJong, G. (1984). Independent living: From social movement to analytic paradigm. In R. Marinelli & A. Dell Orto (Eds.), *The psychological and social impact of physical disability.* New York: Springer.

Fraser, B. A., & Hensinger, R. N. (1983). *Managing physical handicaps.* Baltimore: Paul H. Brookes.

Griffith, E. (1984). Sexual dysfunctions associated with physical disabilities. In R. Marinelli & A. Dell Orto (Eds.), *The psychological and social impact of physical disability*. New York: Springer Publishing Co.

Hardman, M. L., Drew, C. J., Egan M. W., & Wolf, B. (1990). *Human exceptionality*. Needham Heights, Mass: Allyn and Bacon.

La Pointe, L. L. (1986). Neurogenic disorders of speech. In G. Shames & E. Wiig (Eds.), *Human communication disorders (2nd ed.)*. Columbus, Ohio: Charles E. Merrill.

Mysak, E. D. (1986). Cerebral Palsy. In G. Shames & E. Wiig (Eds.), *Human communication disorders (2nd ed.)*. Columbus, OH: Charles E. Merrill.

Peterson, N. L. (1987). *Early intervention for handicapped and at-risk children: An introduction to early childhood special education*. Denver: Love.

Whitmore, J. R., & Maker, C. J. (1985). *Intellectual giftedness in disabled persons*. Rockville, MD: Aspen.

Suggested Readings

Dickey, R., & Shealey, S. H. (1987). Using technology to control the environment. *The American Journal of Occupational Therapy, 41*, 717-721.

Frank, G. (1988). Beyond stigma: Visibility and self-empowerment of persons with congenital limb deficiencies. *Journal of Social Issues, 44*, 95-115.

Hahn, H. (1988). The politics of physical differences: Disability and discrimination. *Journal of Social Issues, 44*, 39-47.

Killilea, M. (1952). *Karen*. Pinebrook, NJ: Dell.

McKinnon, S. (1990). Born on the fourth of July--another man's view. *Accent on Living,* Fall, 30-31.

Schleichkorn, J. (1983). *Coping with cerebral palsy: Answers to questions parents often ask.* Austin, TX: PRO-ED.

Sutherland, A. T. (1984). *Disabled we stand.* Cambridge, MA: Brookline Books.

Waller, S. (1981). *Circle of hope.* New York: M. Evans.

Weis, R. (1988). Disabled communication: The eyes have it. *Science News, 134,* 122.

Exploration

Individual Activities

1. There are many people who have difficulty performing tasks that are usually taken for granted. This activity will give you a perspective on how these people feel and deal with these tasks. Here is what you have to do. Hold one arm behind your back and try to do the following activities: tie your shoes, open a can or a bottle, get dressed, eat something, and play a sport that normally requires two hands. Now, remember, only one hand and no cheating.

   Describe how well you did. Also describe the difficulties you encountered.

   _____
   _____
   _____

2. Assume that you are confined to a wheelchair and about to start your first day in college. But wait. Your college campus is not set up for wheelchairs. How do you feel?

   _____
   _____

   List some of the things that may be obstacles for you.

   _____   _____
   _____   _____
   _____   _____
   _____   _____
   _____   _____

Group Activities

1. As a class, take a trip to the local mall or to your college's student union. Today, you will be physically handicapped. What is that you say? You don't feel like a handicapped person? Well, do what is in store for you and you will. You are to interlock your fingers from both hands and place them on top of your head. Feel silly? Don't worry, everyone else is doing it also! The task assigned to you is to pair off in groups of two with only one person at a time acting as the disabled person. While disabled, have your partner feed you and wash your face. Also, play a video game, bowl, or play some other type of game. As you walk around the mall or union, open doors for yourself and be as independent as possible.

   Reactions:

   _____
   _____
   _____

2. A town meeting is being called to order and your class is the community. Five people need to be appointed to the town council to weigh the information presented to them by the community; namely the rest of the class. The issue of concern in your town is a petition being circulated to keep physically disabled students out of the local public schools. Divide the class into sides; one to argue for these students to be given the right to attend the school and the other side to argue against the action. The town council will be the decision-making body. Before the meeting begins take 5 to 10 minutes and brainstorm ideas supporting your side of the issue. Allow time for opening comments, the actual arguments, rebuttals, and closing comments. After the town council members have made a decision on how they will vote, ask for their reasons.

   Reactions:

   _____
   _____
   _____

Reaction Paper 7.1

You are a world famous inventor and one day you see a little child in a wheelchair. This sight affects you quite deeply and at this moment you decide to dedicate your life to inventing items that will be of use to physically disabled people of all ages. Identify two or three inventions you will create and how they will help physically disabled people.

Continue on back if needed.

Reaction Paper 7.2

Have you ever felt left out? When you were younger, possibly even now, were you ever the last one picked to play a sport? Did people ever laugh at your abilities while you tried to do something such as dancing, reading, drawing, or music? Using your own experiences discuss how a physically disabled person might feel when unable to do a specific task well.

Continue on back if needed.

Notes

CHAPTER 8

PERSONS WHO ARE MENTALLY RETARDED

James McAfee

Introduction

What is mental retardation? If you were to ask 100 people, you would hear nearly 100 different definitions. However, most people would indicate a belief that mentally retarded persons are in some way intellectually limited. Indeed, intellectual limitation is the cornerstone of most definitions of mental retardation, but the concept of mental retardation is much more complex. Is an adult who reads at a fourth grade level mentally retarded? What about a ten year old who just can't seem to master the multiplication tables or the father who can't assemble his child's Christmas toys? All exhibit symptoms of intellectual limitation. However, in no case do we have sufficient information to make a determination of mental retardation.

There are many definitions of mental retardation: medical, legal, psychological, educational, and sociological. Definitions also vary geographically, but the definition offered by the American Association on Mental Retardation (AAMR) (Grossman, 1983) comes closest to being universally accepted, at least in North America. The widespread acceptance of this definition is due to the fact that it represents the input of many disciplines--education, law, medicine, psychology, and sociology. Other organizations use definitions that are essentially variations of the AAMR definition. According to the AAMR, mental retardation is "significantly subaverage general intellectual functioning existing concurrently with deficits in adaptive behavior and manifested during the developmental period" (Grossman, 1983, p. 1). Thus, the AAMR definition includes three critical elements: (a) significantly subaverage general intellectual functioning, (b) deficits in adaptive behavior, and (3) the developmental period.

Significantly subaverage general intellectual functioning refers to performance on an individual test of intelligence. A person is generally considered to be significantly subaverage if his/her score is 70 or below. As IQ tests are not perfectly reliable, individual scores do change.

Deficits in adaptive behavior are measured by instruments such as the AAMD Adaptive Behavior Scale (Nihira, Foster, Shellhaas, & Leland, 1969). A person with adaptive behavior deficits appears to be immature, dependent, or irresponsible. He or she has difficulty meeting the demands of a peer group and sociocultural expectations.

Intellectual and adaptive behavior deficits must appear during the developmental years (conception to 18) to be identified as characteristics of mental retardation. Therefore, an adult with Alzheimer's disease or a 40 year old who suffers head trauma are not considered to be mentally retarded although they might have impaired intellectual functioning and poor adaptive behavior.

Prevalence

Researchers estimate that one to three percent of the population is mentally retarded. Estimates vary because of different definitions and different population bases studied. In a school-aged population, the prevalence of mental retardation is likely to be close to three percent because the intellectual challenges presented by academic tasks lead to identification. Whereas, in a preschool population, developmental variability is often not recognized unless the deviation is great. Therefore, in schools, children with mild intellectual handicaps are apt to be evaluated and identified but in the preschool age range, only those with severe and overt problems will bring attention to themselves. Consistent prevalence figures are not available because no widespread census exists and different entities (states or agencies) use different criteria. For example, some states use an IQ cutoff of 70; others use a cutoff of 75.

Causation

The American Association on Mental Retardation (Grossman, 1983) identified ten categories of causation. They are:

Infection/intoxication. Prenatal and postnatal infections and intoxications are included in this category. Examples are congenital rubella, syphilis, viral and bacterial infections, lead poisoning, maternal tobacco use, cocaine poisoning, and fetal alcohol syndrome.

Trauma. This category includes prenatal, perinatal, and postnatal head injury and hypoxia (lack of oxygen).

Diseases of metabolism. Among the conditions included here are galactosemia, hypoglycemia, phenylketonuria (PKU), thyroid dysfunction, and postnatal failure to thrive.

Gross brain disease. Neurofibromatosis, tumors, Huntington's disease, and cerebrovascular diseases are included in this category.

Unknown prenatal influences. This category includes a host of physical malformations. The origins of these conditions are unknown, but the conditions exist at birth and include microcephaly (small head), craniostenosis (ossification of cranial sutures), and hydrocephaly.

Chromosomal anomalies. Down syndrome (formerly called mongolism) is the most commonly known condition in this category. Among the other anomalies are Turner syndrome and triple X syndrome.

Other prenatal conditions. Low birthweight, fetal malnutrition, high birthweight, and maternal nutritional disorders appear in this category.

Psychiatric disorders. This category includes retardation that follows any psychiatric disorder.

Environmental influences. Retardation resulting from psychosocial disadvantage and sensory deprivation are included in this category.

Other. This category includes retardation resulting from sensory defects and unknown etiology.

Mental retardation is attributed to the last two categories in more than 75 percent of the cases. In most of these cases, professionals cannot identify a specific cause.

Characteristics

The two most commonly used systems for classifying severity are those used by educators and the American Association on Mental Retardation. Generally, educators utilize a three-tier system: (a) educable--individuals with IQs between 51 and 70, (b) trainable--individuals with IQs between 21 and 50, and (c) custodial or severe--individuals with IQs below 20 (Drew, Hardman, & Logan, 1988). The AAMR system includes four levels: (a) mild--individuals with IQs between 56 and 70, (b) moderate--individuals with IQs between 41 and 55, (c) severe--individuals with IQs between 26 and 40, and (d) profound--individuals with IQs below 25 (Grossman, 1983).

Because of the wide range of intellectual functioning among persons with mental retardation, any discussion of characteristics must proceed from the level of severity. In addition, you should remember that, except for the limits associated with below normal intelligence, the variability of human characteristics among persons with mental retardation is as great as it is among persons of normal intelligence (IQ 85-115). It is inappropriate to say that persons with mental retardation possess certain characteristics but rather that these characteristics are apparent more often in persons with mental retardation than in persons who are not mentally retarded.

Physical Characteristics

Most persons who are mentally retarded do not differ in physical appearance from their non-retarded peers. However, a large percentage have some secondary disability (e.g., vision, hearing, motor) (Drew, Hardman, & Logan, 1988). Physical abnormalities are more likely to occur and be severe as the level of retardation becomes more severe. More than 75 percent of persons with mental retardation do not show any sign of brain damage. Members of this group (known as cultural-familial retardation) most often do not exhibit the abnormalities associated with conditions such as Down syndrome or hydrocephaly stereotyped in popular media (e.g., misshapen heads and/or protruding tongues). On the other hand, most mentally retarded persons do exhibit delayed development of motor skills and, in most cases, motor development (e.g., balance, locomotion, coordination, dexterity) remains lower than normal at maturity.

Persons with mental retardation are more likely than non-retarded peers to have conditions such as thyroid dysfunction, diabetes, cardiac abnormalities, and respiratory problems (Drew et al., 1988). In addition, cerebral palsy, epilepsy, visual and hearing impairments, and speech defects are more evident among persons with mental retardation than non-retarded persons. Specifically, about 50 percent of persons with cerebral palsy are mentally retarded; mentally retarded persons are 40 times more likely to have seizures than non-retarded persons; more than 25 percent of mentally retarded persons have a significant hearing loss; and 50 percent of persons with moderate to severe retardation exhibit speech defects. Speech defects are apparent in 8 to 26 percent of persons whose retardation is mild (Westling, 1986).

Learning Characteristics

Do persons with mental retardation learn differently than others? Obviously, there are quantitative differences. Persons with mental retardation learn at a lower rate and they experience lower overall attainment than their non-retarded peers. Interestingly, Fisher and Zeaman (1970) found that while mental age reaches a plateau for most people beginning at age 16-18, for persons with severe/profound retardation the plateau is not reached until age 35 and for persons with moderate/mild retardation, not until age 25. These data reinforce the notion that persons who are mentally retarded benefit from educational programs offered during their late adolescent and adult years.

While the quantitative learning differences are obvious, some researchers have attempted to identify more elusive qualitative differences. Some researchers have concluded that persons with mental retardation learn slowly because they don't approach learning in an efficient manner. For example, most people faced with a long list of words to memorize will organize the list in some meaningful way (e.g., alphabetically or by parts of speech) and then break the list down into manageable chunks. Persons with mental retardation will attempt to learn the list as it is presented without any organization or system. Other researchers have concluded that mentally retarded persons are more rigid in their learning. They have difficulty switching from one task to another and they may continue to do things incorrectly even when they have repeatedly failed by that method (Kreitler, Zigler, & Kreitler, 1990).

Most children learn a great deal from imitating the actions of others. Children also learn from situations where they are not specifically directed to learn (e.g., games). There is evidence that persons with mental retardation do not learn efficiently through imitation or in unstructured situations (Mercer & Algozzine, 1977; Mercer & Snell, 1977).

It is apparent that persons with mental retardation do not learn with the same kind of efficiency and organization as others. It seems that, in addition to learning more slowly, persons with mental retardation do not apply appropriate strategies with consistency and logic.

Personality/Social Characteristics

The personalities of persons with mental retardation are at least as variable as those of other persons. All personality types are represented among persons with retardation, but many researchers have attempted to determine if any personality characteristics occur with greater frequency among those who are mentally retarded. Several researchers have arrived at some general conclusions, but it is important to recognize that there is no "retarded personality type."

Persons who are mentally retarded are more concerned about avoiding failure and less likely to strive for success. Thus, they may be hesitant to try new activities. Persons who are mentally retarded are more likely to look to others for cues on how to behave. Rather than thinking about how they should behave in a given situation, they will often copy the actions of others (Whitman, 1990); they become followers.

Bizarre and abnormal behaviors occur at a higher rate among persons with mental retardation than among the non-retarded population (Beier, 1964) with the most severe disorders occurring most frequently among persons who are profoundly retarded. Behavior patterns such as repetitive rocking, finger twirling, and other motions are known as stereotypical behaviors and occur frequently among persons with profound retardation. Self-injurious behaviors (e.g., biting and scratching oneself, eye gouging) occur most commonly among persons who are profoundly retarded; especially those who are institutionalized. Lack of stimulation may explain the higher rate of self-injurious behaviors among those in institutions.

There are no characteristics that are associated exclusively with mental retardation nor are there any characteristics that are common to all people who are mentally retarded. Therefore, there is no one correct way to educate persons who are mentally retarded or to help them live meaningful and productive adult lives.

Intervention

Generally, persons whose retardation is most severe require a wider array of more intense services than those with mild retardation. Services may be preventive or therapeutic and include nutritional programs, medical interventions, physical therapy, early stimulation and education, parent training, speech therapy, special education, psychological counseling, vocational training, and independent living training.

Prevention

Some cases of mental retardation are preventable through medical treatment or early education. Medical intervention can take three forms: screening for risk, removal of toxic/traumatic agents, and direct treatment. Screening helps prospective parents determine if they are at high risk of producing children with mental retardation or if a child who has been conceived has a condition associated with mental retardation. For example, testing prospective parents for Rh compatibility will allow them to make an informed decision about parenting in which they understand the risk. Similarly, other conditions for which a parent may be a genetic carrier (e.g., Tay-Sachs--a genetically transmitted condition found mostly among Jewish families) can be identified by preconception screening. Medical technology has progressed to the point that prenatal screening through amniocentesis (using a needle to obtain fluid from the amniotic sac) and fetoscopy (using a small flexible scope to examine the fetus in the womb) allows physicians to identify some conditions in fetuses. For a very few conditions, in utero surgery is possible. However, for most conditions current technology only allows parents to prepare for the birth of a child with mental retardation or to consider a therapeutic abortion.

Screening is also applicable to newborns. Most of the damaging effects from PKU (a condition in which the child is unable to metabolize certain proteins) and hypothyroidism (an underactive thyroid) can be avoided if detected at birth. Unfortunately, the incidence of many conditions is so rare and screening so costly that it may not be economically feasible to use the technology.

Mental retardation is sometimes caused by toxins, trauma, or poor health care, and actions can be taken to reduce the incidence of mental retardation. Therapeutic preconception vaccinations have reduced the number of new cases of mental retardation (which is usually severe) due to maternal rubella. Pregnant women can avoid x-rays, alcohol, drugs, and smoking which are linked to mental retardation in newborns. Removal of lead from paint and protection from trauma through use of infant car seats and safely designed cribs and toys also reduce the incidence of mental retardation.

Medical personnel apply direct intervention to some conditions as a means of prevention or ameliorating the severity of retardation. Surgically implanted shunts are used to drain excess cerebral fluid for persons with hydrocephaly. Mothers with herpes deliver children through a caesarian section in order to avoid infection of the newborn. Finally, prenatal nutritional and health care counseling can prevent many cases of mental retardation especially among persons of low income.

Although prevention of mental retardation has reached a sophisticated stage, the actual incidence of mental retardation (i.e., number of new cases) continues to rise because medical advances that aid prevention have also allowed more individuals with retardation to survive.

Early Intervention

Among the most promising approaches to alleviating the symptoms of mental retardation are early intervention programs. Early intervention is so crucial that Congress enacted Public Law 99-457 to require and to help states develop programs to assist preschool children who are handicapped or who are at risk of becoming handicapped. Why would federal and state governments spend a great deal of money on early intervention? The answer is simple: early intervention is much more effective than intervention that occurs in later childhood. Every hour that a child spends in a well-executed infant or preschool program may result in the same gains as three to ten hours in later programs. For children whose intellectual retardation is mild, early intervention may prevent later school failure.

Early intervention programs date back at least 50 years to research begun in the late 1930s (Skeels, 1966). In 1939, Skeels and his associates found that mentally retarded children placed in the care of women specially trained to care for and stimulate the children showed marked improvements in functioning over children who were left in an orphanage. Twenty-five years later the differences remained. Those who had received the special attention were living normal lives and none were considered retarded. On the other hand, the mean educational achievement of those who remained in the orphanage was third grade. More recently, researchers such as Casto and Mastropieri (1986) declared that early sensorimotor stimulation of severely retarded children leads to improvements in functioning in all areas and that these improvements are usually sustained in later years.

Early intervention programs usually include both direct intervention with children and parent training because researchers realize that mental retardation has a profound effect on the way parents interact with their children. Mentally retarded children, especially those who are severely retarded, do not respond to parental attention in the same manner as non-retarded children. Parents of a mentally retarded child may interact less with the child because the child does not smile or show other signs of enjoyment. Early intervention practitioners teach parents how to stimulate their children and how to develop a stimulating environment that includes activities related to later school success (e.g., reading aloud to the child).

Finally, most effective early intervention programs include direct application of medical, health, education, and therapy services. For some children this may mean surgery to correct physical abnormalities or physical therapy to develop ambulation. For others, speech and language development are foci. Nutrition and health care are emphasized so that gains achieved through education and therapy are not eradicated because of illness or injury. Early childhood educators concentrate on development of sensorimotor, language, and self-help skills (e.g., dressing, feeding, toileting) because failure to develop these skills at an early age will prevent development of higher level skills and also negatively influence acceptance of the child by other children and adults.

Education and Therapy Services

A variety of educational and therapy services is required by mentally retarded persons. The types and goals of services depend upon the individual's age, the degree of mental retardation, and individual characteristics (e.g., sensory impairment, gender, living arrangement).

For individuals with severe/profound mental retardation the major goals of education and therapy involve development of capacity to care for oneself. Special education services are aimed at self-help, self-care, communication, and occupational skills. In early childhood, goals include development of independent functioning to the maximum extent possible in feeding, dressing, hygiene, speaking, and listening. Generally, at this level, educators use an approach that involves breaking tasks into small steps (e.g., holding a spoon as a step in learning to self-feed), physical guidance (e.g., holding the child's hand while he/she manipulates the spoon), and reinforcement (e.g., praising the child or giving him/her a "treat" for holding the spoon correctly).

Severely/profoundly retarded children with accompanying physical handicaps receive physical therapy to improve muscle development and skills such as walking and manipulation of objects. Speech and language therapy is also critical to the development of young persons with severe/profound retardation. For some youngsters this may include the use of an augmentative device such as a communication board which is used for children who cannot acquire functional speaking skills.

For severely/profoundly retarded youngsters in middle childhood, educators and therapists maintain efforts in self-help, self-care, and communications and add an emphasis on social development. Thus, learning to interact appropriately becomes an additional focus. This includes recognition of rules and limits, roles, and responsibilities. Interactive play is important at this point.

In adolescence and adulthood, the array and focus of services required by persons with severe/profound mental retardation changes and broadens. While it is likely that language, self-help, and social skills continue to receive attention, other areas become increasingly important. These include development of appropriate social interactions, vocational skills, independent living ability, and survival academic skills such as recognizing warning words. Vocational training is aimed at development of good work habits, acceptance of supervision, specific work skills, and improvement in rate and quality of production. Independent living skills include mobility in the community, basic food preparation, and development of leisure interests.

You should remember that persons with profound retardation possess IQs of 25 or less. For many of these people, lifelong, continuous, and direct supervision is necessary. A small number may never learn to walk, talk, or interact effectively much less perform work for which they earn compensation. However, many severely/profoundly retarded persons do acquire effective communication, self-help, and vocational skills.

Persons who are moderately/mildly retarded are likely to need a broader array of skills because they may become independent or semi-independent as adults (Sedlak & Sedlak, 1985). Self-help, self-care, and communication skills receive emphasis in early childhood services. In addition, academic and preacademic skills are introduced including counting, recognition of the letters of the alphabet, and listening to stories. Because moderately/mildly retarded persons are likely to work and move about the community independently they must learn social skills such as talking to new acquaintances and eating etiquette. Speech and language development goals revolve around conversational skills and following oral instructions such as those one would receive from a work supervisor. Fewer moderately/mildly retarded children require physical therapy than those with severe retardation.

In later childhood, educators emphasize academic development, language, and social interaction. Instruction is focused on functional reading, math, and knowledge of the world (e.g., reading instructions, schedules, computing change, telling time). The array of services and goals broadens greatly. The moderately/mildly retarded adolescent or adult will need to continue academic development and also receive recreational services to develop leisure skills, counseling and instruction in human sexuality, vocational training to obtain and maintain employment, independent living training for the day when he/she is living alone, and genetic/parenting counseling so that he/she can make informed decisions about marriage and parenting. Thus, services are provided by special and regular educators (including those at a postsecondary level), counselors, vocational trainers, employers, social service workers, physicians, parents, recreational workers, and therapists.

During the past 20 years, professionals have learned the value of early intervention. Behavioral methods have succeeded in helping persons with mental retardation learn complex skills. More mentally retarded persons work in competitive employment today than ever before. This is due to greater emphasis on the scientific study of mental retardation.

Technological Advances

Technology associated with mental retardation reaches back many years. In the 1830s, Edouard Seguin, a French physician, developed some of the principles of instruction for persons with mental retardation that are still in use today (e.g., small systematic steps, sensorimotor stimulation). In 1934, researchers discovered the cause of PKU. This tradition of research and technological innovation continues today in both the medical and behavioral sciences. Medical research has resulted in the infancy of in utero surgery to repair conditions such as spina bifida (a condition where the spinal column does not fully close) and hydrocephaly before major damage is done. None of this would be possible without the development of microsurgical techniques and genetic and DNA research. Researchers have begun to understand the mechanisms through which Down syndrome occurs. Some believe that it will be possible through gene splicing and engineering to prevent or undo the effects of genetically transmitted conditions.

Although technological advances in the behavioral sciences are not as spectacular as those in medicine they have a more pervasive effect. A medical breakthrough in the treatment of Down syndrome will directly affect few persons with mental retardation but behavioral interventions that allow more effective instruction can be applied to many. One promising area of research is known as adaptability instruction (Mithaug, Martin, & Agran, 1987). Persons with mental retardation often encounter difficulty generalizing skills to different situations. For example, a mentally retarded individual may perform a job well under one supervisor but experience difficulty with the instructions given by another supervisor. Adaptability instruction involves teaching mentally retarded persons how to identify the critical elements of the task or environment so that they can perform under different conditions. The implications of this research are tremendous for those persons who are about to leave the relative predictability and security of special education for the more complex world of work.

High tech applications have found their way into services for persons with mental retardation. Nowhere is this more apparent than in communications. Many persons with mental retardation experience speech problems. Computer technology allows such individuals to respond and communicate needs by pointing to or touching symbols on a lap board or by using a voice synthesizer (Hogg & Sebba, 1987).

Expectations

Expected achievement for persons with mental retardation varies depending upon the degree of retardation. In addition, achievement is influenced by the presence of secondary handicaps (e.g., blindness, cerebral palsy), the type and length of intervention, and the age at which intervention is begun. These factors compounded with individual differences account for the diversity of achievement.

Persons with profound mental retardation usually achieve some basic skills in self-help (feeding, dressing, and hygiene). In addition, they may be able to perform basic repetitive tasks in a sheltered work setting. This would include sorting, matching, and perhaps simple assembly. They may learn to communicate personal needs and respond to questions and requests with short sentences.

Persons with severe mental retardation will generally achieve up to the level of a five-year-old. They are usually able to feed and clothe themselves, perform routine chores such as making sandwiches, and washing themselves. Language achievement will include participation in simple concrete conversations, expressing their needs and feelings, and responding to spoken instructions. Vocational attainment is likely to include performance of tasks in a sheltered work setting. For some who receive specific and long-term training, there is the possibility of supported employment in a job requiring a narrow range of skills. Some persons with severe retardation achieve the skills necessary to live in a community living arrangement where supervision is available but not constant.

Persons with moderate retardation may achieve basic academic success such as counting money, simple calculations, and basic reading (generally taking the form of recognition of important signs and simple instructions). Language development generally progresses to the point of fluent conversation on an elementary level. In general, the person with moderate retardation can achieve to the level expected of a 6-8 year old child. Achievement is generally higher in concrete areas such as work skills and lower in abstract areas such as reading and academics. Vocational attainment may reach employment in a competitive job after specific job training and support. In addition, persons with moderate retardation have been successful at independent and semi-independent living.

Persons with mild retardation can achieve at a level equivalent to an 8- to 12-year-old. Achievement may be higher in concrete and adaptive behavior and lower in abstract areas and academics. Reading up to about a fourth grade level is expected. They should be able to make change, do computations involving addition, subtraction, and perhaps multiplication. Vocationally, persons with mild mental retardation usually gain competitive employment in unskilled and semiskilled jobs. Most mildly retarded persons begin to blend into the general population as they approach the age of 30. They achieve a level of independent living separate from their parents. By then, they may have married and even may have begun to raise a family.

Expectations have changed drastically over the past 30 years. Because of the work of persons such as Marc Gold (1972), Frank Rusch (1986), and others, professionals have learned that persons with mental retardation can learn more and progress to greater levels of independence if they are taught in more systematic ways and if education begins at an earlier age and continues into adulthood. Thirty years ago, a person with severe mental retardation was unlikely to progress beyond the level of caring for his/her own immediate needs. Today it is not uncommon to see people with severe retardation learning to perform work in competitive employment.

Interactions

How should you behave when you meet a person who is mentally retarded? Obviously it depends on the person's age and level of retardation but there are several guidelines that you should follow. These guidelines adhere to the concept of normalization. That is, you should attempt to treat a person who is mentally retarded as normally as possible.

First, consider the individual's chronological age. Do not engage in childish behavior or childish talk with a mentally retarded person who is an adult. One common problem experienced by persons who work with retarded adolescents and adults is that mentally retarded persons have often been encouraged to hug or otherwise show affection inappropriately. A handshake is much more appropriate. Second, remember that persons with mental retardation may need to have instructions broken down into smaller steps. Giving a person with moderate retardation a series of instructions and expecting that person to carry out those instructions from memory is likely to result in failure. Communication should be less complex and less abstract. Provide examples where possible.

Do not allude to the person's disability during interaction. If the mentally retarded person brings up the subject of his/her limitations, address them in a specific way (e.g., How will the limitations affect job performance if you are considering hiring the person? Does he/she need help reading a bus schedule?). Do not be afraid to ask questions but keep the questions short, concrete, and simple.

As more severely retarded persons move out of institutions and into the community, the likelihood that you will encounter these persons increases. In most cases, these retarded persons will be accompanied by a responsible adult and you should take your cue for interactions from that person.

Summary

Mental retardation is a condition that affects approximately 2-3 percent of the population. It is characterized by impairments in intellectual and adaptive behavior. There are hundreds of known causes of mental retardation but, for most persons who are mentally retarded, a specific cause is unknown. The large majority of people who are mentally retarded have mild impairments and become functioning, self-supporting members of society as adults.

Persons who are mentally retarded exhibit a wide variety of physical, personality, and learning characteristics. Some characteristics (such as speech impairments) appear much more frequently among persons with mental retardation than among other persons. Because of this diversity, interventions take many forms. Prevention of some forms of mental retardation is possible. For others, education, therapy, and counseling are necessary to help the individual realize his/her potential. That potential varies greatly dependent upon the degree of retardation. A person with profound retardation may not learn to communicate or take care of basic needs whereas a person who is mildly retarded may achieve academic skills that are 1/2 to 3/4 of a person with normal intelligence.

Most importantly, you should remember that there are no specific limits to the achievements of persons with mental retardation. Mentally retarded persons can and have become business owners, effective parents, responsible members of the community, and mature adults who participate in the full spectrum of human experience. Your interactions with mentally retarded persons should be comfortable and productive as long as your attitude is positive.

References

Beier, D. C. (1964). Behavioral disturbances in the mentally retarded. In H. A. Stevens & R. Heber (Eds.), *Mental retardation*. Chicago: University of Chicago Press.

Casto, G., & Mastropieri, M. A. (1986). The efficacy of early intervention programs: A meta-analysis. *Exceptional Children, 52,* 417-424.

Drew, C. J., Hardman, M. L., & Logan, D. R. (1988). *Mental retardation: A life cycle approach*. Columbus, OH: Merrill.

Fisher, M. A., & Zeaman, D. (1980). Growth and decline of retardate intelligence. In N. R. Ellis (Ed.), *International review of research in mental retardation* (Vol. 4). New York: Academic Press.

Gold, M. (1972). Stimulus factors in skill training of the retarded on a complex assembly task: Acquisition, transfer, and retention. *Journal of Mental Deficiency, 76,* 517-526.

Grossman, H. J. (1983). *Classification in mental retardation*. Washington, DC: American Association on Mental Deficiency.

Hogg, J., & Sebba, J. (1987). *Profound retardation and multiple impairment*. Rockville, MD: Aspen.

Kreitler, S., Zigler, E., & Kreitler, H. (1990). Rigidity in mentally retarded and nonretarded children. *American Journal on Mental Retardation, 94,* 550-562.

Mercer, C. D., & Algozzine, B. (1977). Observational learning and the retarded: Teaching implications. *Education and Training of the Mentally Retarded, 12,* 345-353.

Mercer, C. D., & Snell, M. E. (1977). *Learning theory research in mental retardation*. Columbus, OH: Merrill.

Mithaug, D. E., Martin, J. E., & Agran, M. (1987). Adaptability instruction: The goal of transitional programming. *Exceptional Children, 53,* 500-505.

Nihira, K., Foster, R., Shellhaas, M., & Leland, H. (1969). *Adaptive Behavior Scale.* Washington, DC: American Association on Mental Deficiency.

Rusch, F. (1986). *Competitive employment issues and strategies.* Baltimore: Paul H. Brookes.

Sedlak, R. A., & Sedlak, D. M. (1985). *Teaching the educable mentally retarded.* Albany, NY: State University of New York.

Skeels, H. M. (1966). Adult status of children with contrasting early life experiences. *Monographs of the Society for Research in Child Development, 31* (No. 3, Serial No. 105).

Westling, D. L. (1986). *Introduction to mental retardation.* Englewood Cliffs, NJ: Prentice-Hall.

Whitman, T. L. (1990). Self regulation and mental retardation. *American Journal of Mental Retardation, 94,* 347-362.

Suggested Readings

Antonak, R. F., Fiedler, C. R., & Mulick, J. A. (1989). Misconceptions relating to mental retardation. *Mental Retardation, 27,* 91-97.

Edgerton, R. E. (Ed). (1984). *Lives in process: Mildly retarded adults in a large city.* Washington, DC: American Association on Mental Deficiency.

Grossman, H. J. (Ed.). (1983). *Classification in mental retardation.* Washington, DC: American Association on Mental Deficiency.

Hogg, J., & Sebba, J. (1987). *Profound retardation and multiple impairment.* Rockville, MD: Aspen.

Sedlak, R. A., & Sedlak, D. M. (1985). *Teaching the educable mentally retarded.* Albany, NY: State University of New York.

Wehman, P. (1981). *Competitive employment: New horizons for severely disabled individuals.* Baltimore: Paul H. Brookes.

Whitman, T. L. (1990). Self regulation and mental retardation. *American Journal of Mental Retardation, 94,* 347-362.

Wolfensberger, W. (1988). Common assets of mentally retarded people that are not commonly acknowledged. *Mental Retardation, 26,* 63-70.

Zigler, E., Hodapp, R. M., & Edison, M. R. (1990). From theory to practice in the care and education of mentally retarded individuals. *American Journal on Mental Retardation, 95,* 1-12.

PERSONS WHO ARE MENTALLY RETARDED 197

Exploration

Individual Activities

1. Have you ever tried to complete a task or participate in an activity and found it beyond your grasp? For instance, playing a sport you were not familiar with, trying to play a musical instrument, or beginning a class in a hard subject. This is a very awkward feeling and, unfortunately, how most retarded individuals feel every day. They have feelings just like you. List 10 feelings that you have felt when placed in uncomfortable situations due to your lack of ability.

   _____   _____
   _____   _____
   _____   _____
   _____   _____
   _____   _____

   Can you now relate to the feelings a mentally retarded individual must have? Put a check in front of those items which are probably similar for persons who are mentally retarded.

2. What does a mentally retarded individual do as he or she gets older? This is quite a big problem. What would you do if you had a mentally retarded person in your immediate family? List 5 job activities that you would have this person do.

   a. _____
   b. _____
   c. _____
   d. _____
   e. _____

Now list three considerations you would have to assist that person with independent living.

a._____

b._____

c._____

Group Activities

1. Make arrangements so your class can spend a day with or, better still, do volunteer work over a period of time with mentally retarded people. This experience will truly give you some tremendous insight into their lives. In addition, the support of your group will allow you to talk to people who have similar emotions. Hopefully, you will find this to be a rewarding and enjoyable activity that you will continue throughout your life.

   Reactions:

   _____

   _____

   _____

2. It is highly probable that many persons in your class know someone or have a family member who is mentally retarded. Ask those classmates to tell everyone about that person's abilities, limitations, and personality.

   Reactions:

   _____

   _____

   _____

Reaction Paper 8.1

There are many misconceptions concerning what mentally retarded people can and cannot do. From your experiences with these people discuss three of these misconceptions and what the truth actually is.

Continue on back if needed.

Reaction Paper 8.2

Your best friend has just called to tell you about the birth of their new baby. Of course you are surprised to learn that the infant is mentally retarded. Write a letter of support to your friends and offer any appropriate suggestions.

Continue on back if needed.

Notes

CHAPTER 9

LEARNING DISABLED INDIVIDUALS

Deborah Simmons

Introduction

Most of you can recall an individual from your educational pasts who seemed quite bright yet had extreme difficulty learning to read, write, or calculate -- that individual who never quite achieved what everyone expected. In the past, that individual may have been characterized as an underachiever, poorly motivated, or uninterested. Today, that same individual might be identified, quite legitimately, as learning disabled (LD). Although the term learning disability was not formally introduced until 1962 by Sam Kirk, individuals whose academic achievement fails to parallel intellectual/cognitive abilities have undoubtedly existed for many generations. Today, learning disability comprises the largest classification of students funded through special education representing 49% of the total exceptional students served (U.S. Department of Education, 1989). No other exceptionality rivals the area of learning disabilities with respect to the number of students served, the number of instructional personnel needed, the ambiguity of the categorical definition, or the disagreement surrounding the optimal methods/placement for educational services.

Despite this rather dubious notoriety, we know a great deal more about learning disabilities than when it gained formal identity in 1962. In this chapter, you will find overviews of (a) what is known about specific dimensions of learning disabilities, (b) issues that continue to perplex the professional community, and (c) how to use most effectively what we know to teach and prepare individuals with learning disabilities for academic and social success.

What is a Learning Disability?

The exceptionality of learning disabilities has stimulated more controversy and attracted more attention than perhaps any other educational exceptionality. Part of this attention is due to the unprecedented number of students identified as learning disabled; part may be due to the complexity of the condition itself. Unlike some exceptionalities in which the features or characteristic behaviors are readily apparent (e.g., visual or physical impairment) or in which the learning problems persist over time and academic areas (e.g., mental retardation), the distinguishing features of a learning disability are often not that apparent and sometimes not that pervasive. In fact, LD has been described as a hidden handicap making the diagnosis and identification quite complicated. Although students with learning disabilities are much more like non-handicapped peers than not, they have one salient difference: they are not achieving as they ought to be (Ross, 1977).

Prevalence and Heterogeneity

As early as 1973, educators reported that LD was reaching epidemic proportions. In 1987-88, 1,917,935 students between the ages of 6 and 20 were identified as learning disabled (U.S. Office of Education, 1989). This burgeoning number of students represents a heterogeneous aggregation of learning problems that ranges from mild to severe, impacts academic domains from reading to mathematical computations, and appears in preschoolers and adults. Because of the range of behaviors that often characterizes individuals with learning disabilities, it has been a very difficult exceptionality to define, to identify causal factors, and to treat.

Theory and Etiology

To assist you in understanding the current state of learning disabilities, it is important to understand the history of the field and the theories that have shaped and continue to influence thinking about learning disabilities. Many theories abound regarding the cause and treatment of learning disabilities. The most prominent and pervasive theory of learning disability is the physiological difference theory that proposes that the learning problem is caused by some biologic pathology within the learner.

Early researchers studied the behavior of brain-injured soldiers and inferred that individuals who demonstrated behaviors similar to brain-injured soldiers must likewise evidence some brain dysfunction. Because the dysfunction was not obvious, the term minimal brain dysfunction was used to describe those individuals who evidenced learning problems without hard signs of impairment. Today, advances in medical technology are allowing researchers to go beyond examining whether brains look different to investigate more subtle but important cellular deviations that may inform us with respect to the causes of learning disabilities and strengthen support for the physiological difference theory.

An alternative to the medically based theory of learning disabilities is the cognitive theory. According to cognitive theorists, individuals with learning disabilities are not organically impaired; instead, they do not use their cognitive resources to control and regulate learning (Hagen, Barclay, & Schwethelm, 1982). For example, individuals who have a list of information to remember and cluster items within the list according to similar features would be using a more advanced cognitive strategy than individuals who simply try to remember the list through repetition. Research suggests that students with learning disabilities do exhibit deficits in cognitive strategies but can be trained to modify their cognitive behavior.

A derivation of the cognitive theme is the individual who fails to monitor and evaluate his/her performance. This failure has been described as a metacognitive deficit. An example of a reader with poor metacognitive skills would be one who reads a story containing many unfamiliar words and concepts but continues to read, never adjusting the reading pace, failing to employ strategies such as rereading, and seldom evaluating passage comprehension. Because these behaviors are sometimes observed in individuals with learning disabilities, they are sometimes described as inactive learners who fail to take action to improve their performance (Torgesen, 1982).

A fourth explanation of learning disabilities derives from an instructional perspective (Engelmann & Carnine, 1982). Some individuals believe the cause of the learning disability is largely irrelevant and that academic failure is principally due to poorly designed and delivered instruction. Consider for example the following sequence of letters: p, b, d. These letters are easily and often confused by beginning readers yet occur in close proximity in many reading curricular programs. Such design features may precipitate learning difficulty. At a more advanced level, how many of you confuse the concepts convex/concave, deductive/inductive, near-sighted/far-sighted, or affect/effect? The principle is the same. When introducing new information, the similarity of the information can influence ability to remember that information, and the simultaneous introduction of similar information can prompt learning failure. There are many dimensions of instructional design that can have a significant impact on what and how efficiently students learn. Ongoing research is investigating optimal means of designing instruction for students who evidence or are at-risk for learning disabilities.

As you can readily deduce (or is it induce?), one's theoretical conception of learning disabilities can significantly influence how one perceives learning disabilities should be treated. For example, if one endorses a within-the-learner, medical deficit theory, then it is likely the methods used to treat the disability would draw upon neurologic and biologic factors. Conversely, attributing the problem to instructional deficits, such as the design of the curriculum, would result in a very different treatment.

Theories of learning disability continue to provide the framework from which all other dimensions are examined. As such, it is important to understand how the field of learning disabilities has been assembled within the past 30 years. Perhaps, one of the most colorful and intricate components of LD that has been shaped by LD theory is the definition.

Definitions

Researchers and practitioners have sought, for the last 30 years, to derive a clear, precise definition of learning disabilities. Such a definition is important because it provides a common frame of reference for researchers, teachers, parents, and individuals with learning disabilities. Definitions specify distinguishing characteristics and, in the case of learning disabilities, largely determine the criteria for special education funding.

It has often been said that we know more about what learning disability is not than what it is. Although there are many variants of LD definitions, most individuals agree that learning disability is not the result of mental retardation, emotional disturbance, cultural deprivation, or instructional inadequacy. Even though we know a lot about what LD is not, a major task of the field of learning disabilities is working toward a definition of learning disability that will satisfy the many disciplines involved.

Because of the breadth and magnitude of learning disabilities, definitions must be somewhat generic. Because less-specified definitions allow for more liberal interpretation, some criticize the field for identifying individuals as LD when perhaps they are more accurately mentally retarded or emotionally disturbed. Because LD is less stigmatizing than other exceptionalities, it often becomes the umbrella for students with mild learning problems whether or not they actually fit LD criteria. Those who want to retain the identity of learning disabilities as a specific exceptionality continue to work for an acceptable definition that distinguishes it from other learning problems.

Hammill (1990) recently reviewed introductory learning disabilities textbooks and found 11 definitions. While there were many commonalities among the definitions, there was sufficient difference to make the identification of learning disability difficult. For example, consider the following definition of learning disability endorsed by the U.S. Office of Education:

> The term "specific learning disability" means a disorder in one or more of the basic psychological processes involved in understanding or in using language, spoken or written, which may manifest itself in an imperfect ability to listen, speak, read, write, spell, or to do mathematical calculations. This term includes such conditions as perceptual handicaps, brain injury, minimal brain dysfunction, dyslexia, and developmental aphasia. The term does not include children who have learning disabilities which are primarily the result of visual, hearing, or motor handicaps, or mental retardation, or emotional disturbance , or of environmental, cultural, or economic disadvantage. (USOE, Federal Register, 1977, p. 65083)

Although this is the most widely accepted definition and the one adopted by most state education agencies, Hammill noted several areas of potential confusion. First, the 1977 USOE definition provided no criteria for determining the central nervous system dysfunction component of the definition. Second, the definition implies that learning disabilities can exist at all ages yet explicitly uses the term children in the definition.

On a positive note, Hammill's (1990) review of the 11 definitions revealed considerable agreement on specific features. For example, 86% of the definitions agreed that students with learning disabilities demonstrate some type of underachievement; 86% also acknowledged some form of central nervous system dysfunction. According to Hammill's analysis, the field of learning disabilities is reaching some consensus that will allow those responsible for studying and treating learning disabilities to progress beyond definitional controversy.

Characteristics

Definitions provide broad parameters; that is, they specify general criteria. From a definition of learning disabilities, you know that an individual underachieves and is suspected to have some form of central nervous system problem. The definition of learning disabilities further specifies it as an academic disability that can affect many domains from listening to mathematics. What definitions do not tell us are the specific behaviors and characteristics of individuals with learning disabilities. In this section, you will become familiar with some of the common characteristics of individuals with learning disabilities. These distinguishing features illustrate some of the behaviors of individuals with learning disabilities but in no way account for all. Before reading this section, it is important to remember the heterogeneous nature of learning disabilities and interpret these characteristics as illustrative. Some individuals demonstrate many of the behaviors mentioned; others evidence very few. First, characteristics in the academic areas will be reviewed. Next, some of the social and vocational attributes of individuals with learning disabilities are described.

Academic Areas

The majority of learning disabilities occur in the domain of reading and language arts; however, a learning disability may exist in any academic area. With respect to reading, results of research suggest that learning disabilities may first interfere with the ability to recognize words. Specific and systematic instruction in word recognition and fluency skills may address students' needs in this area, but it has been theorized that the delay students evidence in word recognition skills negatively impacts their ability to comprehend. For example, Stanovich (1986) described reading disability as a rich get richer and poor get poorer phenomenon. When students read with relative ease, they read more words, develop a broader base of word knowledge, allocate attention to comprehension, and thus increase overall reading skill. Conversely, when word reading is laborious, it delays an individual's ability to interact meaningfully with text. Although early research attributed the reading difficulties of individuals with learning disabilities to visual perceptual deficits, more recent studies indicate the importance of awareness of the auditory components of words. For example, phonological awareness, or the ability to process and act on the sounds of words, has been found to predict later reading achievement. Individuals who can hear the sounds in words and blend those sounds are more likely to develop reading proficiency at an early age.

Another characteristic of many LD students is poor written expression. Written expression is the ability to communicate in writing and spans the range of tasks from writing mechanics, such as handwriting and spelling, to the more complex strategies required to compose letters and essays. Expressive writing is the most complex of language skills, and consequently students with learning disabilities are likely to experience difficulty in a range of writing tasks. As compared to skilled writers, students with learning disabilities may write fewer words, write in simpler sentences, use words repetitiously, spell words incorrectly, spend little time thinking about what to write, fail to revise and rewrite, and write poorly organized products (Isaacson, 1987). Because writing is a primary means of communications, these difficulties may pose serious limitations for individuals with learning disabilities in academic, vocational, and social settings.

Many students with learning disabilities evidence mathematics difficulties. Although some of the problems stem from lack of proficiency with basic computational facts, many additional factors can contribute to mathematical learning problems. Students may fail to understand math-related language, experience problem solving deficits, or evidence difficulty in applying mathematics to functional tasks such as money, time, and measurement. Silbert, Carnine, and Stein (1990) suggested that mathematical learning problems may result because programs provide insufficient practice and schedule too little review for students to master necessary preskills. Additional problems may surface because math is a hierarchical domain. That is, unless one is competent on lower-level skills such as adding one-digit numbers it is quite likely that more complex skills such as adding two-digit numbers with regrouping will be problematic. Therefore, students with LD must establish a solid base of arithmetic and mathematical skills before progressing to more complex skills.

Behavior and Social Skills

By definition, a learning disability is an academic problem. Nevertheless, while the primary handicapping condition must be in an academic area, the effects do not stay within academic boundaries. Accumulating evidence suggests that individuals with learning disabilities show more behavior problems and display less social competence than their nondisabled peers. Once again, it is important to caution against overgeneralizing. Not all individuals with learning disabilities experience social or behavioral problems; however, it is important to recognize the relation between academic and social/behavioral skills. Prolonged failure can affect self-concept and self-esteem. Moreover, because an individual is not likely to gain reinforcement for poor academic performance, it is understandable that an individual might use other means, such as deviant behavior, to gain social attention from the teacher or peers. Teachers and parents of LD children should be attuned to the possible effects of learning disabilities on social behavior.

For instance, children with learning disabilities may show a variety of less acceptable behaviors and consequently receive poor ratings by their teachers and peers on social measures. Students with LD are often distractible, display more negative social behavior, misread social interactions, and display poor role-taking skills. Findings in the area of social behavior are not conclusive; therefore, it is important not to characterize all LD students as having socially inappropriate behavior.

In a related and perhaps more serious dimension of social behavior, research indicates that students with learning disabilities are at higher risk than their non-handicapped peers for involvement in criminal activity. Findings reveal they are also more likely to be victims of crimes (Bryan, Pearl, & Herzog, 1989). Specifically, LD students reported being more involved than non-LD students in stealing and damaging property as well as higher frequencies of having something stolen at school or at home, being assaulted, or carrying something to protect themselves. Such findings indicate the manifestation of learning problems beyond the academic domain.

Expectations

Adolescent and Adult Adjustment

A great misconception of learning disabilities is that the problems go away. Available data suggest this is simply not the case. In 1987-88, 26% of students with learning disabilities between 16 and 21 dropped out of school; 46% graduated with a diploma. One can speculate that both figures stem from these students' histories of academic failure. Of those individuals who do graduate, studies of college students with learning disabilities suggest that academic learning problems persist and present unique problems which adversely affect their academic performance. College-age students demonstrate a variety of problems in the areas of reading comprehension and fluency, mathematical computation and applications, and written expression.

While the vocational training, employment, and long-term follow-up needs of individuals with severe disabilities have been well documented, the same needs of individuals with learning disabilities have not been systematically addressed. It is often assumed that because learning disabilities are a milder handicapping condition, this population of individuals necessarily requires less assistance and follow up. In a recent study, Neubert, Tilson, & Ianacone (1989) found that mildly handicapped individuals, 44% of whom were identified as learning disabled, evidenced need for considerable on-the-job training and follow-up. In addition, 46% of the individuals were unemployed at the end of a 1-year period. Data from the Office of Education further indicated that only 58% of youth with learning disabilities who are out of secondary school maintain gainful employment. The data further suggested that individuals with learning disabilities rely strongly on family for support.

Intervention

Unfortunately, learning disabilities are not obvious until the learner experiences academic failure. Unlike some conditions where the relation between behavior and outcome is quite predictable (for example, the effects of proper nutrition during pregnancy on fetal development, the effects of immunization and contraction of disease, and the effects of cigarette smoking and lung cancer), the causal and preventive factors of learning disability remain less clear. Nevertheless, there exist a number of practices that, when used systematically, can prevent and remediate learning difficulty. The following section reviews selected, promising practices to illustrate the evolution of the field of learning disabilities and the application of knowledge to the treatment of learning problems.

Preventive Methods

A number of different instructional technologies can be used to prevent or minimize the effects of learning disabilities. The following section highlights promising practices including pre-referral intervention, progress monitoring and curriculum-based assessment, early reading experience, and direct instruction and well-designed curricula.

Prereferral intervention. Prereferral intervention is a teacher's modification of instruction or classroom management before referral to better accommodate a difficult-to-teach pupil. This activity is often shared by one or more support staff such as a special educator or school psychologist who works individually with a particular student. Prereferral intervention is designed to eliminate inappropriate referrals and reduce future students' problems by strengthening the teacher's capacity to intervene effectively with a greater diversity of children (Fuchs, Fuchs, Bahr, Fernstrom, & Stecker, 1990). In the prereferral intervention process, teachers may modify instruction in minor or major ways such as altering assignments, providing specialized instruction, reinforcing specific behaviors, or training students to modify their on-task behavior.

Progress monitoring and curriculum-based measurement. Progress monitoring is the systematic method of assessing student performance; curriculum-based measurement (CBM) is a standardized methodology for selecting test stimuli from a student's curriculum, administering and scoring tests, summarizing the assessment information, and using information to formulate instructional decisions in the basic skills areas (Fuchs and Fuchs, 1988). Considerable evidence indicates the importance of monitoring student performance on an ongoing basis. Too often, student progress is not monitored until after prolonged failure. Because many academic skills are based on mastery of prerequisite skills, any extended period of failure sets up a learner for subsequent failure. When teachers have an on-line measure of performance, they can make instructional modifications before the student becomes too discrepant from others in the classroom and too entrenched in the failure cycle.

Early reading experience. Adams' (1990) recommendation for early reading skills suggests that "the single most important activity for building the knowledge and skills eventually required for reading appears to be reading aloud to children regularly and interactively" (Adams, 1990, p. 124). Thus, a logical step to prevent learning disabilities from progressing to advanced stages is to provide children sufficient exposure to print and emerse them in an environment of reading.

Direct instruction and well-designed curricula. One of the less glamourous but consistently effective practices that can be used to promote academic growth is direct instruction. Direct instruction involves three critical dimensions; instructional organization, program design, and teacher presentation techniques (Carnine, Silbert, & Kameenui, 1990). Although research findings suggest that time spent in teacher-directed instruction relates positively to academic growth, other features of direct instruction are equally important. Students must be engaged in academic tasks that are of an appropriate instructional level, adequate time must be allocated, and curricular lessons must be well-designed. As previously discussed, lesson design encompasses multiple components such as the examples used and the practice and review schedules. In addition, findings suggest that direct instruction principles such as mastery of tasks in each stage of learning, teacher modeling of tasks, and consistent correction procedures promote basic skill development in special education students in primary and elementary grades.

Remedial Interventions

All of the previously identified preventive interventions can and should be incorporated in a remedial program. For example, once a student is identified as having a learning disability, the learner's progress should be monitored systematically and the effectiveness of instruction evaluated to determine the need for instructional modification. In addition to preventive interventions, the following treatments hold great promise for remediating learning failure.

Peer-mediated instruction. Peer-mediated instruction refers to a procedure in which students teach fellow students. It is not a replacement for teacher-direct instruction but can supplement teaching resources available in either regular or special education classrooms. During peer-mediated instruction, tutors provide additional practice on material previously introduced during instruction and provide corrective feedback and reinforcement. Variations of peer-mediated instruction include cross-age tutoring in which an older student tutors a younger student and classwide peer tutoring in which all students in a class are paired with a partner for extended opportunities for instruction and practice. Results indicate the potential of peer-mediated instruction to address some of the special needs of students with learning disabilities (Simmons, Fuchs, Fuchs, Pate, & Mathes, submitted for publication).

Cognitive-behavior modification. One area of research with LD students focuses on training students to monitor their own behavior. One objective of cognitive-behavior modification is to change learners from passive to active monitors of behavior who are aware of their performance and take action to modify behavior when things do not go well. Self-monitoring techniques can be used to address a range of deficient behaviors including attention to task and passage comprehension. For example, using a cassette tape that emits intermittent beeps, students can be trained to monitor whether they were on-task at the sound of the tone. The number of on- and off-task tallies can then be used to evaluate on-task performance.

Social skills training. Just as students can improve their academic performance through academic interventions, programs for training social skills hold great promise for teaching appropriate social behaviors. Social skills programs have been designed to teach a range of behaviors from self-control to how to give and receive appropriate criticism. One problem researchers and teachers are now trying to address is how to teach students to use these newly learned behaviors in other settings. Methods are currently being explored which focus not only on the individual but on the contexts in which the social behaviors occur.

Computer technology. Computers represent a potentially effective and accessible means to increase learning. In elementary schools, computer-assisted-instruction can be used for drill-and-practice, tutorials to provide sequenced instruction, simulations to demonstrate events, tool programs to assist in academic work (e.g., word processing), and programming to teach logical sequencing and consequences (Majsterek, 1989). Word processing and spelling checkers can minimize the effects of poor writing expression skills thereby increasing students' motivation toward the writing task. Such capabilities could allow students to focus on the content and process of writing rather than attending to the mechanics of the product. However, further research is needed to determine how best to accommodate the needs of students with learning disabilities. Early reviews indicate that computer-assisted-instruction is most effective as a supplement to teacher-directed-instruction and that careful attention must be paid to the design of instructional software.

Interactions

Learning disability is a complex process, and its causes are difficult to unravel. In recent years, those who interact with individuals with learning disabilities have been encouraged to think of learning disability in a different way. Specifically, it is important not to think of learning disability as a within-the-learner problem that needs to be fixed but from an interactional, contextual perspective. That is, to understand learning disability we must examine more than the learner. This certainly complicates the process because when you expand the focus to other factors you are likely to find more than one variable that causes learning to breakdown. But isn't this a better way to identify causes and design methods of intervention? Learners, be they preschoolers, eighth-graders, or college students, do not fail independently but rather as they interact with factors such as text, mathematics problems, instruction, and language, that do not parallel their skills.

It is important to identify factors that prevent individuals from performing tasks successfully. Such information is likely to require parents and teachers to change their information gathering and evaluation practices in significant ways. This tack to "understanding learning disability" as more than a learner disability provides meaningful information. As such, the learning disability is seen and understood as much more than a learner-based problem.

Guidelines for Interacting with Individuals with Learning Disabilities

Frame problems in terms of variables that you can control (Kameenui & Simmons, 1990). When a problem surfaces, rather than assume the responsibility is learner-based, examine the environment to determine factors that may precipitate the problem (for example, unclear directions or insufficient experience with a task).

Provide sufficient models of any behavior you want demonstrated whether the behavior involves initiating conversations, completing homework, or getting to school on time.

Present information in manageable chunks. That is, do not overload individuals with lengthy lists or series of information.

Structure frequent and cumulative reviews of critical information. Do not assume that one presentation of information will ensure the individual's retention of information.

Reinforce appropriate behavior and ignore inappropriate behavior.

Remember, individuals with learning disabilities most often have average to above-average intellectual skills. Their difficulties stem not from inability to understand but from when information or tasks are unclear. Structure interactions that clearly communicate the information or goals to be accomplished.

Summary

This chapter introduced one of the most perplexing and evolving areas of exceptionality: learning disability. Without question, learning disability represents a great challenge for those who teach, interact with, and quite possibly experience the consequences of academic failure. It is a heterogeneous exceptionality that can impact a range of individuals in a variety of ways. This chapter emphasized the instructional advances made in the area of LD and the importance of viewing learning disability as more than a learner-based problem. Although learning disability, by definition, is an academic deficit, its effects are not restricted to academic outcomes. As with any exceptionality under development, continued research is needed before an acceptable definition and optimal methods can be specified. Given the progress in the area of persons with learning disabilities in the last several years, the promise of methods to remediate and minimize the effects of learning disability certainly appear to be on the horizon.

References

Adams, M. J. (1990). *Beginning to read: Thinking and learning about print.* A summary prepared by S. Stahl, J. Osborn, & F. Lehr, Center for the Study of Reading, The Reading Research and Education Center University of Illinois at Urbana-Champaign.

Bryan, T., Pearl, R., & Herzog, A. (1989). Learning disabled adolescents' vulnerability to crime: Attitudes, anxieties, experiences. *Learning Disabilities Research, 5,* 51-60.

Carnine, D., Silbert, J., & Kameenui, E. (1990). *Direct instruction reading.* Columbus: Merrill.

Englemann, S., & Carnine, D. (1982). *Instructional design: Principles and applications.* New York: Irvington.

Fuchs, L., & Fuchs, D. (1988). Curriculum-based measurement: A methodology for evaluating and improving student programs. *Diagnostique, 14,* 3-13.

Fuchs, D., Fuchs, L., Bahr, M., Fernstrom, P., & Stecker, P. (1990). Pre-referral intervention: A prescriptive approach. *Exceptional Children, 56,* 493-513.

Hagen, J. W., Barclay, C. R., & Schwethelm, B. (1982). Cognitive development of the learning-disabled child. *International Review of Research in Mental Retardation, 11,* 1-41.

Hammill, D. D. (1990). On defining learning disabilities: An emerging consensus. *Journal of Learning Disabilities, 23,* 74-83.

Isaacson, S. (1987). Effective instruction in written language. *Focus on Exceptional Children, 19,* 1-12.

Kameenui, E. J., & Simmons, D. C. (1990). *Designing instructional strategies: The prevention of academic learning problems.* Columbus, OH: Merrill.

Majsterek, D. J. (1989). Computer-assisted instruction for elementary school children with learning disabilities. *LD Forum: Narrowing the Gap Between Research and Practice, 15,* 35-38.

Neubert, D., Tilson, G., & Ianacone, R. (1989). Post-secondary transition needs and employment patterns of individuals with mild disabilities. *Exceptional Children, 55,* 494-500.

Ross, A. (1977). *Learning disability: The unrealized potential.* New York: McGraw-Hill.

Silbert, J., Carnine, D., & Stein, M. (1990). *Direct instruction mathematics.* Columbus: Merrill.

Simmons, D., Fuchs, L., Fuchs, D., Pate, J., & Mathes, P. (Submitted for publication). Effects of four versions of classwide peer tutoring on the reading achievement of students with learning disabilities and other non-handicapped low-achieving elementary-age students.

Stanovich, K. E. (1986). Matthew effects in reading: Some consequences of individual differences in the acquisition of literacy. *Reading Research Quarterly, 21,* 360-406.

Torgesen, J. K. (1982). The learning disabled child as an inactive learner: Educational implications. *Topics in Learning and Learning Disabilities, 2,* 45-52.

U.S. Department of Education. (1989). *Eleventh Annual Report to Congress on the Implementation of the Education of the Handicapped Act.* Washington, DC: Divisions of Innovation and Development, Office of Special Education Programs.

U.S. Office of Education. (1977). Assistance to states for education of handicapped children: Procedures for evaluating specific learning disabilities. *Federal Register, 42,* 65082-65085.

Suggested Readings

Adams, M. J. (1990). *Beginning to read: Thinking and learning about print.* A summary prepared by S. Stahl, J. Osborn, & F. Lehr. Center for the Study of Reading, The Reading Research and Education Center University of Illinois at Urbana-Champaign.

Arter, J. A., & Jenkins, J. R. (1977). Examining the benefits and prevalence of modality considerations in special education. *Journal of Special Education, 11,* 281-298.

Kavale, K., Forness, S., & Bender, M. (1987). *Handbook of learning disabilities: (Vol. I and II).* Boston: College-Hill.

Ross, A. (1977). *Learning disability: The unrealized potential.* New York: McGraw-Hill.

Stanovich, K. E. (1986). Matthew effects in reading: Some consequences of individual differences in the acquisition of literacy. *Reading Research Quarterly, 21,* 360-406.

Notes

LEARNING DISABLED INDIVIDUALS

Exploration

Individual Activities

1. Read the following paragraph quickly.

    Down syndrome si a diseaes dezirertcarahc by wol I.W., shrot and broad hands, and woleb average thgieh. Ti is more birth DNA there is no crue.

    This is how a severely learning disabled individual may see words. Did it take you longer than usual to read and understand it. Imagine having to deal with all reading materials in this fashion.

    Now quickly write the Pledge to the Flag but write all of the words backwards. Do you think learning disabled people feel the way you do now when faced with a difficult task?

    _____
    _____
    _____

2. A learning disability may not just be trouble recognizing words or memory, it may be something such as trouble taking notes. Have a friend read you a short paragraph from your textbook as quickly as a teacher would speak during a lecture. Take notes on this information in the space below. Don't write with your preferred hand. Use the other! Are you LD?

    _____
    _____
    _____
    _____

Group Activities

1. This is an in-class Learning Disability Test. Everyone take out one sheet of clean paper. Now, after each of these tasks, raise your hand when you have finished. Have your instructor read this list off giving only five seconds per event. Work quickly.

    a. Number evens down the left side of the page until you reach the bottom.
    b. Number odds down the right side.
    c. Fold this paper in half, then in half the other way, now rip it into four equal pieces.
    d. Hold one of the pieces up to your forehead and write the word doctor in the center of the paper. About one inch letters should be fine.
    e. Make sure to throw away all papers before you leave class.

    So, how was it? If you didn't finish these tasks before half the class, you could be learning disabled. Don't worry, this isn't a certified learning disability test, but do you get the point?

    Reactions:

    _____
    _____
    _____

2. Gather into groups of 4 or 5. You are the board of directors for a major assembly plant. You have received a call from a teacher of learning disabled students. These students need summer jobs and the teacher is wondering if you can help. The students could do the job just as well as anyone else, but would need a little more training. Discuss the pros and cons of hiring these students with your group members.

    Reactions:

    _____
    _____
    _____

Reaction Paper 9.2

Some learning disabled children are mainstreamed into classes where there are no disabled learners. Others are taught in programs with learning disabled children. What are the pros and cons of both models?

Continue on back if needed.

228

Notes

CHAPTER 10

EMOTIONALLY DISTURBED PERSONS

Tim Landrum

Introduction

Among exceptional individuals, children and adults who are emotionally disturbed are perhaps the most misunderstood. Despite progress in many areas, the education, treatment, and integration of disturbed persons into communities remain subject to debate among parents, community members, legislators, and educators as well. Several misconceptions have contributed to the disagreement regarding appropriate intervention for those who may be emotionally disturbed. Issues on which professionals have yet to reach agreement include such basic matters as the definition of emotional disturbance and the label used to classify individuals who may have emotional or behavioral problems, as well as more philosophical matters of the appropriateness of various educational and treatment approaches, settings, and long-range goals.

In general, persons whose behavior fails to meet the demands of their environment <u>and</u> whose everyday functioning is impaired by these behavioral excesses or deficits may be considered emotionally disturbed. Federal regulations contained in Public Law 94-142 (PL 94-142), The Education for All Handicapped Children Act, describe several conditions which may be indicative of emotional disturbance in school-aged children (e.g., inappropriate types of behavior or feelings under normal circumstances, pervasive mood of unhappiness), although these have been criticized for their vague and even contradictory language (Bower, 1982).

Despite the criticisms of its lack of specificity, the federal definition of emotional disturbance does provide two major guidelines that remain useful in distinguishing those who may be emotionally disturbed from the normal population. First, the behaviors in question must be markedly different in nature, frequency, or intensity from the norm. Second, these behaviors must result in impaired functioning. Because P.L. 94-142 concerns primarily the education of handicapped children, impaired functioning usually refers to school failure, though children may also experience difficulties in their homes or communities. In adults, impaired functioning may include an inability to obtain employment or function independently in the community.

The different labels that have been applied to persons experiencing emotional or behavioral problems also reflect the disagreement that exists among professionals. Adults may be diagnosed with a variety of mental disorders (e.g., paranoia, schizophrenia, depression). These are catalogued in the Diagnostic and Statistical Manual of Mental Disorders - Third Edition Revised (American Psychiatric Association, 1987) which is commonly used by professionals in the mental health field. In contrast, students in school may be labeled conduct disordered, behaviorally disordered, emotionally handicapped, or socially maladjusted, to name only a few (Cullinan, Epstein, & McLinden, 1986; Epstein, Cullinan, & Sabatino, 1977). Federal regulations accompanying P.L. 94-142 use the term seriously emotionally disturbed, and many states have adopted this term as well. Current professional preference, however, is that students experiencing emotional or behavioral problems be referred to as behaviorally disordered. This term is preferred by school personnel because it accurately identifies the problem as one of behavior rather than suggesting that the problem resides within the individual, and because many people believe that this term is less stigmatizing than the term emotionally disturbed (Kauffman, 1989).

Another misconception surrounding emotional disturbance concerns the severity of the behavior problems in question. All children are defiant, fight, or are anxious and fearful at some time in their lives. According to the definition proposed earlier, however, it is only when problem behavior interferes with everyday functioning that it warrants specialized intervention. Generally, the frequency of the problem behavior and the context in which it occurs determine whether a person will be labeled emotionally disturbed. For example, the child who gets into a fight on the playground one afternoon is not emotionally disturbed. If fighting occurs frequently or is of an extremely violent nature, intervention may be necessary. Similarly, occasional temper tantrums in a two-year-old child are certainly less problematic than daily temper tantrums in a 10- or 12-year-old.

Because of the difficulty in determining when problems warrant special intervention, there is also considerable disagreement regarding the number of people who are emotionally disturbed. For many years, the federal government estimated that two percent of the school-aged population could be identified as seriously emotionally disturbed based on their problem behavior. Most experts in the field, however, believe that this is a very conservative estimate. Various researchers have provided prevalence estimates ranging from 3% or 4% to as high as 15% or 20% of the school-aged population. Perhaps the most accepted estimate is that between 3% and 6% of the population may be emotionally disturbed (Kauffman, 1989; Rubin & Balow, 1978).

With adults, the problem of when to intervene may be even more problematic than with children. Adults who experience emotional or behavior problems may not come to the attention of mental health professionals as quickly as children, who are often referred for help by parents or teachers. Individuals' rights are also important. For example, if professionals believe that a person would benefit from therapy or intervention, should they attempt to "force" that person into treatment? A common sentiment among professionals in the mental health field is that all persons in need of services have a right to treatment. The other side of this issue may be that individuals also have the right to refuse treatment (i.e., mental health professionals do not have the right to determine the manner in which others live their lives). For this reason, adults with emotional or behavioral problems may not receive help until their problems infringe on the rights of others or involve violations of the law. Understandably then, the prevalence of emotional problems among adults is also very difficult to estimate.

In the subsequent sections, appropriate intervention for emotionally disturbed children and youth, realistic expectations for school achievement and later life adjustment and employment, and guidelines for interacting with emotionally disturbed persons are discussed. First, a more in-depth discussion of the characteristics of the emotionally disturbed individual may help to answer the question, "What is the emotionally disturbed person really like?"

Characteristics

As mentioned earlier, the most notable characteristic of the child or adult who is emotionally disturbed is that their behavior does not meet the demands of their environment. These discrepancies may involve a lack of appropriate or adaptive behaviors or an excess of inappropriate or maladaptive behaviors. For the child in school, such excesses may include fighting, yelling, destroying property, and defiance of teachers. The student who is emotionally disturbed may be frequently out of his or her seat, may often fail to follow directions or teacher commands, and may be disruptive to others. The adult who is emotionally disturbed may be loud, aggressive, or destructive, and may demonstrate poor social interaction skills (e.g., insult others, use inappropriate language) that limit his or her ability to gain and maintain successful relationships or employment.

Students and adults who are characterized by behavioral excesses are usually very obvious to others. Many people find their behaviors annoying, offensive, or frightening. Because of the disruptive nature of behavioral excesses, it is more often the acting-out child who is referred for special help and consequently identified as emotionally disturbed in school. Similarly the adult with acting-out behavior problems is also more likely to come to the attention of mental health professionals or the authorities.

Although often not as apparent as the person with acting-out problems, emotionally disturbed individuals may also be characterized by behavioral deficits; they do not demonstrate many of the adaptive behaviors typical of their peers. They may be excessively shy and withdrawn, or overly anxious and fearful, even under normal circumstances. Students in school may talk very little or not at all, and may be overly fearful of new tasks, new situations, and adults or even their classmates. Adults who are excessively withdrawn may avoid social situations and interaction with others in employment or community settings. In extreme cases, they may isolate themselves entirely, choosing to remain in their homes and seldom venturing out into the community at all.

Although emotionally disturbed persons may be characterized by either behavioral excesses or behavioral deficits, it is important to remember that only when individuals' functioning is adversely affected by their behavior that they may be identified as emotionally disturbed. Avoiding social gatherings because one prefers to stay home is not a problem in itself. When this behavior results in individuals' failing to maintain employment, shop for themselves, or otherwise participate as community members, they may be in need of intervention.

By definition, students identified as emotionally disturbed in school are usually experiencing academic difficulties. Indeed, federal regulations stipulate that an inability to learn not due to intellectual, sensory, or health factors may be one of the identifying characteristics of emotional disturbance. Moreover, to be identified as seriously emotionally disturbed, children's educational performance must be adversely affected by their behavioral problems. This should not suggest, however, that emotional disturbance is primarily a problem of intelligence or learning. In fact, the intelligence of emotionally persons is usually in the low-average range (Kauffman, 1989). It is true, however, that the school achievement of children with emotional disturbance generally lags behind their measured potential.

The characteristics discussed to this point describe the typical person who has been identified as emotionally disturbed. Much less prevalent, although even more difficult to serve appropriately, are persons who are more severely disturbed. These individuals may be extremely violent, aggressive, or self-abusive to the point that they are dangerous to themselves or others. Or they may be so withdrawn that they lack even daily living and self-help skills (e.g., feeding, dressing, toileting). Such individuals usually require intensive education and training programs, often provided in residential facilities.

Intervention

As with many exceptionalities, it is usually not possible to identify the cause of emotional disturbance, although several factors have been shown to be associated with the development of emotional and behavioral problems. These include lax or inconsistent parental discipline, family or marital discord, family history of mental illness, school failure, and genetic factors (Kazdin, 1987). Researchers believe that each of these factors may cause or contribute to the development of behavior disorders; the child for whom many of the factors are present may be particularly susceptible to the development of behavior problems.

Preventing emotional disturbance, then, represents a great challenge. Early and intensive intervention must be provided for children who are "at risk." Such intervention may involve parenting classes or training parents in the management of problem behavior (Bank, Patterson, & Reid, 1987), family therapy and counseling for families characterized by discord, and early academic and pre-academic intervention for young children who are at risk because of their family background or environment.

Once youngsters are identified as emotionally disturbed, they are most often educated in full- or part-time special classes in public schools. These self-contained classes generally serve a maximum of ten students, and are staffed by a specially trained teacher and teacher's aide. Such classes tend to offer highly structured educational programs with particular emphasis on individualizing instruction to address the specific needs of each student.

Although several treatment approaches have been, and continue to be used, perhaps the most common approach to intervention with persons who are emotionally disturbed involves behavior modification. With emotionally disturbed pupils in particular, behavior modification is often preferred because it addresses the primary problem of such individuals: they behave in ways that are not acceptable. The usefulness of behavior modification as an intervention strategy is also supported by an extensive body of research that has established it as perhaps the most powerful method of changing behavior (Kazdin, 1987).

In its simplest form, a program of behavior modification allows parents, teachers, or therapists to increase appropriate behavior while decreasing or eliminating inappropriate behaviors in the person experiencing behavior problems. In school settings, teachers provide students with clear and precise directions for the tasks they are to complete as well as expectations for acceptable and unacceptable behaviors. Pupils are then rewarded for appropriate completion of tasks or compliance with directions, or they may lose rewards if their behavior is inappropriate. Rewards may include extra recess time, stickers, social praise, or points that may be exchanged for small toys, candy, or other prizes.

The principles of behavior modification also apply to adolescents and adult treatment, with appropriate adaptations according to the age, ability, and interests of the individual. In adolescent treatment centers, for example, it is fairly common to provide clients with opportunities to "earn" weekend outings to movies, shopping malls, or amusement parks by demonstrating appropriate behavior in their academic work, in social situations, or even by participating in therapy sessions.

Parents, or others not familiar with the science of behavior modification, may object to it as little more than bribery. It is important to remember, however, that a major goal of behavior modification is to teach individuals behaviors that they will eventually come to perform without any system of tangible rewards in place. For example, while a program of behavior modification often begins with rewards provided for appropriate behavior, the frequency with which the reward is provided is gradually faded as the person becomes more skilled at a particular behavior. An example of fading might involve providing a child with a small candy and social praise (e.g., "Tommy stayed in his seat for the whole time during reading today!") each time the desired behavior occurs. Gradually, the teacher would eliminate the candy by providing it every other time, and then every third time, that the behavior occurs. Social praise, however, would be provided each time Tommy stayed in his seat during reading. Eventually, the behavior "staying-in-seat" could come to be maintained not by candy but by social praise alone. With more seriously disturbed individuals, behavior modification programs often involve more complex systems of reinforcement, and may necessarily begin with more powerful rewards.

Other treatment approaches that are used with emotionally disturbed children and adults are more concerned with the unconscious motivations for individuals' behavior and may be broadly classified as psychodynamic or psychoanalytic. These approaches emphasize individual psychotherapy and counseling and target a treatment goal of uncovering the underlying cause of the person's emotional or behavior problem. Proponents of this approach believe that the person's behavior is not the problem in and of itself, but rather is only a symptom of underlying mental illness. Unlike the behavioral approach, the psychodynamic model suggests that individuals be allowed to express themselves freely in a permissive environment.

A third treatment approach for many individuals with emotional or behavioral problems involves the use of medications. In cases of emotional disturbance in children medications are predominantly used in cases of hyperactivity, which is often attributed to biological causes. Many children in public schools, some identified as handicapped and some non-identified as well, are currently taking medication to help them control their overactivity. Although the effectiveness of medications has been well documented, professionals caution that medication is not appropriate for all children, and that close monitoring by physicians is essential. In addition to hyperactivity, other mental disorders may be treated with medications as well (e.g. depression, schizophrenia, eating disorders), although these are very specifically prescribed for individual clients and closely monitored by physicians or psychiatrists.

Because students with behavioral disorders are often behind their peers academically, instructional emphasis may rest more heavily on basic skills at the earlier grades with increasing attention to pre-vocational and vocational skills as students move into the upper grades. Throughout the educational program, functional skills--those that will allow students to function in the community, obtain employment, and maintain a home--are stressed. Because students with emotional or behavioral problems are often characterized by poor relationships with others as well, social skills training also receives high priority.

Expectations

Persons who are characterized by chronic behavior disorders early in life have a higher probability for continued problems in later life. Early onset of behavior problems, difficulties in multiple settings (e.g., home, school, community), and a wide variety of problem behaviors are all factors that contribute to this poor prognosis (Kazdin, 1987). Such individuals are more likely to drop out of school, more likely to have contact with the law, and are less likely to be employed in later life than the normal population.

Although discouraging in many ways, this outlook may also serve two purposes. First, it may serve to remind parents, educators, and legislators that early intervention is critical for persons characterized by behavior problems. Intervening with children before they are well entrenched in deviant behavior patterns is essential if we are to increase their chances for normal development and adjustment.

A second purpose that may be served by this relatively bleak outlook for youngsters already characterized by chronic emotional disturbance is to draw attention to the needs of this grossly underserved population. In a pragmatic sense, it is much more cost effective to provide educational and behavioral intervention early in children's lives than to deal with the results of a pattern of antisocial behavior that is well established by adolescence and thus much more difficult to treat.

Despite the pessimistic outlook for many children who have already developed serious emotional disturbance, there is reason for optimism on several fronts. Early intervention and direct instruction in basic skills may provide students with a solid academic background that will enable them to succeed in school. Social skills training programs also have resulted in some success, and the positive effects seem to remain even after the programs are discontinued (Walker, Hops, & Greenwood, 1981).

Parent management training has also met with considerable success. This intervention technique involves training parents first in identifying and defining problem behavior, establishing rules for behavior and then in providing rewards for appropriate behavior and mild punishment for inappropriate behavior (Patterson, 1982). Clearly, research is needed to further develop effective strategies for persons with emotional disorders. Equally important, however, is the need for parents, teachers, and other professionals to be made aware of intervention techniques that have already shown promise.

Interactions

Interacting with the child or adult who is emotionally disturbed raises several difficult issues. By definition, these individuals are often characterized by behaviors that others find inappropriate or offensive. Individuals in the community will have varying tolerance levels, and may react differently when confronted with intolerable behaviors or situations. In general, three broad categories may help to summarize the ways in which you and others might react to the person who is emotionally disturbed: punitive responses, avoidance behavior, and instructive interaction.

There is no denying that a small percentage of persons who are emotionally disturbed display behaviors that are extremely offensive, even to the most tolerant among us. It is important to keep in mind, however, that this is true of a very small percentage of the population, and frequent interaction with such individuals is not likely. When such interactions do occur, it is probably best to avoid responding in a punitive or negative manner. Becoming visibly upset or responding negatively to the person serves no useful purpose, and may only create an even more negative interaction.

The use of punishment provides a good example. If a child or adult displays a behavior that is clearly inappropriate, a punitive response (shouting at or striking the individual) may well stop the behavior from occurring. However, several "side effects" may also be noted. First, the person inflicting the punishment is merely modeling an equally inappropriate behavior; the person being punished may learn that it is acceptable to shout at or strike others. Perhaps more importantly, using punishment may lead children or adults to believe that behavior is controlled by outside authority--that behavior is only wrong if they get caught, or that it is necessary to display appropriate behavior only when those who have some power over them are present.

At the same time it is unreasonable to expect others to be accepting of offensive behavior. Indeed, many professionals argue that it is wrong for persons to act in an accepting manner when disturbed individuals present very unacceptable behaviors. For those who find it difficult to interact positively with emotionally disturbed individuals, avoiding interaction entirely, while not the most positive or constructive choice, is certainly a reasonable alternative. Every person you meet does not become a close friend; you simply do not associate with people whom you do not particularly like. Such may be the case with emotionally disturbed persons, although it is important to maintain the distinction between the person and their behavior. That is, not associating with a person because their personality or interests are different from yours is very different from avoiding a person because they have a behavior problem. As is true of any person with a disability or handicapping condition, the best rule of thumb is to treat that person as you would any other.

Indeed, perhaps the most constructive manner of interacting with emotionally disturbed people is to associate with them as you would with anyone else. Interactions should be natural, not forced, and if particular behaviors are troubling, it is perfectly acceptable to let the person know. If you find profanity offensive, for example, it is much more reasonable to say to the person, "I really don't like that kind of language," than to chastise the person or to avoid interacting with the person in the future. With children in school, special education teachers are encouraged to address behaviors directly so that children learn specifically the behaviors that are required of them, as well as those that are unacceptable. If a child is constantly out of his/her seat for example, the teacher might say, "All students who stay in their seat during reading will be going outside for recess."

It is also important that you do not let a person's behavioral history interfere with day to day interactions. Knowing that a person occasionally behaves in a way that is found to be unacceptable should not come to color your entire relationship with that person. Consider that case of a co-worker who has emotional problems that occasionally result in inappropriate behavior. It would be unfortunate if everyone who worked with this individual ignored or avoided him/her because of these occasional problems, and in fact would probably contribute to the person's difficulties. Co-workers should interact freely with the person in the same manner as they would with anyone else, at least during times when the person is not displaying inappropriate behavior. When inappropriate behavior is a problem, co-workers might simply bring this to the person's attention. Again, if individuals find certain behaviors completely intolerable, choosing not to interact is still preferable to interacting in a negative manner.

Finally, the suggestion that you should treat the individual with emotional disturbance as you would anyone else should also make clear that falsely positive interactions may be as inappropriate as overly punitive responses. Interacting with the emotionally disturbed person in a positive way only because you "feel sorry" for him or her is probably not fair to the individual, and may lead to unnecessary disappointment on the part of both the emotionally disturbed person and those befriending that person for the wrong reasons.

Summary

Persons who are emotionally disturbed present many intriguing questions for both the educational community and the larger society. The characteristics of their exceptionality make them extremely difficult to serve appropriately, especially if they have had many years to develop their deviant behavior patterns. Early intervention is particularly crucial for this population if we are to avert a rather bleak prognosis.

Emotional disturbance may manifest itself in either excessive inappropriate behavior or deficits in appropriate behavior. In school settings, it is most often the disruptive child who is identified as seriously emotionally disturbed, although excessively shy and withdrawn children may also be in need of some type of specialized services. Current professional opinion is that from 3% to 6% of the school-aged population may be seriously emotionally disturbed.

Children identified as emotionally disturbed are usually educated in special education classrooms in the public schools. More seriously disturbed individuals may require more intensive intervention, and are often served in residential settings. Treatment programs for emotionally disturbed children and adults often employ behavioral principles; appropriate behaviors are rewarded while inappropriate behavior may result in the loss of privileges. Academic programs stress basic academic skills, functional and daily-living skills, and social skills.

By definition, emotionally disturbed individuals may present behaviors that most of us find offensive; many people do not want to be around them. Interacting with emotionally disturbed persons may be difficult for some people, but should proceed as naturally as possible. Letting an individual know when behaviors are unacceptable, or simply choosing not to be around the individual when he or she is acting inappropriately are preferable to interacting with the emotionally disturbed person in a punitive or negative way.

Finally, school systems and communities in general find emotionally disturbed people among the most difficult to treat effectively and appropriately. The long-term prognosis for many emotionally disturbed persons is less than positive and the causal factors associated with emotional disturbance seem to be increasing in our society. While it may be discouraging that a population already notoriously difficult to treat may be growing in the future, it is imperative that the knowledge we have today leads to increased efforts toward early and intensive intervention efforts for children and families at risk. That is, while we must continue efforts at improving services and refining treatment programs for emotionally disturbed children and adults, the prevention of emotional disturbance must remain a top priority.

References

American Psychiatric Association. (1987). *Diagnostic and statistical manual of mental disorders* (3rd. ed. rev.). Washington, DC: Author.

Bank, L., Patterson, G. R., & Reid, J. B. (1987). Delinquency prevention through training parents in family management. *Behavior Analyst, 10,* 75-82.

Bower, E. (1982). Defining emotional disturbance: Public policy and research. *Psychology in the Schools, 19,* 55-60.

Cullinan, D., Epstein, M. H., & McLinden, D. (1986). Status and change in state administrative definitions of behavior disorder. *School Psychology Review, 15,* 383-392.

Epstein, M. H., Cullinan, D., & Sabatino, D. A. (1977). State definitions of behavior disorders. *Journal of Special Education, 11,* 417-425.

Kauffman, J. M. (1989). *Characteristics of behavior disorders of children and youth* (4th ed.). Columbus, OH: Charles Merrill.

Kazdin, A. E. (1987). *Conduct disorders in childhood and adolescence.* New York: Sage.

PL 94-142, The Education for All Handicapped Children Act. (1975). 20 United States Code, sec. 1400.

Patterson, G. R. (1982). *Coercive family process.* Eugene, OR: Castalia.

Rubin, R. A., & Balow, B. (1978). Prevalence of teacher identified behavior problems: A longitudinal study. *Exceptional Children, 45,* 102-111.

Walker, H. M., Hops, H., & Greenwood, C. R. (1981). RECESS: Research and development of a behavior management package for remediating social aggression in the school setting. In P. S. Strain (Ed.), *The utilization of classroom peers as behavior change agents.* New York: Plenum.

Suggested Readings

Bower, E. (1982). Defining emotional disturbance: Public policy and research. *Psychology in the Schools, 19,* 55-60.

Council for Children with Behavioral Disorders. (1990). Special issue: Issues in the exclusion of socially maladjusted students. *Behavioral Disorders, 15.*

Kauffman, J. M. (1988). Strategies for the non-recognition of social deviance. In R. B. Rutherford, C. M. Nelson, and S. R. Forness (Eds.), *Bases of severe behavioral disorders of children and youth.* Boston, MA: College-Hill.

Kazdin, A. E. (1984). *Behavior modification in applied settings* (3rd ed.). Homewood, IL: Dorsey Press.

Kazdin, A. E. (1985). *Treatment of antisocial behavior in children and adolescents.* Homewood, IL: Dorsey Press.

Loeber, R. (1982). The stability of antisocial and delinquent child behavior: A review. *Child Development, 53,* 1431-1446.

McAfee, J. K. (1989). Community colleges and individuals with emotional disorders. *Behavioral Disorders, 15,* 9-15.

Patterson, G. R. (1982). *Coercive family process.* Eugene, OR: Castalia.

Walker, H. M. (1979). *The acting-out child.* Boston, MA: Allyn & Bacon.

Wolf, M. M., Braukmann, C. J., & Ramp, K. A. (1987). Serious delinquent behavior as part of a significantly handicapping condition: Cures and supportive environments. *Journal of Applied Behavior Analysis, 20,* 347-359.

Notes

EMOTIONALLY DISTURBED PERSONS

Exploration

Individual Activities

1. Positive reinforcement is often used to control or modify the behavior of emotionally disturbed persons. List 10 reinforcers which would be appropriate to use with children. The list 10 for adults.

   Children

   _____   _____
   _____   _____
   _____   _____
   _____   _____
   _____   _____

   Adults

   _____   _____
   _____   _____
   _____   _____
   _____   _____
   _____   _____

2. Find out how others perceive emotional disturbance by asking five of your friends (who are not in this course) to define emotional disturbance. Write their definitions below. Rate (A,B,C,D,E) each definition's accuracy.

   Definition   Rating

   _____   _____
   _____   _____
   _____   _____
   _____   _____
   _____   _____

Group Activity

1. There has been conversation regarding the opening of a center for emotionally disturbed people in your neighborhood. Form groups of 4-5 people and discuss the pros and cons of the center and its location. Then present your group's ideas to your entire class.

    Reactions:

    _____
    _____
    _____

2. With your same group of 4-5 people develop a list of terms which have been used to label emotionally disturbed persons. Identify those terms which are positive and those which are negative.

    Reactions:

    _____
    _____
    _____

Reaction Paper 10.1

Assume that you have just been told by a psychologist that your child is emotionally disturbed. How would you react to the diagnosis? How would you feel? What would you tell others?

Continue on back if needed.

Reaction Paper 10.2

Assume that you are a camp counselor and you notice that Alex, one of your campers, is always isolated from the others. This troubles you and you decide to appoint Alex as your helper. This attention aggravates him and sends him into a frenzy of kicking, biting, and yelling. Alex may be emotionally disturbed. How would you deal with this situation? What could you do to calm him down? How would you avoid future problems?

Continue on back if needed.

Notes

CHAPTER 11

INDIVIDUALS WITH COMMUNICATION DIFFICULTIES

Carole Zangari

Introduction

If asked to list the disabling conditions which most frequently affect children and adults, you may form mental images of individuals with physical disabilities or visual or hearing impairments. Most likely your list would not include communication impairments, although disorders in speech and language are among the most frequently occurring disability in the United States. When you consider that difficulties in communicating may interfere with the development of social relationships, face-to-face conversation, written expression, learning, self-perception, and employment, it becomes evident that the topic of communication disorders warrants further study. Communication difficulties encompass a broad range of conditions which affect an individual's ability to hear, speak, understand and/or use oral or written language. While some of these conditions are congenital in origin, others are a result of injury or illness. Communication disorders can affect both children and adults. In the United States, one out of every 10 people is affected by a condition which impairs their ability to communicate either orally or in written form. The vast majority of these individuals is only mildly affected; however, there are over two million adults who have such severe communication impairments that they are unable to be gainfully employed.

The average person considers the terms language, speech, and communication to be synonyms, and often uses them interchangeably. To professionals in the fields of language, speech, and hearing; however, the following terms are quite distinct and denote different aspects of development and ability.

Communication is the broadest of these terms and refers to the exchange of information and ideas. Effective communication requires a Sender to encode or create a message which is then transmitted to a Receiver, who deciphers or comprehends the message. While the primary mode of communication is typically speech and language, you can also communicate through gestures, eye contact, facial expression, intonation, and communicative rate.

Speech is one of the primary modes of communication. In order to speak the Sender must have precise control of neuromuscular movements to produce sounds that can be combined into syllables and sequenced into words.

Language is a system of arbitrary symbols and rules that is shared and used by a particular society. Both the symbols and the rules vary according to the society in which they are used, and are generally quite complex. While the most common means of language-based communication is through speech or the written word, some languages are expressed through manual signs (e.g., American Sign Language, British Sign Language, Chinese Sign Language).

Obviously, speech and language are interrelated concepts. Although they are typically used together to communicate thoughts and ideas, speech and language may occur independently of each other in some contexts. For example, a bird trained to imitate spoken phrases is using speech without actually understanding the components of language. The use of language without speech is a far more common occurrence, with printed words and manual sign languages two popular examples.

Speech-language pathologists (also called speech therapists in some settings) and audiologists are the professionals who help individuals with communication difficulties learn to express themselves more effectively. Speech-language pathologists and audiologists may work as a team with other professionals including educators, occupational therapists, and physical therapists in helping communicatively impaired individuals achieve their potential.

Norms for communicative behavior are based on age, sex, cultural expectations, and social contexts, and vary widely from society to society. When a person's patterns of communicating are significantly different from the norms of the society in which he or she resides, that individual is said to have a <u>communication disorder</u>. Difficulties in communicating have traditionally been categorized as being either disorders of speech or language. However, many individuals have problems in both areas.

You will begin your study of individuals who experience difficulties in communicating by discussing some of the specific disorders that interfere with the communication process. First you will consider disorders affecting spoken output (disorders of articulation, fluency and voice) and then address issues related to the impairment of language.

Speech Disorders

Difficulties in producing speech sounds or problems relating to voice quality which attract attention or interfere with the communication process are termed speech disorders. There are several types of speech disorders each of which can affect individuals of any age, and which have a number of different causes.

Articulation Disorders. Articulation disorders refers to difficulties in forming speech sounds, or phonemes. Individuals with articulation problems have difficulty pronouncing individual sounds or sound combinations. This is by far the largest category of any of the speech disorders, affecting an estimated 75% of those with communication impairments (Newman, Creaghead, & Secord, 1985). The prevalence of articulation disorders is higher than the general population among individuals with other disabling conditions.

Most individuals who have articulation difficulties are described as having "functional articulation disorders." This term refers to the absence of an identifiable structural, physiological, or neurological cause within the speech mechanism or its supporting structures. It is thought that the articulation problems experienced by individuals with functional speech disorders are due to either normal variations in anatomy and physiology, by environmental, or psychological factors (Powers, 1971), however, other articulation disorders are known to have specific developmental or physical causes. Some articulation disorders are caused by physical malformations in the mouth (e.g., lip, jaw, teeth, or palate) or throat (e.g., larynx or vocal folds). Damage or injury to specific nerves or parts of the brain are other relatively common physical causes of articulation difficulties (e.g., cerebral palsy, head trauma, stroke).

Fluency Disorders (Stuttering). Interruptions in the flow of the normal rhythm of speech are referred to as dysfluencies. All of us have some instances of disfluency (also called stuttering) when speaking. You may repeat syllables or words occasionally, or fill in pauses with "uh" or "um" as you try to formulate the next phrase or sentence. These normal dysfluencies are differentiated from a fluency disorder only by the frequency with which they occur and the degree of effort it takes the speaker to manage them. When dysfluencies occur so often that they detract from the speaker's intended message or when intense effort is needed to orally express the message, the speaker is described as having a fluency disorder. Approximately one in 100 individuals in the United States is affected by a fluency disorder, with significantly more males than females being affected.

A specific cause for fluency disorders has not been identified, although a number of theories have been advanced. Inherent biological factors, environmental variables, and difficulties with the learning process have all been implicated as causal factors in stuttering behavior. Most researchers now believe that stuttering has a number of different causes and usually arises from a "complex interaction between the stutterer's environment--and the abilities the stutterer brings to that environment" (Conture, 1982, p. 18).

Voice Disorders. Individuals who can articulate clearly and whose speech is fluent may still be considered to have a speech disorder if they exhibit unusual or abnormal acoustical qualities when speaking. If the person's voice differs in pitch, quality, or volume from the norms established for that person's age and sex, a voice disorder may be present.

Speech begins when air from the respiratory system moves upward through the laryngeal system, which modifies the flow of the air stream. It then passes into the pharyngeal-oral-nasal system where it continues to be modified into speech sounds. A voice problem can occur when there is interference in the structure or functioning of these systems.

Abnormal structure or functioning of the phonatory or resonatory mechanisms may have a number of different causes. Organic problems within the laryngeal system, such as the presence of polyps or ulcers, may result in abnormal vocal behaviors. Vocal abuse can cause physical damage to the vocal cords and is a primary cause of voice disorders. Neurological problems and viral laryngitis may also cause voice problems.

Individuals with voice disorders may have problems maintaining an appropriate pitch for their age and sex, or may experience breaks in pitch when they speak. Other voice disorders relate to abnormal acoustical qualities of the voice. Hoarseness, breathiness, harshness, hypernasality (excessive nasal quality), or hyponasality (abnormally reduced nasal quality, as when one has a cold) are dysfunctions which relate to voice quality. Vocal volume which is inappropriate to the context can also be considered a voice disorder in some cases.

Approximately 3% of the school-age population has been identified as having a voice disorder. The prevalence in the total population is less and is estimated at 1%. The disparity between youngsters and adults is probably due to a combination of factors including variations in defining the condition and the fact that voice disorders go undiagnosed more frequently in adults.

Language Disorders

As discussed earlier, the primary tool used for communicating thoughts and ideas is language. Understanding and using language is a complex process requiring a number of distinct skills, involving visual and/or aural perception, processing, learning, memory, and expression. Individuals with language disorders fail to acquire language in a systematic and sequential way, and may have deficits in any of the areas mentioned above. Not all problems with understanding or using language are considered disorders. Individuals who acquire language in a systematic way within the normal sequence of development, but who progress at a slower rate, are considered to have a language delay.

Disorders of language can also be categorized as expressive or receptive. Expressive communication disorders relate to the product of the communicative act, namely speech or the written word. Difficulties in listening and interpreting speech are termed receptive communication problems.

Language has various components which are presented below. Difficulties in mastering any one of them may impair either receptive or expressive communication.

Form. Form refers to the elements of a particular language that integrate sounds and symbols (such as speech or written words) with meaning.

Phonology is the element dealing with the sounds of language and the rules that govern their combination. For example, in English we can only use the sound /ng/ together in the middle or end of a word. Other languages with different phonological rules permit the /ng/ sound to occur at the beginning of a word.

Morphology relates to a system of rules for how words are formed. For example, we use prefixes (such as "un" and "re") and suffixes (such as "er" and "est") to change the basic meanings of root words. Other languages change the basic meaning by altering the tonal quality or adjusting its place in the sentence.

Syntax is another system of rules which govern word order and sentence structure. Syntactic rules tell us how to create complex sentence structures such as compound sentences, embedded forms, questions, imperatives and negative sentences.

Content. Content is the element that is related to meaning of words and sentences.

Use. Use refers to the component involving the social usage of language.

It is evident the different components of language are highly interrelated. Because of this, while most individuals with language disorders have a pronounced problem with one of these elements, it is usually the case that they also have difficulties in one or more of the other components. The interdependency of these components makes accurate diagnosis and effective treatment a complex and time-consuming process.

Because the procedures for defining and assessing language disorders are not yet precise, and because language disorders frequently occur along with other disabling conditions, estimating the prevalence of this disorder is difficult. Current estimates are 5 to 10 % of the child population.

In some cases the etiology of difficulties in spoken or written language can be easily traced to an environmental, sensory, or physiological source. Examples of these causal factors include growing up in an extremely linguistically impoverished environment, hearing impairment, stroke, or head injury. However, in a great many cases it is impossible to identify a precise cause of the language disorder.

Characteristics

Now that you have had an introduction to each of the categories of communication disorders you are ready to examine the characteristics and behaviors exhibited by individuals experiencing these disorders. As these behaviors are discussed keep in mind that the degree of severity of the disorder will affect the extent to which these traits and behaviors occur. As with other impairments, the degree of severity ranges from very mild, in which the difficulties in communicating may not even be noticeable in most contexts, to quite severe, where the affected individual cannot communicate well enough to get personal needs met on a daily basis.

Determining the severity of a communication disorder involves evaluating two important factors; (a) the extent to which the communication skills are deviant for the individual's age, sex, culture, educational level, and socioeconomic background; and (b) the social and emotional impact of the disorder on the functioning of the individual. As would be expected, individuals with more severe impairments will exhibit the behaviors typical of that disorder with more frequency and intensity.

Speech Disorders

The characteristics of individuals with speech disorders are presented in this section. Each category of speech disorder is addressed separately.

Articulation Disorders. Individuals with articulation disorders have one or more of the following types of errors with their speech.

- **Omissions** - only parts of words are pronounced with one or more sounds being omitted:
  "I'm rea-y fo beh now" for "I'm ready for bed now"
- **Substitutions** - words are produced improperly with one sound being substituted for the desired sound:
  "I'm weady now" for "I'm ready now"
- **Distortions** - sounds are produced incorrectly, and are often recognizable, but do not sound right.

Additions - sounds are inserted where they do not belong:
"my best fuhriend" for "my best friend"

The majority of individuals with articulation disorders have mild problems that respond well to treatment and may not impair the person's overall functioning. A few individuals, who have very severe articulation disorders, are intelligible only to family members and close associates or within a known or predictable context. Unfamiliar communication partners, such as store clerks, will probably not be able to understand this person well enough to converse with him or her. Acquaintances, such as classmates or co-workers, may not be able to understand the person with severe articulation problems unless situational cues are available to aid in deciphering the misarticulated message.

Fluency Disorders (Stuttering). Individuals with fluency disorders may have one or more types of interruptions in the rhythm of their speech patterns.

Part-word repetitions - "I wuh-wuh-wuh-want some milk please."
Prolongations - "I want some mmmmmmilk please."
Broken words - "I want some milk p---lease."
Tense pauses - "I want some milk --- please" accompanied by rapid eye blinks, lip posturing, upper body tension, or other distracting mannerisms.

Individuals with fluency disorders may anticipate situations in which they are likely to become dysfluent. They may become anxious when facing situations such as using the phone, speaking in a large group, or calling someone from a distance, and may seek to avoid such situations.

There are many things about fluency disorders which are as yet unexplained. It has been repeatedly observed, however, that there are certain conditions under which an individual with a fluency disorder is less likely to stutter. For example, even individuals with severe fluency disorders rarely stutter when using automatic phrases, when talking without thinking, when talking to one's self, or swearing, or if they speak while distracted. Most people with fluency disorders will also speak quite fluently when provided with a rhythmic bases (e.g., steady beat of a metronome, singing, choral responding). Exactly why the presence of these conditions reduces stuttering behavior still eludes us.

The range of severity of stuttering behavior is wide, ranging from very severe to barely perceptible. Individuals who stutter may approach situations in which they

INDIVIDUALS WITH COMMUNICATION DIFFICULTIES

must speak with varying degrees of anxiety, nervousness, and frustration. Low self-esteem and extreme anxiety may be present in individuals with very severely dysfluent speech (Van Riper, 1978).

Many children between the ages of two and seven go through a normal stage in the development where they exhibit an increased amount of dysfluencies in their speech. Although these children may have an increase in their dysfluencies during this developmental period, the amount of stuttering they exhibit is still less than that of individuals who have a fluency disorder. A child who experiences more than 10 dysfluencies in every 100 words may be considered at risk for a stuttering problem if other symptoms are present.

Voice Disorders. While you may notice an unusual or unpleasant quality in the speech of individuals with voice disorders, you will probably be able to understand them in most instances. The pitch of their voice may be higher or lower than you would expect from a person of that sex and age. They may have a hoarse, breathy, harsh, or nasal quality in their speech. The volume with which they speak may be inappropriate to the context, such as speaking in a whisper when ordering a meal in a restaurant or speaking too loudly during a private conversation.

As with most other communication disorders, the range of severity of this dysfunction is great. You may not even be aware of the problems experienced by some individuals with voice disorders, or you may be aware of them to a minor degree. A small percentage of individuals with voice disorders (such as those whose laryngeal systems have been damaged by injury or disease) have such extreme limitations that their speech is unintelligible.

Language Disorders

Because so many individuals with language disorders also have other disabling conditions (such as learning disabilities or mental retardation), it is difficult to identify behaviors and traits that are characteristic of all or most people with language disorders. Valid generalizations of this group are therefore not possible in most cases. Additionally, many of the individuals with true language disorders may go undiagnosed if some other problem attracts a higher level of attention.

Children who have failed to develop adequate linguistic skills face a unique set of challenges as they enter school. Consider that the focus of the first three years of school is on reading (the written form of language) and other basic skills. If the child has a receptive language disorder he or she may not understand the teacher's instructions, and will most likely lag behind his or her peers in reading ability. The problem is compounded as the child gets older and is expected to have adequate reading skills and to use those skills to acquire information in content areas, such as science, social studies, and English.

Children with receptive communication disorders (who fail to process all or part of what they hear) may be unable to follow directions and may be considered inattentive or uncooperative. As they continue to experience academic failure they may express their frustration through low self-esteem, withdrawal, or inappropriate behavior. Current thinking is that most severe difficulties in academic learning may have problems in language learning and use at the root of the problem (Lee & Shapero-Fine, 1984). Children with expressive communication disorders often have difficulties socializing. Their abnormal patterns of communication may be viewed negatively by their peers and may limit opportunities to develop friendships.

A different set of challenges confronts individuals who have acquired language disorders. One type of acquired language disorder is aphasia, which affects 1.8 million Americans. Caused by injury to the brain, aphasia refers to a partial or total loss of language. Because different areas of the brain are responsible for different areas of language, the way in which language is impaired depends on what part of the brain sustained injury. Two types of aphasia, fluent and nonfluent, can be distinguished by their behavioral characteristics.

Individuals with fluent aphasia are unable to understand much of what they read and/or hear. They usually speak clearly and fluently and use appropriate grammar. However, both their speech and written language is largely devoid of appropriate meaning, as illustrated in the example below.

> Q: When did you first have trouble speaking?
> A: Well, I'll tell you, I couldn't hardly get a cab. You know how it is. It's a greasly bee; that's what I say. Got to hand it to her and look it over, will ya?

By contrast individuals with nonfluent aphasia are able to understand most of what they hear and read. They typically have labored, monotone speech that is poorly articulated and may require intense effort. Their speech is telegraphic in nature (devoid of small, less meaningful words such as articles); often punctuated by pauses and fillers. The content-loaded words occur in the proper sequence, but other grammatically necessary words are missing, as can be noted in the example which follows.

> Q: When did you first have trouble speaking?
> A: Ahh...Jeez........No,no....Oh,last....Jeez...Thanks.....ummmm...Thanks - giving.

Intervention

Some individuals with communication difficulties develop or regain part or all their speech and language skills naturally with the passage of time, regardless of whether or not intervention is provided. This is most often seen with younger children with mild functional articulation disorders, some of whom self-correct their misarticulations and speak normally by the end of their elementary years even without therapeutic intervention. Individuals whose language difficulties are caused by brain injury (e.g., from a car accident or stroke) may also spontaneously recover some skills without therapy.

However, for the vast majority of individuals with communication disorders, a program of intervention carefully planned and implemented by a speech-language professional is needed. The first step toward helping communicatively disordered individuals develop functional communication skills is identification. In the public schools this is typically done through routine speech and language screenings and teacher referrals. Persons outside of school age are often identified as having difficulties by other family members.

When medical problems are present and a communication problem is suspected, a physician may refer the person to a speech-language pathologist. A comprehensive assessment, including a case history, examination of the speech mechanism, standardized testing, informal evaluation, and patient or caregiver interview, is then completed. From the information gleaned in the assessment, the speech-language pathologist prioritizes the individual's needs and establishes objectives leading to skills which address those needs. A treatment plan is then developed and implemented. Re-assessment and any further treatment deemed necessary are the final steps in the intervention process.

Speech Disorders

This section describes methods of therapeutic intervention typically used in remediating communication difficulties. Each category of speech disorder is separately addressed.

Articulation Disorders. Intervention provided to remediate articulation disorders is varied and is often related to the etiology that has been identified. For example, if the misarticulations are a result of a structural anomaly, such as a cleft (or fissure) in the palate, dental, medical, surgical and/or prosthetic options are usually pursued in addition to speech therapy.

Intervention for individuals with functional articulation problems begins by assessing the conditions under which speech sounds are made correctly and incorrectly. Once the error sounds have been identified, the speech-language pathologist helps the individual to discriminate between correct and incorrect pronunciation of the target sound(s). The speech-language pathologist always provides a good model of the target sound and gives explanations and demonstrations of how that sound is formed. Mirrors, pictures, and plastic models of the oral cavity may be used in the teaching process. Specific techniques, verbal instructions, practice, and feedback are generally required to learn new patterns of articulation.

Fluency Disorders. Dysfluent speech is an ancient phenomena which has been documented by the early Greeks and in the Bible. Early attempts at remediation, such as talking with pebbles in the mouth, have been abandoned and, while newer methods are encouraging, a cure for stuttering has remained elusive. Various intervention programs have been used to treat stuttering behavior once a fluency disorder has been identified. While each of those discussed in this section has helped some individuals become more fluent, the current professional focus is on controlling rather than curing fluency disorders.

Prevention of fluency disorders is a topic which has received increased attention in recent years. As discussed earlier, some children go through a normal period of stuttering in the development of communication skills. Professionals now recognize that calling attention to these normal dysfluencies may actually increase their occurrence, putting the child at risk for developing a true fluency disorder. Parents can help prevent their child from developing a disorder by ignoring dysfluencies. Well-intentioned parents, urging a dysfluent child to calm down or speak more slowly, unwittingly encourage the stuttering behavior by calling attention to it.

Behavioral approaches to treating fluency disorders teach the individual to gradually shape approximations of fluent speech. Desensitization programs, with an emphasis on facing rather than avoiding the problem, and relaxation training have been found to be helpful.

Parents and siblings of children who have fluency disorders often participate in counseling to help them learn ways to promote fluent speech. When parents are observed interacting with their dysfluent children it is not uncommon to see them selectively reinforce the stuttering behavior. For example, a child having trouble tying her shoe may call her father several times using fluent speech in requesting his assistance. The father continues his present activity (e.g., watching a ball game on TV) until the child becomes so frustrated that the tension affects her voice ("Duh-duh-duh-duh-dadddddy! Cuh-cuh-cuh-come here!"). Recognizing her distress he immediately gets up and helps her tie her shoe. Her father has unwittingly taught her that dysfluent speech will help her achieve goals (e.g., getting dad's attention) and that fluent speech is likely to be ignored. The goal of family intervention in this situation would be to help the parents recognize the effect of their differential treatment and to learn to respond positively to the fluent speech and ignore that which is dysfluent.

Voice Disorders. Aiding in the prevention of voice disorders is an important role of the speech-language pathologist. It is often the case that the vocal behavior of individuals with voice disorders contributes to the abnormal acoustical qualities of their speech. For example, a young man entering the job market for the first time may force himself to use a lower pitched voice to sound mature and professional. This can cause damage to the laryngeal system, such as contact ulcers on the vocal cords, which can further impair vocal quality. Educating individuals about good "speech hygiene" can go a long way in helping them avoid behaviors that may lead to a voice disorder, and early intervention may prevent significant damage to the vocal mechanism.

Because voice disorders are often related to organic problems with the laryngeal system, a differential diagnosis of the cause of the problem is important prior to initiating therapy. Medical and surgical options are often pursued in cases of disease or structural abnormality. Vocal rest, in which the voice is not used at all, may also be included as part of the treatment.

As previously discussed, vocal abuse is a primary cause of voice problems. Intervention for individuals who abuse their voices often consists of a program designed to make them aware of their abusive behaviors. Yelling, singing at too high or low a pitch, smoking, excessive talking, talking in a noisy environment, and excessive coughing or throat clearing may all cause or contribute to a voice disorder. Individuals with disorders caused by these problems are then trained to use their voices in ways which are not abusive, and taught how to monitor their vocal behaviors. Efforts may also be made to have them avoid situations in which they are likely to further damage their vocal mechanism. Vocal rest is often prescribed in order to allow the damaged mechanism a chance to heal and recover.

It is important that the individual who has recovered from a voice problem continues to utilize the newly learned vocal behaviors even after the voice problem has subsided. If the vocal mechanism is reexposed to damaging behaviors (e.g., yelling, excessive throat-clearing) it is likely that further injury will occur and that the voice problem will return.

Some individuals with severe voice impairments may need the help of an assistive device to be able to speak intelligibly. This is most often seen in individuals whose vocal cords have been surgically removed; a procedure called a laryngectomy. Surgical implants or a vibrator held at the neck may be used as a substitute for the vibration of vocal cords. The speech of a person who has had a laryngectomy will probably sound quite unusual to you, and you may need to pay close attention in order to understand it.

Language Disorders

The focus of intervention for an individual with a language disorder depends on the component(s) in which most difficulty is experienced. In general the speech-language pathologist must consider the communicative contexts in which the individual participates (i.e., What are the environmental demands?) and design a program that will help the individual develop language skills to meet the needs of those environments.

If the individual has problems with linguistic form, intervention may focus on learning rules for how words are formed (e.g., suffixes, plural forms), formulating syntactically correct messages (e.g., passive sentences, question forms). Instruction in the relationships between words may be necessary for the person with difficulties in language content. Treatment may include exercises to teach concepts, word analogies, opposites, object-action relationships, and categories. Individuals who have deficits in the area of language use may benefit from learning when different types of language forms or structures are appropriate for different contextual situations.

The course of treatment for a child with a language disorder is structured differently from the intervention program provided to an adult for several reasons. First, most adults receiving treatment for language disorders spent most of their lives as adequate communicators, but lost those abilities due to accident, illness or injury. In contrast, most children with language disorders never acquired linguistic competency. While adults are in the position of relearning skills they have lost, most children are learning their language skills for the first time. Secondly, because of the difference in age and level of maturity, remedial activities and materials are necessarily different.

Teaching functional language skills in the settings in which they will be used, and working with significant others are factors which are known to significantly improve language learning outcomes (Spradlin & Siegel, 1982). Guided by these principles, speech-language pathologists design a series of activities that give the language disordered individual opportunities to observe and practice the appropriate linguistic structure.

Regardless of the age of the language-disordered individual, the speech-language pathologist may employ a variety of techniques to teach the desired skill. Some common techniques are described below.

> **Correction.** Correction is simply telling the person that his or her response was incorrect, and demonstrating the correct response ("No, that's a red one.")
>
> **Expansion.** Expanding refers to expanding on the original word or phrase, or elaborating on the topic ("A red truck. That's a big red truck.")
>
> **Completion.** This term means providing a linguistic framework for the desired word or phrase ("That truck is .....")
>
> **Replacement.** Replacement means substituting one desired form for another example of the same form ("The truck is red. The ball is red. The cup is red.")

Since communication is comprised of such a sophisticated set of skills it is no surprise that remediating speech and language disorders is a complicated process which needs to be provided by a competent communication specialist. Speech-language pathologists who work with children and adults with communication disorders may be based in a hospital, a medical or university clinic, a school, or they may be in private practice. Intervention may be provided at those sites or at the individual's home.

Augmentative and Alternative Communication (AAC)

A small group of individuals with communication difficulties are so severely impaired that they are unable to use speech to express even their most basic thoughts and needs. Individuals with this degree of impairment may also have multiple physical disabilities, cognitive impairment, or autism. Special techniques and resources are necessary to help nonspeaking individuals acquire functional communication skills.

Augmentative and alternative communication (AAC) refers to a multi-component system of communicating that replaces or supplements the individual's existing communication skills. AAC intervention may include the use of manual signs, gestures, vocalization, and communication aids with pictures or other graphic symbols, such as a specially designed communication book or electronic device with printed or voice output (Blackstone, 1986). Individuals who use AAC generally require long-term intervention as their communication needs grow and change.

Many speech-language pathologists teach new communication skills in an isolated setting, such as a therapy room in a public school, clinic, or hospital. Therapy may be given on an individual basis or in a small group. Once the new communication skills are learned in this isolated setting, the focus is on transferring the use of those skills to everyday living and working environments. Spouses, parents, siblings and teachers may be asked to play a role in this important and difficult step in the therapeutic process by providing opportunities for practice, monitoring performance, and giving feedback and encouragement.

Expectations

The presence of a communication disorder typically does not preclude individuals from attending and succeeding in school or their chosen career, unless the disorder is extremely severe. In most cases the affected individual's life is no different than the rest of us, though activities requiring communication may take more effort and courage. Attitude and self-confidence play an enormous role in the decisions made by individuals with communication impairments. While one college student with a mild fluency disorder may shy away from any speaking activities another may study to be a minister or speech-language pathologist.

Aside from their specific language, articulation, fluency, and voice problems, most individuals with communication disorders have no specialized traits, characteristics, or behaviors that differentiate them from the general populace. If the individual can be understood by unfamiliar communication partners, there is no reason to expect that performance in school, work, and the community would be affected by the disorder.

Individuals with severe disorders (e.g., those who are not intelligible to people other than family members and close associates) may indeed be restricted in their access to a variety of life experiences, and, thus, their ability to function in those contexts may be impaired. Their limitations in communicating their thoughts and ideas will probably affect the decisions they make.

For example, individuals with severe fluency disorders, or those who experience a great deal of anxiety may elect to avoid situations which trigger dysfluent behavior. They may choose to do a written rather than an oral report for an English class, interview for the typing position rather than the receptionist job, or use the fax machine rather than the telephone. They may also capitalize on activities in which their speech is fluent, such as playing guitar and singing or joining a choir. Individuals with a history of voice problems will want to consider avoiding situations that make excessive demands on the vocal mechanism. They may elect not to participate in choir or cheerleading or may choose not to pursue careers such as broadcasting or teaching.

Interactions

When you communicate with people you have certain expectations of them as communication partners. You may expect them to make eye contact, to pay attention to what you are saying, and respond promptly in an encouraging fashion. When your communication partner fails to live up to your expectations, as often occurs in conversing with a person who has a communication impairment, you may feel anxious and uncomfortable. It is natural to feel some apprehension when interacting with someone whose patterns of communication deviate from our expectations. Feelings of inadequacy, self-consciousness, and embarrassment are often experienced by both parties.

You have probably already interacted with at least a few people who had communication disorders. It may have been a child in your neighborhood who was unable to articulate clearly or a classmate who stuttered. You may have encountered a store clerk with an unusually hoarse voice or maybe you have an elderly relative whose language was impaired after a stroke. Your experiences in dealing with these interactions are probably a mixture of positives and negatives and may be as varied as the individuals themselves.

It is important to remember, however, that the attitudes of both parties exert enormous influence on the overall success of the interaction. Altering your attitude and expectations and learning a few strategies will facilitate interactions with individuals who have communication impairments. The following guidelines may ease the flow of interactions you may have with persons with communication disorders.

Communication is possible. You will be able to understand most individuals with communication problems, even though their words and sentences may sound funny or child-like to you. Unless you are so instructed to behave differently there is no reason to alter any of your typical patterns of discourse as long as your interactions are successful. You should use the same nonverbal behaviors (e.g., eye contact, facial expressions), tone, rate of speech, and discuss the same topics as you would if that person's speech and language were completely devoid of errors.

Avoid complex messages. Individuals with receptive language problems are likely to find it difficult following complex conversations. If you become aware that your communication partner is having trouble understanding you, try speaking more slowly, using pauses, and simplifying the complexity of your message.

Adjust your conversation to fit the interaction. In your daily conversations you adjust your speech and language to fit the context of the interaction. You might greet a peer with "Hey, how's it goin'?" but would never address your boss in the same fashion. You automatically consider the age, educational level, culture, social status, and life experiences of a communication partner as you formulate what you will say and how you will communicate it. This is no less important when the partner is someone with a communication impairment. Keep in mind that the presence of a communication disorder is not usually indicative of alertness, intelligence, or enthusiasm.

Be patient. Breakdowns in communication between two people are inevitable and are obviously more likely to occur if either party experiences a communication disorder. Because of the nature of their problem, individuals with communication disorders may need some assistance in clarifying and resolving the issue at hand. By demonstrating your interest and patience when breakdowns occur you will encourage your partner to try again. As your partner formulates a new response, look for other cues to help you understand the message. The context or current topic may help you decipher that which sounded like "tea rose, peas" at the breakfast table was meant to be "Cheerios, please." Facial expressions, gestures, and tone of voice may give you enough additional information to make sense out of an unintelligible message.

INDIVIDUALS WITH COMMUNICATION DIFFICULTIES

Ask questions. If it seems appropriate you may want to ask some specific questions (e.g., "Did you say ....?" "Are you telling me about ...?"). If little progress is being made you may want to suggest an alternate means of clarification (e.g., "Do you want to write it?" "Is it something you can point to?"). As in any social situation, common sense and courtesy will dictate how directive you will want to be.

Respect your partner's wishes. It is usually best to allow your partner to decide whether or not to pursue the topic, since only that person knows how important the message is. (He may not want to spend two minutes trying to tell you about the new cereal he saw advertised, but may elect to continue the process to thank you for the birthday gift.) Respect your partner's wishes to pursue or discontinue the discussion.

Acknowledge communication attempts. It is important to always acknowledge a person who has tried to communicate with you, even if the person's attempts have been unsuccessful. It is almost never acceptable to ignore another person; social rules of etiquette apply regardless of the presence of a disability. We typically do not presume to put words in the mouth of another person, and so you should avoid finishing their sentences for them, or guessing what they are about to say. Those same courtesies should be extended to persons with communication impairments unless they have advised you to do otherwise.

Be direct. If you are unable to understand a person with a communication disorder, try being direct about your failure to understand, (e.g., "I didn't understand you. Can you tell me again?"). Don't ignore the breakdown in communication or pretend that you understood. Remember that if you can't understand the person, others probably can't either. Chances are that the individual is used to being misunderstood and may welcome your direct approach. This lets the person know that you are interested in what he/she is saying, rather than how it is being said, and gives the person another chance to communicate his/her message.

Patience and encouragement assures a successful interaction. A patient, encouraging attitude goes a long way in facilitating successful interaction. It is important that you not interrupt (unless instructed to do so) or act impatiently. Individuals with neurologically-based communication impairments often need additional time to process verbal communication, formulate, and execute their responses. Be aware that this may alter the pace of your discussion. Be patient and allow them the response time they need.

Summary

Communication impairments affect ten percent of our population. Most of those individuals experience problems in articulation, while others have fluency, voice, and language disorders. The causes of these disorders are varied, as are the methods of intervention and treatment. The majority of individuals with communication difficulties are able to participate fully in school, work, and the community, however, activities requiring interaction may be more arduous, time-consuming, and frustrating. Simple strategies, such as those provided in the previous section, can be used to facilitate the interaction process.

References

Blackstone, S. W. (Ed.). (1986). *Augmentative communication: An introduction.* Rockville, MD: American Speech-Language-Hearing Association.

Conture, E. G. (1982). *Stuttering.* Englewood Cliffs, NJ: Prentice-Hall.

Lee, A. D., & Shapero-Fine, J. (1984). When a language problem is primary: Secondary school strategies. In G. P. Wallace & K. Butler (Eds.), *Language learning disabilities in school-aged children* (pp. 338-359). Baltimore: Williams and Wilkins.

Newman, P. W., Creaghead, N. A., & Secord, W. (1985). *Assessment and remediation of articulatory and phonological disorders.* Columbus, OH: Merrill.

Powers, M. H. (1971). Functional disorders of articulation - Symptomatology and etiology. In L. E. Travis (Ed.), *Handbook of speech-language pathology and etiology.* New York: Appleton-Century-Crofts.

Spradlin, J., & Siegel, G. M. (1982). Language training in natural and clinical environments. *Journal of Speech and Hearing Disorders, 47,* 2-6.

Van Riper, C. (1978). *Speech correction: Principles and methods* (6th ed.). Englewood Cliffs, NJ: Prentice-Hall.

Suggested Readings

Calculator, S. N., & Bedrosian, J. L. (Eds.). (1988). *Communication assessment and intervention for adults with mental retardation.* Boston: Little, Brown.

Costello, J. M., & Holland, A. L. (Eds.). (1986). *Handbook of speech and language disorders.* San Diego CA: College Hill Press.

Duguay, M. J., & Ritter, D. H. (1988). *Voice problems: Questions and answers for persons with voice disorders.* Austin, TX: Pro-Ed.

Eisenson, J. (1989). *Understanding stroke and aphasia.* Austin, TX: Pro-Ed.

Fraser, J., & Perkins, W. H. (Eds.). (1987). *Do You stutter? A guide for teens.* Memphis, TN: Speech Foundation of America.

Keith, R. L. (1989). *A handbook for the laryngectomee.* Austin, TX: Pro-Ed.

Lloyd, L. (Ed.). (1976). *Communication assessment and intervention strategies.* Baltimore: University Park Press.

Tanner, D. C. (1988). *The family's guide to stroke, head trauma and speech disorders.* Austin, TX: Pro-Ed.

Notes

Exploration

Individual Activities

1. How important is your speech to you? Try this experiment to find out. Go to a local mall or shopping center and ask a question about an item for sale. Select an item in six different stores. While talking to the six sales clerks keep your tongue pressed to the roof of your mouth or to the back of your front upper teeth. Note, in the spaces provided, what was positive and negative about this experience.

   _____
   _____
   _____

2. Assume that you are sitting in the student cafeteria and someone sits down next to you and wants to chat. You start conversing with this person and realize that he/she has a speech disorder. This should be no problem for you because you've read, in this chapter, some simple strategies used to facilitate the interaction process. List 5 strategies and explain them.

   1. _____
   _____
   _____

   2. _____
   _____
   _____

   3. _____
   _____
   _____

   4. _____
   _____
   _____

5. _____
_____
_____

Group Activities

1. Speech in Front of the Class. Choose four people to get up in front of the class and give speeches on washing a car, playing a sport, a family member, or what they did this weekend. Who does which speech can be left up to the speakers, but they must not be given a chance to practice or too much time to think about what they want to say. It should be spontaneous. The rest of the class will keep track of how many times the person says "umm" or "like" or just hesitates for a long time. How did these people do? You see, everyone has some sort of fluency disorder. Think about how it must feel to have trouble saying what you are thinking all the time.

   Reactions:

   _____
   _____
   _____

2. Get into groups of four or five. You are going to do some translation here, but first you have a little essay to write. Have your group write a nine or ten question/answer dialogue between two people. When finished, a group representative will read it to the class. When writing this dialogue, use slang, street language, or jive. Your job is to try to stump the class on what you mean. The class will try to decipher your slang. When finished, read the dialogue how it would be expressed in proper English. This shows how different expressions of speech can hinder the communication process.

   Reactions:

   _____
   _____
   _____

INDIVIDUALS WITH COMMUNICATION DIFFICULTIES

Reaction Paper 11.2

Complete Individual Activity One. Then, write about your reactions and the reactions of others.

_____

Continue on back if needed.

Notes

CHAPTER 12

GIFTED AND TALENTED INDIVIDUALS

Miriam Adderholdt-Elliott
    and
Donna Wandry

Introduction

Throughout this book, you have had the opportunity to learn about different disabilities. The exceptionality of being gifted and talented is the only field of exceptionality which is not considered to be a disability. However, this field does demand inclusion in the concept of exceptionality, since many identified gifted and talented individuals benefit from special programs. In this chapter, you will learn about the definitions of gifted and talented performance, characteristics of these individuals, special programs for children of all ages as well as adults, and the advantages, as well as the disadvantages, of being gifted or talented.

Defining the concept of giftedness and talent has proven to be an arduous task, and one that has spawned much controversy. Specifically, a large disparity exists in the components of giftedness (Wolf & Stephens, 1986). One of the latest definitions appears in a bill passed by Congress in 1988 (Title IV-H.R. 5) and applies specifically to children and youth:

> The term gifted and talented children means children and youth who give evidence of high performance capability in areas such as intellectual, creative, artistic, or leadership capacity, or in specific academic fields, and who require services or activities not ordinarily provided by the school in order to fully develop such capabilities. (cited in Kirk & Gallagher, 1989, p. 84)

The words high performance capability refer to individuals who might have extraordinary ability, but are not showing it in their performance. The term specific academic ability refers to individuals who might have exceptional ability in one academic area but not in others. The words creative, artistic, or leadership capacity are intended to take the term gifted out of a narrow academic meaning. This definition recognizes not only academic giftedness, but a diversity of talents (Kirk & Gallagher, 1989).

Cohn, Cohn, and Kanevsky (1988) elaborated on this diversity by defining gifted individuals as having extremely high abilities in academic areas, and talented individuals as having superior abilities in non-academic areas such as leadership and the creative or performing arts. Congdon (1985) simply stated that the term "gifted" is perhaps best used as an umbrella term to cover a number of groups of individuals of exceptional ability.

These current definitions indicate a growth from early theories in giftedness. An early definition was tied to performance on the Stanford-Binet Intelligence Scale, which was developed by Lewis Terman after World War I. Individuals who scored above a certain point, an arbitrarily chosen IQ score, were called gifted.

Prevalence

Arbitrary sets of criteria do not lend themselves to a consistent definition of performance levels that are considered "extraordinary" or "superior." Accompanying the discussion of accurate definitions of giftedness must be the question of prevalence. Because the criteria for inclusion as a gifted or talented child or adult is inconsistent at best, it is difficult to determine what percentage of the population may be identified as gifted or talented. Prevalence is determined by what criteria are set and what assessment is used, and by the definitions being used.

For example, an IQ score may be used as a criterion. If the cutoff is set at 180 IQ and above, the resultant identified "giftedness" would apply only to one person in a million. If, however, the cutoff is 115 IQ and above, 15-20% of the school population might be identified as gifted (Wolf & Stephens, 1986). Although the criteria for identification of giftedness are so fluid, general consensus holds that 3-5% of the school population can be identified as gifted (Swassing, 1988).

As you can imagine, it is a bit more difficult still to set criteria for exceptional talent in non-academic areas. When one considers athletic prowess, musical ability, creative thinking, leadership capacity, or visual or performing arts, it may be an insurmountable task to create any cutoff points for what is exceptionally talented and what is not.

Cause

Just as it is difficult to assess giftedness and talent, it is difficult to determine the causes. Unlike other areas of exceptionality, the study of giftedness has yielded no specific etiology (Cohn et al., 1988). In evaluating the possible contributors to giftedness and talent, several questions have been raised by researchers. Are gifted and talented children born or made? What are the contributions of heredity and environment?

Giftedness and talent can be found at every socioeconomic stratum, and in all ethnic, cultural, and racial groups (Wolf & Stephens, 1986). Clark (1988) asserted that giftedness is a biologically rooted concept, with evidence of increased brain growth. However, she further maintained that giftedness is a combination of heredity and environment. How giftedness is expressed depends both on the genetic patterns of the individual and the support provided by that individual's environment. Although researchers make a strong case for the importance of heredity in giftedness, most agree that environment is important as well. Extraordinary talent may be shaped by heredity, but it is nurtured and developed by the environment (Kirk & Gallagher, 1989). This point will be investigated further later in this chapter, within the context of intervention strategies.

Characteristics

Individuals with giftedness or extraordinary talent, as mentioned earlier, can be found at every socioeconomic stratum and within every ethnic or racial group.

Additionally, giftedness spans the life cycle. Aspects of giftedness can be studied in their applicability to infants, school-age children, and adults. There is no one profile that you can identify as belonging to every gifted or talented person, no matter what the age. In this respect, gifted individuals can be referred to as belonging to a very heterogeneous group, as is true of any exceptionality.

Heterogeneity

Giftedness is a complex concept covering a wide range of abilities and traits. Some individuals may have special talents. They may not be outstanding in academics, but they may have special abilities in music, literature, or leadership (Swassing, 1988). Physically, you cannot identify gifted persons. They do not fit the stereotype of a bookworm with glasses, toting advanced literature in quantum physics. They are not pale and sickly social incompetents. They simply learn differently.

Individuals who are gifted may exhibit intraindividual or interindividual differences. For example, a graph of any individual's abilities would reveal some high points and some lower points; scores would not be the same across all dimensions measured (Swassing, 1988). A person who is gifted may have very strong abilities in mathematics, but comparatively lower abilities in written expression. This is an example of intraindividual differences and is certainly true of any gifted individual. However, the gifted individual's pattern of performance may be well above the average for the person's peer group. The levels of performance in all academic subjects, even though highs and relative lows may exist among the subjects, may be generally higher than those of the same age and grade peers. This is referred to as interindividual differences.

Characteristics Across the Life Span

Infants and preschool children. While it is difficult to discern at an early age whether a child is gifted or talented, understanding possible characteristics can lead to recognizing potentially gifted individuals. Exceptionally gifted individuals have a passion for learning, absorbing knowledge from all their experiences. It is important to remember that not all potentially gifted or talented children embody all characteristics discussed.

In their early years, intellectually precocious children may learn to speak and develop sophisticated language patterns, teach themselves to read at a very early age, and exhibit phenomenal perceptiveness to their environment (Cohn et al., 1988). Additionally, they may exhibit long attention spans, abstract reasoning abilities, or specific talents such as art or music.

School-age youth. Gifted or talented students may possess one, several, or all of many possible performance strengths. These include the following:

High verbal ability and an unusually large vocabulary
A questioning attitude and increased curiosity
Increased attention span, persistence, and concentration
Ability to learn basic skills more quickly and retain more information with less repetition
Unusually wide or narrow range of interests
Sensitivity to others and the environment
High level of independence.

It must be remembered that giftedness is not solely a function of intelligence, as some of the traits listed above suggest. It is a combination of intelligence, personality, motivation, and environmental variables (Feldman, 1984).

Gifted and talented adolescents. Within the school years, it is important to consider the unique aspects of adolescents who are gifted or talented. Adolescence is a particularly challenging period of growth, stressing such factors as achievement of independence, exploration and acceptance of sexuality, acknowledgement of intellectual power, development of meaningful interpersonal relationships, and acquisition of life maintenance, career, and self-actualization skills (Clark, 1988).

While all adolescents can be characterized as intense and showing rapid fluctuations in emotion and widely ranging mood swings (partially a result of biochemical changes that are occurring), adolescents who are gifted or talented may confound this behavior by interspersing periods of unusual maturity and marvelous insight (Clark, 1988). When you consider the advanced abilities that gifted adolescents may have, and combine that with the insecurities of growing up, you can see that the teen years may be a time of difficult transition for gifted and talented adolescents. They must deal with such factors as being out of stage (intellectually bored and so focused on success that they are out of touch with their environments), out of phase (aware of differences and distanced from their peer group), and out of sync (feeling a sense of not fitting in) (Clark, 1988).

Giftedness in adults. It might be assumed that gifted or talented children grow up to be gifted or talented adults. A key study by Terman (Terman & Oden, 1976) indicated that this indeed is the case. Terman and Oden stated that the gifted child, with few exceptions, grows up to be the achieving adult. As with children, the ability profiles are generally above those of the general population, but reveal highs and lows. The areas of greatest achievement in gifted or talented adults are in intellectual ability, scholastic accomplishment, and vocational achievements. Physically, gifted adults continue to be above average, experiencing lower mortality rates and stronger health. The delinquency rate is below that of the general population.

The Terman study, which is accepted as the first definitive follow-up study of gifted adults, maintains that these individuals do well not only in school and career, but also in areas like mental health, marriage, and character. Other studies (Kaufmann, 1981; White & Renzulli, 1987) indicated similar findings, stating that the majority of gifted men had entered professions while the women tended to combine career and family, and that these individuals continued to do well academically and most entered professions such as medicine, law, and higher education. However, gifted adults frequently change jobs because of boredom and lack of intellectual stimulation (Willings, 1985). This and other possible difficulties in adult adjustment will be discussed later in this chapter.

Special Groups of Gifted or Talented Individuals

Gifted females. There is a growing belief that gifted girls and women represent one of the largest groups of untapped intellectual potential in this country. A strong social bias exists, affecting attitudes and values (Kirk & Gallagher, 1989). While ability profiles for females are the same as those for males, gifted girls tend to exhibit more fear of success (animosity of classmates, being classified by others as a "brain") and fear of being considered unfeminine (Wolf & Stephens, 1986).

Because of social biases, gifted females often have been expected to operate within the social limitations of sex roles; although this perception is changing. They are entering areas considered historically as more appropriate for males, such as mathematics, engineering, business, and science, and they are succeeding.

Gifted individuals with disabilities. A special situation exists for disabled gifted persons. While the term appears to be a contradiction in terms, giftedness can exist across many exceptionalities. Consider physically impaired, visually impaired, or hearing impaired individuals with no impairment to their cognitive abilities. They may not be able to walk or see or hear, but that does not mean that they cannot be intellectually gifted. It only means that they stand a chance of having their special talents overlooked (Kirk & Gallagher, 1989).

Learning disabled gifted individuals present a very complex set of abilities. Learning disabled gifted children tend to escape identification either as disabled or gifted because of a rather "average" academic record. Although there may be early, recognizable indicators of superior mental abilities, generally they are ignored by the disabled child, the family, and professionals because of a focus on the disability and stereotypic expectations associated with the disability (Whitmore & Maker, 1985). For example, learning disabled children with an inability to interpret symbols may find reading, writing, or arithmetic difficult or impossible in spite of their high intelligence. Through the years of school, a lag between ability and achievement can develop, which may lead to personality or behavior disorders due to frustration, or a pattern of underachievement (Brown-Mizuno, 1990).

Gifted underachiever. As stated above, gifted persons with learning or emotional disabilities may establish a pattern of underachievement. The maladjustment seen in this population is thought to be related to the person, his/her personality and behavior, and the social environment of the home and school (Kirk & Gallagher, 1989; Wolf & Stephens, 1986). Increased lags between ability and achievement may affect self-esteem and emotional stability, rendering a self-perception of being "crazy and bright" (Brown-Mizuno, 1990). By this, the authors were implying that a gifted and talented person may be perceived by others as being odd or "crazy," when that person may be struggling to understand the inconsistencies in his or her own environment.

Four major characteristics are believed to separate the underachievers from the achievers. These are greater feelings of inferiority, less self-confidence, less perseverance, and a loss of a sense of life goals (Kirk & Gallagher, 1989). A summation of the literature on the distinctive personality and behavioral traits that describe many underachievers yields the following characterization: "A negative self-concept, low self-esteem, expectations of academic and social failure, a sense of inability to control or determine outcomes of efforts, and behaviors that serve as mechanisms for coping with the tension produced by conflict for the child in school" (Whitmore, 1980, p. 189).

Interestingly, the underachieving behavior may be self-induced, yielding a deliberate performance below potential. In essence, this individual has "learned to underachieve." This decision may be induced by the social "safeness" of not being different, the lack of interesting or challenging tasks, or the fact that peer and parent relationships may not be based on expectations of superior achievement (Swassing, 1988).

Culturally different gifted or talented individuals. Even though gifted children may be found in every socioeconomic and cultural group, the schools have been more successful in identifying those in the majority or dominant culture (Wolf & Stephens, 1986). Negative teacher attitudes toward minority persons may result in fewer referrals of these groups for assessment to identify giftedness.

However, several unique traits that exist in culturally different gifted or talented persons have been identified. These include (a) dependence on controls from their environment rather than control from "within"; (b) loyalty to their peer groups; (c) ability to "rebound" from environmental hardships; (d) verbal persuasiveness, humor rich with symbolism, language rich in imagery; (e) logical reasoning and problem-solving ability; (f) social intelligence and activity regarding justice; and (g) sensitivity and alertness to movement (Swassing, 1988).

Interventions

Early Intervention

Although giftedness or talent cannot be explained, three factors that do seem to contribute are heredity, prenatal and postnatal care, and early childhood environment (Wolf & Stephens, 1986). Early stimulation is particularly important during the first two years. While this is important for all children, this point, as it specifically relates to giftedness, is discussed here. Home environment and parents exert a strong influence in the development of potential. Those children who exhibit traits of giftedness addressed earlier in this chapter, referred to as potentially gifted and talented, need early recognition and nurturance in order for full potential development (Cohn et al., 1988).

Early learning nurtures giftedness. Stimulation must be provided in the baby's environment; this includes safe but free exploration. The tendencies to pretend, create, and imagine should be encouraged. Expensive toys are not necessary, since the truly creative and imaginative child will make castles out of blankets and horses out of chairs. However, early indications of interests or strengths in specific directions may be facilitated by appropriate materials, such as books or art materials.

The number of formal intervention programs with interest in this age group at all levels of ability is growing. "Gifted preschools" are characterized by well-defined identification procedures, clearly defined program goals, a conducive learning environment, ample materials, and continuity after moving into regular schooling (Cohn et al., 1988). The purpose of these elements is to provide more opportunities for young, highly able learners to participate in structured educational experiences before entering the general educational system.

School-age Interventions

Support for programs for gifted students has risen dramatically since the late 1950s, following the launch of the satellite Sputnik. Increasing research into the most effective programs for gifted and talented students has occurred. These school-based interventions must be discussed in two arenas: academic interventions and emotional/social interventions.

Academic interventions. The complexity and individuality of each gifted and talented individual's ability profile, as well as the special groups of persons that fall under the umbrella of giftedness and gifted education, combine to create the necessity for highly individualized curriculums and instructional approaches. For this reason, students who fall within this population need special services above those provided by the general school setting, just as students from other exceptionality groups described in this book require special services. There is no one special way in which the educational needs of all students and their families can select options which are most appropriate to their needs, resources, and constraints (Cohn et al., 1988).

There are a variety of options available, including increasing the speed with which students pass through the curriculum, or enriching the student's present learning environment. The first main alternative, grade or materials advancement, is called acceleration. This option may include starting kindergarten or first grade earlier, grade skipping, early college entrance (entering at an earlier age or taking college courses while still in high school), taking Advanced Placement courses, or compacting the amount of time needed to complete course sequences.

The second main alternative, adapting the present learning environment and augmenting existing curriculums, is called enrichment. This allows students to investigate topics or interests in much greater detail than is ordinarily possible with the standard school curriculum (Swassing, 1988). Enrichment may include more complex problem solving in the classroom (providing more complex ideas and problems within coursework designed for the student's age level), exploration (creating awareness of various disciplines available for further study), or role-modeling (affiliation with a mentor possessing similar interests) (Cohn et al., 1988). As mentioned earlier, the simultaneous enrollment in high school and college courses frequently is an option, and may be used to enrich high school study in specific areas. Some colleges and universities offer the opportunity to start the freshman year of college, full-time, during the senior year of high school; upon completion of the first year of post-secondary study, the high school diploma is awarded along with the credits earned for one year of college work.

Social/emotional interventions. Counseling is an important concern for all gifted and talented children. A number of crises can occur during childhood and young adulthood, including differences between intellectual and emotional and physical growth, underachievement and fear of success, expectations of others, social "fitting in," and educational or career decisions. While the need for counseling, either in the school setting or outside the school, is not a foregone conclusion for all gifted and talented youngsters, it may be a necessary option for some.

Bibliotherapy, a counseling approach particularly suited to gifted children, is a technique of providing reading material on ways of dealing with problems. Because many gifted children are avid readers, teachers and counselors may help them resolve personal crises by directing them to appropriate articles or books (Wolf & Stephens, 1986). Such an approach may help open up discussions and opportunities to express feelings.

Adult Interventions

You read earlier in this chapter that highly able children carry extraordinary abilities into adulthood. While many positive facts concerning gifted and talented adults were presented, special interventions may be necessary or desired to circumvent difficulties that may arise.

The emerging gifted and talented adult, as evidenced by follow-up studies, is almost certain to go on for further schooling. The choice of career, however, may be confounded by the existence of multipotentiality. This means that the individual may have strengths and aptitudes in many areas, and may have a difficult time deciding which path to follow. For this reason, career counseling is a frequent practice for gifted and talented adults.

Additionally, a delay in becoming financially and societally independent, which is a strongly developed trait in many gifted individuals, may occur because of further schooling (Kirk & Gallagher, 1989), and may cause frustration. Once schooling is completed and the career is started, some gifted and talented persons may, by virtue of their high standards for themselves, transfer their drive and motivation to the workplace. If the remuneration is not considered to be in line with the output, if the job does not offer intellectual stimulation or challenge, or if the use of independent thinking is not accepted by coworkers and supervisors, career dissatisfaction may occur. In these cases, the need for counseling may be seen, either on a vocational or a personal basis.

Besides the need for intellectual stimulation in the workplace, a need may exist for similar stimulation in leisure activities. This may be assuaged through personal pursuits that conform to the interest areas of the individual, or through organizations that provide interactions with other individuals of high abilities. One such organization is Mensa (derived from the Latin word for "round table"), which makes membership dependent upon superior performance on an intelligence test.

Expectations

Like any exceptionality, giftedness carries with it its own set of stereotypes. Because gifted and talented individuals show advanced abilities and, in many cases, career and personal success, many people may assume that they have no flaws, no personal crises, or no need for outside support. Gifted people are just that--people. Despite their demonstrated ability to make friends and adapt well, and achieve academic/professional success, gifted people encounter some difficult burdens that stem from their exceptionality (Kirk & Gallagher, 1989).

Several aspects of being gifted or talented which may be considered negative, and to which societal stereotypes may contribute, are:
- **Unrealistic expectations placed on them by others**
- **Finding others who share similar interests**
- **Boredom in standard school and work settings**
- **Self-inflicted isolation in choosing activities**
- **Struggling against rules and standardized procedures**
- **Possible violation of societal mores and structures in seeking avenues for expression.**

As with any exceptionality, a need exists to improve society's attitudes and perceptions regarding gifted and talented individuals. The common stereotype of the socially ineffective "brain" with poor health is inaccurate and contributes to the feeling that many gifted persons have that they are different, outcast, or free of everyday concerns that we all face.

Interactions

As stated earlier, gifted people are people. They do not respond favorably to being called by an assortment of names that negatively connote studiousness, achievement levels, or social interactions. They do not look strange, nor does genius breed mental illness.

You may have met intellectually advanced or talented people in your classes, while in school, or in the workplace. Perhaps they always have been the first ones to raise their hands, or to complete an assigned task; this may have caused feelings of jealousy, frustration, and irritation among other members of the group. It would be unjust, however, to assign stereotypical attributes to the individual, just as it would be to assign stereotypes to anyone.

Gifted and talented people do not wish to be socially shunned; they desire to be included in the social activities of their peers. Enjoy the different perspective they may bring to your group activities. Encourage and congratulate them on their achievements, but look beyond those achievements to find the person within. Perhaps you are gifted academically or talented. Share your insights with others; show them you are a person, also.

Summary

In this chapter, you have become acquainted with gifted and talented individuals. Gifted persons, whether they be academically advanced or possess high abilities in non-academic areas, comprise a very heterogeneous group. As with any person, and any exceptionality, there is no one consistent type or profile. Giftedness spans socioeconomic barriers, genders, and disabilities; there is no definite etiology, although most researchers favor a combination of hereditary and environmental factors.

Gifted and talented persons of any age benefit from special interventions. These may be provided in the home, the school, the workplace, and in leisure settings. Societal perceptions, stereotypes, expectations, and interactions affect the degree to which a gifted or talented individual may perceive his or her own abilities and the degree to which interventions may be needed. As with any exceptionality, the important issue is that everyone is a person, deserving of the same respect and opportunities we would expect for ourselves.

References

Brown-Mizuno, C. (1990, Fall). Success strategies for learners who are learning disabled as well as gifted. *Teaching Exceptional Children*, pp. 10-12.

Clark, B. (1988). *Growing up gifted*. Columbus, OH: Merrill.

Cohn, S. J., Cohn, C. M. G., & Kanevsky, L. S. (1988). Giftedness and talent. In E. W. Lynch & R. B. Lewis (Eds.), *Exceptional children and adults*. Glenview, IL: Scott, Foresman.

Congdon, P. (1985). Why identify gifted children? *Early Childhood Development and Care, 21,* 107-109.

Feldman, D. (1984). A follow-up of subjects scoring above 180 IQ in Terman's Genetic Studies of Genius, *Exceptional Children, 50,* 518-523.

Kaufmann, I. (1981). The 1964-1968 presidential scholars: A follow-up study. *Exceptional Children, 48,* 164-169.

Kirk, S. A., & Gallagher, J. J. (1989). *Educating exceptional children* (6th ed.). Boston: Houghton Mifflin.

Swassing, R. H. (1988). Gifted and talented students. In W. L. Heward & M. D. Orlansky (Eds.), *Exceptional children* (3rd ed.) (pp. 405-438). Columbus, OH: Merrill.

Terman, L. M., & Oden, M. H. (1976). The gifted child at midlife. In W. Dennis & M. Dennis (Eds.), *The intellectually gifted: An overview.* New York: Grune and Stratton.

White, W., & Renzulli, J. (1987). A 40 year follow-up of students who attended Leta Hollingworth's school for gifted students. *Roeper Review, 10*(2), 89-93.

Whitmore, J. R. (1980). *Giftedness, conflict, and underachievement.* Boston: Allyn and Bacon.

Whitmore, J. R., & Maker, C. J. (1985). *Intellectual giftedness in disabled persons.* Rockville, MD: Aspen.

Willings, D. (1985). The specific needs of adults who are gifted. *Roeper Review, 8*(1), 35-38.

Wolf, J. S., & Stephens, T. M. (1986). Gifted and talented. In N. G. Haring & L. McCormick (Eds.), *Exceptional children and youth* (4th ed.). Columbus, OH: Merrill.

Suggested Readings

Adderholdt-Elliott, M. R. (1987). *Perfectionism: What's bad about being too good.* Minneapolis: Free Spirit.

Clark, B. (1988). *Growing up gifted.* Columbus, OH: Merrill.

Davis, G. (1986). *Creativity is forever.* Dubuque, IA: Kendall-Hunt.

National Commission on Excellence in Education. (1983). *A nation at risk: The imperatives for educational reform* (Report to the Nation and the Secretary of Education). Washington, DC: U.S. Government Printing Office.

Whitmore, J. R., & Maker, C. J. (1985). *Intellectual giftedness in disabled persons.* Rockville, MD: Aspen.

Notes

GIFTED AND TALENTED INDIVIDUALS

Exploration

Individual Activities

1. Think about a person whom you know who is gifted or talented. List five characteristics of this individual.

    1. _____
    2. _____
    3. _____
    4. _____
    5. _____

2. When you think of gifted persons, what descriptors or labels cross your mind? List the first 10 thoughts that come to mind. Then check the ones which are accurate labels for gifted persons.

1._____	6._____
2._____	7._____
3._____	8._____
4._____	9._____
5._____	10._____

Group Activities

1. Divide up into groups of five or six students. Your assignment is to brag. Have each person describe his/her special talents. You will probably be surprised to learn how many of your fellow students are gifted in specific areas.

    Reactions:

    _____
    _____
    _____

2. Stay in your same group. Develop a list of at least 20 persons (historical or contemporary) who are gifted or talented. Identify how each is gifted.

    Reactions:

    _____
    _____
    _____

Reaction Paper 12.1

Some have said that gifted children, who are not identified and who do not receive appropriate school interventions, may be our most wasted resource. Do you agree or disagree with this statement? Why?

Continue on back if needed.

Reaction Paper 12.2

What do you think makes an individual gifted? Is giftedness an inherited quality or does one come by it through experience and hard work?

Continue on back if needed.

304

Notes

CHAPTER 13

SPECIAL EDUCATION

Beth Tulbert

What is Special Education?

Thomas Dewey (cited in Turnbull, 1986) stated that the "goal of American education is to value each child as equally an individual and entitled to equal opportunity of development of his own capacities, be they large or small" (p. ix). Special education grew out of this belief and is the means for equalizing the opportunity of intellectual, physical, social, and vocational development for exceptional individuals.

What is so special about special education?

Special education implies that there is something "special" happening with students in schools. The "special" part of education can be defined by answering four questions (Heward & Orlansky, 1988):

Who needs "special" education?
What is "special" about the curriculum?

How is "special" education instruction different from
regular education instruction?
Where does "special" education take place?

Who needs "special" education?

Children or adolescents whose needs or abilities require an individualized program of education are placed in special education (Heward & Orlansky, 1988). These students receive some or all of their education from teachers who have completed specialized teacher training programs. Special education teachers are expected to have expertise in several areas (Hallahan & Kauffman, 1986):

Academic instructional techniques for children/adolescents with learning problems

Behavior management techniques for use with children/adolescents with serious behavioral problems

Technological advances, such as computers and other adaptive equipment

Special education laws, rules and regulations at the local, state, and federal government, and the rights of parents and students.

Many other professionals, such as school psychologists, speech and language therapists, and physical therapists, may also work with these exceptional students.

What is "special" about the curriculum?

Special education is often differentiated from regular education by what is taught (Heward & Orlansky, 1988). Intensive, systematic instruction is used to teach exceptional students skills that others acquire naturally (Kirk & Gallagher, 1986). For example, students with behavior problems may be taught social skills in a special education class because they have not learned those skills during their social interactions with others. Also, students with physical limitations may be taught how to dress and feed themselves by special education teachers because they could not learn to do these things by themselves. And, students who are mentally retarded may be taught job related skills, such as time, money, and transportation.

The individual needs of each student will dictate the curriculum, which will be more individualized than that for a regular education student. Curriculum for students with mild handicaps more closely resembles "regular school curriculum" and may include additional content and/or a different focus. Students with mild mental retardation may need to be taught social skills (additional content) as well as have their social studies class emphasize community instead of world geography (different focus). Curriculum for students with severe handicaps is greatly different than the "regular school curriculum" and emphasizes completely different content. Students with severe mental retardation, for instance, may need to be taught hygiene and basic safety skills (different content). Curriculum for individual students in special education varies greatly because the needs of each student are so different.

How is "special" education instruction different from regular education instruction?

Special education instruction differs from regular education instruction in two ways--the teacher who delivers the instruction and the instruction that is delivered. First, special education teachers usually complete different teacher training programs than regular education teachers. Special educators are certified in different areas of exceptionality such as learning disabilities, mental retardation, hearing impairment, and behavior disorders. Coursework in typical special education programs includes a survey course of all exceptionalities, methods and materials for instruction in the different areas of exceptionality, curriculum for students in the different areas of exceptionality, behavior management, assessment, precision teaching, special education law and legislation, technology, and teaming or consultation with other school professionals. This coursework enables special education teachers to fulfill their roles in serving exceptional children

Special education teachers are expected to evaluate the academic abilities and disabilities of students, participate in team conferences, write and implement individual educational plans, communicate with parents and school personnel, and participate in due process hearings and negotiations (Hallahan & Kauffman, 1986). Special education teachers must also have expertise in academic instruction of children with learning problems, adaptation of curriculum, management of serious behavior problems, use of technological advances, and knowledge of special education law (Hallahan & Kauffman, 1986).

In addition, different instructional methods are used in special education classes, but for the most part, special education teachers use the same effective teaching skills that all good teachers use (Heward & Orlansky, 1988). Exceptional students, however, need additional interventions in order to be successful in school and later in life. Interventions available in special education fall into three categories which include preventive, remedial, and compensatory interventions (Heward & Orlansky, 1988).

Preventive intervention helps keep a disability from becoming a serious handicap. This type of intervention is most effective when begun early in life and often is used by early childhood special educators. Teaching parents developmental games to play with their infants at risk of developing a disabling condition is an example of a preventive intervention.

Remedial intervention is used when a student does not have skills commensurate with his/her peers. Remediation, also referred to as rehabilitation, can occur with academic, vocational, social, or personal skills and is necessary if the exceptional person is to succeed in the "normal" world. Teaching social skills is an example of remediation.

Compensatory intervention teaches the exceptional student a new way of dealing with a problem. A substitute skill is taught or device is provided that allows the person to circumvent their disability or reduce the handicap caused by the disability. An example of a compensatory device would be a calculator used to complete math problems.

Where does "special" education take place?

Some exceptional children may also need a different, special learning environment. Most exceptional students (approximately 66%) are taught in regular classes, but some (approximately 33%) require instruction in a different setting (Heward & Orlansky, 1988). Many exceptional students remain in the regular class all or most of their school day with a minimum amount of time spent in a special education class where they receive individualized instruction. Students with more severe problems may need to be taught in separate special education classes, in residential schools, or in specialized day schools. Special education also takes place in environments not typically thought of as "school," such as the home (early childhood special education and home bound education) and community and job sites (vocational special education).

As you can see, there is much that is "special" about special education. Exceptional students receiving special education have an individualized curriculum taught by specially trained teachers. Effective teaching methods are used in special education along with additional assessment and close monitoring of student progress. Some special education students also may require a special learning environment, but many exceptional students are placed in regular classes. This is a general overview of special education, and before continuing this discussion, a clear understanding of several important terms is necessary because a variety of terminology is used to discuss special education and exceptional children.

Terminology

Special Education. Special education refers to an individually planned and carefully monitored arrangement of physical settings, special equipment and materials, teaching procedures, and other interventions designed to help exceptional children achieve personal self-sufficiency and academic success (Hallahan & Kauffman, 1986; Heward & Orlansky, 1988). In its broadest sense, special education refers to the provision of services aimed at assisting children to achieve their fullest potential, and can include such things as curriculum enrichment or special materials. The most widely used interpretation of "special education" is more narrow in focus and refers to the use of specifically designed instruction, curricula, and materials which allow exceptional children to receive an appropriate education (Davis, 1986).

Exceptional Children. Exceptional children or adolescents differ from average children or adolescents in mental characteristics, sensory abilities, communication abilities, social behavior, or physical characteristics to such an extent that they require a modification of school practices to achieve success (Kirk & Gallagher, 1986; Taylor & Sternberg, 1989). These modifications of school practices is what is meant by special education. The term exceptional refers to children or adolescents who have:

Auditory or visual impairments
Learning disabilities
Speech and language impairments

Intellectual differences, either mental retardation or
      gifted/talented
   Behavioral differences
   Physical differences, either in mobility or physical
      vitality
   Multiple handicaps.

Exceptional. Exceptional is used as a label for persons with a disability or impairment as well as for a person who is gifted or talented. Exceptional really means differing from average or normal, either above or below; however, it is important to remember that normal and exceptional are relative terms and tell very little about the individual (Haring & McCormick, 1986). The term exceptional can also be used to describe all ages, and is not limited to the kindergarten through twelfth grade school population.

Disorder. Disorder is the broadest term and refers to a disturbance in normal academic, psychological, or social functioning. Students could be described as having reading disorders when their functioning in reading is below normal.

Disability. Disability usually refers to a physical disorder (a reduction in function or loss of a particular body part or organ), but is also used with learning or behavior problems that may or may not have a physical cause. Students are described as having a physical disability if they are either totally or partially paralyzed. A learning disability is so named because a physical cause was suspected at one time.

Impairment. Impairment is used to describe a sensory deficit. Students would be described as having a visual or auditory impairment if they were blind or deaf.

At-risk. At-risk is a term that refers to an individual who is not currently identified as exceptional, but who is considered to have a greater than usual chance of developing a handicapping condition (Heward & Orlansky, 1988). Infants may be identified as at-risk for several reasons, such as trauma at birth or a delay in normal development.

Handicap. Handicap refers to a problem or set of problems which is caused by a disorder or disability. People have handicaps when their environment does not accommodate for their needs. A goal should therefore be the reduction of the handicap. Everyone has had a handicap at one time or another. For example, a

SPECIAL EDUCATION

student who is blind has a handicap in a classroom where the teacher writes notes on the board and does not lecture.

You now should have an understanding of the "special" nature of special education and be familiar with the terminology used in talking about exceptional students. The next concern relates to accessing the services provided by special education.

How Is Special Education Accessed?

Accessing special education and related services is a carefully regulated and controlled process. Great care is taken to ensure that decisions made are appropriate for the student and not arbitrary or biased in any way. This section will include information on the steps for placement into special education and their time-line, the individual educational plan, the triennial evaluation, and the rights of parents and students.

Placement into Special Education

The eligibility process for accessing special education services is long and involved. A referral leads to screening and assessment by professional staff members of the school or school district. A multidisciplinary team determines eligibility and an individualized educational plan is designed.

Referral

Children who have severely handicapping conditions usually are identified as needing special education services before they start school (Taylor & Sternberg, 1989). These children are identified by parents or physicians and are receiving some sort of services at home or in a preschool setting. Students having mildly handicapping conditions are usually identified as needing special education after they begin school.

The process of identifying a school age student for special education starts with a referral. This referral begins a screening and assessment process which will determine whether or not the student fits into one of the previously mentioned categories of special education and is therefore eligible for special education services.

The decision to refer a student for evaluation to determine eligibility for special education services is a serious decision. A referral usually leads to placement in special education for these two reasons (Taylor & Sternberg, 1989):

1. **Definitions of handicapping conditions and criteria for labeling students are often ambiguous.**
2. **Many students score poorly on tests used in determining eligibility due to anxiety, poor motivation, or biased tests.**

Because of these problems, some schools establish a pre-referral program to help a student who is experiencing difficulties by assessing the student's needs and trying various modifications and strategies in the student's classes before a referral is made. The goal of a pre-referral program is to find a way for the student who is having problems to be successful in the regular education classroom. If the problem can be remedied, the student remains in the regular education placement.

Anyone working with students may make a referral but, it usually is initiated by a parent or teacher. If the referral is initiated by school personnel, the parents usually are notified before the referral is made. The referral consists of several things:

A reason for the referral
A statement of the perceived problem
Current academic level
Previous test scores
Other important data (number of absences, previous schools attended, health/medical data, and special programs attended)
The current classroom environment (method of instruction, classroom management techniques, and student response to feedback and correction)
Strategies and modifications which have been attempted and their results.

Noting the previously used strategies and modifications is important because this demonstrates an attempt to alleviate the student's problem before making a referral for special education. If these interventions fail or the problem is serious enough to need immediate attention, the referral is made.

Screening

The referral goes to the Child Study Team which is comprised of several school related personnel, such as the school principal or his/her designee, regular and special education teachers, school counselors and psychologists, and various specialists. The student's referral is screened or reviewed to decide whether or not an evaluation to determine eligibility for special education is needed (Hammill, 1987). Additional information may be gathered so that an informed decision can be made. The Child Study Team can recommend several things:

Consultation with one of the school personnel (counselor, teacher, psychologist, social worker, nurse, etc.)
Educational modifications within the regular school program
No action at that time
Additional time, noting a future date for re-screening
Referral for an evaluation to determine eligibility for special education.

A copy of the screening report is sent to the parents regardless of the committee's recommendation. If a referral for evaluation is made, a form to obtain the parents' permission for the evaluation is sent along with the screening report. The permission-to-evaluate form contains a detailed list of the assessment components of the evaluation and a copy of the parents' rights. The evaluation cannot be made without the parents' permission.

Evaluation

The evaluation for determining eligibility for special education has several requirements which act as safeguards to ensure a fair, appropriate, multifaceted assessment (Heward & Orlansky, 1988; Taylor & Sternberg, 1989). First, the evaluation must be a multidisciplinary evaluation. Multidisciplinary means that the professionals completing the assessments must have different areas of expertise. Examples of professionals on a multidisciplinary team include psychologists, special education teachers, regular education teachers, guidance counselors, speech and language therapists, physical therapists, occupational therapists, medical doctors, and vocational evaluators. No determination of eligibility can be made on the recommendation of one or two people--it is a team decision. Second, all tests must be administered by trained professionals.

Third, the evaluation must assess various areas of educational need. Educational and psychological assessment would include achievement and intelligence tests. A sociological report is completed to gather information about the student's behavior at home and to allow the parents a chance to provide input. Fourth, this evaluation must assess all areas where the student may have a disability. This includes hearing, vision, motor, medical, and speech and language assessments. A physical examination by a doctor is required. Fifth, a wide range of test instruments must be used. An evaluation such as this can not be accomplished by using one or two tests. Observations, standardized tests, teacher made tests, and intelligence tests are examples of assessment techniques that can be used. It is important to remember that this evaluation should not be limited to finding the student's disabilities (weaknesses), but must identify the student's abilities (strengths) as well (Hammill, 1987; Heward & Orlansky, 1988).

And finally, tests included in this evaluation can not be discriminatory by either race, culture, or language. For example, if a student's primary language is Spanish, the tests must be administered in Spanish. Finding tests that do not discriminate against students with special needs, such as visual or auditory impairments, can be difficult.

Eligibility

After all the assessments are complete, the Child Study Team meets again to determine the student's eligibility for special education services. Parents are usually invited to attend the eligibility meeting, but some parents do not choose to attend. The team approach is used here to provide for unique professional perspectives, enhance problem solving, and act as insurance against erroneous or arbitrary placement decisions (Heward & Orlansky, 1988).

Findings from the various assessments are analyzed and discussed to determine if the student has an educational need not being met by the current educational placement, and as a result of which, requires some sort of special education and/or related service. The student must meet eligibility criteria for one of the handicapping conditions, including mentally retarded, hard-of-hearing, deaf, speech impaired, visually impaired, emotionally disturbed, orthopedically handicapped, other health impaired, multiply handicapped, learning disabled, or deaf-blind (Taylor & Sternberg,

1989). If determined to fit the eligibility criteria, the student is labeled or classified as having one of the above handicapping conditions and becomes eligible for special education and related services.

The act of labeling students has created quite a bit of controversy (Haring & McCormick, 1986; Taylor & Sternberg, 1989). Labels are used to categorize individuals. Labeling has several benefits in special education:

> **Facilitates communication of student needs to professionals**
> **Helps get needed services and programs for students**
> **Helps get funding and improves legislation**
> **Helps develop advocacy agencies**
> **Provides a general idea of the needs of students.**

But, labeling also has some negative side effects:

> **Low self-esteem and poor self-concept of labeled students**
> **Lower teacher expectations for labeled students**
> **Peer rejection of labeled students**
> **High number of minority students labeled.**

Most school districts continue to label students, but some districts have tried a noncategorical approach where students are only labeled as to the severity of their handicapping condition (mild/moderate or severe/profound).

Placement

The parents, if not in attendance at the eligibility meeting, are sent a copy of the eligibility report at the conclusion of the meeting. If the student is found eligible for special education and labeled, a permission form must be signed by the parents. It is sent home with the eligibility report if the parents did not attend the eligibility meeting. This permission form describes the proposed placement for the student, why that placement is the most appropriate, and a list of the reports used as a basis for the proposed placement. The parent must give permission for a change of placement from the student's current placement (regular education) to the proposed placement (special education and/or related services) before any change can be made.

Individualized Educational Plan

When permission for placement has been given by the parents, a meeting is held to write the student's Individual Educational Plan (IEP). Every student receiving special education or related services must have a current IEP (Davis, 1986). The first IEP is a product of the Child Study Team (the student's teachers, parents, the child if appropriate, a representative of the school district, and other support staff if needed) and is written before special education services are begun. The IEP must include (Haring & McCormick, 1986; Heward & Orlansky, 1988; Hewett & Forness, 1984; Taylor & Sternberg, 1989):

Current level of performance (academic, social, pre-vocational, vocational, motor, and self-help skills)
Annual goals
Short term goals (instructional objectives which must be measurable)
Specific services needed by the student
Date services begin and length of time services are to be given
Extent the student will participate in the regular education program
Evaluation criteria, procedures, and time schedule for determining when short term objectives have been met
Justification for the student's placement
List of individuals responsible for implementing the IEP.

IEPs must be reviewed, revised, and updated at least yearly. The student's parents are asked to attend the IEP meeting to help write the IEP, and they must approve it. They receive a copy of the IEP at the meeting or in the mail if they did not attend.

Timeline

The identification, assessment, and eligibility process has certain time restrictions placed on its various steps. This insures both parent and school district

SPECIAL EDUCATION

rights. This process can not be unnecessarily delayed but must be completed in a reasonable length of time.

Many states have established timelines. The following is an example of the timeline used in Virginia.

> **From the time that a referral is completed and submitted to the appropriate person, there are 10 administrative working days for the screening meeting to be held.**
>
> **If the screening committee makes a referral for evaluation for special education, there are 5 working days for that referral to be received by the special education coordinator or other designated person.**
>
> **From this day, there are 65 administrative working days allotted to complete the assessment and hold the eligibility meeting.**
>
> **If the decision is to place the student into special education, there are 30 calendar days for notifying parents and holding the IEP meeting.**
>
> **The maximum time allowed from the initial referral to the IEP meeting and subsequent placement of the student into special education is 80 administrative working days plus an additional 30 calendar days; however, this process is often completed in a much shorter length of time.**

Parent and Student Rights

Parents and students are guaranteed procedural safeguards in the process of identification, evaluation, and placement for special education. These rights of due process (shown below) ensure that decisions made about the student are fair and just, and allow a means of resolving disagreement and conflict.

> **All records related to the identification, evaluation, and placement of students in special education are maintained in a confidential manner.**
>
> **Testing and evaluation materials utilized for the purpose of classification and placement of students into special**

education are selected and administered so as not to be racially or culturally discriminatory.

The parents have the right to inspect and review all the educational records relating to this process.

The parents have the right to an independent educational evaluation of their child and information on getting such an evaluation will be provided by the school district.

The school or the parent has the right to initiate a hearing when a disagreement occurs in matters relating to this process. The request for such a hearing is made in writing to the local school board. The decision by the hearing officer is final unless either party appeals the decision by contacting the State Board of Education and requesting a review of the hearing. Civil action may be initiated by either the parents or the school in response to the review of the hearing.

During the identification, assessment, and eligibility process, and/or during the hearing process, the child must remain in the present educational placement unless otherwise agreed upon by the parent and school district.

Each school district must make its parents aware of their rights.

The initial evaluation for eligibility for special education is only the beginning. Continuous monitoring of each student's progress is required to ensure that the student's placement continues to be appropriate.

Triennial Evaluations

Once students are placed in special education, they must be re-evaluated every three years. These triennial evaluations require that the process described above be repeated to decide if the students are still eligible for special education. This insures that students are appropriately placed by monitoring their progress and making changes in their placement as needed. The triennial evaluation must follow the same timeline as the initial evaluation.

As you realize, the process for accessing special education programs and services is not easy nor fast, but it is regulated in an attempt to ensure that appropriate decisions are made. When a student is found to be eligible for special education services, a decision must be made as to the most appropriate level of services.

What Service Models Are Available?

Because exceptional students have a wide variety of abilities and disabilities, more than one level or type of special education service is needed. This range of services is called a cascade or continuum of services and uses a variety of different service models. Placement of exceptional students in the continuum of services is governed by the idea of least restrictive environment.

Least Restrictive Environment

Least restrictive environment (LRE) is defined as "that educational setting which maximizes the . . . student's opportunity to respond and achieve, permits the regular education teacher to interact proportionally with all students in the classroom, and fosters acceptable social relations between non-handicapped and [handicapped] students" (Heron & Skinner, 1981, p. 116). The idea behind LRE is that exceptional students should be taught with non-handicapped students to the maximum extent possible (Davis, 1986). The least restrictive placement is determined by assessing the needs of the exceptional child and matching those needs to the environment that can best meet them (Taylor & Sternberg, 1989). Central to the idea of LRE is that of integration which is the opposite of segregation and implies an interaction between handicapped and non-handicapped students.

Education in the LRE is often confused with the idea of mainstreaming. Mainstreaming implies that students in special education are integrated into the regular education program for some or all of the day. Placement in the LRE is not necessarily the same as mainstreaming, although it can be. The important difference between LRE and mainstreaming is that the LRE is a program placement determined by the needs of the student, while mainstreaming is just one of many program placements.

Different Service Models

The variety of different service models or placement choices can be conceptualized as a continuum containing several different placement options (Hallahan & Kauffman, 1986):

Regular classrooms
Regular classrooms with consultation
Regular classrooms with itinerant services
Regular classrooms with resource room services
Self-contained
Special education classes
Special day schools
Residential schools.

These service models "cascade" down a continuum from less restrictive program placements (e.g., regular classrooms) to more restrictive program placements (e.g., residential schools). More students are placed in the regular classroom options (less restrictive) than are placed in self-contained classes or special schools (more restrictive).

The different service models available in the continuum of services shown above include (Hallahan & Kauffman, 1986):

Regular classroom (the expertise of the regular teacher is all that is needed and there are no direct services by special education personnel; integrated with non-handicapped peers all day)
Regular classroom with consultation (special education teacher consults with the regular education teacher and/or the special education student concerning other resources, strategies, or methods to use in the regular education class; integrated with non-handicapped peers)
Regular classroom with instruction by an itinerant specialist (direct services or consultation is provided for the regular class teacher or the special education student on a regular schedule by a specialist such as speech therapist, physical therapist, or occupational therapist; integrated with non-handicapped peers)

Regular classroom with time spent every day in a resource room (direct services for part of the day by a special education teacher in a resource room; integrated with non-handicapped peers most of day)
Self-contained special education classroom (direct instruction all or most of the day by a special education teacher in a classroom of 15 or fewer exceptional students; segregated all or most of day from non-handicapped peers)
Special day school (all day instruction in a special school; segregated from non-handicapped peers)
Residential school (24 hour a day care in a residential facility away from home with academic instruction as well as management of daily living; segregated from non-handicapped peers).

Other services not described above include hospital and homebound instruction, and diagnostic/prescriptive classrooms (Hallahan & Kauffman, 1986). Hospital and homebound instruction is provided for students with physical or psychological problems that prevent them from attending school. Usually these services are needed for a short time only.

Diagnostic/prescriptive classrooms are used for short term evaluation (2-6 weeks). Students attend these classes so that a plan of action, often called a written prescription, can be formulated and recommendations for placement can be made.

A wide variety of service models is available to fit the diverse needs of exceptional students. Appropriate placement in school is determined by the individual student's needs. But consideration must be given to the services needed after school years.

What is the Extent of Services Offered?

Most people think that special education is something available only in public schools, grades K-12, but this is not the case because legislation mandates special education services for individuals with handicapping conditions from birth to age 22. Some services are available outside of school, such as pre-school early intervention programs or community-based adult programs. Early intervention services are provided for infants and toddlers identified as being at-risk (Salvia & Ysseldyke, 1988). The children receive direct services, and the parents are trained and counseled by a variety of specialists. These services are available from birth until the child enters a school program. Community based adult services include on-the-job training, training in independent living skills, social skills training, and transition planning.

Other services span the lifetime of the exceptional individual, such as transition services. Transition refers to changes in a person's life such as the transition from being at home to starting school, the transition from elementary school to high school, and the transition from school to work. Transition planning can be included as a part of every exceptional student's IEP. As you have seen, special education services are provided not only by a continuum of service delivery models, but also on a continuum of time.

How Many Students Are in Special Education?

The total number of individuals in special education is hard to estimate at any given time, but one common method is with prevalence. Prevalence refers to the "total number of individuals who are in a given category [of special education] at a particular point in time" (Taylor & Sternberg, 1989, p. 2), and is a percentage of the general population. Prevalence figures for the categories of exceptionality are listed in Table 13.1. (From Taylor, R. L., & Sternberg, L. (1989). *Exceptional children: Integrating research and teaching.* New York: Springer-Verlag.)

Table 13.1
<u>Prevalence Figures</u>

<u>Category</u>	<u>Prevalence Rate</u>
Gifted	3%-5%
Speech or Language Impairment	3%-4%
Mental Retardation	2%-3%
Learning Disabilities	2%-3%
Emotional Disturbance	2%-3%
Hearing Impaired	<1%
Physically Impaired	<1%
Multiple Handicapped	<1%
Visually Impaired	<1%

Overall, 11%-12% of the population is considered to have a handicap (Heward & Orlansky, 1988; Taylor & Sternberg, 1989). Combine that with the 3%-5% of the population considered to be gifted and the prevalence of exceptional students is 14%-17% of the general population (Taylor & Sternberg, 1989). In The 1990 World Almanac and Book of Facts, the population of the United States was estimated to be 247.1 million people as of January 1, 1989. Using the 14% figure, there were approximately 34.6 million exceptional individuals that year.

Summary

Special education is "special" in many ways. Exceptional students receiving special education services have impairments or disabilities which require a change in what and how they are taught, and perhaps where they are taught. Special education and related services are accessed through an eligibility process orchestrated by a multidisciplinary team. Each student receiving special education and related services has an individualized education plan which specifies the "special" components of his/her education. A variety of program placements, other that the regular education classroom, are available, but the program choice is made by identifying the least restrictive environment. Every student's progress in special education is monitored and changes in placement are made as needed. The processes, procedures, and options described in this chapter help ensure that each individual is allowed the opportunity to develop his/her capacities to their fullest.

References

Davis, W. E. (1986). *Resource guide to special education: Terms/laws/assessment procedures/organizations.* Boston: Allyn and Bacon.

Hallahan, D. P., & Kauffman, J. M. (1986). *Exceptional children: Introduction to special education.* Englewood Cliffs, NJ: Prentice-Hall.

Hammill, D. D. (1987). Assessing students in the schools. In D. D. Hammill (Ed.), *Assessing the abilities and instructional needs of students* (pp. 5-37). Austin, TX: Pro-Ed.

Haring, N. G., & McCormick, L. (1986). *Exceptional children and youth: An introduction to special education.* Columbus, OH: Merrill.

Heron, T. E., & Skinner, M. E. (1981). Criteria for defining the regular classroom as the least restrictive environment for LD students. *Learning Disabilities Quarterly, 4,* 115-121.

Heward, W. L., & Orlansky, M. D. (1988). *Exceptional children: An introductory survey of special education.* Columbus, OH: Merrill.

Hewett, F. M., & Forness, S. R. (1984). *Education of exceptional learners.* Boston: Allyn and Bacon.

Hoffman, M. S. (1990). *The world almanac and books of facts.* New York: Pharos Books.

Kirk, S. A., & Gallagher, J. J. (1986). *Educating exceptional children.* Boston: Houghton Mifflin.

Salvia, J., & Ysseldyke, J. E. (1988). *Assessment in special and remedial education.* Boston: Houghton Mifflin.

Taylor, R. L., & Sternberg, L. (1989). *Exceptional children: Integrating research and teaching.* New York: Springer-Verlag.

Turnbull, H. R. (1986). *Free appropriate public education: The law and children with disabilities.* Denver: Love.

Suggested Readings

Hallahan, D. P., & Kauffman, J. M. (1986). *Exceptional children: Introduction to special education.* Englewood Cliffs, NJ: Prentice-Hall.

Haring, N. G., & McCormick, L. (1986). *Exceptional children and youth: An introduction to special education.* Columbus, OH: Merrill.

Heward, W. L., & Orlansky, M. D. (1988). *Exceptional children: An introductory survey of special education.* Columbus, OH: Merrill.

Hewett, F. M., & Forness, S. R. (1984). *Education of exceptional learners.* Boston: Allyn and Bacon.

Howell, K. (1983). *Inside special education.* Columbus, OH: Merrill.

Kirk, S. (1986). *Educating exceptional children.* Boston: Houghton Mifflin.

Knoblock, P. (Ed.). (1987). *Understanding exceptional children and youth.* Boston: Little Brown.

Orlansky, M. D., & Heward, W. L. (1981). *Voices: Interviews with handicapped people.* Columbus, OH: Merrill.

Payne, J. S., Patton, J. R., Kauffman, J. M., Brown, G. B., & Payne, R. A. (1987). *Exceptional children in focus.* Columbus, OH: Merrill.

Notes

SPECIAL EDUCATION 329

Exploration

Individual Activities

1. Now that you know more about special education, consider the expertise and skills needed by a special education teacher. Assume that you are Director of Personnel for your local school district. Develop a special education teacher job description and list the skills needed.

   _____
   _____
   _____
   _____
   _____
   _____

2. Develop a list of those things that are special about special education.

   _____
   _____
   _____
   _____
   _____
   _____
   _____

Group Activities

1. Make arrangements so your class can visit and observe in special education classes in your local school district. While observing, look for the items you listed as being special about special education.

   Reactions:

   _____
   _____
   _____

2. Arrange for a panel of individuals with different types of exceptionalities to visit your class. Ask the panel for their assessment of special education.

   Reactions:

   _____
   _____
   _____

SPECIAL EDUCATION

Reaction Paper 13.1

Assume that you are a political leader and you have to make a decision whether to support or oppose a bill to give more money to special education. How would you vote and why?

Continue on back if needed.

SPECIAL EDUCATION

Reaction Paper 13.2

An important part of special education is mainstreaming. How do you feel about this idea? How does mainstreaming benefit disabled students? Non-disabled students?

Continue on back if needed.

Notes

CHAPTER 14

RELATED SERVICES AND SUPPORT PROFESSIONALS

Glenn Buck

Introduction

This chapter focuses on the variety of services that is available to people whose physical, social, emotional, and cognitive capabilities are different from the norm. The first section provides background knowledge concerning related services (e.g., factors that affect the number of services disabled people receive). The second section explores the various types of therapies that people with disabilities require. References are provided so that you can solicit further information regarding each type of therapy. The final section provides an opportunity to identify and recognize the contributions of the varied professionals who care for and support disabled persons.

Background

People having little experience or interaction with disabled people may be surprised by the large number of support professionals and therapies that are available. For example, Robert, a fifth grader with cerebral palsy, receives services from a regular classroom teacher, special education teacher, physical education teacher, school nurse, physical therapist, occupational therapist, guidance counselor, music therapist, and speech therapist. Because he has chronic health problems, he also requires the support of a number of medical professionals. By the time Robert is a teenager, he will be familiar with a wide array of therapists and other support professionals.

Obviously, not all exceptional people require a large number of services. For example, a person with a mild articulation problem may only require the services of a speech therapist. Contrastingly, a person with multiple disabilities (like Robert) requires the services of a variety of therapists. As a general rule, the more severe a person's disabilities, the more likely he/she will need extensive services and therapies.

Another factor in the number and type of therapies and support services a person receives is age. Over the life-span of an individual, therapies may change in type and number. For instance, because at-risk infants are usually medically fragile and require a great deal of medical intervention, they will receive most of their services from medically-related professionals (e.g., nurses, neonatologists, family counselors, and infant specialists). As these infants grow into the preschool period (generally considered between one and five years), services will take on more of a developmental dimension; though medical services will still be very important. Occupational and physical therapists may help these children reach developmental milestones such as crawling, standing with and without assistance, or walking. A speech therapist may work on a child's speech and language development. Additionally, if a child attends a preschool program, transportation may become an important service.

When disabled children reach the school-aged period, therapies gradually become more concerned with helping them to be successful with academic tasks (although reaching developmental milestones may still be important goals of different therapies). During this period, schools are most likely to provide speech therapy, occupational therapy, physical therapy, and counseling services for disabled students (Strickland & Turnbull, 1990). Not only do therapists offer direct services to disabled students (e.g., an occupational therapist who teachers a student to hold and control a pencil, ask directions, and maintain attention during class), but they are also helpful to teachers by providing information about each disabled student's individual learning style and suggesting ways to adapt instruction and improve the classroom environment to maximize academic success.

As disabled adolescents grow into the adult-period, services take on more of a vocational and independent-living dimension. Counseling, recreation, and job training become the major emphasis of the adult support services. Therapists (e.g., recreational therapists) and support professionals (e.g., psychologists) develop programs that help disabled people enjoy their leisure time, get around the community, and develop healthy interpersonal relationships. These professionals will also teach disabled people how to behave appropriately in job and social settings.

RELATED SERVICES AND SUPPORT PROFESSIONALS

Types of Therapies

Before 1950, many therapies, such as physical and occupational therapy, were not commonly available to disabled people. Only within the last two decades have these therapies been incorporated into the educational and habilitative programs of many exceptional people. In 1975, the passage of Public law 94-142, The Education of All Handicapped Children Act, mandated that such needed therapies (usually referred to as related services) be provided to disabled individuals within the school setting. In settings other than schools, therapies and support professionals are found in such places as acute care hospitals, rehabilitation centers, psychiatric hospitals, halfway houses, community living arrangements, community mental health centers, long-term care facilities, nursing homes, senior citizen centers, children's hospitals, sheltered workshops, vocational training centers, burn treatment centers, community recreation agencies, and in private practice.

The following therapies are those most often encountered by people with disabilities. These therapies are accessed by referrals from either the disabled person, teachers, parents, or counselors. Physical therapy, however, is one therapy that can only be accessed by the recommendation and/or referral of a physician.

Physical and Occupational Therapy

Because of having many characteristics in common, these two types of therapies are frequently thought to be the same. Both therapies help children and adults who have motor disabilities (motor meaning the body's ability to move, coordinate, position, and balance itself) and can be found in schools, hospitals, diagnostic clinics, and nursing homes. In school settings, a child can only receive these therapies if the motor disabilities are somehow interfering with educational performance (such as a child with cerebral palsy who can not keep up with writing assignments due to poor hand and finger control).

Despite the common practice of referring to physical and occupational therapies together, it should be understood that they are fundamentally different. Generally, an occupational therapist is more concerned with teaching a disabled person activities for daily living (ADL) rather than strengthening or relaxing certain muscles. As an example, an occupational therapist may teach disabled people how to feed, dress, and care for themselves with minimal assistance. Occupational therapists are also involved with providing training in perceptual skills and visual-motor training (Cusick, 1991). Such training helps disabled people to improve their eye-hand coordination, handwriting, and small-muscle (e.g., finger) dexterity.

A physical therapist, on the other hand, is more apt to be concerned with the relaxing, strengthening, and moving of individual groups of muscles. The physical therapist will focus on developing motor skills and functional activities such as positioning, handling, sitting, ambulation, and lifting and transferring.

Goals and objectives for physical and occupational therapy are often quite varied, but basically they are oriented toward teaching the disabled person to move and function as normally as possible. Structured experiences are provided that encourage the person to use movement to initiate interactions with and control different aspects of the environment, and to gain as much independence as possible (Hanson & Harris, 1986). With some children, therapists focus on weak and dysfunctional muscles in order to reduce the chances of physical deformity as the disabled person becomes older (especially true for people with cerebral palsy and other neuromuscular disorders). In other instances, therapists help disabled people learn how to use compensatory devices, such as crutches, wheelchairs, grasping devices, or braces.

Besides providing direct intervention to the disabled person, therapists from both fields can be extremely helpful in the evaluation and consultation process (Kohn, 1982). For example, a physical or occupational therapist can provide a parent with recommendations, such as how to best carry their child that is non-ambulatory, how to feed their child, and how to purchase adaptive equipment (e.g., wheelchairs). Therapists can also instruct a teacher on how to best meet the special needs of a physically disabled student in the classroom (e.g., positioning a child in a wheelchair to prevent body sores that result from remaining in one position for an extended period of time). Therapists can consult with teachers on adapting games, playground equipment, and sports and physical education activities. Serving on the multidisciplinary team, therapists can make recommendations concerning compensatory technological devices (e.g., motorized wheelchairs, computers, and communication devices), and suggest appropriate educational placements consistent with the child's motor and intellectual levels. Physical and occupational therapists can also help assess prevocational and vocational skills in relation to body strength, endurance, and motor coordination (Cusick, 1991). Moreover, these therapists can help plan for transportation needs by making recommendations concerning proper seat restraints and positioning of the child in the seat.

For more information about these two therapies, you are encouraged to contact:

> The American Occupational Therapy Association, Inc.
> 1383 Picard Drive
> P.O. Box 1725
> Rockville, MD 20850-0822
> (301) 948-9626
>
> American Physical Therapy Association
> 1111 N. Fairfax Street
> Alexandria, VA 22314
> (703) 684-2782

Speech and Language Therapy

Like physical and occupational therapy, speech and language therapists can be found in schools, hospitals, diagnostic clinics, and nursing homes. Unlike the previous therapies, however, speech and language therapy is only concerned with the production and functional use of speech and language. People who require this type of therapy may have one or more of a variety of difficulties, such as receptive and expressive language delays, misarticulations, dysfluencies, or voice-quality disorders. It is also very common for speech therapists to work with stroke and accident victims.

Speech and language therapists will often identify children and adults with speech and language disorders by means of screening activities conducted at day care centers, school settings, hospitals, speech and hearing clinics, or nursing homes. Once identified, therapists will diagnose and appraise specific speech or language difficulties and develop individualized therapy programs. In severe cases, they may refer clients for medical or other professional attention.

Like the physical and occupational therapist, the speech and language therapist can also serve as a consultant to classroom teachers and parents. For example, the therapist can counsel a teacher or parent of a child who stutters on how to respond to their child's dysfluencies--such as slowing their own rate of speaking and avoiding telling the child to stop and think of what he/she is going to say.

For more information, you are encouraged to contact:

American Speech and Hearing Association (ASHA)
10801 Rockville Pike
Rockville, MD 20852
(301) 897-5700

Music Therapy

Within the last few decades, the recognition and acceptance of music as a viable mode of therapy and instruction for disabled people has increased. Music therapists can now be found in a variety of settings. For instance, public schools and rehabilitation/community-based centers have developed music therapy programs which offer people with disabilities opportunities to participate in singing groups, develop musical abilities, and acquire leisure-time skills (e.g., knowledge and ability to access and enjoy community musical events such as concerts). Therapy typically includes such activities as playing hand-bells, strumming a guitar, or moving to music.

Music therapy not only fulfills aesthetic needs, but also helps people with disabilities to improve speech and language skills, decrease inappropriate behavior, and enhance social development. Furthermore, music therapy can improve recreational skills, academic performance, and emotional stability. With people who are physically disabled, music therapy helps to improve body positioning, increase or decrease muscle tone as needed, and increase fine and gross motor coordination.

For more information concerning music therapy, you can contact:

National Association for Music Therapy
505 Eleventh Street, S.E.
Washington, DC 20003
(202) 543-6864

American Association for Music Therapy
136 Ruwmfort Road
Philadelphia, PA 19119
(215) 242-4450

Dance Therapy

Similar to music therapy, dance therapy can be found in a variety of settings. Goals for dance therapy include the development of socialization, self-expression, speech-language skills, fine and gross motor coordination, and aesthetic responses. Like music, dance is an excellent medium that offers any person with a disability an opportunity to release emotions and tensions and gain a sense of personal pride and self-satisfaction. Dance is also an effective way of increasing imitation skills and appropriate behavior for more severely disabled people.

For people with physical disabilities, dance therapy can be especially beneficial in helping to improve motor control and stimulating circulatory systems. Using activities similar to those used in most aerobic exercises, the dance therapist can combine music with repetitive body movements to work on skills such as stretching limbs and muscles, reaching and grasping for objects, and crawling and rolling. For people confined to wheelchairs, wheelchair dancing is a popular activity that combines music and movement. In this type of dance, either the disabled person moves his or her own wheelchair, or another person moves the chair from behind. In the latter case, the person in the wheelchair is free to express him or herself to the music by swaying arms, hands, fingers, head, or any other mobile body part. With the increasing use of motorized wheelchairs, some disabled people are expanding the concept of dancing in very creative ways.

For more information on dance therapy, you can contact:

American Dance Therapy Association
200 Century Plaza
Columbia, MD 21044
(301) 997-4040

American Alliance for Health, Physical Education,
Recreation, and Dance
1900 Association Drive
Reston, VA 22091
(703) 476-3481

Art Therapy

Unlike music and dance therapy, art therapy primarily has been associated with the mental health field and is typically found in hospitals or rehabilitation settings for mentally ill persons. Established in the 1930s, art therapists have been concerned with providing opportunities for emotionally disturbed and psychotic patients to explore and reconcile emotional conflicts through drawing, sculpting, and painting activities (Liebmann, 1986). Consequently, this form of therapy has been viewed as a therapeutic tool of psychotherapy. Interestingly, it has only been in the last few decades that professionals have begun to realize the potential that art therapy holds for all disabled people.

Art therapy can have a tremendous impact on the physical, emotional, and cognitive development of any disabled person. Through art activities disabled people can develop fine motor coordination, better self-awareness, and social interaction skills. For a withdrawn person, art can be a strong motivator for group participation. Contrastingly, for an aggressive person, art can provide a constructive outlet for feelings of frustration and anger. For a person with cerebral palsy, art can be a means of developing muscle strength and coordination. (You are encouraged to read the life story about Christie Brown, a famous painter and writer, who due to athetoid cerebral palsy, did all of his work with his feet. The movie about his life is called "My Left Foot.")

One of the values of art therapy for disabled people is the way in which the therapist emphasizes the process of creating rather than the production of aesthetically pleasing end products. Disabled persons are encouraged to select the materials to be used and the subject matter on which to base their work. As a result, art provides one means by which disabled people can develop a feeling of independence and control over their lives.

For more information regarding art therapy, you can contact :

American Art Therapy Association
1202 Allanson Road
Mundelein, IL 60060
(312) 949-6064

Recreation Therapy

Like other types of therapists, recreational therapists provide services in a variety of settings, such as medical, community-based, educational, and rehabilitative settings. Usually referred to as therapeutic recreation, this type of therapy is concerned with helping disabled people facilitate an independent lifestyle through leisure time and recreational activities. Specifically, recreational therapists provide individual and group counseling, consult with families and other professionals, and adapt games, arts and crafts, and sports activities to accommodate physical, mental, or emotional disabilities of people within all age groups.

According to the National Therapeutic Recreation Society (1986), therapeutic recreation can have many benefits for disabled people. Through therapy, individuals learn to improve abilities that make participation in recreational activities possible. For example, a person who has just lost an arm or leg in a car accident may need help in discovering what leisure time activities are available and easily accessible. Recreation therapists will train these people to actively participate in sports such as swimming, wheelchair basketball, and bowling. Therapists will also counsel these individuals to help them realize and reduce many of their fears and apprehensions about participating in such leisure time activities. By promoting health and growth in a rewarding and enjoyable manner, recreational therapists help disabled individuals to be as active and independent as possible, thereby making like more satisfying and fun.

Recreation therapists also provide their clients with information about public and private programs that provide recreational outlets, such as scouting, camping, sports, social clubs, and leisure type courses at community colleges. They can also provide information about agencies that sponsor these types of programs, such as YMCA, YWCA, church and synagogue groups, city and county recreation departments, and Kiwanis, Lions, and Rotary Clubs.

For more information regarding therapeutic recreation, you can contact:

National Therapeutic Recreational Society
Suite 1200
3101 Park Center Drive
Alexandria, VA 22302
(703) 820-4940

Now that you have become familiar with the various types of therapies, it is important to learn about the many support professionals frequently encountered by people with disabilities. Disabled people access these professionals through self, parent, teacher, counselor, or physician referral.

Support Professionals

As stated before, the number of professionals that a disabled person may be involved with will depend upon the type and severity of the person's disability. Specific responsibilities for each of these types of professionals may vary from state to state and may change over any given period of time. The various professionals are presented in the next sections of this chapter.

Audiologist

The audiologist is involved with the identification of children and adults with hearing loss. The audiologist determines the range, nature, and degree of hearing loss. Once a hearing loss is detected, the audiologist refers the family to appropriate medical professionals for medical treatment. In addition, the audiologist can provide habilitative activities such as fitting, dispensing, and maintaining hearing aids, language habilitation, auditory training, and speech or reading.

Dentist

As one might assume, dentists provide routine checkups, prophylactic mouth hygiene, and general treatment. Since some people with disabilities suffer from oromaxillary abnormalities (e.g., teeth, mouth, and jaw deformities), dentists also serve as consultants to other professionals. For instance, dentists may collaborate with plastic surgeons and speech therapists regarding a person who has a cleft lip.

Dietitians

With the increasing awareness of how nutrition can affect human development and general well being, dietitians are gaining more attention in the care of people with disabilities. Dietitians are knowledgeable of the kinds and amounts of foods needed for proper health. This information is especially helpful to parents and professionals who are concerned with improving the growth and development of children with developmental delays. Dietitians also have knowledge about food allergies that may affect a child's behavior (e.g., hyperactivity and levels of attention). For older people, risks of disease can be reduced when dietitians help individuals control their cholesterol and saturated fat intake. Dietitians will often serve on an assessment team and consult with counselors, teachers, and parents regarding the regulation of a disabled person's diet.

Neonatologist

Neonatologists are specialized pediatricians concerned with the care and follow up of severely handicapped and at-risk infants in the hospital setting. Specifically, they work in and around Neonatal Intensive Care Units, often referred to as NICUs. Neonatologists are primarily involved with the care of critically ill and low birthweight infants. Like other pediatricians, the neonatologist plays an important role in assessing the infant's medical status and providing information to the family.

Nurse

Due to the increasing number of health impaired and disabled children in early intervention, school, and rehabilitative programs, nurses are being called upon to provide more direct care and consultative services in non-medical settings. The nurse is often involved in reviewing medical histories, administering medication, and communicating with the pediatrician. Since the nurse has knowledge of different types of treatments, and how those treatments affect individuals, the nurse helps set up health and medical policies and procedures in these various settings. For example, a nurse may be directly involved with helping a public school develop policies and procedures for dealing with students who may have contagious diseases. A nurse may also be responsible for providing such activities as the catherization of a student or monitoring a student for signs of physical abuse.

Ophthalmologist

An ophthalmologist is a physician who specializes in diseases and disorders of the eye (e.g., cataracts, glaucoma, or inflammatory conditions). The ophthalmologist will perform surgical procedures on the eye structures. Similar to optometrists, ophthalmologists also test acuity, prescribe lenses, and develop individualized programs and procedures for treating people with muscular vision problems (e.g., recommending exercises for weak eye muscles).

Optometrist

The role of the optometrist varies from state to state, and in many places, is becoming similar to that of the ophthalmologist. Generally, the optometrist is concerned with eye assessment and care. The optometrist will assess visual acuity and other eye problems. Optometrists will also prescribe corrective lenses, adjust eye glasses, and consult with parents, teachers, and other professionals involved in the care of disabled people. In some cases, the optometrist will prescribe medication for eye treatment and provide follow-up care after eye surgery. Optometrists may also evaluate a person to determine if a visual problem is the cause of a suspected learning disability.

Orthodontist

Taken from the Greek language, 'orthos' meaning straight, an orthodontist is a specialized dentist who is concerned with correcting and preventing irregularities of the teeth. Specifically, orthodontists straighten the alignment of teeth and oral structures. Using braces and other functional appliances (e.g., plastic molds), orthodontists will modify the growth and development of teeth and other oral structures, as well as correct the alignment of these structures when deformity is due to accident or injury. The orthodontist will often play a key role with persons who have structurally caused speech disorders.

Orthopedist

Whether due to accident, birth defect, or disease, some people require the services of an orthopedist to straighten or replace parts of the body. Specifically, an orthopedist is a physician who specializes in the correction and prevention of deformities involving the structures of the body used for movement, especially the skeleton, joints, muscles, fascia, and other supporting structures such as ligaments and cartilage. Treatments may include medical, surgical, or physical interventions. For instance, an orthopedist may recommend a prosthetic device (a device that replaces a missing body limb--e.g., an artificial leg) or an orthotic device (an instrument that straightens and supports a dysfunctional body limb--e.g., leg brace) to facilitate ambulation.

Otologist

An otologist is a physician who is concerned with the hearing mechanisms and diseases of the ear. When a person's hearing difficulty is due to birth defect, obstruction, or disease, the otologist may prescribe medication and/or perform surgery to correct and prevent further damage of the hearing mechanisms. Otologists will also conduct follow-up treatment after surgery and consult with audiologists and other professionals.

Pediatrician

A pediatrician is a medical doctor who specializes in the care of children and the treatment of their diseases. The role of the pediatrician is growing due to two current developments: (a) improved technology is maintaining the lives of low birthweight and severely disabled babies; (b) the number of health impaired children is increasing due to such factors as AIDS, toxification of the environment (e.g., increased air pollution that is resulting in greater numbers of respiratory problems), and poor pre-natal and post-natal care. Pediatricians play a major role by assessing the medical status of children and trying to determine how this status will influence their physical, cognitive, and emotional development. Pediatricians also search for etiological factors (causes for the disabilities). Though the etiology of disabilities is often very difficult to determine, technology is making many breakthroughs in this area. For instance, research in genetics is having a profound impact on the detection of genetic factors involved in various disabilities. As a result, couples are getting better counseling concerning genetic histories that might put them at high risk for having a child with a disability.

Pediatricians also play a major role as consultants to early intervention programs and school districts. Teachers and parents are requiring more information about such issues as normal and abnormal child development, administering medication and possible side-effects, and behavior management in home and school settings. In some instances, pediatricians are being asked to serve on multidisciplinary teams (however, this is limited due to time constraints common to their profession).

Psychiatrist

Unlike the psychologist, psychiatrists are specialized physicians trained to tell the difference between physical and emotional diseases, to order laboratory tests, and prescribe medications. Because many serious physical diseases, such as cancer or body toxins, can produce symptoms that resemble mental illness, psychiatrists (because of their dual training in physical and psychological illness) are able to distinguish between the cause and nature of the two and recommend appropriate treatment (Florida Psychiatric Society, 1988). Treatments commonly used by psychiatrists include medicine, psychotherapy (structured interactions between the psychiatrist and client characterized by listening, understanding the client's difficulties, and helping the client to find relief from emotional stress), psychoanalysis (generally, more longer-term treatment that focuses on the client's thoughts, feelings, and dreams to resolve underlying emotional conflicts and bring about personality change), and hospitalization (Florida Psychiatric Society, 1988).

RELATED SERVICES AND SUPPORT PROFESSIONALS

Psychologist

Whether in a clinical, private, or school setting, a psychologist will be involved in a wide variety of job responsibilities. For instance, a psychologist will typically be involved in the identification, assessment, and diagnosis of children suspected of having one or more handicapping conditions. A psychologist will also assist in the certification of school-aged children for special education eligibility as a member of the school's assessment team. With students currently placed in special education, a psychologist may do follow-up assessment procedures to measure what the individual's cognitive and adaptive behavior levels are and help other professionals plan and deliver appropriate services.

Psychologists also provide individual and group counseling in a variety of settings. This may involve counseling a group of disabled people in how to get along better with other people. In more clinical settings, the psychologist may assess the dynamics of the disabled person's family and provide family therapy. Psychologists also work with younger children in what is known as play therapy. Play therapy is a type of non-intrusive therapy in which a disturbed child works out and resolves inner emotional conflicts that are caused by such things as family problems, abuse, neglect, fantasies, and childhood schizophrenia and neurosis.

Social Worker

Typically, the social worker services as a liaison between the disabled person's family and service agencies. For example, the social worker may help the family secure information on respite care (temporary care in order for the parents to have an opportunity to get away and relax) for their disabled child or adult. Additionally, the social worker may provide counseling for the disabled person and the family. Counseling may be oriented around problems of personal hygiene, transportation, or child care. Usually, the social worker will deal with those types of problems in the environment that are affecting the individual and/or family. This may mean that the social worker conducts home or school visits. The social worker is also responsible for making disabled people and their families aware of community resources and helping them access those resources.

Vocational Counselor

Since many people with disabilities experience difficulties in securing employment (either due to lack of job training or direct/indirect discrimination), vocational counselors are important support professionals for them. These counselors are concerned with assessing, training, placing, and monitoring clients who are employed in a variety of job settings. Counseling can begin as early as the high school years by helping students to assess their physical limitations, mental abilities, interests, and specific skills, thereby helping these students to make appropriate and realistic career choices.

You should now be able to (a) identify the many therapies and support professionals that are available and necessary for disabled people, and (b) understand the role of each type of therapy and support professional as they relate to disabled individuals. This chapter was intended to serve only as an introduction to these services. For more information, you are encouraged to write to the addresses presented or talk to professionals in your local area.

Summary

Due to their diverse problems, people with disabilities require many different types of therapies and support professionals. Only within the last few decades, however, have such therapies and professionals have been made consistently available to them. Currently, communities and school systems continue to provide and expand these services. Through the efforts of many therapists and support professionals, people with disabilities are learning to adjust to social and physical environments, attain vocational and career skills, and improve general physical and mental health. Understanding the roles and responsibilities of these services will help you to advocate for such services in your own community.

References

Cusick, B. (1991). Therapeutic management of sensorimotor and physical disabilities. In J. L. Bigge (Ed.), *Teaching individuals with physical and multiple disabilities* (3rd ed.) (pp. 16-49). New York: Merrill.

Florida Psychiatric Society. (1988). *What is psychiatry?* Tallahassee, FL: Florida Psychiatric Society.

Hanson, M. J., & Harris, S. R. (1986). *Teaching the young child with motor delays.* Austin, TX: Pro-ed.

Kohn, J. G. (1982). Multiply handicapped child: Severe physical and mental disability. In E. E. Bleck & D. A. Nagel (Eds.), *Physically handicapped children: A medical atlas for teachers* (pp. 380-381). New York: Grune & Stratton.

Liebmann, M. (1986). *Art therapy for groups: A handbook of themes, games, and exercises.* Cambridge, MA: Brookline Books.

National Therapeutic Recreation Society. (1986). *About therapeutic recreation.* Alexandria, VA: National Therapeutic Recreation Society.

Strickland, B. B., & Turnbull, A. P. (1990). *Developing and implementing individualized education programs* (3rd ed). Columbus, OH: Merrill.

Suggested Readings

Boxill, E. H. (1985). *Music therapy for the developmentally disabled.* Rockville, MD: Aspen Systems.

Clark, P. N., & Allen, A. S. (Eds.). (1985). *Occupational therapy for children.* St. Louis: C. V. Mosby.

Espenak, L. (1981). *Dance therapy: Theory and application.* Springfield, IL: C. C. Thomas.

Esterson, M. M., & Bluth, L. F. (Eds.). (1987). *Related services for handicapped children.* Boston: College-Hill.

Kalish, R. A., & Presseller, S. (1980). Physical and occupational therapy. *Journal of School Health, 50,* 264-267.

Katzen, G. (1981). Your professional: The recreational therapist. *The exceptional Parent, 11,* 27-29.

Levy, F. J. (1988). *Dance/movement therapy: A healing art.* Reston, VA: National Dance Association, American Alliance for Health, Physical Education, Recreation, & Dance.

Michel, D. E. (1985). *Music therapy: An introduction, including music in special education.* Springfield, IL: C. C. Thomas.

Rubin, J. A. (Ed.). (1987). *Approaches to art therapy: Theory and technique.* New York: Bruner/Mazel.

Exploration

Individual Activities

1. Develop a list of six types of problems which disabled persons and their families may face. Identify a service agency or type of therapy which can assist with each problem.

_____ _____

_____ _____

_____ _____

_____ _____

_____ _____

_____ _____

2. Select one type of therapist (not support professional) which is discussed in the chapter. List what you feel to be the positives and negatives of that professional position.

Positive	Negative
_____	_____
_____	_____
_____	_____
_____	_____
_____	_____

Group Activities

1. Therapeutic Recreation is concerned with helping disabled people have a full and complete life through leisure time experiences and recreational activities. One of the best activities of this nature is Special Olympics. As a class, donate your time as "huggers" and other types of volunteers to the Special Olympics in your area.

    Reactions:

    _____
    _____
    _____

2. Make arrangements so that all members of your class can volunteer, on a regular basis, with an organization or agency which serves persons who are disabled. Keep a journal of your experiences.

    Reactions:

    _____
    _____
    _____

Reaction Paper 14.1

Therapy can take many different forms. Two types of therapy are occupational and physical. What are the differences between the two? What are the similarities?

Continue on back if needed.

Reaction Paper 14.2

Therapists are now using music, dance, and art as methods to assist severely disabled people. How do you feel about these types of therapy? Do you think they are as effective as other methods such as physical and occupational therapy?

___

Continue on back if needed.

360

Notes

CHAPTER 15

COMMUNITY AND CONSUMER GROUPS

Donna Wandry

Introduction

The purpose of this chapter is to acquaint you with community resources available for exceptional individuals and their families. These resources, which usually are in the form of agencies and organizations, play a vital role throughout the lifespan of the individual. The most recent amendments to Public Law 94-142 (Education for All Handicapped Children Act) show a greater sensitivity for integrated, coordinated services for children from birth to six and for older adolescents moving from educational to work settings (Mallory, 1986). While many services are provided in the educational setting during the school years, exceptional individuals and their families may seek support from outside sources both during the school years and in the years preceding and following the formal educational service paradigm.

In this chapter, you will become familiar with (a) reasons for accessing community services, (b) types of community agencies and organizations at the federal, state, and local levels, (c) the special importance of community services during the adult years, and (d) the responsibility of all citizens to be informal community resources for exceptional individuals.

Using Community Resources Throughout the Lifespan

There are many reasons why exceptional individuals and their families seek out community agencies and organizations. Often these persons need information concerning the exceptionality and support in adjusting to the changes and stresses in the family structure that the exceptionality may cause. Specific agencies may offer legal advice concerning the civil rights of the disabled individual, as well as advocacy techniques. Many organizations issue publications that serve as sources of current information such as legislation and available programs.

Mallory (1986) suggested additional reasons why community agencies and organizations can play a vital role in planning support services for both individuals and the family systems within which they live. These include increased likelihood that available services will be utilized and enhanced equity in the relationships between professional service providers and the families. Additionally, organizations and agencies have funds, equipment, and contacts beyond the school setting. While such resources are not intended to supplant the services offered by the school, they can enhance and support any services the individual enjoys through the traditional school system.

An important function of community services is the responsibility to counteract the general public's negative attitudes and misconceptions toward exceptional individuals. Because these agencies and organizations exist within the community, opportunities for public relations and positive attitude building are numerous. Additionally, these groups can afford many opportunities for people with disabilities to observe others as role models, to have direct contact with them, and eventually to develop a network of acquaintances and friendships that may be beneficial during both the school years and adult years (Lippert, 1987).

Types of Community Resources

Federal Agencies

Tindall and Gugerty (1989) pointed out that there are literally hundreds of public and private agencies and organizations at the national level that collaborate in assisting exceptional youth and adults. Nearly every disability group has a nationally recognized professional advocacy organization; these include Association for Retarded Citizens (ARC), Association for Children and Adults with Learning Disabilities (ACLD), and Council for Exceptional Children (CEC). In Appendix A you will find a listing of many such organizations with addresses and telephone numbers.

State and Local Agencies and Organizations

Many of the federal organizations have state and local branches. According to Anderson and Strathe (1987), the responsibilities of resources found in the community vary depending on the nature of the services provided by specific agencies. For example, it is a service agency's responsibility to provide special needs individuals with services deemed appropriate by parents, guardians, advocates, service providers, and the individuals themselves. The foci of these agencies may include:

Recreational services
Residential services
Guardianship
Transportation
Work activity
Sheltered work
Case management.

Recreational services. The philosophy of recreation for persons with disabilities is to provide comprehensive services in order to facilitate individual development and greater participation of disabled students and adult members of the community in their leisure time pursuits (Madison Metropolitan School District, 1987). Community agencies can work independently or collaboratively with school programs in providing (a) leisure education, leisure counseling, and participation opportunities; (b) information on accessible facilities as well as support in advocating for necessary changes in existing facilities; and (c) an avenue for self-expression and personal satisfaction.

Residential services. State and local organizations and agencies may be involved in supervising and, in some cases, providing a continuum of residential options for exceptional individuals. These options range from the most restrictive environment of institutional care to the least restrictive one of independent living. Within this continuum of living options is group home living, supervised by a professional who either lives on the premises or checks in frequently, or living with the family or a guardian.

Often, decisions regarding the best living arrangement is a major source of stress for families of special needs individuals. Families may be confronted with early separation of disabled offspring if out-of-home placement is chosen prior to adulthood, or the family cycle may be disturbed if the handicapped member remains at home after the normal age of launching into the adult world (Mallory, 1986). Besides the possible involvement of state and community agencies in the operation of alternative living facilities, they also may be involved in counseling the client and family members during the decision-making process and adjustment to decision outcomes.

Guardianship. When persons with disabilities reach the age of 18, they have the same adult rights and responsibilities as any other individual. This includes the right to marry, live and work independently, and enjoy sole decision making for their lives.

When an individual is incapable of living independently, guardianship often is granted through the courts. This must be petitioned by the parent or legal guardian. The courts must decide, with information from parents and involved professionals, if continued supervision is needed for the individual. If so, continued guardianship is granted and the parent or guardian serves as the direct provider and decision maker for that individual.

Transportation. State and local community agencies and organizations may be involved in advocating for or providing specialized or modified transportation for individuals with special needs. This modified transportation may include wheelchair lifts on buses and door-to-door bus service. Also, community agencies may work in collaboration with local transportation companies in arranging reduced rates and special pick-up locations.

Work settings. Although this topic will be discussed in greater depth in Chapter 17, it is mentioned here that a major responsibility and function of community agencies and organizations is the successful transition of individuals with special needs into a satisfying work setting. Federal programs and agencies often oversee the structure of work programs and funding for such programs and it may fall to the state and local community branches to execute the successful daily functioning of the programs and make them an accepted part of the local community.

Case management. Anderson and Strathe (1987) stressed that one of the most important services needed by many individuals with handicaps is case management. A case manager is a professional who assumes responsibility for a group of clients who are in need of support services but lack the knowledge or skill to assess and utilize services independently. During the school years, case management usually is a function of the school system. However, during those years preceding or following the formal educational process, an outside resource often found in the community is the case manager, who acts as an information source, advocate, or liaison with other community resources in acquiring the most appropriate support services for the client.

Other Community Resources

Early Intervention Programs

For families of the under-three-year-old child with disabilities, the most frequent and influential contact remains the pediatrician, who often makes the initial decision to refer for special services such as early intervention programs. Examples of early intervention programs include those operated by The Association for Retarded Citizens and by Head Start.

The Early Intervention Program operated by the Association for Retarded Citizens is designed to serve disabled children from birth to three years of age. Doctors, parents, or agencies involved with the family can make the referral to this program, for which there is no direct charge to the child's family. Services such as physical and occupational therapy, speech therapy, and play therapy (described in Chapter 14) are offered as part of the daily activities. Additionally, staff members work with families in developing advocacy techniques once the child leaves the early intervention setting and is placed in the school system.

Head Start provides comprehensive educational and social services, parent involvement, and health services (including medical, dental, nutrition, and mental health services) to preschool children, ages 3-5. At least 10 percent of the nationwide enrollment in Head Start must consist of children who have disabilities and require special services (U.S. Department of Education, 1989).

Parent Support Groups

Stagg and Catron (1986) stated that very little is known about how individuals use support available to them, particularly the strategies and skills that individuals employ to obtain the support they need from a network. However, it is clear that many parents of individuals with special needs do access networks. These networks help them deal with the stresses associated with having disabled individuals in their families.

Often the greatest support can be found among other parents of individuals with special needs, where fears of stigma and misunderstanding do not exist. One of the most common forms of family support and involvement is parent support groups (Mallory, 1986). Many communities have informal parent support groups, as well as local chapters of state and federal organizations (such as Parent to Parent, Inc.). These groups can offer emotional support, information, and a very important conduit for awareness of respite care options.

Respite Care

Respite care is an alternate, short-term form of caring for individuals with special needs, and is especially beneficial for parents of children with more severe handicaps. Respite care has emerged since the mid-1970s in response to the deinstitutionalization movement and the resulting reliance on family-based care for children and adults with disabilities. A range of formal models of respite care was described by Upshur in 1982, and included:

Respite placement agencies which train community providers to work in a client's home or their own home

Group day care or family day care outside of the handicapped person's home

Community residences where a few beds are reserved for overnight respite

Residential treatment facilities with a few beds reserved for respite

Group respite facilities that only provide respite care

Pediatric nursing homes or hospitals that provide emergency respite care during crises

Private respite providers, without organizational affiliation, who care for children in their own homes

State institutions that provide a few respite beds for former residents.

Respite care was recognized by Cohen (1982) as leading to improved family functioning, more hopefulness about the future, a more positive attitude toward the family member, and an increased ability to cope with the daily demands caused by the handicapped person.

Community Agency Involvement in Transition

Definition of Transition

Current legislation, in the form of Section 626 of Public Law 98-199, defines transition services as:

> a coordinated set of activities for a student, designed within an outcome-oriented process, which promotes movement from school to integrated employment (including supported employment), post-secondary education, vocational training, continuing and adult education, adult services, independent living, or community participation. The coordinated set of activities shall be based upon the individual student's needs, taking into account each student's preference and interests, and shall include, but not be limited to, instruction, community experiences, the development of employment and other post-school adult living objectives, and when appropriate, acquisition of daily living skills and functional vocational evaluation. (H.R. 1013, 1990)

Since the goal of transition is the successful movement into the community (as depicted by Figure 15.1), it becomes clear that the role of community resources becomes even greater at this time of the exceptional individual's life.

Although the educational system is playing an increasing role in the provision of programming that facilitates successful movement into the workplace and community, the school system's involvement ends with graduation or exit from the formal school setting. Primary responsibility for transition services then falls upon community resources at the federal, state, and local levels. In order to understand the framework within which these agencies and organizations function, a description of several of these support services is needed.

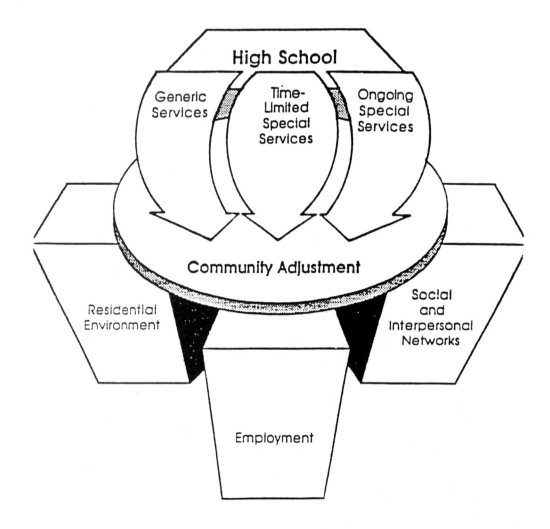

Figure 15.1. Community adjustment model. Halpern, A. (1985). Transition: A look at the foundations. *Exceptional Children, 51,* 479-486. (Used with permission.)

Table 15.1 depicts several agencies important to career development and adult adjustment of individuals with handicaps. These agencies have state and many times local branches that may be accessed through the telephone directory. A brief description of some of these agencies is offered following the table.

Table 15.1
Transition Resources

Type of Organization	Resources Available
Private Agencies	Respite Facilities Rehabilitation Facilities Sheltered Workshops
Federal and State Agencies	Vocational Rehabilitation Social Security Administration Job Training Partnership Act Agencies Developmental Disabilities Agencies
Service Organizations	Volunteer--The National Center Special Olympics Fraternal Organizations
National, State, and Local Organizations	Association for Retarded Citizens Parent Support Organizations Association for Children and Adults with Learning Disabilities National Easter Seal Society

---

Vocational Rehabilitation

Sitlington (1986) described vocational rehabilitation (VR) as primarily serving individuals who have been classified as handicapped or whose disabilities interfere with obtaining and retaining employment. She further stated that vocational rehabilitation primarily serves a post-school population, but, according to the Vocational Rehabilitation Act of 1984, this discipline also must work with in-school youth who are preparing to make the transition to employment. Involvement with special needs individuals may begin as early as age 16. For those VR counselors who are involved with clients while they are still in the school system, service provision may include (a) career counseling; (b) consultation with special and vocational education teachers, school counselors, and other professionals; (c) work adjustment counseling; and (d) specialized planning and links with postsecondary programs and support services for students with disabilities (Szymanski & King, 1989).

Once the client is outside the school system, vocational rehabilitation agencies identify which services are needed by these adults with disabilities, and purchases these services on a contractual basis from other agencies. Sitlington listed several examples of services that can be funded by vocational rehabilitation. These include:

Medical and vocational evaluation

Medical treatment or prosthetic devices to make the person more employable

Academic support services related to instruction in a vocational training program

Specific vocational skill training

Other services related to support in vocational training programs, including transportation during the training period, tools, and textbooks.

Vocational rehabilitation agencies receive federal funding for their operation, and are highly effective through their connection with adult service providers and community employers. Vocational rehabilitation agencies do not provide their own vocational training, but rely on those existing services in their local communities to provide needed programs for work preparation. The involvement of vocational rehabilitation is on a time-limited basis; that means that client interaction with the agency ends shortly after employment is achieved.

Job Training Partnership Act (JTPA) Agencies

JTPA programs, which stem from the Job Training Partnership Act of 1982 (Public Law 97-300), mostly serve economically disadvantaged adolescents and adults. However, many states have made provisions to consider individuals with special needs as a "family of one" (a person who is solely responsible for him/herself financially), making them eligible for JTPA services regardless of income. Like vocational rehabilitation, JTPA often identifies the needs of individual participants, then purchases services from existing training programs. Additionally, on-the-job training and employer incentives for hiring special needs individuals is emphasized (Sitlington, 1986).

Services that can be funded by JTPA agencies include (a) job search assistance and counseling; (b) vocational exploration and work experience, and on-the-job training; (c) specific skill training in an existing vocational program; and (d) programs to develop positive work habits and attitudes. Like vocational rehabilitation, JTPA services are on a time-limited basis.

Developmental Disabilities Programs

Developmental disabilities programs make use of existing services in health, welfare, education, and rehabilitation to provide for the long-range needs of people with developmental disabilities. These disabilities are defined as severe, chronic disabilities attributable to mental or physical impairment, which are manifested before age 22, and require services over an extended period (U.S. Department of Education, 1989). Developmental disability (DD) agencies primarily serve youth and adults with disabilities such as cerebral palsy, epilepsy, mental retardation, autism, or behavioral disorders. These agencies are funded through state grants, with a designated agency to administer the developmental disabilities program as well as provide protection and advocacy for individuals with developmental disabilities and their families.

Developmental disability agencies are involved in providing group living arrangements for these individuals as they become adults. Many times, these persons have difficulty living independently, and living with a family member is not an option. Since institutionalization is too restrictive an environment for many developmentally disabled individuals, group living arrangements with full or limited supervision is a viable alternative. In addition to living arrangements, developmental disabilities agencies may be involved in diagnosis and treatment, training for jobs, recreation programs, social and legal services, information and referral to services, and transportation. More information can be obtained about these programs through the organizations listed in Appendix A.

Social Security Administration

Under Social Security, the definition of disability is related to the ability to work. A person is considered disabled when he or she has a severe mental or physical impairment or a combination of impairments that prevents working for a year or more or that is expected to end in death. Because this description applies to many exceptional individuals, they often are eligible for Social Security benefits.

These benefits may take the form of Supplemental Security Income (SSI), which is available to both children and adults with disabilities. If the individual is able to work, SSI may still be received at a reduced rate if the earnings are low enough. An additional benefit from Social Security is Medicaid, to assist in paying costs of hospital care and physicians' services. Usually, a person who is eligible for SSI can also receive Medicaid. Persons receiving SSI may also be able to get social services from the state or county, including housekeeping help, arrangements for meals, or transportation (U.S. Department of Health and Human Services, 1990).

Sources of Information

Many other agencies exist that offer community resources to exceptional individuals. The ones described above provide only a glimpse of the possible options available to these persons. Efforts by different groups have yielded several source guides that may be accessed to provide information and services about varying exceptionalities and special interest groups. This section lists some of these publications, with further listings provided in Appendix A.

National Clearinghouse on Postsecondary Education for Individuals with Handicaps Resource Directory. Sponsored by the Higher Education and Adult Training for People with Handicaps (HEATH) Resource Center in Washington, the *National Clearinghouse on Postsecondary Education for Individuals with Handicaps Resource Directory* (1989) offers over 150 annotated references and resources for education and training after high school. The HEATH Resource Center receives funding from the United States Department of Education, and operates under legislative mandate to collect and disseminate information nationally about disability issues in postsecondary education. This information is valuable for parents, exceptional individuals, educators, and anyone seeking information about agencies and organizations.

Updated regularly, the HEATH Resource Directory includes organizations and directories that provide information on access and awareness, resources regarding specific disabilities, community integration, technology, funding, and legal assistance. Pertinent laws and regulations are described and Department of Education Regional Technical Assistance Offices are listed so that additional materials can be requested. Also included is a toll free telephone listing of various organizations and agencies. A single copy of the HEATH Resource Directory (with a nominal charge for

COMMUNITY AND CONSUMER GROUPS

additional copies) can be obtained through the following address and telephone number:

>Higher Education and Adult Training for People
>   with Handicaps Resource Center
>One Dupont Circle, Suite 800
>Washington, DC 20036-1193
>(800) 544-3284

National Information Center for Handicapped Children and Youth (NICHCY). The National Center for Handicapped Children and Youth provides a wide selection of written information including (a) information sheets including names and addresses of public groups serving handicapped children and youth within each state, (b) fact sheets on specific disabilities and resources for further information, (c) legal fact sheets on children's rights, including rights to education, (d) parent information on direct children's services and advocacy and support groups, (d) teacher-parent information on educational concerns, (e) student information on careers in special education and related services, and (f) general information on organizations and publications about handicapping conditions.

NICHCY also distributes resource sheets which list the names and addresses of the key individuals and agencies serving exceptional individuals in each state. NICHCY may be accessed by writing the following address:

>National Information Center for Handicapped Children
>   and Youth
>P. O. Box 1492
>Washington, DC 20013

Directory of National Information Sources on Handicapping Conditions and Related Services. This major reference is sponsored by the United States Department of Education, Office of Special Education and Rehabilitative Services (OSERS), Clearinghouse on the Handicapped (Publication No. E-82-22007). It provides information about national government organizations, advocacy, consumer, and volunteer health organizations, special facilities, schools and clinics, and religious and sports organizations for exceptional individuals and their families. This directory is available from the U.S. Government for a minimal charge. The address is:

>U.S. Government Printing Office
>Washington, DC 20401

The information in these directories, as well as from specific organizations such as those found in Appendix A, is extremely helpful to exceptional individuals, their families, and the professionals with whom they are involved. However, they also may serve as important information resources for the general public. Citizens in every community have many opportunities for interaction with exceptional individuals, whether it be as an acquaintance, a friend, an employer, or a customer. You will benefit from broadening your knowledge base about exceptional individuals as you assist their integration into the community.

The Role of Community Resources

Employment Opportunities for Exceptional Individuals

Changes in the business economy and demographic factors, such as greater numbers of jobs with fewer qualified workers to fill them, will offer those professionals involved in transition services for special needs persons increased opportunities to establish productive partnerships with the community. However, many employers have stereotyped images of persons with disabilities as being potentially unemployable and unproductive (Johnson, Warrington, & Melberg, 1989). In order for transition efforts to be effective, those in the business community must make every effort to rid themselves of these stereotypical attitudes, and thus provide valuable work experiences for individuals with disabilities.

These goals may be accomplished through interacting with professionals in the school setting and in vocational training programs. Cooperative networking with other businesses may also be an effective method of providing an employment base for those exceptional individuals entering the work force.

Volunteer Efforts

Many of the organizations listed in Appendix A, as well as other organizations that exist in local communities, offer the opportunity for volunteer activities.

Individuals may choose to take part in such activities as Special Olympics, a nationally recognized sports competition for individuals with physical and developmental disabilities. Volunteers are given opportunities in coaching, organizing, and conducting competitions, and interacting in fun and challenging sports with the competitors.

Additionally, local organizations such as the Association for Retarded Citizens often sponsor recreation programs and community outings for members and clients. Municipal parks and recreation offices may have information on special recreational programs for individuals with handicaps.

The chances for volunteer participation are numerous. Because each community varies in the number and types of organizations, and the types of activities offered, it is suggested that interested individuals contact local organization chapters or offices to identify the available opportunities. These organizations often can be found in the local telephone directory. A good example is Volunteer--The National Center, which is a nationwide network, with local offices throughout the United States. Their national office address is:

> Volunteer--The National Center
> 111 N. 19th Street
> Suite 500
> Arlington, VA 22209
> (703) 276-0542

Summary

You have become acquainted with the various types of community resources available to exceptional individuals and their families, as well as opportunities for every citizen to become a valuable individual resource. Each one of us has a support network in our activities at work, at home, and at play. Whether this network is of a formal (organizations and clubs) or an informal (friends and contacts) nature, we would not enjoy a high quality of life without them. This also is true of exceptional individuals, and may be even more so because of the added challenges they may face.

The role of community resources is to maintain a high quality of life for those that access their services. Needs may change throughout the life span, but the main goal is to become part of the community. This may be illustrated by the following description of normal life that we all seek, and which the accessing of community resources may help us achieve:

> Normalization means . . . a normal rhythm of the day. You get out of bed in the morning, even if you are profoundly retarded and physically handicapped; you get dressed, and leave the house for school or work; you don't stay home. . . .
>
> Normalization means . . . a normal rhythm of the week. You live in one place, go to work in another, and participate in leisure activities in yet another. You anticipate leisure activities on weekends, and look forward to getting back to school or work on Monday. . . .
>
> Normalization means . . . having a range of choices, wishes, and desires respected and considered. Adults have the freedom to decide where they would like to live, what kind of job they would like to have and can best perform, and whether they would prefer to go bowling with a group, instead of staying home to watch television.
>
> Normalization means . . . the right to normal economic standards. All of us have basic financial privileges and responsibilities. . . . We should have money to decide how to spend on personal luxuries or necessities.
>
> Normalization means . . . living in normal housing in a normal neighborhood. . . . Normal locations and normal-size homes will give residents better opportunities for successful integration with their communities. (Mallory, 1986, pp. 334-335)

References

Anderson, R. L., & Strathe, M. L. (1987). Transition from school to work and community. In G. D. Meers (Ed.), *Handbook of vocational special needs education* (2nd ed.) (pp. 315-329). Rockville, MD: Aspen.

Cohen, S. (1982). Supporting families through respite care. *Rehabilitation Literature, 43,* 7-11.

Halpern, A. (1985). Transition: A look at the foundations. *Exceptional Children, 51,* 479-486.

HEATH Resource Center. (1989). *National Clearinghouse on Post-Secondary Education for Individuals with Handicaps: Resource Directory.* Washington, DC: Author.

Johnson, D. R., Warrington, G. J., & Melberg, M. L. (1989). Job developing, placement, and follow-up services. In D. E. Berkell & J. M. Brown (Eds.), *Transition from school tow work for persons with disabilities* (pp. 161-186). New York: Longman.

Lippert, T. (1987). *The case management team: Building community connections* (Publication No. 421-88-011). St. Paul, MN: Metropolitan Council Developmental Disabilities Program.

Madison Metropolitan School District. (1987). *Recreation programs for people with disabilities staff manual.* Madison, WI: Madison School-Community Resources.

Mallory, B. L. (1986). Interactions between community agencies and families over the life cycle. In R. R. Fewell & P. F. Vadasy (Eds.), *Families of handicapped children: Needs and supports across the life span* (pp. 317-356). Austin, TX: Pro-Ed.

Sitlington, P. L. (1986). *Transition, special needs, and vocational education* (Contract No. NIE-C-400-84-0011). Columbus, OH: the Ohio State University, National Center for Research in Vocational Education.

Staff. (1990, Winter-Spring). Will the real "Transition Services" please stand up: The reauthorization of the transition amendment (PL 98-199). *Policy Network Newsletter*, The George Washington University, p. 8.

Stagg, V., & Catron, T. (1986). Networks of social supports for parents of handicapped children. In R. R. Fewell & P. F. Vadasy (Eds.), *Families of handicapped children: Needs and supports across the life span* (pp. 279-296). Austin, TX: Pro-Ed.

Szymanski, E., & King, J. (1989). Rehabilitation counseling in transition planning and preparation. *Career Development for Exceptional Individuals, 12*(1), 3-10.

Tindall, L. W., & Gugerty, J. J. (1989). Collaboration among clients, families, and service providers. In D. E. Berkell & J. M. Brown (Eds.), *Transition from school to work for persons with disabilities* (pp. 127-160). New York: Longman.

Upshur, C. C. (1982). Respite care for mentally retarded and other disabled populations: Program models and family needs. *Mental Retardation, 20*, 2-6.

U.S. Department of Education. (1982). *Directory of national information sources on handicapping conditions and related services* (Publication No. E-82-22007). Washington, DC: Office of Special Education and Rehabilitative Services, Clearinghouse on the Handicapped.

U.S. Department of Education. (1989). *Pocket guide to federal help for individuals with disabilities* (Publication No. E-89-22002). Washington, DC: Clearinghouse on Disability Information.

U.S. Department of Health and Human Services. (1990). *SSI* (SSA Publication No. 05-11000). Washington, DC: Social Security Administration.

Suggested Readings

Esterson, M. M., & Bluth, L. F. (1987). *Related services for handicapped children.* Boston: Little, Brown.

Fewell, R. R., & Vadasy, P. F. (Eds.). (1986). *Families of handicapped children: Needs and supports across the lifespan.* Austin, TX: Pro-Ed.

Healy, A., Keesee, P. D., & Smith, B. S. (1989). *Early services for children with special needs: Transactions for family support.* Baltimore: Paul H. Brookes.

Janicki, M. P., Krauss, M. W., & Seltzer, M. M. (1988). *Community residences for persons with developmental disabilities: Here to stay.* Baltimore: Paul H. Brookes.

Lippert, T. (1987). *The case management team: Building community connections* (Publication No. 421-88-011). St. Paul, MN: Metropolitan Council Developmental Disabilities Program.

Perske, R., & Perske, M. (1981). *New life in the neighborhood.* Nashville, Abingdon.

Stewart, J. C. (1986). *Counseling parents of exceptional children.* Columbus, OH: Charles E. Merrill.

U.S. Department of Education. (1989). *Pocket guide to federal help for individuals with disabilities* (Publication No. E-89-22002). Washington, DC: Clearinghouse on Disability Information.

Wilson, M. (1990). *You can make a difference: Helping others and yourself through volunteering.* Boulder, CO: Volunteer Management Associates.

Notes

COMMUNITY AND CONSUMER GROUPS

Exploration

Individual Activities

1. Develop a list of ten community and consumer groups in your area. The Yellow Pages of your phone directory should be helpful.

    1. _____
    2. _____
    3. _____
    4. _____
    5. _____
    6. _____
    7. _____
    8. _____
    9. _____
    10. _____

2. Define normalization. Then list six things that can be done to promote normalization in your community or on your campus.

    Definition:_____

    _____

    1. _____
    2. _____
    3. _____
    4. _____
    5. _____
    6. _____

Group Activities

1. Arrange yourselves into groups of about six people. You know that there are not enough social activities in your community for disabled persons. Brainstorm and identify five social activities which can be developed.

   1. _____
   2. _____
   3. _____
   4. _____
   5. _____

2. Arrange for a representative from your local J.T.P.A. to attend your class. Ask that person to describe their program and its benefits for disabled people.

   Reactions:

   _____
   _____
   _____

Reaction Paper 15.1

Assume that you are going to run for governor. One major component of your campaign is your stand on the facilitation of more services for disabled people. Explain and justify this part of your platform.

Continue on back if needed.

Reaction Paper 15.2

You have recognized that respite care is helpful for persons who are disabled and for their families. Write a news release which announces the opening of your new respite care facility. Fully describe your facility and your objectives.

Continue on back if needed.

Notes

CHAPTER 16

LAWS AND LEGISLATION

Carl Cameron

Introduction

The previous chapters of this book have focused on a variety of aspects related to the understanding of individuals with disabilities and the types of services that are available to ensure full participation in the mainstream of American life. There have been references in almost every chapter to federal and state laws; rules and regulations that mandate rights and services for individuals with disabilities. This focus on law and legislation is not incidental, but is at the heart of the social change that has resulted in increased opportunity for individuals with disabilities.

While there is truly no one point in history that constitutes the beginning of the development of legislation related to individuals with disabilities, it is apparent that during the period from the late 1950s to the early 1960s there was a new awakening in the United States to social issues that included the rights of individuals who were members of minority groups; racial, sex, and persons with handicapping conditions. While the issues and concerns voiced by these groups were not new, the increased interest in changing the conditions under which minorities lived grew out of a dissatisfaction with their inability to participate fully in the new quality of life being experienced throughout the rest of the nation. From a review of history, it is apparent that much of the general public was first made aware of the social movement by

African Americans in this country with the civil rights movement in the late 1950s. This movement provided the model for the social change that was to follow--the women's movement, movements related to sexual preference, and the disability movement.

There are many common elements among these movements for social change; among the most predominant is the fight against personal, social, and economic discrimination. While there were also many ways in which this discrimination has been, and continues to be addressed, a major factor in the redress of grievances has been through the court system in this country, and the legislation that was brought about by that litigation.

In this chapter, the emphasis is on the importance of the court system and the development of state and federal law that has provided opportunities for individuals with disabilities in securing and maintaining employment, accessing appropriate education opportunities, and securing appropriate health and other medically related services. The obtaining of opportunity through the court system, or the litigation process, in many cases was not finally resolved until decisions were handed down by state or federal supreme courts. It was the large number of court decisions that established rights for individuals with disabilities that pressured the state governments and the federal government to begin establishing public policy through the passage of state and federal legislation.

It has not been easy to obtain rights for individuals with disabilities. The courage that many private citizens demonstrated when they attempted to bring suit against agencies, organizations, and ultimately the state and federal government has rarely been observed in other areas of advocacy. Hallahan and Kauffman (1978) suggested that only through the sustained efforts of parents and advocates of exceptional children has legislation and increased funding become available for individuals with disabilities.

Disability Related Litigation

Litigation has played a pivotal role in the development of public policy related to individuals with disabilities. During the period of time from the early 1950s through 1975, the major impact of litigation was in its influence on the developing and passage of disability legislation. With the passage of major pieces of federal legislation in the mid-1970s, litigation evolved into predominantly a tool to define and refine the existing legislation.

The litigation focused on individuals with disabilities has its roots near the turn of the century when specific court decisions focused primarily on excluding children with handicaps from school (Watson v. City of Cambridge, 1893 and Beattie v. State Board of Education, 1919). It was not until 1954 that Brown v. Board of Education established that segregated schools were inherently unequal, which paved the way for a variety of lawsuits that challenged the right of schools to exclude students based on their handicapping condition.

A major court case that radically affected the educational opportunities for individuals with disabilities was Mills v. Board of Education in 1972, which ruled that students could not be excluded from school because of a handicapping condition and that handicapped children have a right to a "constructive education" including appropriate specialized instruction. In 1972, Pennsylvania Association for Retarded Children (PARC) sued the Commonwealth of Pennsylvania over the rights of mentally retarded students to attend school. This landmark case established the right of mentally retarded students to an education, no matter how severe the handicapping condition.

A series of landmark court decisions followed the PARC v. Commonwealth of Pennsylvania case which established rights of parents to a fair and orderly process in determining if a student is handicapped and the determination of the type of special services that should be provided. In addition to the establishing of an appropriate evaluation and placement process (now usually referred to as due process), a series of decisions followed PARC v. Commonwealth of Pennsylvania focused on the right of individuals with disabilities to live in communities outside residential institutions. For instance, the case of Halderman v. Pennhurst (1977) resulted in the ruling that ordered the closing of state institutions for mentally retarded persons and the establishment of community residential options for all the institutionalized residents. These rulings have established what has become to be known as the deinstitutionalization/ normalization movement in this country and established the rights of individuals with severe handicaps to live in an integrated environment.

The focus of litigation related to the provision of services for individuals with disabilities changed with the passage of the Education of All Handicapped Children Act of 1975 (PL 94-142), when litigation became more important as a tool in defining, implementing, and enforcing existing legislation than in providing the basis for the development of new legislation. One area of ongoing litigation following PL 94-142 attacked the disproportionate number of minority individuals in special education classes. Litigation such as Larry P. v. Riles (1974), PASE v. Hannon (1980) and

Lora v. New York City Board of Education (1978) sought to define an unbiased assessment and placement process to ensure that other cultural differences were the basis for problems in school achievement, and not a handicapping condition. While a great deal of progress has been made in the appropriate identification of minority youngsters, minority and economically disadvantaged youngsters continue to be over-represented in special education. Public Law 94-142, or the Education of All Handicapped Children Act of 1975, along with its later amendments, will be discussed in more detail in the next section.

Disability Related Legislation

The legislation that began to appear in the 1960s included an emphasis on access to appropriate public school education for children and youth with disabilities. This legislation focused on the provision of special education services, and the inclusion of services for students with disabilities within vocational education.

Special Education

Providing appropriate education for children and youth with handicaps has been a major focus of disability legislation. The initial legislation, related to the mandatory provision of special education services, emanated from individual states in the early and mid-1960s. Testimony at public hearings regarding the implementation of new public education legislation for handicapped children during the 1970s revealed that there were more than eight million school-aged handicapped children and youth who were not receiving an adequate education and one million children who were excluded from school because of their handicapping condition (Nystrom & Bayne, 1979). As a result of litigation, pressure from parent and advocacy organizations, and state initiated legislation, the Education of All Handicapped Children Act (PL 94-142) became law in 1975. This landmark piece of legislation was designed to:

> **Guarantee the availability of special education programs to children and youth with handicaps**
> **Assure that educational decisions related to children and youth with handicaps are fair and appropriate**

Financially assist the efforts of the state and local government to provide special education through the use of federal funds.

Under PL 94-142, schools must provide appropriate elementary and secondary education to children and youth with disabilities from the ages 6 to 21. This law has since been amended to include all children from age three. States are also required to provide special education to infants and toddlers (birth to three years of age) if they receive funds under Part H of this law.

The Federal Law guarantees that children and youth with handicaps have the right to a free appropriate public education. This ensures the right of parents to participate in the educational decisions related to their child. These educational decisions (explained more fully in Chapter 13) include the process of determining if their child is handicapped, and therefore eligible for special education services, decisions on where the special education services will take place, determining the instructional program, evaluating the effectiveness of the special education services, and determining if their child should remain in special education. The legislators involved in the enactment of PL 94-142 realized that parents have a special insight into their children's needs, that parents can learn through involvement in making decisions, and that children benefit when parents and educators work together. The parent has the right and responsibility to participate in the educational decision making as part of a team comprised of teachers, the principal, specialists such as psychologists, occupational therapists, physical therapists, and other medical personnel. At any stage in the process, a parent may challenge the decisions of the team through a series of procedural safeguards called Due Process. The Due Process provisions provide a series of options to the parents that include complaint mediation, a formal due process hearing, and even resolution within the judicial system.

PL 94-142 is a public law that has been amended on several occasions, including the amendments PL 98-199 and PL 100-457, which emphasized two major target populations in special education: (a) the education of infants, toddlers, and preschoolers and (b) services for adolescents who are leaving school programs and beginning their adult life. PL 94-142 and the subsequent amendments now authorizes special education for children from birth through the age of 21. The federal law provides additional resources to assist local schools in serving infants and toddlers and provides new resources to guarantee services to adolescents who are entering the world of work. The guarantees include a requirement for the educational program of a student with a disability to include a plan for transitioning to post-secondary life. One important aspect of the transition plan is the inclusion of appropriate assistive technology that is of benefit to the student. This provision focuses on the selection, purchase, and training in the use of assistive technology like an adapted microcomputer, alternative speech devices, and keyboards.

Vocational Education

Vocational education has a long history of focusing on the special needs of students who are disadvantaged or handicapped. Through the history of vocational education legislation, other special populations have been the focus of the vocational education legislation. These targeted groups include:

Men/women entering non-traditional occupations
Adults in need of training or retraining
Single parents and displaced homemakers
Students with limited English proficiency
Individuals who are incarcerated.

The most recent legislation in vocational education, the Carl D. Perkins Vocational Education Act (PL 98-524) provides federal funds to each state that operates vocational education programs. One of the ongoing provisions in the vocational education legislation has been the specific funding for programs for both disadvantaged and handicapped persons. The Carl D. Perkins Vocational Education Act provides specific federal funds to support the additional costs of the vocational education of handicapped and disadvantaged students--over and above what is provided for all students who are enrolled in vocational education.

The Carl D. Perkins Vocational Education Act is currently being reauthorized by Congress, and this reauthorization is expected to eliminate funds specifically mandated by the law to serve students with handicaps, but encourages each state to provide funding through the basic state grant for the special programs and services for students with disabilities. Many special needs teachers and education professionals are concerned about this change from providing set-aside federal funds to allowing states the discretion to determine the extent to which vocational funds will be used to serve the special needs of students with handicaps. This reauthorization also will rename the Carl D. Perkins Vocational Education Act to focus on the theme of "Applied Technology Education" to emphasize the changing emphasis from vocational subjects to the focus on high technology and changing technology applications in the work world.

Employment

Employment continues to be one of the most critical challenges for individuals with disabilities in the United States. Extremely high rates of unemployment continue to be reported by every study that looks at the employment needs of persons with disabilities--rates of 60-70% unemployment are often cited (Rusch & Phelps, 1987).

At the same time employers continue to express their needs for more and more workers--there are, in many communities, help wanted signs everywhere and at relatively high hourly rates. This demand for workers is also accompanied by a new experience for many in the field of employment of individuals with disabilities; employers are actively pursuing non-traditional workers such as non-English speaking persons, and individuals with severe handicaps.

Another factor in the employment debate surrounding persons with disabilities is the issue of under-employment of individuals. Rusch and Phelps (1987) reported that individuals with disabilities are 75% more likely to be employed part-time than their non-disabled peers. From follow-up studies of students leaving special education, it is apparent that temporary and part-time employment make up a large percentage of the few jobs that youth with disabilities are able to obtain (Ryan, 1988).

In order to confront this long standing need, the federal government has addressed employment of individuals with disabilities in a variety of ways; most of which has been legislation and fiscal appropriations designed to provide some measure of federal financial assistance. This federal legislation, while providing resources, such as funding for job training programs in local communities, has not been without its critics, some who are state or local service providers. A major criticism of federal financial assistance is that federal funding is often accompanied by an infinite number of federal mandates and reporting requirements that do not necessarily bring with them equal amounts of new federal dollars to implement them. For example, the Department of Labor requires an extensive accountability system within the Job Training and Partnership Act that most training professionals do not find fits with the needs of their clients. Possibly more of a problem than the limitation of federal resources and the excessive documentation is the frustration that occurs as states and regions attempt to interpret federal mandates that appear to be confusing, overlapping, or even contradictory.

For example, there is a requirement for a planning process in almost all transition related legislation or in the implementing regulations. There is a requirement for an Individual Education Program in special education, the Individual

Vocational Plan in vocational education, and the Individual Work Rehabilitation Plan in the Department of Rehabilitation Services, all which may be required in providing transition services to a single adolescent who is the recipient of federal support from these three different sources.

This example describes what appears to be at the very least a confusing relationship between state and federal agencies. It is also important to note that, federal, state and local agencies can, and do, work together in an effective and efficient manner. In fact, one of the really unique features of employment legislation is that interagency cooperation is mandated within all of the major pieces of federal legislation that focus on providing transition services. It is also important to examine the role that the state plays in implementing the federal regulation with its own priorities, and the role the state plays in supporting and monitoring local implementation.

The legislation that focuses on the employment of individuals with disabilities encompasses both legislation that focuses specifically on individuals with disabilities and an even broader area of legislation related to employment that includes rules and regulations for individuals with disabilities. In addition, legislation focuses on education and training, followed by legislation that serves students with disabilities but may be primarily focused at other target populations; such as, economic disadvantage, other unemployed but not disabled students, and adolescents or adults who have left school.

There are a variety of sources of state and federal legislation that provide support for employment and training activities. Two which provide the majority of the legislation and related support are the U.S. Office of Special Education and Rehabilitation Services and the U.S. Department of Labor.

Vocational Rehabilitation

Vocational Rehabilitation had its beginnings with World War I, where legislation was passed to assist in the rehabilitation of soldiers injured in conflict. The emphasis of vocational rehabilitation for many years was on the rehabilitation of individuals who were injured on the job or in the military. The Vocational Rehabilitation Act of 1973 (PL 93-112, and its subsequent amendments; Public Law 93-516, 95-602, 98-221) increased the emphasis on individuals with developmental disabilities (those who were disabled at birth or during the formative years). The Vocational Rehabilitation Act in its current form has established a priority for persons who are the most severely disabled, and actively supports a cooperative relationship with special education. The federal support is provided through basic state grants that support efforts in counseling, vocational evaluation, work adjustment, mental and physical rehabilitation, education, vocational training, job placement, and post-employment services.

In addition to the Basic grants provided to each state, the Vocational Rehabilitation Act authorizes:

Support for the most severely disabled individuals in their transition to independent living through the funding of supported employment. Supported employment emphasizes employment in community based business and industry, with long-term support by employment and training specialists. Supported employment is not training for employment, but is permanent employment that included training on the job.

Support for the National Institute of Disability and Rehabilitation Research, to support and promote research related to rehabilitation of individuals with disabilities.

Support for a nationwide network of Independent Living Centers that provide assistance to individuals with disabilities in their attempts to live independently.

Provision of resources to provide assistive technology for individuals who require assistance in order to obtain and maintain employment. A companion piece of legislation called the Technology Related Assistance for Individuals with Disabilities Act of 1988 (PL 100-407) assists states in developing and implementing statewide programs of technology-related assistance for meeting the needs of individuals with disabilities. The legislation includes funds to states to examine delivery of assistive technology and for national level activities such as technical assistance to states currently receiving support.

One very important feature of the Vocational Rehabilitation Act is the provisions in Sections 503 and 504 of the act, that are sometimes referred to as the legislation providing for a "Barrier Free Environment." These specific sections mandate that facilities and programs be accessible to individuals with disabilities. Included in the Vocational Rehabilitation Act is the prohibition against discrimination in access to any program or activity using federal funds because of a handicapping condition. This applies to any aspect of a program including recruitment, testing, admissions, and treatment. The removal of architectural barriers is also part of this legislation, and requires that programs, services and activities that receive federal funds be accessible to individuals with disabilities. This provision has been the basis for the development of wheelchair ramps, braille markings on elevators, and accessible bathrooms.

The Job Training and Partnership Act

The Job Training and Partnership Act (PL 97-300) provides an opportunity for employment and training services for persons with limited income. This legislation authorizes the use of federal funds administered by the Department of Labor to support local and regional employment assistance efforts. The type of programs and services provided in each area is determined by the Private Industry Councils (PIC's), or local policy making councils comprised of a wide variety of citizens from both public and private agencies and corporations. Programs and services for individuals with disabilities can be included in the priorities of the PIC's through a unique provision of the law, which entitles individuals with disabilities to automatically qualify as a family of one, regardless of their living arrangements. This allows disabled individuals, regardless of their family's income, to qualify for services based solely on their own personal income.

Tax Reform Act of 1986

The Tax Reform Act authorizes a program called the Targeted Jobs Tax Credit. This program provides a unique opportunity for employers to realize a business tax credit for hiring an individual belonging to any one of a number of targeted groups, such as 16-19 year old youth, economically disadvantaged individuals, students participating in cooperative education programs in school, or individuals with disabilities.

Fair Labor Standards Act of 1980

The Fair Labor Standards Act of 1980 distinguishes between an employee and a trainee and provides an opportunity for employers to hire individuals with severe disabilities at non-competitive wages. This legislation has had significant impact on the ability of rehabilitation and other disability professionals to provide supported employment services to adolescents and adults with severe disabilities.

Access to Programs and Services

One other major area of legislation that affects the lives of individuals with disabilities is the access to programs and services and the mandated role that public agencies and services play in providing and monitoring the effectiveness of the services.

Developmental Disabilities Act (PL 98-537)

The Developmental Disabilities Act, as amended in 1988, authorizes the use of federal resources for a variety of research, development, training, policy development, and advocacy activities for individuals with developmental disabilities. Developmental disabilities refers to disabilities that appear during the developmental period and usually involve moderate, severe, or multiple disabilities. One of the components of the Developmental Disabilities Act is the authorization of and support for the Developmental Disabilities State Planning Councils. The councils are components of state governments that develop policy and monitor the implementation of services for persons with disabilities. The planning councils are usually selected by the governor of each state and provide a focus for interagency planning and the monitoring of existing services. Each of the councils supports special development activities based on both federal and state priorities.

The Developmental Disabilities Act also provides authorization and support for the Protection and Advocacy organizations in each state. The Protection and

Advocacy agencies are charged with providing advocacy and direct support for disabled individuals who need assistance in securing their rights under federal and state law. For example, individuals with a disability may enlist the assistance of a Protection and Advocacy agency if they feel they have been discriminated against in employment due to a handicapping condition.

Research, development, and professional training is provided by the Developmental Disabilities Act through the nationwide system of University Affiliated Programs (UAP's). UAP's are federally funded programs usually associated with a university or medical school program and are designed to provide interdisciplinary training to professionals who serve developmentally disabled individuals. For example, UAP's would typically provide advanced training for pediatricians, nurses, audiologists, dentists, and psychologists to work specifically with individuals with developmental disabilities.

In addition to the above activities, the Developmental Disabilities Act supports a variety of special projects that emanate from priorities developed by the Administration for Developmental Disabilities. These priorities include employment, case management, and early intervention.

Social Security Act

Social security legislation provides direct support to individuals with disabilities through two basic entitlements; Social Security Disability Insurance (SSDI) and Supplemental Security Income (SSI).

Social Security Disability Income (SSDI) provides social security payments for individuals who are disabled over the age of 16. While this income has provided basic support for individuals who are unable to work, it has been criticized in recent years for providing a disincentive for disabled people who are attempting to enter the work force. Recent changes in the legislation have resulted in the removal of some of the disincentives, including the ability to continue SSDI benefits during a trial work period of 9 months and to continue coverage by medicare for 24 months after employment.

Supplemental Security Income (SSI) also offers financial support for individuals with disabilities, including a unique program called the SSI Plan for Achieving Self Support, or PASS, which enables a SSI recipient to continue to receive benefits while establishing and implementing a vocational goal, and may set aside personal income or resources to be used in completing that goal. This income and/or resources is not considered when determining the amount of SSI a recipient will receive while completing the plan.

Section 1619(a) of the Social Security Legislation allows an SSI recipient to continue receiving SSI payments until the recipient reaches an income level that is about twice the level of their original SSI benefits. In addition, medicaid coverage is allowed to continue even while working.

Medicaid Reform Act

Of particular interest to individuals with disabilities is Medicaid reform legislation sponsored by Chaffee (1988, 1989, 1990). This act has focused on the inclusion of medicaid payments for individuals with disabilities who live in community settings such as group homes and supervised apartments. Currently Medicaid payments are concentrated on support for individuals who live in institutions or Intermediate Care Facilities for the Mentally Retarded (ICFMR's) and create a disincentive to individuals attempting to move from institutional life to community living in a group home or other more independent situations. In addition, these attempts at reform are also focused on providing Medicaid support for supported employment activities where individuals need long term employment supervision, or specific adaptation to their work environment in order to remain employed.

Americans With Disabilities Act

Last, but certainly not least, is the recently enacted Americans With Disabilities Act or ADA (PL 101-336). This controversial legislation is considered a "civil rights bill" for individuals with disabilities and may have a profound effect on access to employment for a greater number of disabled individuals. The controversy involves the assurances related to non-discrimination in the workplace for persons with disabilities. The ADA also gives civil rights protection to individuals with disabilities in all public services, public accommodations, transportation and telecommunications. A major feature of the new legislation is the requirement that employers provide reasonable accommodations for employees with disabilities. While there has been very vocal opposition to the requirement that employers make reasonable accommodations, this objection is primarily based on an employer's concern that accommodations may be extremely costly. It has, however, been demonstrated that most workplace accommodations are relatively low in cost, with an average cost of under $500.00. The ease of adjusting the workplace is often cited as an objection to workplace accommodation, but most accommodations are relatively unobtrusive in the workplace, allowing employees with disabilities to work harmoniously with their co-workers.

Summary

The development of litigation and legislation in this country has had a profound effect on social change for persons with disabilities. The enactment of this legislation is a tribute to people with disabilities, their families and friends, and the professionals who have dedicated their lives to advocacy and training. The pioneers in changing the law, rules, and regulations in this country were more than silent partners in this process; they deliberately sought to challenge 'business as usual' for persons with disabilities and over a period of 30 years, have completely reshaped disability policy. This by no means infers that the existing public policy is adequate. A wide variety of issues remains to be challenged, clarified, and developed as we seek full participation by all citizens, regardless of race, religion, ethnic background, age, sex, sexual preference, or handicapping condition. In the future, new issues will emerge, and will continue to emerge. For example, the issues of contagious diseases like AIDS, the impact of drug abuse related disabilities, and the expanding assistive technological applications will continue to challenge our public policy for people with disabilities.

Litigation

Brown v. Board of Education, 347 U.S. 483 (1954)

Larry P. v. Riles, 343 F. Supp. 1306 (N.D. Cal 1972) aff'd, 502d 963 (9th Cir. 1974)

Lora v. New York City Board of Education, 456 F. Supp. 1211, 1275 (E.D. N.Y. 1978)

LAWS AND LEGISLATION

Mills v. Board of Education of the District of Columbia, 348 F. Supp. 866 (1972)

PASE v. Hannon, 74C3586, (N.D.Ill. 1980)

Pennsylvania Association for Retarded Children (PARC) v. Commonwealth of Pennsylvania, 334 F. Supp. 1257(E.D. Pa. 1971); 343F. Supp. 279(E.D. Pa. 1972)

Legislation

Americans With Disabilities Act of 1990 (uncoded)

Carl D. Perkins Vocational Education Act of 1984, 20 U.S.C. 2301

Developmental Disabilities Act of 1984, 42 U.S.C. 7501

Education of All Handicapped Children Act of 1975, 20 U.S.C. 1400

Education of the Handicapped Act Amendments of 1986, 20 U.S.C. 1400

Fair Labor Standards Act of 1980, 29 U.S.C. 201

Job Training and Partnership Act, 29 U.S.C. 201

Rehabilitation Act of 1973, 29 U.S.C. 700

Social Security Act, 29 U.S.C. 1001

Tax Reform Act of 1986, 26 U.S.C. 1

Technology Related Assistance for Individuals with Disabilities Act of 1988, 29 U.S.C. 2201

References

Chaffee, J. (1988, 1989, 1990). *Medicaid home and community quality services act,* U. S. Congress.

Hallahan, D., & Kauffman, J. (1978). *Exceptional children: Introduction to special education.* Englewood Cliffs, NJ: Prentice Hall.

Nystrom, D. C., & Bayne, G. K. (1979). *Occupation and career education legislation* (2nd ed.). Indianapolis: Bobbs-Merrill.

Rusch, F. R., & Phelps, L. A. (1987). Secondary education transition from school to work: A national priority. *Exceptional Children, 53*(6), 487-488.

Ryan, R. D. (1988). School to work transition for special needs students. *The Journal for Vocational Special Needs Education, 11*(1), 9.

The White House Working Group on Disability Policy. (1983). Washington, DC: U.S. Government Printing Office.

Suggested Readings

Affirmative action to employ handicapped people. (1976). Washington, DC: The President's Committee on Employment of the Handicapped.

Council for Exceptional Children. (1990). Americans with Disabilities Act of 1990: What should you know? *Exceptional Children, 57*(2), supplement.

Pocket guide to federal help for individuals with disabilities. (1987). Washington, DC: U.S. Department of Education, Clearinghouse on the Handicapped.

The rights of individuals with handicaps under federal law. (1989). Washington, DC: U.S. Department of Education, Office of Civil Rights.

LAWS AND LEGISLATION

Exploration

Individual Activities

1. When PL 94-142 was passed it was a monumental day for disabled people across the country. What do you see as the strengths and weaknesses of this legislation?

   Strengths: Weaknesses:

   _____   _____
   _____   _____
   _____   _____
   _____   _____
   _____   _____

2. As you go through your daily activities you often notice the accommodations made for disabled people; ramps, lower water fountains, and braille on elevator buttons, etc. You are a politician who would like to design a bill to help disabled persons further. Describe legislation that you would sponsor to better the quality of exceptional people's lives.

   _____
   _____
   _____
   _____
   _____
   _____
   _____
   _____

Group Activity

1. A bill is being debated concerning disabled people's rights. This bill, if passed, will grant disabled people free college education and low cost housing. Your class is the deciding body for this law. Choose six members of the class to make the final decision based upon the arguments presented by the rest of the class. Arrange to have half the class argue the pros of this bill and the other half the cons.

    Reactions:

    _____
    _____
    _____

2. Invite a few disabled persons and one or two attorneys to your class. Ask your speakers to discuss the implications of the Americans with Disabilities Act.

    Reactions:

    _____
    _____
    _____

LAWS AND LEGISLATION

Reaction Paper 16.1

The Americans with Disabilities Act is legislation that is a civil rights bill for disabled people. It states that the work-place must be made to accommodate disabled persons. How do you feel about this bill? Is it fair to make employers modify their places of business? Support your position.

Continue on back if needed.

410

Reaction Paper 16.2

Some persons believe that laws and legislation are needed to improve the quality of life for persons with disabilities. Others would argue that it shouldn't take laws and legislation; that this should be natural for members of our society. What is your position? Why?

Continue on back if needed.

Notes

CHAPTER 17

THE EXCEPTIONAL ADULT

Jeanne B. Repetto

Introduction

A moving van pulls up to the house next door and begins to unload your new neighbor's belongings. Although you have not met the family, by watching the truck being unloaded you learn that two children will be living next door. Also, you have learned, through the "neighborhood grapevine" that your new neighbor is a manager for a local computer firm and his wife is a realtor. Having come to the conclusion that this family will be a positive addition to your neighborhood, you are anxious to meet them. However, your meeting has been delayed several weeks because of your family's vacation. Finally, you are able to invite them to dinner. When your new neighbors arrive at your door you are confused because he is in a wheelchair. You struggle to be polite, when all you can think is, how could someone in a wheelchair live such a seemingly normal life?

Your confusion is not uncommon and is, in part, due to a lack of knowledge regarding adults with exceptionalities. Although legislation assures that equality is given to Americans with disabilities, inequities still exist. The real struggle is not with legal issues, but rather with misperceptions of the abilities of exceptional people. Most everyone is guilty of one of the following misperceptions: (a) persons who are hearing impaired are less intelligent, (b) persons who are visually impaired should be content to work at fast food establishments because they are lucky to have jobs, (c) individuals in wheelchairs are asexual, (d) individuals who are mentally impaired need to be protected, (e) exceptional individuals are more loyal employees, and (f) all visually impaired individuals have the same needs. This list of myths could go on and on. Even the most educated readers are guilty of believing in one of these myths at some time in their lives. The problem is that the rights and opportunities of exceptional people are diminished when the general public fosters any of these misperceptions.

The following real-life scenarios which occurred within the last two years should demonstrate that these misperceptions do still exist:

> An accountant, who is hearing impaired, asked her boss for a volume amplifier for the phone in her office (this was the only job modification she required). Though she was immediately issued a set of keys to the elevator, it took several months to receive the volume amplifier. Her employer's misperception was that all individuals with handicaps needed keys to the elevators because they are unable to walk up and down a flight of stairs. In fact, this individual had the ability to climb stairs, but was unable to converse on the phone without a voice amplifier. Although this employer made an attempt to accommodate the needs of the employee, lack of understanding that individuals with handicaps do not all have the same set of needs caused her to limit her employee's job performance.

> A neighborhood protested the opening of a supervised group home for adults with disabilities. The community feared that a group home might lower the property values and raise the crime rate in the neighborhood. Once the community realized that exceptional adults are rarely criminals and that property values are not lowered by group homes, the group home was allowed to open. However, during the year it took to educate the community, exceptional adults, already working in the community, had to be transported to their jobs from the institution in which they were living. The community's misperceptions caused a group of exceptional adults, who had the skills to function within a community setting, to remain in a more sheltered living environment than was necessary. In essence, they were forced to put their lives on hold for a year.

These are just a two of many similar situations that happen on a daily basis to exceptional people. Every time that these events occur they infringe on the rights of individuals with disabilities. Their rights are the same as everyone else's and include the right to:

> **be viewed as people first**
> **experience love and friendship**
> **be able to communicate with others**
> **move freely throughout the community**
> **be given dignity and respect**
> **have opportunities to make choices**
> **live in decent homes**
> **be productive members of society**
>
> (Governor's Planning Council on Developmental Disabilities, 1987)

In an effort to promote a better understanding of exceptional adults, this chapter will provide you with information on exceptional adults in three domains: employment, living environments, and social networks (Halpern, 1985). All of these areas combine to form the fabric of our lives. Without one of these components, our lives somehow are not whole. Therefore, in studying exceptional adults, it is important to address all the components of adulthood. It is expected that by learning more about the lives of these individuals, your misperceptions will diminish and the exceptional adult will be given a chance to the same quality of life as all adults.

Exceptional Adults

When reading this chapter it is important to note that not all exceptional adults are identified as handicapped. Once individuals with handicaps leave the school system it is their choice as to whether or not they wish to be identified as handicapped. As adults, if they need support services, they must apply to the agency providing the needed services. Prior to becoming a client of that agency it must be determined if they meet the criteria, set by that agency, to receive services. Therefore, though they have disabilities, many adults may not be identified as handicapped because they have not applied for services or did not meet the criteria to receive services.

Exceptional adults fall into four main groups: (a) adults identified as disabled, (b) adults no longer identified as disabled, (c) unidentified exceptional adults, and (d) individuals who become disabled as adults. Each of these groups has different characteristics and needs. In this chapter you will learn about those individuals who have been identified as exceptional either early in their lives or later due to an illness or an accident. Although those exceptional individuals who remain unidentified might benefit from the services to be described in this chapter, without being identified as exceptional, these services will not be available to them. To further clarify these groups of exceptional adults each will be briefly described.

Adults identified as disabled. These adults were identified while in school as handicapped and in need of support services to be successful in the school setting. Upon exiting the school system they applied for adult support services because such support was necessary for them to be able to function in the community. After being evaluated it was determined that they met the criteria to receive services from adult service providers. Sue, for example, who received job support services while in school, needed continued job support after exiting the school system to be a successful employee. Therefore, Sue applied for and received support from Vocational Rehabilitation, whose staff provides her with the needed job support.

Adults no longer identified as disabled. These individuals were identified as handicapped while in the school system, but did not apply for any adult services, did not qualify for any adults services, or simply decided to make it on their own without adult services. For example, many individuals who were identified as mildly handicapped while in school choose to try making it on their own before applying for support services. As long as they do not apply for support services they will not be identified as disabled.

Unidentified exceptional adults. These are adults who may have some type of disability, but were able to "pass as normal" in the school systems or dropped-out of school; avoiding being identified as handicapped. As adults, they may continue to have problems, such as poor reading skills. Companies are spending approximately $200 billion per year on training programs for their employees (Harkins & Giber, 1989). Many of these programs are designed to promote literacy among their workers. Technological advances have caused companies to retrain a large portion of their workforce. One of the first steps in retraining is the assessment of employees' strengths and weaknesses. Through this assessment, many companies have found that employees who have worked for their company for many years are unable to read. The job that they previously held did not require them to read more than a few phrases, which could easily be memorized. For the first time in their lives, many of these people are being labeled and identified as having special needs.

Individuals who become disabled as adults. This group includes individuals who become disabled during adulthood through an accident or illness. Every year more than 780,000 U.S. workers sustain injuries or illnesses that disable them for at least five months. Furthermore, approximately half of these workers never return to work (President's Committee on the Employment of Persons with Disabilities, 1989). Many of these disabling injuries are job related, such as orthopedic or visual impairments. However, other disabling conditions that may have their onset during adulthood include diabetes, heart conditions, arthritis, and hypertension (National Institute on Disability and Rehabilitation Research, 1989). In fact, 70% of all Americans will, at some time in their lives, be so disabled that they will be unable to climb a flight of stairs (President's Committee on the Employment of Persons with Disabilities, 1989).

Cooperative Planning

Central to the provision of adult services is cooperative planning. Like non-disabled people, individuals who are disabled have many areas in their lives they need to coordinate such as employment, living environments, and social networks. The difference is that individuals who are disabled may need assistance in coordinating these pieces into a whole. There are issues to deal with in each of these areas. For example, non-disabled individuals probably have mornings timed so that they can get out of bed, get dressed, eat breakfast, drive to work, and begin work within about an hour's time frame. Once they have this routine learned they do it automatically with little thought to its components. However, individuals who are disabled may need assistance getting dressed, or help eating, or the bus that is accessible may only arrive on their corner once in the morning. Therefore, before exceptional adults' morning routines become "second nature" several issues must be addressed and coordinated. Often this takes planning and cooperation among several adult service providers such as Vocational Rehabilitation and the Association for Retarded Citizens.

One method of coordinating these services is through transition planning. Planning for the transition of an exceptional individual from school to the world outside of school is the focus of this coordination. Through early identification and coordination of needed support in areas such as employment, transportation, and living arrangements it is anticipated that individuals will have a better chance to achieve independence once they leave school (Brown, Halpern, Hasazi, & Wehman, 1987). Starting transition planning while individuals who are disabled are still in school allows professional educators to assist with applications to adult service providers. Early application can mean that a student who receives support while in school will be able to continue to receive that service upon leaving school without any interruption in service.

Once an individual has left school and qualifies for adult services the agencies providing the services will establish a method to coordinate various services. It should be noted that not every exceptional adult needs a variety of services. Some adults may simply need assistance in minor job modifications; for example, a voice amplifier on the phone. Other exceptional adults will require many services that are planned for and well coordinated in order for them to live as independent adults. Independence is a relative term. For some exceptional adults it means living a life much like you live including working and renting an apartment. However, for other exceptional adults it might be limited to mean only being able to dress and feed themselves.

It is important to remember that exceptional adults are not a homogeneous group. As has been discussed so far in this chapter, adults with exceptionalities vary in abilities and needs. In this respect they are not unlike the general population of adults which needs many different working and living opportunities in order to accommodate the uniqueness each person. Fortunately, there are a variety of employment, living environments, and social network arrangements available to exceptional adults to suit their individual abilities and needs. In the following section you will read about each of these arrangements in detail.

Employment

Recent employment statistics indicate that (a) 67% of all adult Americans with disabilities do not work, (b) exceptional adults who are employed are 75% more likely to be employed part-time, and (c) 67% of those adults with disabilities who are unemployed would work if the opportunity existed (Rusch & Phelps, 1987). Further, Edgar (1987) concluded that less than 15% of individuals with handicaps obtained employment at or above the minimum wage. When persons are employed part-time they do not receive benefits or job security. Therefore, adults who are underemployed are not being given the opportunity to reach their full potential. These statistics not only indicate that exceptional individuals are not working, but that they are not being given the opportunity to be contributing members of society. Fostering independence in the workplace means adding tax paying employees to the workforce. In a society such as ours that measures human worth by the jobs people hold, it is important to offer exceptional individuals the opportunity to work in order to enhance their feeling of self-worth. Exceptional people have the right to have an answer to the proverbial question: "So, what is it that you do?"

Work Settings

A cascade of work settings available to exceptional people will be discussed in this section. The work settings that are most like the settings available to non-disabled adults will be listed first; then the list will progress to the most sheltered setting. Exceptional individuals can move up and down this list as their needs indicate. The following list of work settings was compiled from lists offered by Clark and Kolstoe (1990) and Gaylord-Ross (1988).

Competitive employment. With time-limited (offered for a specified short period of time) services the majority of individuals with disabilities will be able to obtain and retain jobs in the competitive workplace similar to the positions held by individuals who are not handicapped. These services are designed to assist an individual in four areas: (a) evaluating strengths and weaknesses to determine appropriate jobs, (b) training prior to job placement to teach job readiness skills, (c) securing a job, and (d) adjusting to the demands and setting of the job. Once it is determined that an individual has adjusted to the job site services are terminated.

Supported competitive employment. For those individuals who may be able to retain a job in the competitive workforce with ongoing support services, supported competitive employment is an option. Services are considered ongoing if they include permanent follow-along by adult service professionals. These services, designed to foster independence in the workplace, are preplanned and include: (a) locating an appropriate job, (b) training on the job site, and (c) ongoing follow-up which may include retraining. An example of supported employment is a "job coach" who matches a client to a job, works alongside the client until the job is learned, and regularly checks to make sure the client is able to do the job. If the client is having problems completing the job, or the job changes, the "job coach" starts the training process over again. These services are available to clients as long as they are employed and in need of them. Agencies that offer these services include Vocational Rehabilitation, Developmental Disabilities, and private Adult Service Providers.

Work enclaves. Work enclaves are an option for those individuals not likely to be independently competitively employed, but are able to adjust to a competitive job site. A work enclave consists of six to eight workers with disabilities grouped together within a normal business or industry. This group is provided with continuous supervision by a trained human service professional or host company employee. Enclave members work alongside "regular" workers and perform the same jobs. Agencies that offer these services include Developmental Disabilities and private Adult Service Providers.

Mobile work crews. Individuals with severe disabilities who are mobile and display the ability to complete tasks may be able to function as members of a mobile work crew. Mobile work crews are teams of four to six clients who spend their day in the community working. Each team has a supervisor who is responsible for securing work and assuring that the jobs are completed to required standards. This supervisor remains with the work crew all day training and supervising its members. Typically, jobs contracted by work crews include groundskeeping, janitorial, and home maintenance tasks. Agencies that offer these services include Developmental Disabilities and private Adult Service Providers.

Sheltered workshops. Individuals with severe disabilities who are not ready for competitive employment or work within the community have the option to work in a sheltered workshop. These workshops contract for outside work to be brought to their site. For example, a sheltered workshop may contract with a hair supply company to package combs. Supervisors train and oversee clients in the completion of this work. Sheltered workshops are considered a training site to increase clients' personal, social, and job skills so that they can progress to a less sheltered work site. Agencies that offer these services include Developmental Disabilities, the Association for Retarded Citizens, Goodwill Industries, and private Adult Service Providers.

Training Options

Just as you have several training options from which to choose, so do individuals with disabilities. In reviewing the following list, it becomes clear that the training options available to exceptional people are the same as the options available to everyone. The difference may lie only in the support services exceptional people may need to be successful. Clark and Kolstoe (1990) offered the following listing of these training options.

Colleges and universities. As with the general population, some individuals with disabilities go to college and become lawyers, teachers, engineers, doctors, and professionals in all other possible fields. In order to accommodate the diverse needs of college students with disabilities, many universities offer support services such as tutoring and adapted instruction to assist the college students in successfully completing coursework.

Postsecondary vocational, community colleges, and technical schools. Individuals with disabilities wishing to learn specific job skills and/or earn an Associates Degree can attend postsecondary vocational training in public or private institutions. Much like universities and colleges, post-secondary vocational schools, community colleges, and technical institutes provide support services such as tutoring and adapted instruction to students with disabilities.

Adult education. Typically, adult education programs do not offer comprehensive vocational training programs. Adult education courses are often held in the evening at the local high school. However, for individuals wishing to learn a specific skill, such as bookkeeping, this may be an option. Usually these programs are designed more for leisure or home maintenance offering courses such as microwave cooking, bicycle repair, and personal finance.

Specialized training in the military. Those disabled individuals who qualify for the military are eligible for the same training and advanced degree work as all military personnel. Although this may be an option for only a small percentage of individuals with disabilities, for those few who qualify it can offer a promising future.

Job training and apprenticeship programs. Training programs provided under the Job Training and Partnership Act (JTPA) of 1982 (PL 97-300), the Job Corps (administered by the U.S. Department of Labor), and labor union apprenticeship programs are options available to those individuals who qualify. Disadvantaged and disabled populations are targeted for services by both JTPA and the Job Corps. Many adults with disabilities who are unemployed qualify as disadvantaged. Therefore, they would be qualified to receive services from both JTPA and the Job Corps.

Living Environments

The living environment is a component of how the general population defines its independence; this is also true for exceptional adults. As economics dictates where non-disabled adults live, so does it for exceptional adults. Many adults with disabilities are underemployed or employed part-time, causing them to live at or below the poverty level. Therefore, they often must live at home or in subsidized government housing. Added to economic factors are accessibility and attitudinal barriers. When choosing apartments, adults with disabilities must consider additional factors such as closeness to accessible buses, ramped entrances, and understanding managers. Group homes need to be located near public transportation and in neighborhoods willing to accept their clientele as neighbors. The main goal of providing a variety of living options is to give exceptional adults the opportunity to live as independently as possible and to become a part of the community. In this section you will read about the range of residential options (Clark & Kolstoe, 1990).

Independent living. This option is for individuals who are able to live independently in homes and apartments. These people may live with roommates or family. Often times they are married and have children. They lead seemingly "normal" lives.

Semi-independent living. The only difference between these adults and those living independently is that they may require someone to check in on them periodically or they may need to have a live-in helper. This helper might assist them in getting dressed or in fixing meals. Although needing this assistance, these individuals with disabilities are able to lead relatively independent lives.

Living at home. Many exceptional adults, who have the skills to live independently, continue to live at home as economics become tight or parents find it difficult to allow them to live independently. This is a trend that is occurring in the non-disabled population as well, as finances become restrictive.

Group homes. Group homes are usually located in neighborhoods, allowing exceptional adults access to the community and work sites. Group homes are for those adults who require minimal supervision. Typically, six to eight adults live in the home along with one or more supervisors.

Family or foster care. This living arrangement is for those exceptional adults who need close and continual supervision. These adults live at home because they are not able to live independently, not because of finances.

Institutional care. Although there has been a push towards deinstitutionalization over the past 15 to 20 years, this type of residential placement remains an option for some exceptional adults (usually those persons who are severely disabled).

Social Networks

If you were to list the members of your social network, most likely the list would include family, friends, co-workers, and significant others. Your network is comprised of people who offer you love, support, and friendship. Social networks of adults with disabilities would be similar except these relationships may be more difficult to build. One reason is that individuals who are more severely disabled may have been isolated from the mainstream of society. This isolation may not have allowed them to practice the social skills needed to be accepted in society and to build friendships. Two other possible barriers to the ability of exceptional adults in building friendships are (a) isolation due to transportation problems, and (b) lack of organized activities that provide for their individual needs so that they can participate. Leisure activities designed to provide opportunities to exceptional adults to make friends, have a good time, relax, and feel part of a community are becoming more commonplace. The following is a list of a few of these activities.

Travel services. Travel services include agents that specialize in helping travelers who are disabled, specialized travel books, and government brochures. These services assist the disabled traveler in locating accessible hotel rooms, identifying the sites that are accessible, listing accessible restaurants, and providing other needed services.

Sports. Sports leagues for exceptional adults have become commonplace. These leagues include wheelchair basketball, "beeper" baseball for visually impaired persons, and hand-cranked bikes. For example, members of numerous university wheelchair track teams participated in the 1988 Olympics in Seoul.

Recreational clubs. These community centered and participant oriented programs offer exceptional adults the opportunity to socialize with friends in restaurants, bowling alleys, and movie theaters (Schloss, Smith, & Kiehl, 1986). Recreational clubs are similar to the many clubs offered to the non-handicapped individual wishing to become part of the community such as newcomers clubs, and bridge clubs. Similarly, these clubs offer opportunities for single adults to meet other single individuals.

Families

Similar to the general population, individuals with disabilities have a wide range of relationships with their families. Each family is unique in its interactions with the disabled relative ranging from full acceptance of the exceptional adult's independent lifestyle to wanting to shelter their relative from the outside world. Factors that influence how families interact with their disabled relative include the (a) seriousness of the disability, (b) exceptional relative's behavior, (c) family's emotional state, (d) family's characteristics such as size, and (e) availability of community support services (Bradley & Agosta, 1985).

Although the family support offered to adults with disabilities varies, it is important that they have someone to give them this needed support. A follow-up study conducted by Edgerton, Bollinger, and Herr (1984) concluded that the prime influence to the success an exceptional adult met in adjusting to the community was their ability to locate and hold a benefactor (someone who offers emotional support and helps to solve problems). Like non-disabled adults, if this support is not provided by family members, it will be sought from friends or spouses.

The need for this family support may lessen as individuals with disabilities form their own community of friends and/or marry and start their own families. This natural progression, which occurs throughout society, is part of the maturation process. Although many exceptional adults choose to remain single, others choose to marry and have children. Like many non-disabled couples, physical impairments may not allow some individuals with disabilities to have children. However, many disabled couples have children and are able to raise them alone or with support from a benefactor.

Assisting in Fostering Independence

If asked to define independence, most people are able to offer personal accounts that define what independence means to them. Believing that individuals with disabilities would be able to give personal definitions of independence, Rock (1988) asked six exceptional adults to define independence. Their answers fell in five main areas:

Risk taking - Examples given included being able to go out alone, cooking, and possibly injuring oneself.

Privacy - Examples given included being able to lock one's door, and having space to be alone.

Decision making - Examples given included not having to constantly asking permission to do things, and handling one's own money.

Control - Examples given included determining meals and bedtimes for oneself, and being able to undertake tasks unaided.

Encouragement - Examples given include being helped to maintain independent levels of functioning, and being encouraged to develop hobbies.

Summary

Having read this chapter you should have gained some understanding of the lives that exceptional adults live. This knowledge will assist you, as exceptional adults become your friends, co-workers, employers, and neighbors, to foster independence rather than build barriers through misperceptions. The following are a few simple guidelines to follow when meeting exceptional adults:

Be friendly
Rather than avoid the issue, discuss their disability
Before offering help, ask if they want assistance

Include the exceptional adult when decisions are made about their work, home, or social environments

Ask before assuming they will not be able to do something

Accept all individuals as equals.

The future is bright for individuals with disabilities due to increased options for employment, living arrangements, and social interaction. These have occurred for several reasons, including the (a) decrease in the American workforce causing business to view every worker as a valuable resource, (b) education of the American public in better understanding disabilities, (c) advocacy efforts of exceptional adults to be treated as other adults, (d) passage of legislation that has assured equal rights for individuals with disabilities, and (e) increased knowledge of the needs and abilities of exceptional adults by the professionals working with them.

The following statement made by President Bush, as he signed the Americans with Disabilities Act of 1990, sets the stage for a bright future for individuals with disabilities:

> America welcomes into the mainstream of life all of our fellow citizens with disabilities. We embrace you for your abilities and for your disabilities, for our similarities and indeed our differences. (Devroy, 1990, p. 1)

References

Clark, G. M., & Kolstoe, O. P. (1990). *Career education and transition education for adolescents with disabilities.* Boston, MA: Allyn and Bacon.

Bradley, V. J., & Agosta, J. M. (1985). Keeping your children at home: The case for family support. *Exceptional Parent, 15*(7), 10-22.

Brown, L., Halpern, A. S., Hasazi, S. B., & Wehman, P. (1987). From school to adult living: A forum on issues and trends. *Exceptional Children, 53*(6), 546-554.

Devroy, A. (1990, July 27). Bias against disabled banned. *The Gainesville Sun,* pp. 1,12.

Edgar, E. (1987). Secondary programs in special education: Are many of them justified? *Exceptional Children, 53*(6), 555-561.

Edgerton, R., Bollinger, M., & Herr, B. (1984). The cloak of competence: After two decades. *American Journal of Mental Deficiency, 88*(4), 345-351.

Gaylord-Ross, R. (Ed.). (1988). *Vocational education for persons with handicaps.* Mountain View, CA: Mayfield.

Governor's Planning Council on Developmental Disabilities. (1987). *A new way of thinking.* St. Paul, MN: Author.

Halpern, A. S. (1985). Transition: A look at the foundation. *Exceptional Children, 51,* 479-486.

Harkins, P. J., & Giber, D. (1989). Linking business and education through training. *Training & Development Journal, 43*(10), 69-71.

National Institute on Disability and Rehabilitation Research. (1989). *Chartbook on disability in the United States.* Washington, DC: Author.

President's Committee on the Employment of Persons with Disabilities. (1989). *Economics of Disability.* Washington, DC: Author.

Rock, P. J. (1988). Independence: What it means to six disabled people living in the community. *Disability, Handicap & Society, 3*(1), 27-35.

Rusch, F. R., & Phelps, L. A. (1987). Secondary education transition from school to work: A national priority. *Exceptional Children, 53*(6), 487-488.

Schloss, P. J., Smith, M. A., & Kiehl, W. (1986). Rec club: A community centered approach to recreational development for adults with mild to moderate retardation. *Education and Training of the Mentally Retarded, 21*(3), 282-288.

Suggested Readings

Berkell, D. E., & Brown, J. M. (1989). *Transition from school to work for persons with disabilities.* New York, NY: Longman.

Biller, E. F. (1988). *Understanding adolescents and young adults with learning disabilities: A focus on employability and career placement.* Springfield, IL: Charles C. Thomas.

Janicki, M. P., Krauss, M. W., & Seltzer, M. M. (1988). *Community residences for persons with developmental disabilities: Here to stay.* Baltimore, MD: Paul H. Brooks.

Kallembach, S. C. (Ed.). (1989). *Resources to facilitate the transition of learners with special needs from school-to-work or postsecondary education.* Berkeley, CA: University of California, National Center for Research in Vocational Education.

Meers, G. D. (Ed.). (1987). *Handbook of vocational special needs education* (2nd ed.). Rockville, MD: Aspen.

O'Brien, J., & Stern, D. (1988). Economic issues in employing persons with disabilities. In R. Gaylord-Ross (Ed.), *Vocational Education for Persons with Handicaps* (pp. 257-295). Mountain View, CA: Mayfield.

Pati, G. (1988). The business perspective on employing persons with disabilities. In R. Gaylord-Ross (Ed.), *Vocational Education for Persons with Handicaps* (pp. 257-295). Mountain View, CA: Mayfield.

Rusch, F. R. (Ed.). (1990). *Supported employment: Models, methods, and issues.* Sycamore, IL: Sycamore.

Sarkees, M. D., & Scott, J. L. (1985). *Vocational special needs* (2nd ed.). Homewood, IL: American Technical Publishers.

Exploration

Individual Activities

1. Assume that you are an exceptional individual who uses a wheelchair. List 10 occupations that you could do equally well, if not better, than a non-disabled person.

   1._____   6._____
   2._____   7._____
   3._____   8._____
   4._____   9._____
   5._____   10._____

2. Do the same as #1 but with the assumption that you are blind.

   1._____   6._____
   2._____   7._____
   3._____   8._____
   4._____   9._____
   5._____   10._____

Group Activities

1. Schedule a field trip for your class to a local sheltered workshop. While there observe to find out the disabilities the clients have and the types of work which are being done.

    Reactions:

    _____

    _____

    _____

2. There has been a tremendous outcry by the people in your community for more governmentally supported workshops and group living homes for the exceptional adults in your area. Choose five people to be the deciding government panel and then divide the class in half with one side arguing for these services and the other against them. Each side will be allowed opening statements, then general remarks, and finally closing arguments. Allow the panel members to give their decisions individually with reasons for their vote.

    Reactions:

    _____

    _____

    _____

Reaction Paper 17.1

All business should hire disabled workers. If you were a business person, how would you feel if a law were passed supporting this idea? Do you think it would be a good or bad idea? Why?

Continue on back if needed.

Reaction Paper 17.2

Assume that you are a disabled person. You go looking for a job and all that people seem to be aware of is your limitation instead of your ability. How do you feel? What could you do to give yourself a fair chance at employment?

___

Continue on back if needed.

Notes

CHAPTER 18

THE FUTURE

Stuart E. Schwartz

Introduction

Now that you are about to conclude your study of persons who are exceptional, you have to decide what you will do with the information you have gained and with the attitudes you have adjusted. It would be unfortunate for you to end your study of this critically important topic without a plan to be certain that you and others will benefit from your efforts.

Although it appears that people have generally become more understanding of human differences over the past years, it is still common for individuals to fear and ridicule those persons who are different. For example, someone may be critical of a person with a visible disability who eats in a restaurant. Another person may be concerned about a group living home for exceptional persons being established in their neighborhood. Unfortunately myths and negative attitudes about exceptional individuals still exist.

Steady progress has been made toward establishing equal rights for exceptional persons. But that does not mean that persons who interact with disabled persons will be kind, considerate, or comfortable. Part of the problem with society seems to be related to attitudes which were instilled during early childhood by parents. Now you are in the position to adjust those attitudes for yourself and others. You are equipped to insure that society makes additional progress which goes beyond all of the laws and legislation which have assisted disabled people. Wouldn't you prefer to live in a society where people don't stare at disabled people? Where everyone, regardless of whether different due to race, ethnic or religious background, sex or sexual preference, age, intellectual ability, or disability type or level, is treated with respect? Where persons are evaluated based upon how pleasant and skilled they are rather than on what labels they wear? You have the ability and opportunity to influence our society so that fair treatment is afforded to all persons.

The purpose of this final chapter is to assist you in developing strategies which will enable you to assist others as they deal with exceptional individuals. Remember that you may need to take the leadership role in this area as you are now the 'educated' one. You have taken a course and read this book about exceptional persons and have taken a bold step toward confirming that, as an educated person, you will be a leader of others. Each of the sections in this chapter offers you ideas and encouragement as you begin to modify society so that everyone, including those persons who wear the label of exceptional, has respectful and comfortable interactions with others.

Your Comfort Level

Each chapter author has stressed the importance of being comfortable when interacting with those persons who are exceptional. Comfort logically follows the reduction of fear and myths and the development of knowledge. You have had the opportunity to do that. The next steps toward being comfortable around people who are different include those listed below.

Make your own decision that you desire to be comfortable when interacting with those persons who are different from you. It is not sufficient to have the desire to be comfortable. You must make a firm decision that that is what you want to accomplish.

Continue to learn more about exceptional individuals. Consider taking additional courses about disabled persons. It would be wise to take sign language classes so that you can easily converse with people who utilize this form of communication. Review technological advances as well so that you are well versed

THE FUTURE

in the rapidly developing technology which is doing much to broaden opportunities for persons with disabilities.

Interact with exceptional individuals. You should be able to find many opportunities to socialize with or work with exceptional people. At your college or in your neighborhood there may be an agency or organization which provides social activities for disabled people. For instance, you may find a basketball team for persons who use wheelchairs or there may be a group of persons who are blind and who bowl or dance regularly. Such groups would be happy to have your participation.

When you make friends with persons who are exceptional don't be afraid to talk with them about their exceptionality. Ask the questions you want to ask. Raise the issues you want to raise. Being open and honest with exceptional persons are just as important toward developing friendships as they are with those who are not exceptional.

Assist persons who are exceptional through volunteer organizations. This is another opportunity for you to get to know those persons who are exceptional. Try a visit to your local Volunteer Center. A counselor there should be able to provide you with a list of agencies which would be delighted to have your assistance with a variety of projects or activities involving disabled persons.

Include persons who are exceptional among your acquaintances and friends. Don't be afraid to invite that disabled person to a social function. If you are going to a movie and want to invite a blind friend, do so. Or, if you are going shopping in a local mall, don't hesitate to invite that person you met last week who happened to be a wheelchair user. Don't worry if your sign language skills are weak; ask that deaf person to a social event. In every case the person who is exceptional would more than likely be pleased to have been invited. And, if that person doesn't care to join in, he or she will politely tell you.

Finally, just be yourself around persons who are exceptional. If you are false, they will readily recognize it. Don't worry about your mood; disabled people know that others have good and bad days. (Remember they have good and bad days too.) Also, don't adjust your vocabulary. If you are with a blind person, feel free to say, "It's great to see you." While with a deaf friend you can be very comfortable saying or signing, "Have you heard about such and such?" Or with a friend who has ambulation difficulties and uses a wheelchair, don't worry about saying, "Let's walk down to the lake and watch the sunset." In other words, be yourself and the disabled person will quickly see that you are comfortable.

You are on your way toward comfortable interactions. But it is important to consider the attitudes of others. That may be just as important due to your newly defined leadership role and, hopefully, your new goal of making life more fair and comfortable for all persons who are different.

Your Friends' Attitudes and Behaviors

You probably have been studying about exceptional individuals with friends of yours. All of you are now better prepared to interact correctly and comfortably with exceptional persons. But think about all of your friends and acquaintances who have not read this text or who have not taken a course about persons who are different. Their behaviors will probably demonstrate that they have a severe lack of knowledge and some attitude adjustment needs. In fact, you may be appalled by certain behaviors and attitudes which you will now notice being exhibited by your friends. Are you ready for the next time that a friend of yours cracks a joke about disabled persons or indicates to you that a friend of yours, who happens to have a disability, is not welcome at a social function? The suggestions which follow should assist you with these friends and acquaintances.

Be an excellent role model for your friends and they will learn by following your example. Every time you involve a friend with a disability in your social group and treat that friend in a respectful, comfortable, and normal style, others around you will learn from you. You will be demonstrating to your friends how they can simply be themselves and go on with their everyday activities while including exceptional people in their lives.

Invite your acquaintances to participate in activities with your disabled friends. An excellent opportunity for your friends to improve their attitudes is to have them get to know those persons who are different. Once they interact with these people they will quickly realize how alike they are to themselves and they will probably do what you have done, forgotten about that label.

Be tough with those friends who continue to joke or ridicule people who are different. This is a difficult suggestion to follow as this requires that you challenge your friends when they treat persons who are different in an inappropriate fashion. Interrupt someone who is about to tell a joke at the expense of one who is different with a comment such as, "If you don't mind, I would appreciate your not telling that type of joke as it is demeaning and disrespectful to other persons." If you don't want to stop inappropriate behavior then you can at least leave the group where such negative attitudes are being displayed as your presence may be construed as approval. In fact, it may be best to tell your friends why you are leaving so they fully understand that their ridicule of other people is not acceptable to you.

Teach your friends and acquaintances whenever the opportunity arises. Try to use your social sessions as lessons for those who need some knowledge development or attitude adjustment. If you and your friends are watching a TV show which includes a disabled person or you observe a person with a visible disability while shopping, use those opportunities to encourage positive interactions and respect for persons who are different. Your friends know that you have been studying about exceptional persons and they probably will appreciate your input.

These suggestions should assist you with friends and acquaintances. Of course there are many other ideas you might try based upon your skills and personality. In the next section you will have the opportunity to consider an issue that may appear to be more serious; that of being a parent of an exceptional child.

On Being a Parent

You probably have considered having children someday or you may already be a parent. Most adults, when planning for a family, imagine that they will have perfect little babies who will grow up and be successful at anything and everything. Too often the reality that a baby may be different from that which is expected is not considered and parents are shattered when their hopes and dreams are not realized. However, many persons have found that raising a child who is exceptional can be rewarding and filled with love. Those parents most probably have supportive friends and family, have learned about the proper interventions for reducing the effects of the disability (the handicap), and have found joy in watching and promoting the progress of their child.

Many support groups and service agencies now exist to assist parents of exceptional persons. But the most important assistance may come from family members and friends. You may someday be that family member or friend. The keys to being successful in that role are simple to follow and include the following:

- **Give your friends or family members ample opportunities to talk about their joys and problems with their child.**
- **Make appropriate suggestions but don't suggest that your ideas are better or that you could handle problem situations more easily.**
- **Be cautious that you don't down play the significance or impact of any problems which the parents are having with the child.**
- **Welcome that child into your home in exactly the same way as you would other children.**
- **Respect the disabled child as a person and focus on the child's abilities and accomplishments.**
- **Continue your friendship or relationship with the parents in a manner that is the same as before the child was born with a disability or became disabled.**

Aside from assisting friends and family, it is important to recognize your potential role as a community member. That area will be discussed in the next section.

As a Professional Community Member

Now, or in the future, you will be in the position of having a significant influence upon your community. You most probably will belong to numerous civic, religious, and professional groups. Perhaps you will be a city commissioner, a state legislator, or a leader at the federal level. You may hold a leadership position in an industrial or business setting and have responsibility for hiring or influencing the careers of others. What wonderful opportunities you may have to make a positive impact upon the lives of those who are disabled.

As a member of a civic, religious, or professional group you certainly can set an example for others regarding their interactions with exceptional individuals. In fact, all of the suggestions given in the previous sections of this chapter should also apply with community groups. It is important to realize that exceptional individuals have every right to fully participate in such community groups but some disabled persons may need special facilitation to accomplish successful membership.

For instance, if you belong to a civic group which meets in a hall which is not fully accessible to those people who use wheelchairs then you may want to consider a new meeting place. Some might argue with you that it is not necessary for your group to change meeting places if you do not presently have any physically disabled members. However, the reason these physically disabled persons are not attending may not be due to a lack of desire or interest, but may be due to accessibility difficulties. Change your location so that you send a "you are welcome" message to disabled community members.

Likewise, your civic, religious, or professional group may be sponsoring a special speaker and may be opening the presentation to the community as a public service. Be sure to hire a sign language interpreter, and include that information in your advertising, so that those members of your community who require the use of an interpreter will be motivated to attend. Again, be prepared for arguments from those who will point out that deaf people have not come to your programs in the past so that it would be an unnecessary expenditure to hire an interpreter. You see the lack of logic in that argument even though your fellow member may be very sincere.

Should you enter the political arena, you will have many opportunities to significantly influence funding of programs, the establishment of procedures for service development and service provision, and the design of laws or legislation which directly affect the lives of disabled people. Whether on the local, state, or federal level, you are urged to follow two simple rules. The first is that persons who are exceptional deserve every opportunity to lead the most normal life possible and desired. The second is that disabled people should not simply be tolerated or accepted; they need to be respected as community members who are given opportunities equal to those provided to their non-disabled peers. As an individual who is influential in your community's, state's, or in our nation's political structure, you just may be in the position to make decisions which have great and positive impacts.

As a professional in business or industry you will often be in the unique position of hiring individuals for employment. This is an excellent opportunity for you to demonstrate to your company that individuals who are exceptional are great for business. Although you may meet some skepticism from others, in most cases a disabled employee will quickly prove to co-workers that exceptional persons are good workers.

Be creative as you make any needed modifications to the work place in order to accommodate the person you are hiring. Usually only simple changes are needed such as a ramp up to a piece of equipment (or the lowering of that equipment) for a person who is a wheelchair user, a piece of string taped to a machine so that the worker can see (rather than hear) when a unit has stopped, or a template as a finished product example for those who may not learn or remember easily.

Providing fair and equal treatment in the employment sector is an excellent way to assist exceptional persons in their quest for a life which is satisfying and rewarding. But exceptional people deserve opportunities, equal to those of their non-disabled peers, in all areas of life. They have every right to expect and receive respect, good employment opportunities, normal challenges of life, and the ability to enjoy living. You are in the position to insure that our society continues to improve in these and all other areas so that those persons who wear the label "exceptional" every day will succeed. Whatever you do today and in the future to assist our society in improving services for and attitudes toward exceptional people will benefit all people and have a profound effect on future generations.

Careers With Exceptional People

Before closing your study of exceptional individuals why don't you consider your future. If you are not already solidly decided upon a career path, think of entering a profession which deals directly with persons who are disabled. Many of those professionals have been introduced to you throughout this book. Consider special education, music therapy, speech and language therapy, sheltered workshop management, sign language interpreting, or any other career where you can make meaningful contributions toward improving the lives of disabled people. If interested, visit with a few professionals in the area of your choice and you just may be on your way to a rewarding and exciting career.

Personal Perspectives

To assist you as you began your study of exceptional individuals you had the opportunity, in Chapter One, to read a number of Personal Perspectives. It seems very appropriate to conclude your study with a number of additional real-life, true essays. Enjoy reading these Personal Perspectives which were written by exceptional people, members of their families, and their friends. They are the experts!

"No Time for Sorrow"
Dale Spencer

I look back to my accident in amazement. I wonder how I survived my fall. It happened on December 2, 1988. I was walking across a railroad trestle. When I had reached the middle, I must have slipped on some ice or grease, fell over and through the middle of the two tracks. I fell forty feet into the Kishwaukee River. I quickly attempted to get up only to realize that my legs were not moving. I then, with my arm strength, dragged myself to the side of the river. I immediately yelled to my friends to help me. They called a police officer who, in turn, called an ambulance and brought me to Kishwaukee Hospital.

I was then transferred, by helicopter, to Northwestern Memorial Hospital. The X-rays showed that I had fractured my DT-12 vertebrae on the spinal cord. The attending doctor went to the waiting room, where my parents were waiting anxiously, and proceeded to tell them that I would never walk again. My mother moved in a burst of rage, pushed the doctor against the wall, and called him every name in the book. My father had to pull her off of him. I think it was harder for her to accept it than myself. Mom and I have a very close relationship. She thought that something like this could never happen to someone like me. That first morning, when she walked into that intensive care unit and saw me for the first time since the accident had happened, she wanted to be so strong for me. But, she could not help but to cry. I feel that it was the best thing to let our emotions out into the open.

The next few days were critical. I was put on a striker bed (a bed, where every hour, I have to turn over from my back to my front and vice-versa). This was incredibly uncomfortable. I had no choice but to deal with it because the bed prevented my back from being further injured. This went on until the night before my operation. That night I was literally going insane. There were thousands of thoughts going through my mind at the same time. The doctors assured me that everything was going to be fine. Luckily, a nurse helped me through the whole night. Well, the operation was a success. They took the smashed bone out, and took bone grafts from my right hip and my left fibula. They also fused two twelve inch Herrington rods into my spine. The operation took twelve hours.

My recuperation took two months. I was transferred to the Rehabilitation Institute of Chicago for physical therapy. The first two weeks I spent most of my time in bed. My family and the personnel thought that I was giving up hope. WRONG!!

I was in so much pain because of my back brace (it covered my whole torso), that I could not even bend over. Actually, the pain lasted until I got the brace off three months later.

Now I have a different pain. Picture this; take a fire poker and put it into a lit fireplace until it is white hot. Then stick it into your leg. That's how it feels. The doctor said it is not good and it is not bad. But these things don't keep me down. I believe that my attitude has been great since this whole ordeal started. It was hard to go out in public at first but I realized that I don't need to worry what other people have to say. I rarely think of myself as being handicapped. The only time I dwell on it is when people come up to pity me. I don't need people like that. I need people to be my friends; people to rely on.

Right now I am more active than ever. I am currently in a fraternity (Delta Sigma Phi), I am the Executive Vice President of the InterFraternity Council of Northern Illinois University and I am a Teaching Assistant for EPSE 200 (Exceptional People in Society). I also work out and exercise five days a week and I am taking five classes in my major (Political Science) this semester. I have a pretty busy schedule.

I would like to conclude by quoting an individual who is a double amputee. He plays "Lifeguard" on the show "Wise Guy." He was on the Pat Sajak show recently. He explains, "Don't feel sorry for yourself, you have no time for it."

"Little Buttercup"
Debra Hamilton

If we were lucky, most of us crossed paths in our school days with one or two special teachers who saw something extra in us and drew it out. While most of these teachers were gifted with insight and caring, it seems to me that my special teacher also taught me something about self-confidence and risk-taking by her example.

Her name was Mrs. Bishop and she was the music teacher for our small, rural elementary school in upstate New York. Though I used a wheelchair due to a non-progressive form of muscular dystrophy, I had been "mainstreamed" from the beginning due to my parents' vigilance and probably due to the directness of a small community. It was 1964, long before there were any laws about disabled kids, and I was a 5th grade member of the school chorus. I sang alto and I was pretty good.

Neither was I particularly shy, but I never would have auditioned for the school musical--Gilbert and Sullivan's H.M.S. Pinafore--because, well, what role could there possibly be for me? But Mrs. Bishop was more imaginative and, I think, more courageous.

After chorus one day, she asked me to try out for the part of "Little Buttercup" and after duly auditioning me and a few other girls, she gave me the role, a major one in the show. She persuaded me that I was perfect to sing the part and that my wheelchair even fit in with the character, who was a gypsy-like saleswoman on some English waterfront. Hmmm. But whatever else the character was, she had a terrific solo number and I threw my adolescent heart and soul into it.

The musical was a local hit, I didn't miss a note, and I've never forgotten the experience. Over the next few years, on my own initiative, I went on to perform in piano recitals and as a guitar-playing member of a vocal duet in another school show. I had plenty of other opportunities during my teen years to get up in front of people for things like 4-H Club demonstrations and the usual class reports, and I've done a considerable amount of public speaking in my adult life. I know that I owe a lot of my confidence in these situations to Mrs. Bishop and her faith in me, and her daring to be different in choosing me way back in the fifth grade.

"Welfare Woes"
Diana Mathews

I met her at a peer counseling workshop, and she opened up another world for me. Her child struggled with chronic illness, and Mom was literally on call 24 hours a day. Asthma treatments and sudden migraines formed the pattern of the weeks. Woven into this existence were Mom's constant struggles to survive on the welfare payments she received. Her low-income housing had no central heat or air-conditioning; this with a chronically ill child. One summer she had no money to buy a battery for the car, and she worried about how she would get her child to the emergency room if an attack occurred that Mom could not get under control. According to a Congressional Hearing, the number of children whose activities are limited by a chronically disabling condition has dramatically increased. I don't suppose that this mother is alone with her problems.

She told me she had gotten used to the rude stares and comments people would make when she used foodstamps, but she continued to be upset by the comments people would make about work. After all, everyone knows that the way to get off welfare is to go to work. Of course, Mom knew this. She had worked before her daughter was born and became chronically ill. In fact, if anyone would have told this woman that she would be on welfare, she would have replied, "Never in a million years." Sorry to say, she, too, was once one of the people who did not understand welfare woes, and sometimes she felt that her harsh judgments had simply come back to haunt her. Nevertheless, she tried everything she could think of to change her circumstances. By the way, her husband left her when he realized the child had a seriously chronic condition.

So, like many women with chronically ill or disabled children, she found herself struggling to survive. The hardest part was the lack of compassion in so many around her because she was on welfare. If she dared to complain about a shortage of funds, people would suggest that she should work. Not that she had not tried to do so, either. But she had discovered that employers needed to rely upon her to be on the job more than she was off of it. Also, she had trouble finding child care for a chronically ill child. Very few people were specialized in providing the medical treatments the child needed. Mom had learned how to give medicine and lots of other little things that few sitters wanted to learn. For that matter, most people are frightened by the thought of caring for a child with these problems. The logical caregiver would be a nurse, and Mom could never really earn enough at a job to pay for that kind of care.

But wait, maybe she could. A college education would enable her to get a professional job that paid more. Being a spunky lady who qualified for the college assistance some people on welfare can get, she eagerly returned to classes. The only problem was that her child did not seem to understand that asthma attacks and serious migraines had to happen between semesters. While Mom's professors tried to understand, she fell too far behind in her studies. Another door closed in her face, and she fought back the feelings of bitterness that threatened to overwhelm her. She was smart enough to get a college education, but she was so often treated as if she was too dumb to get off welfare. She was determined, however, to hold on to a positive outlook on life. While I may not have any answers right now, I do know that the next time anyone sees a woman using foodstamps, it might be worthwhile to remember that she could be doing the best she can.

"Very Much Alone"
Joan C. Allen

Mary Elizabeth is a profoundly retarded 26 year old, with the mentality of a 6-9 month old, and requires 24 hour care. If I had known what the future held in store for me, I would have given more thought, as to the alternatives of caring for her myself. I have to place her in a residential facility. I've had comments as to how it will be great to be free after all these years, but, it is going to hurt me, not her. Mary is happy as long as her needs are taken care of. I have two younger boys, now in their 20's and it has not been easy on them growing up with a retarded sister. When they were small and wanted to bring friends home, they'd have to pick friends who *would be understanding. If they didn't, they'd get teased in school the next day for having a RETARD for a sister. My time was limited with them because of the extra care Mary needed. I couldn't go to work to help supplement my husband's salary so that has hurt us a lot financially.*

Mary has mood swings and loud noises and confusion around her make her scream. So, it's hard to take her anywhere. The older Mary gets, the more trouble I have with her toileting. Basically my life is controlled by Mary. She's with me alone, I have no help. I feel very much alone. My husband and boys are free to go and come as they please and I am with Mary. I haven't had a vacation in 15 years. Mary was home for four years between leaving a special school at 21 and attending a day-care type of facility that was opened up at a workshop. I have to sit with her every night until she falls asleep otherwise she just sits up and won't stay laying down.

I love Mary with all my heart. She's got a happy little squeal that tugs at your heart. She's helpless and dependent on me. I'm her eyes, ears, and voice. I have to place her somewhere so I know before I die that she's safe, happy, and well cared for. I worry that she might not get the proper care, that she'll just be another retarded adult that doesn't know anything so she has no feelings. I wish that I could live one day longer than her, so that I could die in peace.

It's been hard on me with her, I've had no life, only an existence, but she has shown me what love is. I get no sympathy, the attitude seems to be, you chose to keep her, so deal with it. My husband and boys only think of her as a burden. It hasn't been easy dealing with taunting kids in the stores and stares from everyone. Some professionals (doctors, dentists, etc.) treat these kids as if they had no feelings, and have no sympathy. I wish parents would teach their children that not everyone is PERFECT, and it's very, very rude to stare. This has always been hard for me to handle. I want to shield Mary from their eyes, or stare them down, until they realize what they're doing and turn away.

Some of Mary's habits are very nerve-racking. Sometimes she stands and rocks in place, and sometimes she shuffles her feet, and sometimes she screeches real loud or even makes low moaning sounds. This annoys the family while they're trying to concentrate and I have to try and keep her quiet or remove her to another part of the house, just to keep things running smoothly.

When it is time to give up my child, it is going to hurt so much, and I don't know how I will be able to handle it. I hope somewhere there is a support group for other parents like me that are forced to give up their children because we will no longer be able to care for them, or because if we die, there is no one.

"Entering the World of Indiscernible Darkness"
Howard R. Behar

For just a moment, I wished to enter that other world where days and nights are blended into one realm of indiscernible darkness. I was eager to feel and experience what it is like to lose one's sight. I pulled the sinister cloth (required by a class assignment) over my eyes and darkness fell upon my world. The cloth robbed me of all light and vision, and the pervasive fear of uncertainty engulfed me. The world I eventually entered into became a far different place, where my own self-sufficiency was undermined and my dependency upon others was increased. Having temporarily lost my sight is much like losing an element of one's humanness, there is an immediate feeling of incompleteness and anxiety. The sensation of danger that pervaded me with every step became the sole agent of my blinded experience. No longer could I engage in the normal activities and lifestyles of most people. No, I would need to adjust and conform to a non-conforming world. With blindness, I surrendered the dependence upon myself to create my own path in the world; I now relied upon the sight and decisions of others.

Curiosity became the most pronounced sensation during my blinded experience. I was eager to know every facet of the environment including the color and size of all objects. I learned to see with my hands, which would instinctively reach forward, and attempt to foresee any danger. All my other senses flourished as well, and allowed me to determine location through hearing echoes and smelling my surroundings.

With blindness, life immediately deviated from normalcy, and I became a product of fear and misconception. Futile efforts to hide my blindness were in vain, I was ultimately different now. No longer could I engage in the classic lifestyle of society, now I had become the exception and a source of stares and whispers. I could not hope to blend in the menagerie of people, I was exceptional and was to be dealt with in a unique way. I knew the only strength I could ever hope for stemmed from the isolated few, who like me, lived with the stigma of being different. All around me the world passed by absorbed in their own existence, rarely concerned about my incapacities. All they could offer were suspicious stares or even worse; condescending gestures of assistance. Society is able to manage effectively without my presence so I knew I must manage without them.

A blind person can master all the possibilities available to them (both mental and physical) in order to reach a state of complete independence. It appears that a man with no sight is much like a man with no purpose. All around one can sense the product of man's sight, he has created an environment both of function and beauty. Like many other blind people, I will learn to open doors for myself, thus I will also be opening the doors to endless opportunities for improving my life and showing all those around me that I am still human.

To be lost in total blackness, where every step brings with it the possibility of detriment and hazard was overbearing at times. When I surrendered my sight I was also losing my independence. Yet, I learned I must also lose those misconceptions and fear of others, thereby giving me light in their strength and support.

"To Billy, With Love"
Pat Rickeart

Billy is a 24 year old young man with Down Syndrome who is around the age of 5 socially and mentally. After meeting in Nashville for a vacation at Opryland, Billy received the following letter from his aunt.

Dear Billy,

I just wanted to thank you for making my vacation so wonderful. You would make a great ambassador because of your love of people, the respect you have for the flag, and the love of God that shows in your face. When you arrived, you took my hand and held on to it and showed me a good time--through your eyes.

We visited President Andrew Jackson's home. The first thing you did was salute the flag and stand at attention for a few minutes. I saw no other person do this. This made me pause and remember what the flag stands for and how lucky we are to live where it flies so freely. We all tend to take it so for granted. I felt very humble. We enjoyed the rest of the tour. Later that day we went to the Grand Ole Opry. We all came out a little disappointed in the show, but not you. "Great show, great show" came from your lips. You were teaching us not to be so critical. That evening we had the best meal ever, as always, because for you each meal is the best.

Next day we toured Opryland. You took my hand and went up to people and introduced yourself. Then you introduced me as your "Boss." Through you I never met a stranger. We met people from New York, Wisconsin, Tennessee, Florida, Ohio, and, yes, Amsterdam. Yes, I met all these people through the eyes of a child that loved everyone just as they were.

We rode the rides with child-like enthusiasm. On the airplane ride when you yelled "Holy Mackerel, we're taking a nosedive!" you made the ride more fun for the rest of the people who were riding. Then on to the swings where we flew through the air. First we were Superman, then we were in Happyland! I was a kid again with you.

We were off to see some of the shows--Rock and Roll and Country Western-- which we really enjoyed. Then we watched the Gospel show and when they sang "How Great Thou Art" you made the sign of the cross and turned your eyes toward heaven. I have never felt so close to God as I did that day. You had such a spiritual look that I felt like God had just reached down and touched you. It was a very special moment.

We went on to ride the bumper cars and antique cars with just as much vigor as the other rides.

On to the Brenda Lee Show, "The Spirit of America." It was a great show and enjoyed by all. When she told us her age, we thought she looked older. But what did you have to say--"Beautiful show! Beautiful woman!" and you really beamed when you had your picture taken with her.

Billy, thank you again for taking my hand and leading me into a beautiful experience and for showing me how to enjoy life as a child again. Thank you for showing me the love and trust and acceptance as only a child can have, but what more adults need to have.

Love, Boss

"It's Not Easy Bein' Green"
Harold Gertner III (age 13)

Kermit the Frog frequently sings "It's Not Easy Bein' Green." He sings this song in an attempt to tell the whole world that it is all right to be different, even though it is sometimes hard. Whether it is the color of your skin, as in Kermit's case, or a physical or mental handicap, being different is often a challenge to the individual and the society in which the person lives.

My brother, Jeffrey, was born with Down Syndrome. That simply means that he was born with a genetic mistake of an extra Number 21 Chromosome, and yet that one small addition makes him very different. Jeffrey fits very well into our family and I am proud to have him as my brother. My other brothers, Morris and Logan, and I have learned that handicapped children are often more like normal children than they are different. I am glad that Jeffrey has been able to go to school in a regular classroom. He has always had neat teachers who are loving, patient, and demanding of his skills as well as his behavior. He now has many friends at his present school. Probably Jeffrey's favorite thing to do is swim. He has taken swimming lessons since has was very small from a super friend and fan of his. He now swims and dives very well. He also enjoys basketball (with the goal at his own level), blowing bubbles, swinging and riding his bike. He also goes to a special gymnastics class and loves that. *Together we work on our Apple IIGS computer and I try to modify some of our learning games for him.*

Jeffrey's speech developed slowly. As he learned sign language, so did the rest of my family. Although his speech is much improved now and he signs very little, my mom often calls on me to interpret. Jeffrey and I are great pals and he enjoys my friends when they come over to visit. Perhaps they have the opportunity to see that "Bein' Green" is not as different as they might think.

Jeffrey's handicap has shown me the importance of the national campaigns such as the March of Dimes and international events such as the Special Olympics. Perhaps one day Jeffrey could swim in the Special Olympics competition. He has helped me to be more tolerant and understanding of differences in all people. Someday I would like to be able to help families who have special children. I might become a geneticist or a developmental pediatrician. I wish people could understand how much Jeffrey means to me. So, I guess if being "Green" means having Jeffrey for a little brother, like Kermit would say, "That will do just fine for me!"

Summary

Here is a test of your attitude and your ability to respect and assist those who are considered by some to be exceptional.

If you were being wheeled into a hospital's emergency room with a critical, life-threatening injury and your life depended on the ability of the one on-duty doctor, which one of the following labels would you want that person to have?

Male   Female   Christian   Jewish   Homosexual   Heterosexual   Black

White   Hispanic   Older   Younger   Foreign   Disabled   Expert

What is you answer?

Option 1. Given your desire to live you probably would only care that the doctor is an "expert" and is able to save your life. You probably would not be concerned, at that moment, with any other label that person may own. It is doubtful that you would refuse life-saving treatment from a doctor who owned "expert" and one of the other labels as well. If that is so, and if you are able to ignore labels at other times and in other situations, then it appears that you are a positive individual who is ready to treat all persons who are different with respect.

Option 2. If you would not accept emergency treatment from a person who owned any of the other labels in addition to "expert" or you would accept treatment but you would not be respectful toward that person in other situations, then it may be beneficial for you to rethink your attitudes about people who are different. Isn't it rather hypocritical to accept life-saving treatment from a person but not respect that person in other circumstances?

Every expectation is that you fit the scenario in Option 1. After your study of exceptional persons you are probably most eager to accept and respect all of those persons in society who are different. Your challenge is to do what you can to insure that every exceptional person is treated with respect and is fully accepted into our already diverse society. Everyone who has worked on this book hopes that you accept the challenge. Consider this your opportunity to begin to make this world a better place for all people--including those who are different.

Suggested Readings

Ausello, E. F., & Rose, T. (1989). *Aging and lifelong disabilities: Partnership for the 21st century.* College Park, MD: University of Maryland.

Brown, S. L., & Moersch, M. S. (Eds.). (1978). *Parents on the team.* Ann Arbor, MI: The University of Michigan Press.

Buckley, J. (1989). Fixing the teaching, not the kids. *U.S. News and World Report, 106,* 61-62.

Cain, E. J., & Taber, F. M. (1987). *Educating disabled people for the 21st century.* Boston, MA: Little, Brown.

Fish, J. (1985). *Special education: The way ahead.* Philadelphia: Open University Press.

Howard, J. (1989). All I ever wanted was a shot. *Sport Magazine, 80,* 26-29.

Meyen, E. L. (Ed.). (1984). *Mental retardation: Topics of today--Issues of tomorrow.* Reston, VA: Council for Exceptional Children.

Turnbull, A. P., & Turnbull, H. R. (1990). *Families, professionals, and exceptionality: A special partnership.* Columbus, OH: Merrill.

U.S. Congress, Senate Committee on Labor and Human Resources. (1990). *The developmental disabilities assistance and bill of rights act of 1990: Report* (GPO No. 2008-D). Washington, C: U.S. Government Printing Office.

Notes

THE FUTURE

Exploration

Individual Activities

1. What are some things that you have done in the past in regard to exceptional people that will be different in your future. List five things. For example, you formerly may have stared at someone with a disability and now you will not. (Don't use this one!)

   1. _____

   2. _____

   3. _____

   4. _____

   5. _____

2. List six things that you have learned, while taking this course, that have assisted you in improving your comfort level when interacting with disabled people.

   1. _____

   2. _____

   3. _____

4. _____
_____

5. _____
_____

6. _____
_____

Group Activities

1. In a few years all of you are going to hold important positions in your community. Get together in small groups and discuss what you will do to make your community a better place for all exceptional persons. Present these actions to your entire class.

    Reactions:

    _____
    _____
    _____

2. Invite a panel of exceptional persons and parents of exceptional persons to your class. Discuss and evaluate the suggestions regarding the improvement of your comfort level which were given in the chapter.

    Reactions:

    _____
    _____
    _____

Reaction Paper 18.1

In the summary of the chapter you were asked about labels and an emergency room doctor who could save your life. Which option did you choose? Why?

Continue on back if needed.

APPENDICES

APPENDIX A

LIST OF AGENCIES

Access Unlimited
3535 Briarpark Drive, Suite 102, Houston, TX 77042
(713) 781-7441
>Access Unlimited Speech Enterprises, a charitable non-profit special technology organization, provides information on computer resources. The information is of value to children or adults with disabilities, or to their parents or trainers.

Administration on Developmental Disabilities
Office of Human Development Services
U.S. Department of Health and Human Services
200 Independence Avenue, S.W., Washington, DC 20201
(202) 245-2890
>The Administration on Developmental Disabilities administers the Developmental Disabilities Assistance and Bill of Rights Act whose programs and services assist persons with developmental disabilities to achieve independence, productivity, and integration into the community.

Alexander Graham Bell Association for the Deaf
3417 Volta Place, N.W., Washington, DC 20007
(202) 337-5220
>The Alexander Graham Bell Association for the Deaf is an organization which encourages hearing-impaired people to communicate by developing maximal use of residual hearing, speech-writing, and speech and language skills. It also promotes better public understanding of hearing loss in children and adults, and helps oral deaf adults and parents of hearing-impaired children.

American Association on Mental Retardation
1719 Kalorama Road, N.W., Washington, DC 20009
(202) 387-1968 or 1-800-424-3688
>The American Association on Mental Retardation is an interdisciplinary association of professionals and individuals concerned about the field of mental retardation. Founded in 1876, AAMR promotes the well-being of individuals with mental retardation and supports those who work in the field.

American Cancer Society
1599 Clifton Road, N.E., Atlanta, GA 30329
(800) ACS-2345

    The American Cancer Society is the nationwide voluntary health organization dedicated to eliminating cancer as a major health problem by preventing cancer, saving lives from cancer, and diminishing suffering from cancer through research, education, and service.

American Lung Association
1740 Broadway, New York, NY 10019
(212) 315-8700

    The American Lung Association, the Christmas Seal People, is the oldest nationwide voluntary health agency in the United States. Founded in 1904 to combat tuberculosis, the Association is dedicated to the conquest of lung disease and the promotion of lung health.

American Printing House for the Blind
P. O. Box 6085, Louisville, KY 40206-0085
(502) 895-2405

    The American Printing House for the Blind (APH) is the world's largest company devoted solely to producing products for people who are visually impaired. Under the federal act to promote the Education of the Blind, APH is the official supplier of educational materials for visually impaired students in the U.S.

American Speech-Language-Hearing Association
10801 Rockville Pike, Rockville, MD 20852
(800) 638-8255 or 301-897-8682 (Voice or TDD)

    This group provides information and referral on a broad range of speech, language, and hearing disorders, a toll-free telephone number for consumer assistance and referrals, and a consumer newsletter, "Let's Talk."

Association for the Care of Children's Health
7910 Woodmont Avenue, Suite 300, Bethesda, MD 20814
(301) 654-6549

    ACCH is a multi-disciplinary membership organization advocating family-centered, psychosocially sound, and developmentally appropriate health care for children. ACCH promotes meaningful collaboration among families and professionals across all disciplines to plan, coordinate, deliver, and evaluate children's health care systems.

Association for Education and Rehabilitation of the Blind and Visually Impaired
206 N. Washington Street, Suite 320, Alexandria, VA 22314
(703) 548-1884

> The Association for Education and Rehabilitation of the Blind and Visually Impaired is the only professional membership organization dedicated to the advancement of education and rehabilitation of blind and visually impaired children and adults.

Association for Retarded Citizens of the U.S.
2501 Avenue J, Arlington, TX 76006
(817) 640-0204

> The Association for Retarded Citizens is the nation's largest volunteer organization solely devoted to improving the welfare of all children and adults with mental retardation and their families.

Autism Society of America
8601 Georgia Avenue, Suite 503, Silver Spring, MD 20910
(301) 565-0433

> ASA is a national umbrella organization of 160 local chapters serving the needs of autistic citizens of all ages.

Canine Companions for Independence
P. O. Box 446, Santa Rosa, CA 95402-0446
(707) 528-0830

> Canine Companions for Independence trains dogs to assist persons who are physically handicapped. These dogs not only help people up when they fall, open doors, turn on lights, pull wheelchairs, and retrieve objects when needed, but they also become loving companions.

Captioned Films/Videos for the Deaf
Modern Talking Picture Service
5000 Park Street North, St. Petersburg, FL 33709
(800) 237-6213 (Voice/TDD)

> Open-captioned educational and entertainment films and videos are offered on a free-loan basis to hearing-impaired persons. These are made available by the U.S. Department of Education and distributed by contract with Modern Talking Picture Service.

Cleft Palate Foundation
1218 Grandview Avenue, Pittsburgh, PA 15211
(800) 24-CLEFT or (412) 481-1376

>This foundation provides information and referral to individuals with cleft lip and palate or other craniofacial anomalies. Referrals are made to local cleft palate/craniofacial teams for treatment and to parent support groups. Free information on various aspects of clefting is available.

The Council for Exceptional Children
1920 Association Drive, Reston, VA 22091
(703) 620-3660

>The Council for Exceptional Children (CEC) is a special education professional association whose purpose is to advance the quality of education for all exceptional children and to improve the conditions under which special educators work.
>
>Divisions of the Council for Exceptional Children:
>
>**Council of Administrators of Special Education (CASE)**
>**Council for Children with Behavioral Disorders (CCBD)**
>**CEC Division for Research (CEC-DR)**
>**CEC Division on Mental Retardation (CEC-MR)**
>**CEC Pioneers Division (CEC-PD)**
>**Council for Educational Diagnostic Services (CEDS)**
>**Division for Children with Communication Disorders (DCCD)**
>**Division on Career Development (DCD)**
>**Division for Culturally and Linguistically Diverse Exceptional Learners (DDEL)**
>**Division for Early Childhood (DEC)**
>**Division of International Special Education and Services (DISES)**
>**Division for Learning Disabilities (DLD)**
>**Division for Physically Handicapped (DPH)**
>**Division for the Visually Impaired (DVH)**
>**The Association for the Gifted (TAG)**
>**Technology and Media Division (TAM)**
>**Teacher Education Division (TED)**

APPENDIX A

Council for Learning Disabilities
P. O. Box 40303, Overland Park, KS 66204
(913) 492-8755
> The Council for Learning Disabilities is the only national professional organization dedicated solely to professionals working with individuals who have learning disabilities. The main purpose is to aid all LD educators in the exchange of information through publications and conferences.

Epilepsy Foundation of America
4351 Garden City Drive, Landover, MD 20785
(301) 459-3700; 1-800-332-1000 (Information); 1-800-332-4050 (Library)
> The Epilepsy Foundation is dedicated to the well being of persons with epilepsy. It sponsors research and provides toll free information service to lay and professional inquirers. Local affiliates offer support groups, employment assistance, and other direct services.

Federation for Children with Special Needs
95 Berkeley Street, Suite 014, Boston, MA 02116
(617) 482-2915 or (413) 562-5521
> The Federation is composed of a coalition of 11 statewide parent organizations that act on behalf of children and adults with a variety of special needs. It was established to represent the expressed interest of parents and their organizations and encourages parental input in all aspects of their child's needs.

Immune Deficiency Foundation
P. O. Box 586
Oakland Mills Village Center Office Building
5865 Robert Oliver Place, Suite 212
Columbia, MD 21045
(301) 730-8837
> IDF is a non-profie, volunteer organization which supports research and education for the primary immune deficiency diseases. The Foundation has available various publications on these diseases, including a newsletter. IDF periodically supports research grants, medical meetings, and physician training.

Institute for Child Behavior Research
4182 Adams Avenue, San Diego, CA 92116
(619) 281-7165
> ICBR conducts and fosters scientific research into causes and treatments for autism. It publishes a quarterly newsletter and serves as an information and referral service for people worldwide.

Juvenile Diabetes Foundation International
432 Park Avenue South, New York, NY 10016
(212) 889-7575 or 1-800-JDF-CURE
> The Juvenile Diabetes Foundation International was founded in 1970 by parents of diabetic children who were convinced that, through research, diabetes could be cured. Today, JDF is a voluntary health agency with membership in the tens of thousands.

Learning Disabilities Association of America
4156 Library Road, Pittsburgh, PA 15234
(412) 341-1515
> The Learning Disabilities Association of America is a national information center and referral service that has affiliates in all 50 states and 750 local chapters. This group offers an information packet free of charge and publishes a newsletter and journal.

Muscular Dystrophy Association
810 Seventh Avenue, New York, NY 10019
(212) 586-0808
> The Muscular Dystrophy Association (MDA) is a voluntary health organization which provides comprehensive patient care throughout its nationwide network of 230 MDA clinics. MDA also supports an international research program to find the causes and treatments for muscular dystrophy and related neuromuscular diseases.

National Association of the Deaf
814 Thayer Avenue, Silver Spring, MD 20910
(301) 587-1788 (Voice) or (301) 587-1789 (TDD)
> The National Association of the Deaf is the oldest and largest consumer organization of disabled persons in the United States, with more than 22,000 members and 50 affiliated state associations. It serves as an advocate for the millions of deaf and hard-of-hearing people in America.

National Association of the Physically Handicapped, Inc.
Bethesda Scarlet Oaks, #117
440 Lafayette Avenue, Cincinnati, OH 45220-1000
(513) 961-8040
> NAPH's purpose is to advance the social, economic, and physical welfare of physically handicapped persons in the United States. NAPH is composed of handicapped and non-handicapped persons who are trying to bring about awareness of the needs of disabled people and support legislation for their benefit.

APPENDIX A

National Association for Visually Handicapped
22 West 21 Street, New York, NY 10010
(212) 889-3141
> This organization provides services for partially seeing persons, including informational literature (much in large print) for the lay person and professionals, large print loan library (by mail), and newsletters for adults and children (in large print).

National Braille Association, Inc. (NBA)
1290 University Avenue, Rochester, NY 14607
(716) 473-0900
> NBA provides continuing education to groups and individuals who prepare reading materials for handicapped persons through seminars, workshops, consultations, publication of instruction manuals; and provides braille textbooks, music, career and technical materials at below cost to blind college students and professionals.

National Information Center for Children and Youth with Handicaps
P. O. Box 1492, Washington, DC 22013
(703) 893-6061; 1-800-999-5599; (703) 893-8614 (TDD)
> NICHCY collects and shares information and ideas that are helpful to children and youth with disabilities and to the people who care for and about them. NICHCY publishes a <u>News Digest</u> and assorted issue papers.

National Multiple Sclerosis Society
205 East 42nd Street, New York, NY 10017
(212) 986-3240
> This organization funds research into causes and cures for multiple sclerosis, provides a variety of publications, and has local chapters throughout the country. <u>Inside MS</u>, published quarterly, covers general topics of interest for those with multiple sclerosis, daily living aids, research legislation, and treatments.

National Organization for Rare Disorders, Inc.
P. O. Box 8923, New Fairfield, CT 06812
(203) 746-6518
> NORD is a clearinghouse for information on over 5,000 rare disorders.

Office of Special Education Programs
330 "C" Street, S.W., Washington, DC 20202
(202) 732-1007

>The Office of Special Education Programs administers programs authorized under the Education of the Handicapped Act, including state-administered grant programs and discretionary grants which are awarded for research, training, demonstration, and technical assistance relating to special education.

Pathfinder Resources, Inc.
Midtown Commons, Suite 105
2324 University Avenue West, St. Paul, MN 55114
(612) 647-6905

>Pathfinder Resources, Inc. works to improve the health and well-being of children and adults with chronic health conditions. Pathfinder activities fall into four categories: networking, education, publications, and technical assistance.

Recording for the Blind
The Anne T. MacDonald Center
20 Roszel Road, Princeton, NJ 08540
(609) 452-0606

>Recording for the Blind is a nonprofit organization providing recorded textbooks, library services, and other educational resources to individuals who cannot read standard print because of a visual, physical, or perceptual disability. RFB's 77,000 volume master tape library is steadily augmented by 4,500 volunteers in 32 RFB recording studies.

Tourette Syndrome Association
42-40 Bell Boulevard, Bayside, NY 11361-2861
(800) 237-0717

>TSA is the only national voluntary, nonprofit organization dedicated to identifying the cause, finding the cure, and controlling the effects of TS, a neurological disorder. TSA provides information, referral, education, direct services, and medical research for people with Tourette Syndrome.

APPENDIX B

SIGN LANGUAGE

Knowing sign language will greatly assist you in your future interactions with deaf persons who utilize signing as their means of communication. Find out if there is a sign language club or if courses are offered on your campus, or in your community, as these are excellent ways to develop your sign language skills.

To assist your learning of basic sign language you will find drawings of fingerspelling on the next two pages. Practice these with a friend or in a mirror. Be sure to learn your letters in random order so that you do not depend upon sequence to recall a specific letter. While practicing, say the word (not the letters) as you fingerspell.

The second section of the appendix is designed to assist you in learning some common words. Find each listed word in a sign language book and draw (or describe) the sign configuration in the provided space. Then practice these words with a friend. You will probably be surprised at how quickly you will learn the words if you practice.

Below are suggested sign language books which you should be able to find in a library or bookstore. There are many others, so choose the one which you like best.

    Bornstein, H., Saulnier, K., & Hamilton, L. (1983). *The comprehensive signed English dictionary.* Washington, DC: Kendall Green.

    Costello, E. (1983). *Signing: How to speak with your hands.* New York: Bantam.

    Riekehof, L. (1987). *The joy of signing.* Springfield, MO: Gospel.

    Sternberg, M. (1987). *American sign language dictionary.* New York: Harper and Row.

    Sternberg, M. (1990). *American sign language: A concise dictionary.* New York: Harper and Row.

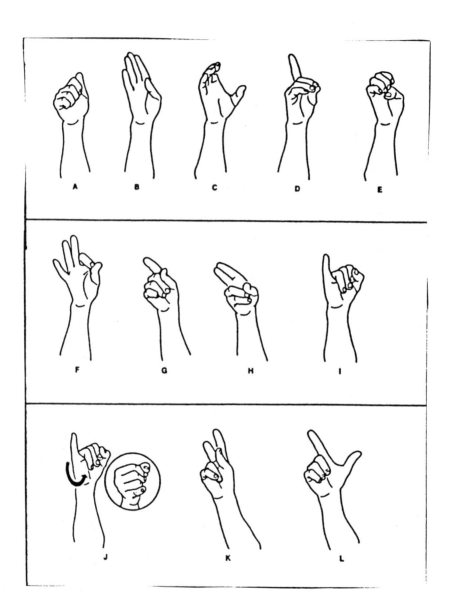

APPENDIX B

family	group	yesterday
today	week	year
morning	afternoon	evening
later	again	like/similar

APPENDIX B

hot dog	hamburger	egg
spaghetti	soda	milk
coffee	tea	popcorn
thirsty	hungry	drink

eat	pay attention	dance
help	see	talk
cry	finish	feel
work	give	want

APPENDIX B

sign language	school	book
house	tree	bathroom
doctor	airplane	music
kiss	name	car

neighbor	embarrass	good
bad	fine	dirty
large	small	sick
broken	happy	afraid

APPENDIX B

hot	cold	man
woman	baby	who
what	when	where
why	how	please

mother	father	sister
brother	parents	grandmother
grandfather	agree	home
beautiful	please	thank you

STUDENT STUDY GUIDE

Kurt Lischka

This study guide has been designed to further your understanding of the book's content and to assist you as you prepare for exams on each chapter. The guide should also compliment the text's goal of helping you understand and interact with exceptional people.

In each chapter of this guide you will find four sections of exercises. The **Terminology** section will give you an opportunity to review the new terms and concepts which were presented in the chapter. Try to define each term without referring to the chapter; then check yourself. In the **True/False** and **Multiple Choice** sections, all you have to do is circle the correct responses. When finished, check your answers with the Key located at the end of the guide. Be sure to go back to the chapter and review the content if you missed any items. The fourth section, **Essay Practice**, offers questions designed to assist you as you prepare for essay style test questions. Outline and write your responses and you should be ready for essay style questions on the chapter's content.

You should attempt to complete all the exercises without referring to the text. Then go back and concentrate on those areas that proved to be difficult. If you still have problems or questions, be sure to address those with your instructor.

Chapter One

In Chapter One you were given a look at part of what makes the world go around--being different. Hopefully you're intrigued and ready to learn more. Before continuing the study of people who are exceptional, see what you have learned so far by doing a few exercises.

Terminology

These are important terms from Chapter One which you should know. Try defining the terms in the provided spaces before referring to the chapter or other references.

Exceptional: _____

_____

Gifted/Talented: _____

_____

Mentally Retarded: _____

_____

Developmentally Delayed: _____

_____

Disabled: _____

_____

Handicapped: _____

_____

Visible Disability: _____

_____

Hidden Disability: _____

_____

STUDENT STUDY GUIDE

True/False

Here's a chance to test your knowledge by circling the correct response. Try for 100% correct.

T F 1. It's possible that you could be labeled exceptional right now or in the future.

T F 2. Labels should be avoided when describing exceptional individuals, because labeling always conveys a negative connotation to those individuals.

T F 3. The term handicap is used for a person who has a permanent disability.

T F 4. In general, children should be encouraged to talk about people who are different.

T F 5. Children should not be allowed to talk directly to exceptional individuals about their differences.

T F 6. You should be careful to alter your behavior around exceptional individuals to keep from offending them.

T F 7. It is a good idea to substitute words you might ordinarily use with less offensive ones, to avoid embarrassing exceptional individuals.

T F 8. You should expect normal behavior and achievement from exceptional people.

Multiple Choice

Here's another chance to see what you've learned from Chapter One. Circle the best of the possible answers.

1. Why are labels important in our society?
   a. So we can identify people that are different.
   b. To compare the possible achievements of others with our own.
   c. So that professionals can communicate with each other about differences.
   d. Because people have an inherent need to classify and organize individuals within a societal group.

2. Why are labels with negative connotations often misleading?
   a. They confuse family members and professionals when communicating about exceptional individuals.
   b. They create reduced expectations of exceptional individuals and poor attitudes toward them.
   c. They are often confused with labels issued by the National Bureau of Labels and Standards.
   d. They are often offensive but never misleading.

3. Which would be considered as having a visible disability?
   a. A person who is deaf.
   b. A person with epilepsy.
   c. A person with a learning disability.
   d. A person who uses a wheelchair.

4. Whom should you not invite swimming with you?
   a. A person who is mentally retarded.
   b. A person who is blind.
   c. A person with epilepsy.
   d. A person who can't swim.

5. If you were the only person in the world who didn't use a wheelchair, what would you prefer to be labeled?
   a. Disabled.
   b. Handicapped.
   c. Chairless.
   d. Exceptional.

6. When dealing with an exceptional person you should:
   a. Forget labels and concentrate on the person.
   b. Keep labels in mind in order to limit expectations.
   c. Alter your behavior, being careful not to offend.
   d. Alter your expectations so you won't embarrass the exceptional person.

STUDENT STUDY GUIDE   489

7. Which would not be proper action when responding to a child's curiosity toward exceptional people?
   a. Telling the child to ignore people with differences.
   b. Allowing the child to ask people about their differences.
   c. Encouraging the child to talk about differences.
   d. Telling the child not to fear people with differences.

8. Which of the following could be labeled exceptional or different?
   a. Helen Keller.
   b. Your instructor.
   c. Yourself.
   d. Any of the above.

Essay Practice

These activities will help you learn more about exceptional people.

1. Imagine you are to give a lecture to parents and their children at a local day care center. As preparation for the lecture, write down guidelines concerning the improvement of attitudes toward exceptional people.

   _____
   _____
   _____
   _____
   _____
   _____
   _____
   _____
   _____
   _____

2. Discuss the positive and negative effects of labels. Also, suggest reasons why some labels are necessary.

STUDENT STUDY GUIDE 491

Chapter Two

Haven't you felt different at one time or another? Maybe it was the people you were with, or the situation that made you feel out of place. One key to being different and enjoying life is feeling in place, and through this chapter you can help others and yourself achieve that goal.

Terminology

Here are some terms that will help your understanding of Chapter Two. Write the definitions for the terms in the provided spaces.

Sign Language: _____

_____

Handicap: _____

_____

Congenital: _____

_____

Adventitious: _____

_____

The Education for All Handicapped Children Act of 1975 (PL 94-142): _____

_____

Multiple Sclerosis (MS): _____

_____

Mainstreaming: _____

_____

Muscular Dystrophy (MD): _____

_____

Learning Disability: _____

_____

True/False

Try to get as many of these correct as you can without looking back at Chapter Two. Circle your answers.

(T) F 1. Congenital disabilities are present at birth.

T (F) 2. Adventitious disabilities appear only in adulthood.

T (F) 3. The Education for All Handicapped Children Act of 1975 states that all Handicapped Children be educated in a segregated manner.

(T) F 4. Relationships, for many people with disabilities, can be experiences that include rejection and isolation.

T (F) 5. Feelings toward people who are different usually come from instinct rather than what is learned.

T (F) 6. Perceptions about exceptional people are usually objective and well thought out.

T (F) 7. A visible disability is more accepted by people than a hidden disability.

STUDENT STUDY GUIDE

Multiple Choice

This exercise will help at test time.

1. The restrictions placed on people with disabilities has mostly to do with:
   a. A function of the disability.
   b. The attitude of the individual.
   c. A function of the attitudes of society.
   d. What makes disabled people different.

2. Gordon (1974) says that handicaps are created by:
   a. Congenital or adventitious disabilities.
   b. The physical limits on the individual.
   c. The attitudes of the individual.
   d. Society at large.

3. The effect of The Education for All Handicapped Children Act of 1975 (PL 94-142) is that:
   a. Most children with handicaps must be segregated.
   b. All children with handicaps should spend a majority of the school day with their non-handicapped peers.
   c. All children with handicaps should be assigned to a special education classroom for part of the school day.
   d. Most children with handicaps should spend all or part of the school day in the regular classroom.

4. Perceptions and attitudes toward people who are exceptional are typically:
   a. Subjective and arbitrary.
   b. Objective.
   c. Rational.
   d. Conscious judgments.

5. People who are different are constrained mostly by:
   a. Their self image and confidence.
   b. Their physical and mental characteristics.
   c. Those closest to them.
   d. The attitudes of society.

6. Which has contributed the most toward segregation of people who are different?
   a. Societal definitions of what is different.
   b. Governmental laws and agency guidelines.
   c. Stereotypes, myths, and fears.
   d. Professional diagnosis and systematic institutionalization.

7. What will be the likely effect of mainstreaming?
   a. People with differences will become more accepted by society.
   b. The general level of education will be lowered.
   c. People will remain uncomfortable around people with differences.
   d. Only those with hidden handicaps will succeed.

Essay Practice

Give these questions some careful thought before your write your responses in the provided spaces. They'll help you gain a fuller understanding of Chapter Two.

1. In Chapter Two you met several pairs of people; in each pair one person was exceptional. Imagine you are a junior in college and have a friend who will be a freshman next semester. You want to show your friend firsthand what campus life is all about. What kind of difficulties might you and your friend, who is blind, encounter?

2. Identify some famous persons who have been disabled. What influence did they have on attitudes toward disabled people?

Chapter Three

Chapter Three provides a look at how families react and interact when challenged by a disability. It is a challenge that must be met with courage and determination by the whole family.

Terminology

These are important terms and concepts from Chapter Three to learn. Identify each term in the space provided.

Disability: _____

_____

Long-term planning: _____

_____

Empowerment: _____

_____

Least restrictive environment: _____

_____

Respite care: _____

_____

Special Olympics: _____

_____

True/False

Test your knowledge of Chapter Three by circling the correct response. Can you get all seven correct?

T (F) 1. Wise professionals often withhold information about a disability to lessen the impact on the family.

(T) F 2. Featherstone (1980) says the four most prominent emotional reactions to a family member's disability are fear, anger, loneliness, and guilt.

(T) F 3. When families undertake future planning, it is important that they involve the person with the disability to the maximum extent possible.

T (F) 4. Educational integration for adults is legally mandated by the federal government.

T (F) 5. Most early litigation and legislation leading to special services and protection for people with disabilities did not involve action by family members.

T (F) 6. Family members should avoid technical materials when researching a disability.

T (F) 7. It is a good idea for parents to protect their children by holding back information about their sibling's disability.

Multiple Choice

If you've carefully read Chapter Three, you shouldn't have any problem with these. Circle the correct responses.

1. Which statement is not true about the emotional stages families undergo when faced with a disability?
   a. Stages oversimplify the intricate dynamics within a family.
   (b.) Stages happen at the same time for different family members.
   c. Grief is a very common initial reaction.
   d. Stages of emotional reaction are not unique.

STUDENT STUDY GUIDE

2. Which is not a suggested step in approaching long-term planning?
   a. Defining the problem or need.
   b. Creating a list of possible solutions.
   c. Having a professional counselor evaluate the alternatives and choose one.
   d. Implementing the chosen alternative.

3. Which is not a guideline in financial planning for a family facing a disability?
   a. Determining the family's assets.
   b. Involving other family members and professionals in planning.
   c. Considering the whole family when planning.
   d. Investing in government bonds.

4. Which is not a suggested element in a strategy for helping children deal with teasing and rejection of their exceptional sibling by their peers?
   a. Ignoring the teasing.
   b. Not joining the teasing.
   c. Stating that joking about a handicap is unfair.
   d. Stating something positive about the sibling who is exceptional.

5. Which emotion is widely reported as an initial reaction to the news that a family member has a disability?
   a. Grief.
   b. Anger.
   c. Guilt.
   d. Fear.

6. When faced with a family member who has a disability, parents, grandparents, brothers, and sisters prominently experience:
   a. Fear, denial, guilt, anger.
   b. Fear, loneliness, guilt, denial.
   c. Anger, guilt, fear, loneliness.
   d. Anger, denial, loneliness, fear.

7. Which is not suggested as a source of information about disabilities?
   a. Books and periodicals.
   b. Parent and professional organizations.
   c. Department of Education parent information and training centers.
   d. Family members and other relatives.

8. Which factor is not suggested as contributing to marital stress in regards to a child with a disability?
   a. Time limitations on working parents.
   b. Emotions associated with the disability.
   c. Perceived parental failure.
   d. Reorganization of the family.

Essay Practice

Here are two exercises to help you gain a better understanding of Chapter Three. Provide your responses on the lines below both questions.

1. Explain what respite care is and how it can benefit a family.

STUDENT STUDY GUIDE 501

2. Families of disabled persons have much to consider. These may include such things as long-term planning, finances, and the needs of other family members. Discuss the impact of the three areas.

_____
_____
_____
_____
_____
_____
_____
_____
_____
_____
_____
_____
_____
_____
_____
_____
_____
_____
_____
_____
_____
_____
_____

STUDENT STUDY GUIDE

Chapter Four

Hearing impairment is a common and often misunderstood form of disability. See what understanding you've gained from Chapter Four by doing the following exercises.

Terminology

Here are some terms from Chapter Four that will help you with the subject of hearing impairments. Define each term.

Deaf: _____

Hard of hearing: _____

Hearing impaired: _____

Prelingual hearing impairment: _____

Postlingual hearing impairment: _____

Conductive loss: _____

Sensorineural loss: _____

Audiological exam: _____

True/False

Circle the correct response. You should know all of these.

T F 1. Hearing is the sense primarily responsible for the development of language and speech.

T **F** 2. Most people with hearing impairments have no speech skills.

T F 3. The cause of 25% of all hearing losses remains unknown.

T F 4. Noise-induced hearing loss is currently the leading cause of a sensorineural impairment.

T F 5. A postlingual hearing loss may leave language and speech unaffected.

T **F** 6. Investigators have suggested that lower scores on intelligence tests by those with hearing impairments reflect inherent cognitive defects.

T F 7. A child can become hearing impaired as a result of conditions present during the birth process.

Multiple Choice

Circle the best of four possible answers. Good luck with these.

1. A conductive hearing loss is one in which:
    a. Is located in the inner ear.
    b. Damage is evident in the auditory nerve.
    c. Sounds will be heard without distortion through proper amplification.
    d. Sounds will be distorted even with amplification.

2. A sensorineural hearing loss is one in which:
    a. Typically results from damage to the cochlea or auditory nerve.
    b. It is located in the outer or middle ear.
    c. Sounds will be heard without distortion through proper amplification.
    d. Sensitivity to sounds is normal with proper amplification.

STUDENT STUDY GUIDE

3. A hearing loss that disables a person but does not prohibit the development of speech and language skills is termed:
   a. Deafness.
   b. A prelingual hearing impairment.
   c. A postlingual hearing impairment.
   d. Hard of hearing.

4. Hearing losses are generally categorized as:
   a. Mild, moderate, severe, profound.
   b. Mild, moderate, moderately severe, profound, profoundly severe.
   c. Mild, moderate, moderately severe, severe, profound.
   d. Mild, moderate, severe, severely profound.

5. A hearing loss which makes speech beyond 5 feet difficult to understand would be classified as:
   a. Mild.
   b. Moderate.
   c. Severe.
   d. Severely profound.

6. A hearing loss in which the person can't hear a loud voice if it is more than one or two feet away would be classified as:
   a. Moderately severe.
   b. Severe.
   c. Profound.
   d. Profoundly severe.

7. Which is not one of the major speech problems experienced by individuals with severely impaired hearing, according to Ling (1976)?
   a. Limited pitch.
   b. Limited intensity.
   c. Slower rates of speech.
   d. Difficulties with the production of vowels and consonants.

8. What percentage of students with hearing impairments achieve levels of academic competence comparable to their hearing peers?
   a. 10%
   b. 25%
   c. 43%
   d. 80%

Essay Practice

Here's another chance to see what you've learned from Chapter Four. Write out your answers in the provided spaces.

1. List and briefly describe the different communication philosophies.

2. Technological interventions, available to those who are hearing impaired, can be very beneficial. Describe at least three uses of technology for hearing impaired persons.

STUDENT STUDY GUIDE 509

Chapter Five

By scanning the list of terms describing visual disabilities in Chapter Five, you can see that the subject is not as simple as it may appear at first glance. Look over the chapter again, then see if you can answer these exercises correctly.

Terminology

Did you notice the terms related to sight in the paragraph above? Here are some more. Identify each.

Distance visual acuity: _____

Legally blind: _____

Visual field: _____

Visually handicapped: _____

Albinism: _____

Cataracts: _____

Microphthalmos: _____

Diabetic retinopathy: _____

True/False

Here's a chance to test your knowledge by circling the correct responses.

(T) F 1. A normal visual field encompasses a horizontal arc of 160 to 180 degrees.

(T) F 2. The fastest growing population of people with visual disability is newborns.

(T) F 3. In adults, most visual impairment is caused by aging.

(T) F 4. A person with a central visual acuity of 20/200 must be as close as 20 feet in order to see what a person with normal vision sees at 200 feet.

T (F) 5. People who are totally blind comprise about 50% of the total number of people considered to have visual disabilities.

(T) F 6. The best prevalence estimate for visual impairment among the school-age population is about 1%.

T (F) 7. Most causes of visual impairment in children are adventitious.

Multiple Choice

Circle the best of four possible answers. Try to answer all eight correctly without referring to the chapter.

1. Estimates of the proportion of people with visual disabilities, who also have additional disabilities, range from:
   a. 23-30%
   b. 33-39%
   (c.) 48-66%
   d. 45-62%

STUDENT STUDY GUIDE

2. Barraga (1983) estimated the percentage of the legally blind population that may actually be able to use vision as their primary means of getting information as:
   a. 25%
   b. 40%
   c. 50%
   d. 75%

3. The Education of the Handicapped Act (PL 94-142) defines the term visually handicapped as a visual impairment that adversely affects a child's:
   a. Ability to read.
   b. Ability to perform daily living skills.
   c. Educational performance.
   d. Ability to use vision as a primary means for acquiring information.

4. The best prevalence estimate for school-age children with visual impairments is:
   a. .1%
   b. 1%
   c. 2%
   d. 3.6%

5. Prevalence estimates for people over 18 who have visual impairments range from:
   a. 1-12%
   b. 2-18%
   c. 3-16%
   d. 4-23%

6. The fastest growing population of people with visual disability is:
   a. Newborns.
   b. School-age children.
   c. That part of the population with additional disabilities.
   d. Elderly.

7. Which limitation did Lowenfeld (1973) not suggest as affecting people with visual disabilities?
   a. The range and variety of experiences available.
   b. The ability to perform daily living skills.
   c. The ability to move about.
   d. The control of the environment and the self in relation to it.

8. When interacting with a person who has a visual disability, you should:
    a. Assume they need help with difficult tasks.
    b. Speak loudly so the person can tell where you are.
    c. Give tactual clues.
    d. Avoid terms such as look and see.

Essay Practice

These will provide an additional test of what you know about visual disabilities.

1. State why prevalence figures for people who are visually impaired are hard to determine. Include in your discussion the various agencies and organizations that issue such figures.

2. Discuss proper actions and behaviors when interacting with a person who has a visual disability. Use social situations as examples of your suggestions.

STUDENT STUDY GUIDE

Chapter Six

In Chapter Six you received an overview of the complex topics related to people who have health impairments. Try these exercises to test what you've learned.

Terminology

These are some important terms and concepts from Chapter Six. Define each one.

Orthopedic Impairments: _____
_____

Health Impairments: _____
_____

Physical Disability: _____
_____

Diabetes: _____
_____

Cystic Fibrosis: _____
_____

Asthma: _____
_____

Epilepsy: _____
_____

AIDS: _____
_____

True/False

Is it right or wrong? If you've carefully read Chapter Six, you'll know. Circle either T or F.

(T) F 1. It has been estimated that chronically ill children compromise approximately 50% of pediatric practice.

T (F) 2. The time of the onset of a disability has no effect on the reaction to the disability.

T (F) 3. Too much insulin in the system results in the form of diabetes known as hyperglycemia.

(T) F 4. Cystic Fibrosis is the most common hereditary disease of childhood.

(T) F 5. Exercise can precipitate an asthma attack.

(T) F 6. Current educational policy and legislation supports education in the least restrictive environment.

T (F) 7. Most often, people with health impairments appear different and cannot engage in most typical life activities.

Multiple Choice

Take your time with these. Hopefully you can get them all right. Circle your choices.

1. The Education for All Handicapped Children Act of 1975 (PL 94-142) divides physical disabilities into which two categories of impairments?
   a. Orthopedic and pediatric.
   (b.) Orthopedic and health.
   c. Health and pediatric.
   d. Geriatric and pediatric.

STUDENT STUDY GUIDE

2. Health impairments that are treatable but incurable are called:
   a. Acute.
   b. Extended.
   c. Chronic.
   d. Orthopedic.

3. Why are prevalence figures of health impairments difficult to determine?
   a. Because many health impairments are classified as disabilities.
   b. Because health impairments can occur in combination with other disabilities.
   c. Because of the rapid changes within the health-care industry.
   d. Because of poor communication between the health-care industry and the federal government.

4. When you have popcorn and soda during a movie, the normal reaction is the level of:
   a. Glucose in your blood rising, and less insulin being produced.
   b. Glucose in your blood rising, and more insulin being produced.
   c. Glucose in your blood falling, and less insulin being produced.
   d. Glucose in your blood falling, and more insulin being produced.

5. Recent research indicates that an asthma attack is a hyper-response occurring when a person has:
   a. Inflamed bronchial tubes.
   b. Foreign objects in the lungs.
   c. An infection in the throat.
   d. Excessive antibodies.

6. AIDS is viral in nature and acts by attacking and weakening the body's:
   a. Immune system.
   b. Reproductive system.
   c. Neurological System.
   d. Glandular functions.

7. Traditionally, occupational therapists are concerned with fine motor development, activities of daily living and:
   a. Career enhancement.
   b. Job skill training.
   c. Sensorimotor integration.
   d. Training in the use of adaptive devices.

8. The current method of placing children with health impairments in the proper learning environment is based on:
   a. The medical model.
   b. Regular education guidelines.
   c. The least restrictive environment.
   d. The decisions of health-care professionals.

Essay Practice

Try these to help further your understanding of health impairments.

1. Recall what you have learned about AIDS. Discuss prevention activities and myths.

_____
_____
_____
_____
_____
_____
_____
_____
_____

2. What guidelines would you suggest for interacting with persons who are health impaired? Use examples of different types of health problems in your response.

520

STUDENT STUDY GUIDE

Chapter Seven

In Chapter Seven the author indicated that it is important to remember that a person with physical disabilities is a person first. Those are wise words to remember about people with all forms of disabilities.

Terminology

Here are some terms from Chapter Seven to learn. Try to define each term without referring back to the chapter.

Orthopedic impairments: _____

_____

Cerebral palsy: _____

_____

Limb deficiencies: _____

_____

Multiple sclerosis: _____

_____

Muscular dystrophy: _____

_____

Spina bifida: _____

_____

Spinal cord injuries: _____

_____

True/False

Test your knowledge by circling the correct response. Try to get all seven correct!

(T) F 1. Cerebral palsy is actually a group of movement difficulties, rather than a single disorder.

T **(F)** 2. Acquired limb deficiencies result most frequently from disease.

(T) F 3. Spinal cord injuries are more common in males than in females.

(T) F 4. People with moderate cerebral palsy are able to ambulate with assistance.

T **(F)** 5. The effects of a spinal cord injury depend mostly on two major factors; the amount of damage to the spinal cord and the lapse of time between injury and treatment.

T **(F)** 6. Multiple sclerosis is a progressive disease of the muscular system.

T **(F)** 7. Spina bifida cystica is caused by genetic abnormalities.

Multiple Choice

Here are some questions about physical disabilities. Circle the best of four possible answers.

1. How many forms of cerebral palsy are known?
   a. Three.
   (b.) Six.
   c. Two.
   d. Five.

2. Which is not a form of cerebral palsy?
   a. Athetosis.
   b. Rigidity.
   c. Mixed.
   (d.) Duchenne.

STUDENT STUDY GUIDE

3. In addition to causing muscle weakness, spasticity, and balance difficulties, multiple sclerosis can also cause:
   a. Visual impairments.
   b. Pulmonary difficulties.
   c. Speech disorders.
   d. Immune system deficiencies.

4. How many major types of muscular dystrophy are known?
   a. Two.
   b. Three.
   c. Four.
   d. Six.

5. Which is not a known form of muscular dystrophy?
   a. Limb-girdle.
   b. Facioscapulohumeral.
   c. Athetosis.
   d. Myotonic.

6. How many major types of spina bifida are known?
   a. Two.
   b. Three.
   c. Four.
   d. Five.

7. Of every 1,000 people born, how many will have spina bifida?
   a. 1.4
   b. 2
   c. 3
   d. 6.9

8. Approximately what percent of the population of people with cerebral palsy tests as mentally retarded?
   a. 10%
   b. 23%
   c. 50%
   d. 65%

Essay Practice

These activities will help prepare you for an exam on physical disabilities. Write out your complete answers.

1. List and give characteristics of each major type of cerebral palsy.

2. Some types of physical disabilities can be prevented. Identify at least two types and describe the prevention intervention for each.

STUDENT STUDY GUIDE

Chapter Eight

Chapter Eight's author points out that most people are intellectually deficient in one area or another and to different degrees. The degree of deficiency and adaptive behavior level are factors to seriously consider when discussing mental retardation.

Terminology

These are important terms from Chapter Eight you should know. Try filling in the blanks first before referring to the chapter or other reference.

Mental retardation: _____

Down syndrome: _____

Educable: _____

Trainable: _____

Custodial: _____

Mild mental retardation: _____

Moderate mental retardation: _____

Severe mental retardation: _____

Profound mental retardation: _____

True/False

You should be able to get all of these right if you've studied Chapter Eight.

(T) F 1. The most accepted definition of mental retardation is offered by the American Association on Mental Retardation.

T (F) 2. Researchers estimate that from 10% to 12% of the population is mentally retarded.

T (F) 3. The American Association on Mental Retardation has identified eight categories of causation for mental retardation.

(T) F 4. About 50% of people with cerebral palsy are mentally retarded.

T (F) 5. About 40% of people with moderate to severe retardation exhibit speech defects.

(T) F 6. Some cases of mental retardation are preventable through medical treatment or early education.

T (F) 7. People with profound mental retardation never achieve basic self-help skills.

(T) F 8. Early intervention programs for people who are mentally retarded date back to the late 1930s.

STUDENT STUDY GUIDE

Multiple Choice

Circle the best of four possible answers. Get all eight and you're great!

1. Researchers estimate that the percentage of the population that is mentally retarded ranges from:
   a. 1-3% ✓
   b. 2-4%
   c. 6-9%
   d. 7-10%

2. The estimate of school-age population that is mentally retarded is:
   a. 1%
   b. 2%
   c. 3% ✓
   d. 4%

3. Examples of conditions that could result in mental retardation from the infection/intoxication causation category include syphilis, lead poisoning, and:
   a. Galactosemia.
   b. Epilepsy.
   c. Rubella. ✓
   d. Hypoglycemia.

4. Included in the metabolic disease category of causation are galactosemia, phenylketonuria, and:
   a. Hypoxia.
   b. Neurofibromatosis.
   c. Hydrocephaly
   d. Hypoglycemia. ✓

5. Included in the chromosomal abnormality category of causation are Down syndrome, triple x syndrome, and:
   a. Microcephaly.
   b. Neurofibromatosis.
   c. Turner syndrome. ✓
   d. Thyroid dysfunction syndrome.

6. People with profound mental retardation are classified as a result of having IQ scores:
   a. Between 41 and 55.
   b. Between 26 and 40.
   c. Below 35.
   d. Below 25.

7. People with mental retardation considered educable are classified as a result of having IQ scores between:
   a. 51 and 70.
   b. 21 and 50.
   c. 71 and 90.
   d. 91 and 110.

8. Which is not one of the medical interventions suggested for mental retardation?
   a. Screening for risk.
   b. Antibiotic treatment.
   c. Removal of toxic/traumatic agents.
   d. Direct treatment.

Essay Practice

Do these exercises to check what you know about Chapter Eight.

1. Explain the personality/social characteristics of people who are mentally retarded.

_____
_____
_____
_____
_____
_____

2. What technological advances have benefitted people who are mentally retarded? What others would you suggest need to be developed?

STUDENT STUDY GUIDE

Chapter Nine

The X axis derivative of the square root of the hypotenuse multiplied by the Y axis derivative minus the slope equals mass multiplied by the speed of light squared.

If you've ever had a problem understanding what in the world your teacher was talking about, you've gained some insight about people who are learning disabled. If you miss too many of the exercises below, you're not necessarily learning disabled. Try going over the chapter again.

Terminology

These are important terms and concepts to learn from Chapter Nine. Define each in the provided spaces.

Learning disabled: _____

_____

Physiological difference theory: _____

_____

Cognitive-based theory: _____

_____

Metacognitive deficit theory: _____

_____

Instructional deficit theory: _____

_____

Instructional design: _____

_____

Pre-referral intervention: _____

_____

Progress monitoring: _____

_____

True/False

Test your knowledge by circling the correct responses.

(T) F 1. Learning disability comprises the largest classification of students funded through special education.

T (F) 2. The number of students who are learning disabled represents 53% of students served through special education.

T (F) 3. Research indicates that students with learning disabilities exhibit deficits in cognitive strategies and can not be trained to modify their cognitive behavior.

(T) F 4. The majority of learning disabilities occur in reading and language arts.

T (F) 5. Only 23% of youth with learning disabilities who are out of secondary school maintain gainful employment.

T (F) 6. Peer-mediated instruction refers to students learning job skills from peers on the job.

T (F) 7. According to cognitive theorists, people with learning disabilities are organically impaired.

STUDENT STUDY GUIDE

Multiple Choice
These are good practice for an exam about learning disabilities. Circle the best of four possible answers.

1. What percentage of students served through special education are classified as learning disabled?
   a. 23%
   b. 34%
   c. 49%
   d. 53%

2. The theory that proposes that learning disabilities are caused by some biologic pathology within the learner is the:
   a. Physiological difference theory.
   b. Cognitive-based theory.
   c. Metacognitive deficit theory.
   d. Instructional deficit theory.

3. The theory that claims people with learning disabilities do not use their cognitive resources to control and regulate learning:
   a. Physiological difference theory.
   b. Cognitive-based theory.
   c. Metacognitive deficit theory.
   d. Instructional deficit theory.

4. Those who believe that learning disabilities are a result of poorly designed teaching materials subscribe to the:
   a. Physiological difference theory.
   b. Cognitive-based theory.
   c. Metacognitive deficit theory.
   d. Instructional deficit theory.

5. The theory based upon the premise that people with learning disabilities are inactive learners is the:
   a. Physiological difference theory.
   b. Cognitive-based theory.
   c. Metacognitive deficit theory.
   d. Instructional deficit theory.

6. The intervention strategy that is aimed at preventing future learning disabilities by emersing children in an environment of reading is known as:
   a. Early reading experience.
   b. Direct instruction.
   c. Curriculum-based measurement.
   d. Remedial interventions.

7. Which one of the following is not a component of the direct instruction method?
   a. Direct teacher presentation techniques.
   b. Well designed curricular lessons.
   c. Practice and review sessions.
   d. Exploratory learning activities.

8. Considerable evidence indicates the importance of monitoring student performance on a(n):
   a. Ongoing basis.
   b. Sporadic basis.
   c. Infrequent basis.
   d. Inconsistent basis.

Essay Practice

Here are two exercises about learning disabilities. Give your complete answers in the spaces below each question.

1. Discuss the four theories of causation pertaining to learning disabilities.

   _____
   _____
   _____
   _____
   _____
   _____

2. List and describe at least five intervention strategies for people with learning disabilities.

Chapter Ten

Chapter Ten covers a sensitive topic. Hopefully you've gained some insight about people whose behavior differs from the norm. Try these exercises to see what you've learned.

Terminology

Fill in the blanks with what you know about each term or concept.

Emotionally disturbed: _____

_____

Behavior modification: _____

_____

Parent management training: _____

_____

Punitive responses: _____

_____

Avoidance behavior: _____

_____

Instructive interaction: _____

_____

True/False

These are either correct or incorrect statements. Test your knowledge by circling the correct response for each item.

(T) F 1. Generally, the frequency of a problem behavior and the context in which it occurs determine whether a person will be labelled emotionally disturbed.

T (F) 2. The most accepted estimate of people who are emotionally disturbed is between 4 and 6%.

T (F) 3. Students and adults who exhibit behavioral excesses are usually not very obvious to others.

(T) F 4. Students identified as emotionally disturbed usually experience academic difficulties.

T (F) 5. The intelligence of people, who are emotionally disturbed, is usually in the average range.

(T) F 6. It is usually not possible to identify the cause of an emotional disturbance.

(T) F 7. Early intervention and direct instruction in basic skills may provide students with a solid academic background that will enable them to succeed in school.

Multiple Choice

Circle the best of four possible answers.

1. The most accepted estimate for people who are emotionally disturbed is between:
   a. 1 and 4%
   b. 2 and 4%
   (c.) 3 and 6%
   d. 4 and 6%

STUDENT STUDY GUIDE

2. Which is not one of the factors associated with emotional disturbance?
   a. Genetic influences.
   b. Family or marital discord.
   c. School failure.
   d. Strict parental discipline.

3. Which is not a suggested intervention component in the parent management training approach?
   a. Moderate to severe forms of punishment for inappropriate behavior.
   b. Defining problem behavior.
   c. Providing rewards for appropriate behavior.
   d. Mild punishment for inappropriate behavior.

4. A system of rewards for appropriate actions or completion of tasks is part of:
   a. Behavior modification.
   b. Instructive interaction.
   c. Academic intervention.
   d. Psychoanalytic treatment.

5. A reaction to people who are emotionally disturbed that often causes an even more negative interaction is called:
   a. Avoidance behavior.
   b. Punitive response.
   c. Direct instruction.
   d. Instructive interaction.

6. When interacting with a person who is emotionally disturbed, a good rule of thumb is to treat the person as you would any other. This is a good way to avoid:
   a. Avoidance behavior.
   b. Punitive response.
   c. Direct instruction.
   d. Instructive interaction.

7. When special education teachers address behaviors directly, they are employing:
   a. Avoidance behavior.
   b. Punitive response.
   c. Direct instruction.
   d. Instructive interaction.

8. The two factors which determine whether a person will be labeled emotionally disturbed are:
   a. The intensity and context of the problem behavior.
   b. The frequency and context of the problem behavior.
   c. The intensity and frequency of the problem behavior.
   d. The frequency and disruptiveness of the problem behavior.

Essay Practice

Here are two essay style questions to assist you in your review of the chapter.

1. Describe the federal definition of people who are emotionally disturbed.

   _____
   _____
   _____
   _____
   _____
   _____
   _____
   _____
   _____
   _____
   _____
   _____
   _____

2. Explain what behavior modification is, when it is used, and how it is used.

Chapter Eleven

Most of us take speech and language for granted. We don't even think about it unless we've said too much, or said something we regret. In contrast, people who have speech and language disorders often struggle to communicate effectively. Review your knowledge of this topic by completing these exercises.

Terminology

If you can fill in these blanks, then you know your stuff.

Communication: _____

_____

Speech: _____

_____

Language: _____

_____

Communication disorder: _____

_____

Speech disorder: _____

_____

Articulation disorder: _____

_____

Fluency disorder: _____

_____

Voice disorder: _____

_____

Language disorder: _____

True/False

Test yourself by circling the correct responses.

~~T~~ F 1. Speech and language disorders are among the most frequently occurring disability in the United States.

T ~~F~~ 2. Articulation disorders result in problems related to the natural rhythm of speech.

T ~~F~~ 3. Most people who have articulation disorders are described as having functional articulation disorders.

~~T~~ F 4. More males than females have fluency disorders.

T ~~F~~ 5. About 5% of the school-age population has been identified as having a voice disorder.

~~T~~ F 6. The majority of people with articulation disorders have mild problems that respond well to treatment and may not impair the person's overall functioning.

T ~~F~~ 7. Aphasia refers to a partial or total loss of language resulting from an injury to the vocal cords.

STUDENT STUDY GUIDE

Multiple Choice

As a review, circle the best of four possible answers for each question.

1. What percentage of people in the United States is affected by a fluency disorder?
   a. 1%
   b. 1.5%
   c. 2%
   d. 3%

2. Which communication disorder is characterized by a person failing to process all or part of what they hear?
   a. Voice disorder.
   b. Receptive communication disorder.
   c. Stuttering.
   d. Expressive disorder.

3. What percentage of the school-age population has been identified as having a voice disorder?
   a. 1%
   b. 2%
   c. 3%
   d. 4%

4. Which component of language is the element that integrates sounds and symbols with meaning?
   a. Form.
   b. Phonology.
   c. Morphology.
   d. Syntax.

5. Which component of language deals with the sounds of language and the rules that govern their combination?
   a. Form.
   b. Phonology.
   c. Morphology.
   d. Syntax.

6. Which component of language governs word order and sentence structure?
   a. Form.
   b. Phonology.
   c. Morphology.
   d. Syntax. ✓

7. Which component of language relates to how words are formed?
   a. Form.
   b. Phonology.
   c. Morphology. ✓
   d. Syntax.

8. The current estimate of the number of children with language disorders is between:
   a. 1 and 3%
   b. 3 and 12%
   c. 5 and 10% ✓
   d. 8 and 12%

Essay Practice

1. Identify and discuss the errors in speech associated with people who have articulation disorders and voice disorders.

_____
_____
_____
_____
_____
_____
_____
_____

2. Explain the difference between speech and language problems. Use specific examples in your discussion.

550

STUDENT STUDY GUIDE

Chapter Twelve

Just as most people are intellectually deficient in one area or another to some degree, so are they gifted or talented in some way. The exercises below are provided to test your knowledge of gifted and talented people.

Terminology

Here are some terms to help you with Chapter Twelve. Define each.

Gifted and talented persons: _____

High performance capability: _____

Specific academic ability: _____

Intraindividual differences: _____

Interindividual differences: _____

Academic intervention: _____

Social/emotional intervention: _____

Adult intervention: _____

True/False

Test your knowledge by circling the correct response. If you get all seven, consider yourself gifted.

(T) F 1. A general consensus indicates that 3-5% of the school population can be identified as gifted.

T (F) 2. Giftedness is not found across all socioeconomic levels.

(T) F 3. Giftedness is a complex concept, covering a wide range of abilities and traits.

T (F) 4. A person who has strong abilities in math but comparatively lower abilities in written expression would be described as exhibiting interindividual differences.

T (F) 5. Giftedness is solely a function of intelligence.

(T) F 6. It is possible for a person to have learning disabilities and still be considered gifted or talented.

T (F) 7. The intervention strategy known as enrichment allows students to take courses at a faster pace than usual.

Multiple Choice

Did you get all seven? Now let's see if you're talented in multiple choice style too.

1. The definition of gifted and talented children legislated by congress includes children and youth who give evidence of high performance capability in all but which one of the following areas?
   a. Creativity.
   b. Intelligence.
   (c.) Diversity.
   d. Art.

STUDENT STUDY GUIDE

2. The term which refers to people who might have extraordinary ability but are not showing it in their performance is:
   a. High performance capability.
   b. Gifted or talented potential.
   c. Specific academic ability.
   d. Leadership capacity.

3. Congdon (1985) stated that the term "gifted" is perhaps best used as an umbrella term to:
   a. Determine who is eligible for special education programs.
   b. Label those people with scores above 150 on the Stanford-Binet intelligence scale.
   c. Define individuals who have extremely high abilities in academic areas.
   d. Cover a number of groups of individuals of exceptional ability.

4. The percentage of the school population considered gifted is:
   a. 2-4%
   b. 1-5%
   c. 3-5%
   d. 3-8%

5. The term that best describes the entire population of people who are gifted is:
   a. Homogeneous.
   b. Heterogeneous.
   c. Ethnically diverse.
   d. Academically superior.

6. Which trait would not ordinarily belong to a school-age student who is gifted?
   a. High level of independence.
   b. Confusion about career choices.
   c. Long attention span.
   d. Sensitivity to others.

7. One characteristic commonly separating underachievers from overachievers is:
   a. The ability to comprehend and complete complex tasks.
   b. Feelings of inferiority.
   c. Vocabulary size.
   d. Attention span.

8. Which is not a characteristic difference shown by culturally different gifted or talented people, when compared with their culturally average peers?
   a. Loyalty to their peer groups.
   b. Verbal persuasiveness.
   c. Dependence on controls from within rather than control from their environment.
   d. Logical reasoning.

Essay Practice

Fully answer both essay questions as a test of your grasp of the topic of giftedness.

1. In what areas may one be gifted or talented? Define and give examples for each area mentioned.

2. What are the negative and positive consequences of being gifted? Fully discuss each consequence which you list.

STUDENT STUDY GUIDE

Chapter Thirteen

Special education is a significant component of the educational system. Demonstrate your knowledge of special education by completing these exercises.

Terminology

Here are some terms to know from Chapter Thirteen. Define each in the provided spaces.

Special education: _____

_____

Preventive intervention: _____

_____

Remedial intervention: _____

_____

Compensatory intervention: _____

_____

Multidisciplinary team: _____

_____

Referral: _____

_____

Noncategorical approach: _____

_____

Individualized Education Plan: _____

_____

Due process: _____

Integration: _____

Mainstreaming: _____

Least restrictive environment: _____

True/False

Test your knowledge by circling the correct response.

T (F) 1. Special education is often differentiated from regular education by the academic setting.

T (F) 2. Curriculum for individual students in special education varies greatly because of differing standards across the nation.

(T) F 3. Special education differs from regular education in two ways -- the teacher who delivers the instruction and the student who receives it.

(T) F 4. Sixty-six percent of exceptional students are taught in regular classes.

T (F) 5. At-risk is a term that refers to a person who is identified as exceptional.

T (F) 6. The identification, assessment, and eligibility process has certain geographical guidelines.

(T) F 7. Once students are placed in special education, they must undergo a triennial evaluation every three years.

STUDENT STUDY GUIDE

Multiple Choice

Circle the best of four possible answers.

1. Which intervention method is most effective when begun early in life?
    a. Remedial intervention.
    b. Compensatory intervention.
    c. Multidisciplinary intervention.
    d. Preventive intervention.

2. The term that refers to services provided to individuals to help them make life changes such as changing from school to work:
    a. Transition services.
    b. Remedial education.
    c. Early intervention.
    d. Chapter I.

3. Which intervention method teaches substitute skills?
    a. Remedial intervention.
    b. Compensatory intervention.
    c. Multidisciplinary intervention.
    d. Preventive intervention.

4. The name of the service model that provides 24-hour-a-day care in a facilty away from home:
    a. Self-contained special education classroom.
    b. Residential school.
    c. Special day school.
    d. Resource special education classroom.

5. What is the technical/formal term that refers to the total number of individuals who are in a given category of exceptionality (SE) at a particular point in time?
    a. Incidence.
    b. Prevalence.
    c. Current supply.
    d. Proportion.

6. One professional not usually included as a member of a multidisciplinary team is:
   a. Special education teacher.
   b. Psychiatrist. ✓
   c. Guidance counselor.
   d. Vocational evaluator.

7. Which assessment technique is not commonly used in an evaluation for determining eligibility for special education?
   a. Psychiatric evaluation. ✓
   b. Observation.
   c. Teacher-made tests.
   d. Intelligence tests.

8. Which would not be a benefit of labeling in special education?
   a. Labels help to get funding.
   b. Labels help to determine expectations from others. ✓
   c. Labels help develop advocacy agencies.
   d. Labels provide a general idea of the needs of students.

Essay Practice

Try writing what you know about each of these.

1. Discuss the components of the individualized education plan. Also indicate who develops the plan and the procedure for its development.

_____
_____
_____
_____
_____
_____

2. Explain the difference between mainstreaming and least restrictive environment. Provide specific examples of both models.

STUDENT STUDY GUIDE

Chapter Fourteen

Here are some of my friends--teacher, nurse, physical therapist, guidance counselor, psychologist, pediatrician, music therapist, social worker, vocational counselor, and recreation therapist. This set of exercises will test your knowledge of their roles with disabled persons.

Terminology

Fill in the blanks with information found in Chapter Fourteen.

Physical therapy: _____

_____

Occupational therapy: _____

_____

Speech and language therapy: _____

_____

Music therapy: _____

_____

Dance therapy: _____

_____

Art therapy: _____

_____

Recreation therapy: _____

_____

Play therapy: _____

_____

True/False

Check what you've learned by circling the correct responses in these seven items.

T **F** 1. The Education of All Handicapped Children Act states that related services be provided to people with disabilities within the home environment.

T F 2. Physical therapy can only be accessed by the recommendation and/or referral of a physician.

T **F** 3. A child with motor disabilities can only receive physical and/or occupational therapy in school settings if such therapy does not interfere with educational programming.

T F 4. A physical therapist is involved with the relaxing and strengthening of individual groups of muscles.

T F 5. It is very common for some speech therapists to work with stroke and accident victims.

T F 6. Some pediatricians play a major role as consultants for early intervention programs and school districts.

T **F** 7. An Otologist is a physician who determines the range, nature, and degree of a hearing loss.

Multiple Choice

Circle the best of four possible answers. Can you get all eight correct without referring to the chapter?

1. Which therapy often uses screening activities to identify clients?
    a. Occupational therapy.
    b. Speech and language therapy.
    c. Recreational therapy.
    d. Physical therapy.

STUDENT STUDY GUIDE

2. A therapy designed to teach a person with disabilities activities for daily living is:
   a. Occupational therapy.
   b. Speech and language therapy.
   c. Recreational therapy.
   d. Physical therapy.

3. Which therapy focuses on developing motor skills and functional activities?
   a. Occupational therapy.
   b. Speech and language therapy.
   c. Recreational therapy.
   d. Physical therapy.

4. A therapy that trains people to participate in activities such as swimming and bowling is:
   a. Occupational therapy.
   b. Speech and language therapy.
   c. Recreational therapy.
   d. Physical therapy.

5. A medical doctor who specializes in the care and treatment of children is a:
   a. Neonatologist.
   b. Pediatrician.
   c. Orthopedist.
   d. Otologist.

6. Which specialist is primarily concerned with the hearing mechanisms and diseases of the ear?
   a. Neonatologist.
   b. Pediatrician.
   c. Orthopedist.
   d. Otologist.

7. The specialist primarily involved with the care of critically ill and low birth-weight infants is the:
   a. Neonatologist.
   b. Pediatrician.
   c. Orthopedist.
   d. Otologist.

8. Which specialist would be involved in recommending prosthetic devices?
   a. Neonatologist.
   b. Pediatrician.
   c. Orthopedist.
   d. Otologist.

Essay Practice

These questions will test what you know about related services and support professionals. Be sure your responses are thorough.

1. Explain the difference between occupational and physical therapy. Give specific examples of the objectives and activities of each discipline.

2. Identify and discuss the roles of at least five support professionals who deal with disabled people.

STUDENT STUDY GUIDE 569

Chapter Fifteen

A community of any size or scope is created when people help people. The agencies and organizations described in Chapter Fifteen provide vital help to people with differences. Here is your opportunity to review these agencies and organizations.

Terminology

Here are some important terms and concepts concerning community and consumer organizations.

Case manager: _____

_____

Early intervention programs: _____

_____

Parent support groups: _____

_____

Time-limited services: _____

_____

Vocational rehabilitation: _____

_____

Job Training Partnership Act: _____

_____

Developmental disabilities programs: _____

_____

True/False

A little hint -- five are true. Circle the correct answers.

T F 1. The provision of case management for people with disabilities is the responsibility of state and local agencies and organizations.

T F 2. State and local agencies and organizations may be involved in supervising, and in some cases, providing residential options for exceptional individuals.

T F 3. When people with disabilities reach the age of 18, they have the same rights and responsibilities as any other adult.

T **F** 4. When a person is incapable of living independently, guardianship is often granted through state and local agencies and organizations.

T F 5. During the school years case management is usually a function of the school system.

T F 6. Developmental disability agencies are involved in providing group living arrangements for adults with developmental disabilities.

T **F** 7. A person who is eligible for Supplemental Security Income usually is not eligible for Medicaid.

Multiple Choice

Find out what you've learned by circling the best of four possible answers. Sorry, no hints this time.

1. State and local agencies and organizations do not focus on:
   a. Recreational services.
   b. Guardianship.
   c. Therapeutic services.
   d. Case management.

STUDENT STUDY GUIDE

2. Which agency or organization type includes special olympics?
   a. Private agencies.
   b. Federal and state agencies.
   c. National, state, and local organizations.
   d. Service organizations. ✓

3. Which agency or organization type includes the Association for Children and Adults with Learning Disabilities?
   a. Private agencies.
   b. Federal and state agencies.
   c. National, state, and local organizations. ✓
   d. Service organizations.

4. Which agency or organization type includes Job Training Partnership Act agencies?
   a. Private agencies.
   b. Federal and state agencies. ✓
   c. National, state, and local organizations.
   d. Service organizations.

5. Which agency or organization type includes the Association for Retarded Citizens?
   a. Private agencies.
   b. Federal and state agencies.
   c. National, state, and local organizations. ✓
   d. Service organizations.

6. Which agency or organization type includes respite facilities?
   a. Private agencies. ✓
   b. Federal and state agencies.
   c. National, state, and local organizations.
   d. Service organizations.

7. Funding for medical treatment or prosthetic devices to help a person with a disability become employed could come from:
   a. Job Training Partnership Act agencies.
   b. Vocational rehabilitation agencies. ✓
   c. Social Security Administration.
   d. Developmental disabilities programs.

8. Disabilities termed as severe, chronic, attributable to mental or physical impairments, which are manifested before age 22 and require long-term services are commonly referred to as:
   a. Developmental disabilities.
   b. Reoccurring disabilities.
   c. Acute disabilities.
   d. Diversified disabilities.

Essay Practice

These essay exercises will help at test time. Take your time with these.

1. Define respite care and discuss at least four models for providing respite care.

STUDENT STUDY GUIDE

2. Discuss the concept of transition services and describe the agencies which are involved in transition. Be sure to provide the role which each agency plays in transition.

STUDENT STUDY GUIDE 575

Chapter Sixteen

Now that you've learned about the laws and legislation regarding people with disabilities, you can see that much has been done to protect their rights and interests. But ask some, and you'll find that the battle has just begun. Begin your battle with a test of your knowledge.

Terminology

Fill in the blanks with what you know about these acts.

Education of All Handicapped Children Act of 1975 (PL 94-142): _____

Carl D. Perkins Vocational Education Act (PL 98-524): _____

Vocational Rehabilitation Act of 1973 (PL 93-112): _____

Technology Related Assistance for Individuals with Disabilities Act of 1988 (PL 100-407): _____

Job Training and Partnership Act (PL 97-300): _____

Fair Labor Standards Act of 1980: _____

Developmental Disabilities Act (PL 98-537): _____

Medicaid Reform Act: _____

_____

True/False

Test your knowledge by circling the correct responses.

T **(F)** 1. Mills v. Board of Education ruled that students who are mentally retarded have a right to an education.

(T) F 2. The Education of All Handicapped Children Act was designed in part to financially assist the efforts of state and local government in providing special education through the use of federal funds.

(T) F 3. PL 94-142 and amendments authorize special education for disabled children from birth through age 21.

(T) F 4. The Vocational Rehabilitation Act of 1973 provides support for the National Institute of Disability and Rehabilitation Research.

T **(F)** 5. Private Industry Councils are local councils designed to aid in implementing the Technology Related Assistance for Individuals with Disabilities Act of 1988.

T **(F)** 6. The Fair Labor Standards Act of 1980 forces employers to hire people with disabilities at competitive wages.

(T) F 7. The Developmental Disabilities Act provides support for protection and advocacy organizations in each state.

STUDENT STUDY GUIDE

Multiple Choice

Here are some questions that will test what you know about the laws and legislation designed to protect the rights and interests of people with disabilities. If you get all eight correct, you must be a law student!

1. The case that established the right of students who are mentally retarded to receive an education is:
   a. Mills v. Board of Education.
   b. Pennsylvania Association for Retarded Children v. the Commonwealth of Pennsylvania.
   c. Lora v. New York City Board of Education.
   d. Halderman v. Pennhurst.

2. The case which resulted in the closing of state institutions for people who are mentally retarded, and established community residential options for the institutionalized residents is:
   a. Mills v. Board of Education.
   b. Pennsylvania Association for Retarded Children v. the Commonwealth of Pennsylvania.
   c. Lora v. New York City Board of Education.
   d. Halderman v. Pennhurst.

3. One case which sought to define an unbiased assessment and placement process to ensure that cultural differences were the basis for problems in school achievement, and not a handicapping condition, is:
   a. Mills v. Board of Education.
   b. Pennsylvania Association for Retarded Children v. the Commonwealth of Pennsylvania.
   c. Lora v. New York City Board of Education.
   d. Halderman v. Pennhurst.

4. The case which ruled that students could not be excluded from school because of a handicapping condition is:
   a. Mills v. Board of Education.
   b. Pennsylvania Association for Retarded Children v. the Commonwealth of Pennsylvania.
   c. Lora v. New York City Board of Education.
   d. Halderman v. Pennhurst.

5. The act that ensures availability of special education for children and youth with handicapping conditions is the:
   a. Vocational Rehabilitation Act of 1973 (PL 93-112).
   b. Job Training and Partnership Act (PL 97-300).
   c. Education of All Handicapped Children Act (PL 94-142).
   d. Fair Labor Standards Act of 1980.

6. The act that provides support for a nationwide network of independent living centers is the:
   a. Vocational Rehabilitation Act of 1973 (PL 93-112).
   b. Job Training and Partnership Act (PL 97-300).
   c. Education of All Handicapped Children Act (PL 94-142).
   d. Fair Labor Standards Act of 1980.

7. The act that provides an opportunity for employment and training services for people with limited income is the:
   a. Vocational Rehabilitation Act of 1973 (PL 93-112).
   b. Job Training and Partnership Act (PL 97-300).
   c. Education of All Handicapped Children Act (PL 94-142).
   d. Fair Labor Standards Act of 1980.

8. The act that has had a significant impact on the ability of rehabilitation and other disability professionals to provide supported employment services to adolescents and adults with severe disabilities is the:
   a. Vocational Rehabilitation Act of 1973 (PL 93-112).
   b. Job Training and Partnership Act (PL 97-300).
   c. Education of All Handicapped Children Act (PL 94-142).
   d. Fair Labor Standards Act of 1980.

STUDENT STUDY GUIDE

Essay Practice

These essay questions are a real challenge.

1. Explain how people with disabilities benefit from laws and legislation. Give examples of specific cases and laws in your response.

2. Discuss the features of the Americans With Disabilities Act (PL 101-336), and why it is considered the disabled person's civil rights bill.

STUDENT STUDY GUIDE

Chapter Seventeen

You will encounter many exceptional adults in your future. Let Chapter Seventeen be your guide for understanding disabled adults and for completing these exercises.

Terminology

These are categories and concepts from Chapter Seventeen. Use what you've learned to fill in the blanks.

Adults identified as disabled: _____

_____

Adults no longer identified as disabled: _____

_____

Unidentified exceptional adults: _____

_____

Individuals who become disabled as adults: _____

_____

Cooperative planning: _____

_____

Work enclaves: _____

_____

Mobile work crews: _____

_____

Sheltered workshops: _____

_____

True/False

See what you know about exceptional adults by circling the correct response for each question.

T (F) 1. Remedial planning is the term used to refer to the coordination of services between school and work.

(T) F 2. Recent statistics allow for the conclusion that 67% of all adult Americans with disabilities do not work.

(T) F 3. Companies spend about $2 billion per year on training programs for their employees.

(T) F 4. Every year more than 780,000 U.S. workers sustain injuries or illnesses, which disable them for at least 5 months.

(T) F 5. Seventy percent of all Americans, at some time in their lives, will be so disabled that they can't climb a flight of stairs.

T (F) 6. Work enclaves require intermittent supervision by a trained professional.

T (F) 7. Institutional care has increased 23% over the last 10 years.

Multiple Choice

Circle the correct response.

1. What is the type of work setting that contracts for outside work to be brought into the work site and employs workers with severe disabilities?
   a. Sheltered workshops.
   b. Mobile work crews.
   c. Work enclaves.
   d. Supported competitive employment.

STUDENT STUDY GUIDE

2. Adults who do not apply for services are classified as:
   a. Adults identified as disabled.
   b. Adults no longer identified as disabled.
   c. Unidentified exceptional adults.
   d. Individuals who become disabled as adults.

3. Adults who received services in school and continue to receive services after completion of school are termed:
   a. Adults identified as disabled.
   b. Adults no longer identified as disabled.
   c. Unidentified exceptional adults.
   d. Individuals who become disabled as adults.

4. Disabled adults who avoid being labeled as disabled are called:
   a. Adults identified as disabled.
   b. Adults no longer identified as disabled.
   c. Unidentified exceptional adults.
   d. Individuals who become disabled as adults.

5. Adults who become disabled from an accident or illness are labeled:
   a. Adults identified as disabled.
   b. Adults no longer identified as disabled.
   c. Unidentified exceptional adults.
   d. Individuals who become disabled as adults.

6. What percentage of adult Americans with disabilities do not work?
   a. 23%
   b. 31%
   c. 57%
   d. 67%

7. Which category would describe a living situation in which adults require someone to check in periodically?
   a. Independent living.
   b. Semi-independent living.
   c. Living at home.
   d. Group homes.

8. Which category would describe a living situation in which adults require constant supervision?
   a. Independent living.
   b. Semi-independent living.
   c. Living at home.
   d. Group homes.

Essay Practice

Just two more, then ahead to the future in Chapter Eighteen.

1. Describe the five main areas exceptional people use to define independence. Give examples of activities which would clearly identify each area.

2. Discuss the five major work settings available for adults with disabilities. Be sure to explain each thoroughly.

586

Chapter Eighteen

The nature of the material in Chapter Eighteen is not easily shaped into true/false or multiple choice exercises. Therefore, there will only be two essay practice questions for this chapter.

Essay Practice

1. Assume that friends of yours have been negative toward disabled persons. What guidelines can you practice to assist your friends in improving their attitudes. Give specific examples.

2. Fully discuss "the doctor is an expert" concept. Explain the implications of the concept for disabled people and for those people who interact with disabled people.